CODE:BREAKER

Volume 1

Akimine Kamijyo

Translation and Adaptation by
William Flanagan

Lettered by
North Market Street Graphics

DEL REY

Ballantine Books · New York

Honorifics Explained

Throughout the Del Rey Manga books, you will find Japanese honorifics left intact in the translations. For those not familiar with how the Japanese use honorifics and, more important, how they differ from American honorifics, we present this brief overview.

Politeness has always been a critical facet of Japanese culture. Ever since the feudal era, when Japan was a highly stratified society, use of honorifics—which can be defined as polite speech that indicates relationship or status—has played an essential role in the Japanese language. When you address someone in Japanese, an honorific usually takes the form of a suffix attached to one's name (example: "Asuna-san"), is used as a title at the end of one's name, or appears in place of the name itself (example: "Negi-sensei," or simply "Sensei!").

Honorifics can be expressions of respect or endearment. In the context of manga and anime, honorifics give insight into the nature of the relationship between characters. Many English translations leave out these important honorifics and therefore distort the feel of the original Japanese. Because Japanese honorifics contain nuances that English honorifics lack, it is our policy at Del Rey not to translate them. Here, instead, is a guide to some of the honorifics you may encounter in Del Rey Manga.

-san: This is the most common honorific and is equivalent to Mr., Miss, Ms., or Mrs. It is the all-purpose honorific and can be used in any situation where politeness is required.

-sama: This is one level higher than "-san" and is used to confer great respect.

-dono: This comes from the word "tono," which means "lord." It is an even higher level than "-sama" and confers utmost respect.

-kun: This suffix is used at the end of boys' names to express familiarity or endearment. It is also sometimes used by men among friends, or when addressing someone younger or of a lower station.

-chan: This is used to express endearment, mostly toward girls. It is also used for little boys, pets, and even among lovers. It gives a sense of childish cuteness.

Bozu: This is an informal way to refer to a boy, similar to the English terms "kid" and "squirt."

Sempai/
Senpai: This title suggests that the addressee is one's senior in a group or organization. It is most often used in a school setting, where underclassmen refer to their upperclassmen as "sempai." It can also be used in the workplace, such as when a newer employee addresses an employee who has seniority in the company.

Kohai: This is the opposite of "sempai" and is used toward underclassmen in school or newcomers in the workplace. It connotes that the addressee is of a lower station.

Sensei: Literally meaning "one who has come before," this title is used for teachers, doctors, or masters of any profession or art.

-[blank]: This is usually forgotten in these lists, but it is perhaps the most significant difference between Japanese and English. The lack of honorific means that the speaker has permission to address the person in a very intimate way. Usually, only family, spouses, or very close friends have this kind of permission. Known as *yobisute*, it can be gratifying when someone who has earned the intimacy starts to call one by one's name without an honorific. But when that intimacy hasn't been earned, it can be very insulting.

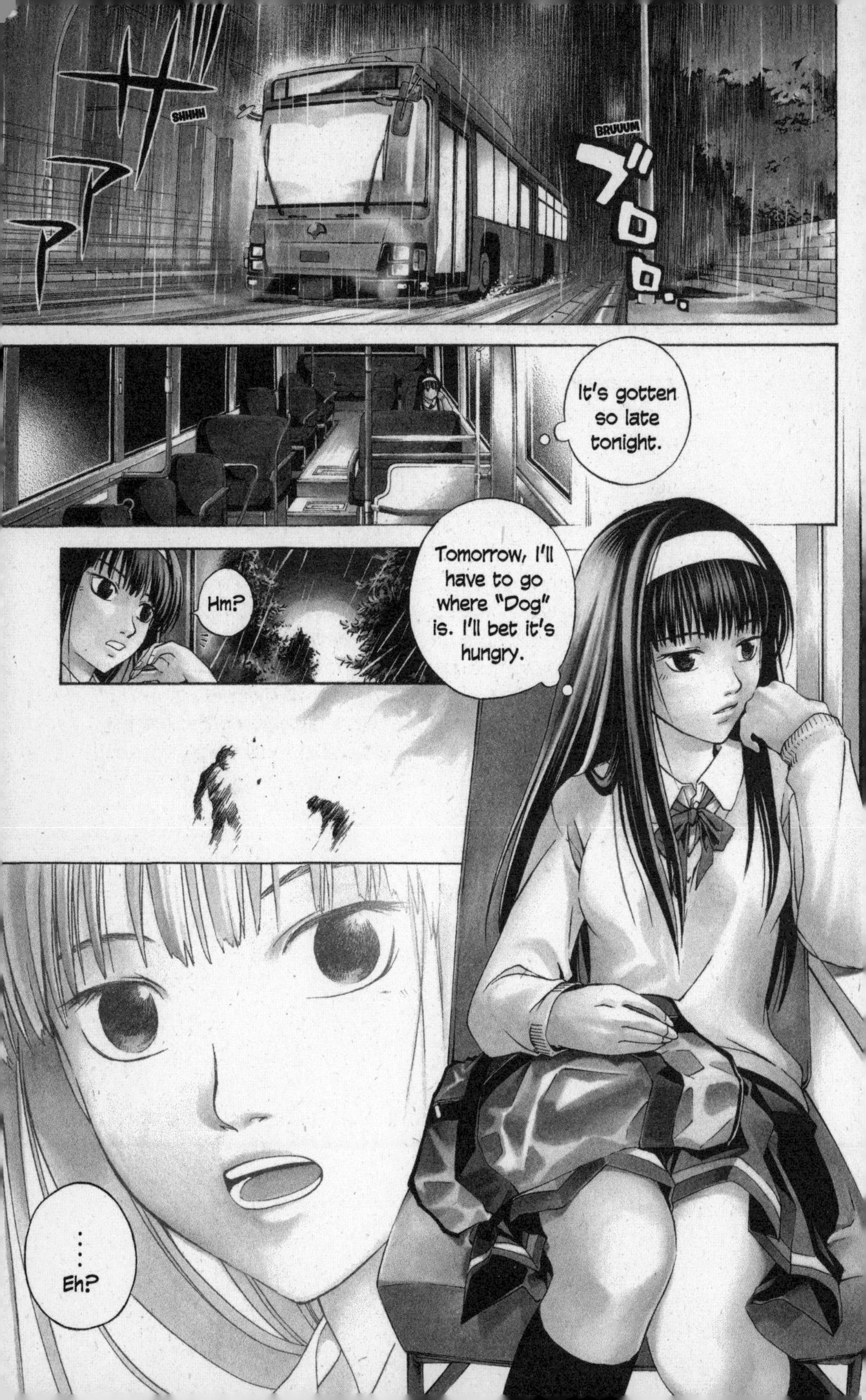
BRUUUM
SHHHH
It's gotten so late tonight.
Tomorrow, I'll have to go where "Dog" is. I'll bet it's hungry.
Hm?
.... Eh?

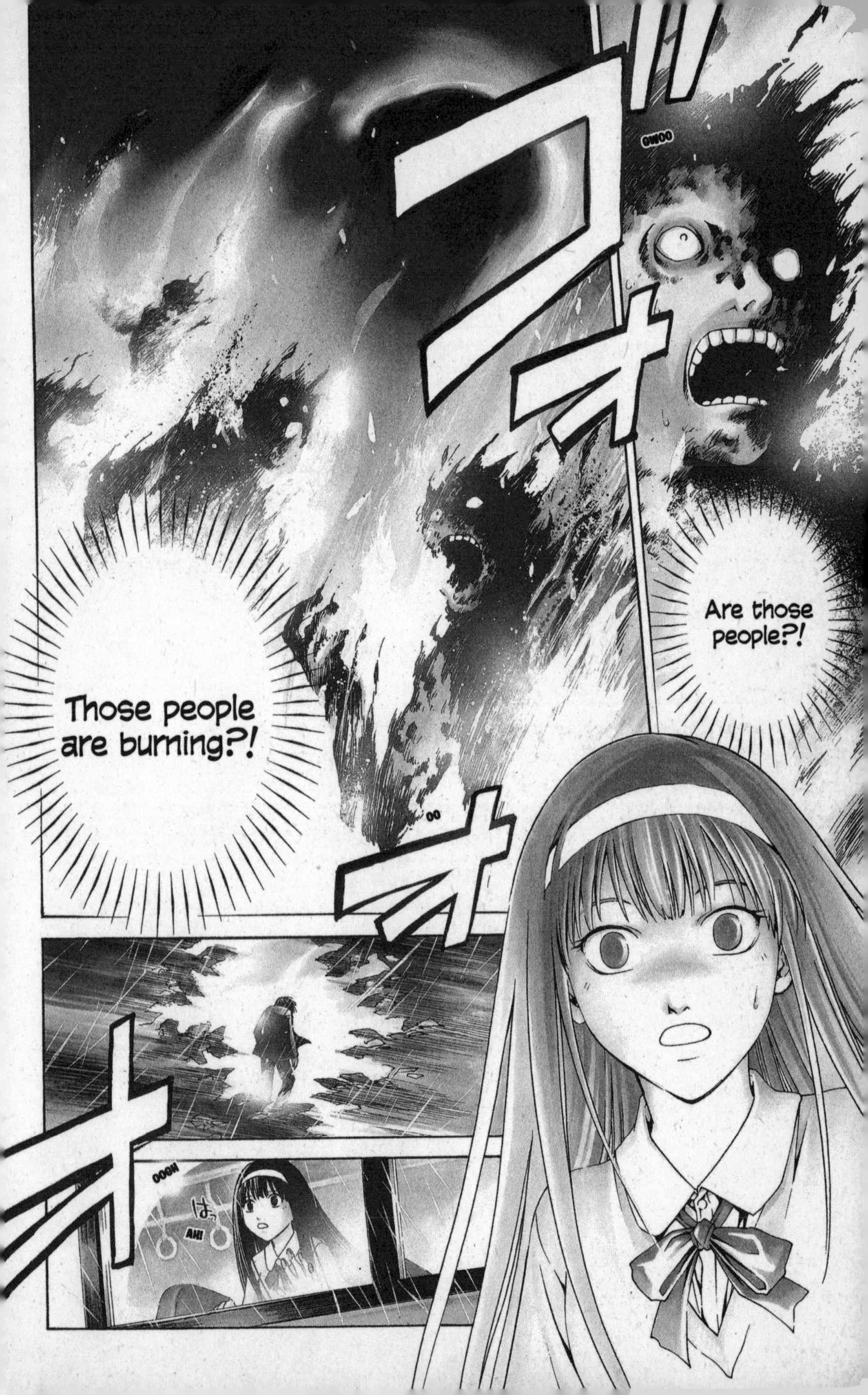
OWOO
Are those people?!
Those people are burning?!
OO
OOOH
はっ
AH!

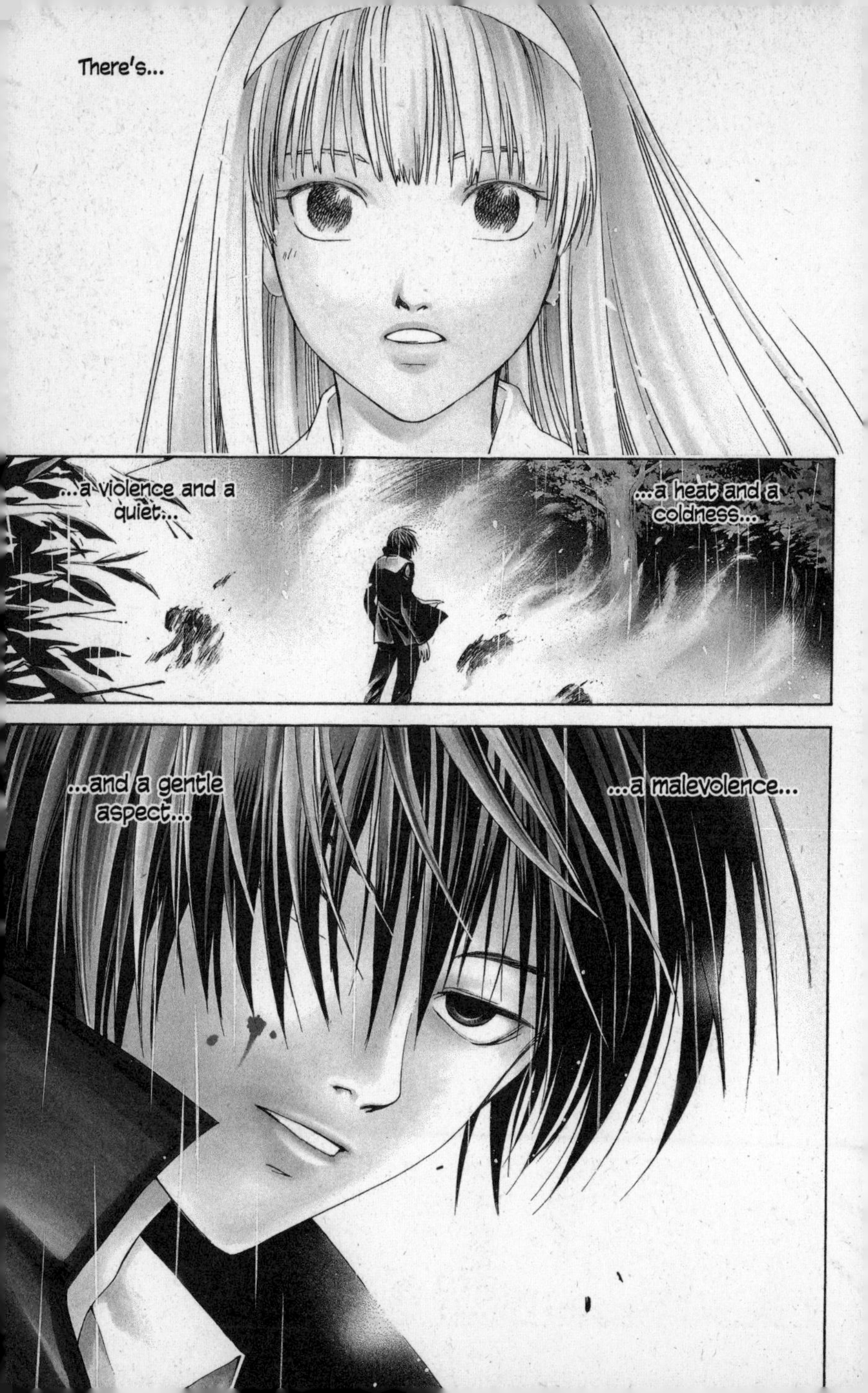
There's...
...a heat and a coldness...
...a violence and a quiet...
...a malevolence...
...and a gentle aspect...

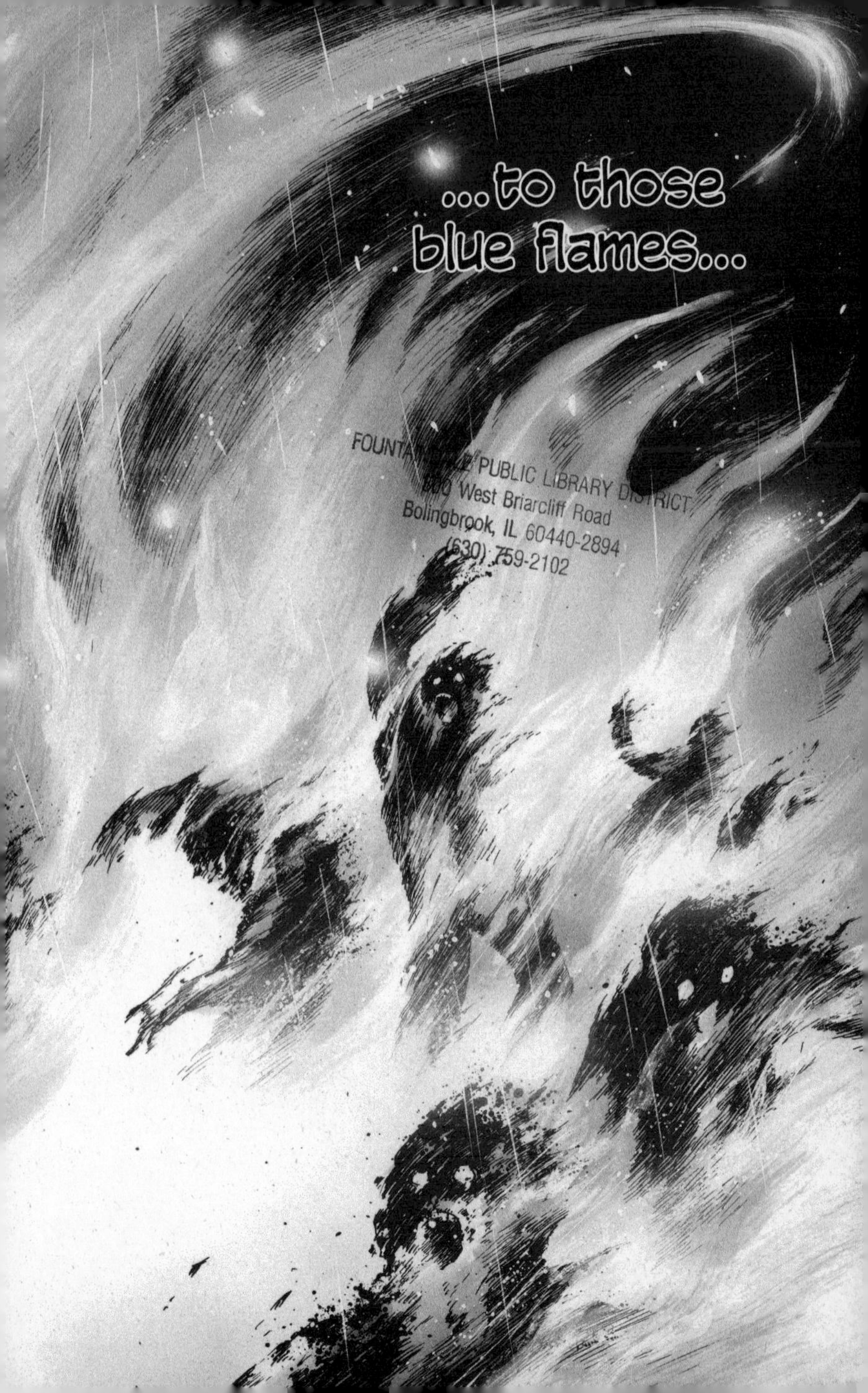
...to those blue flames...

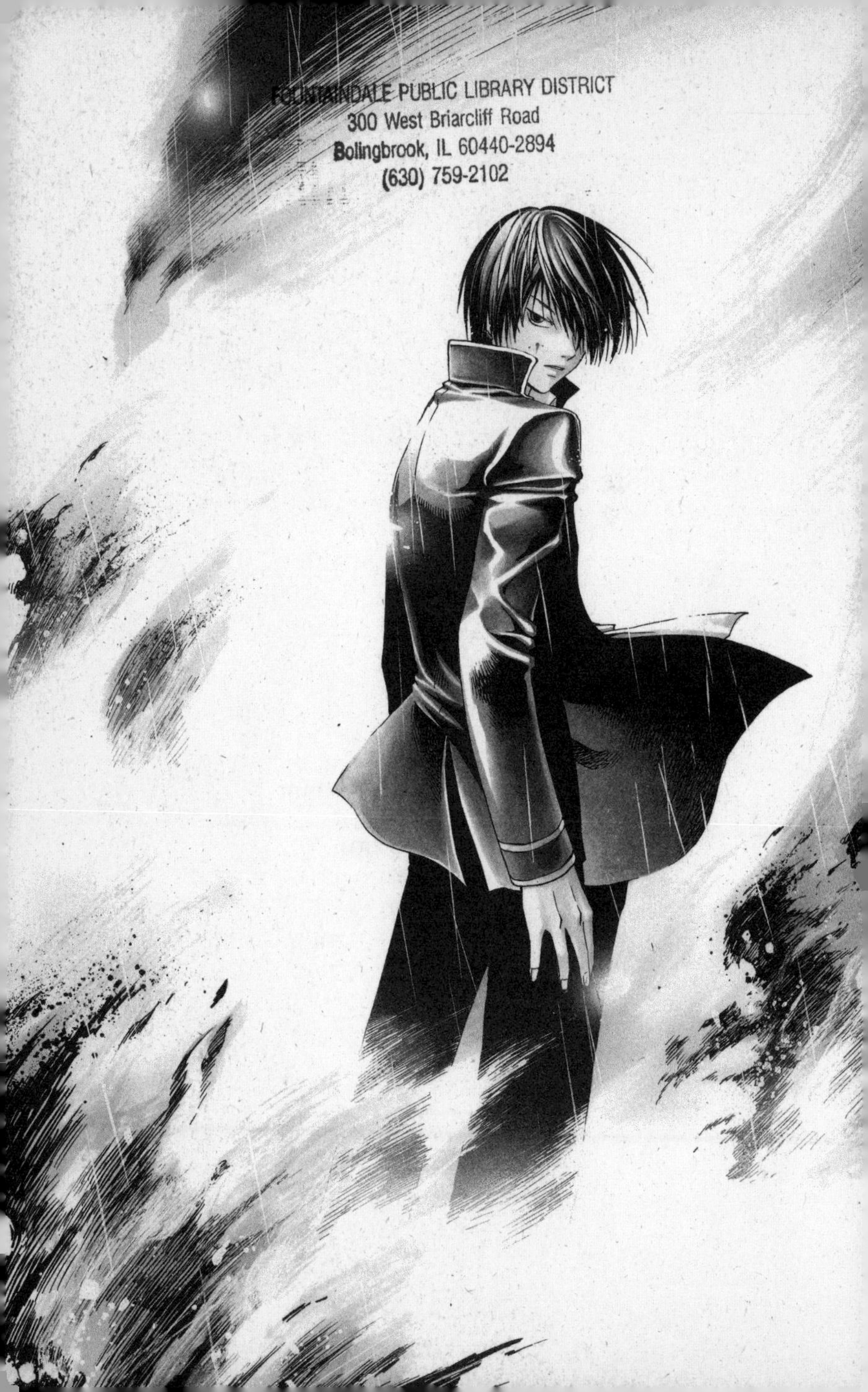

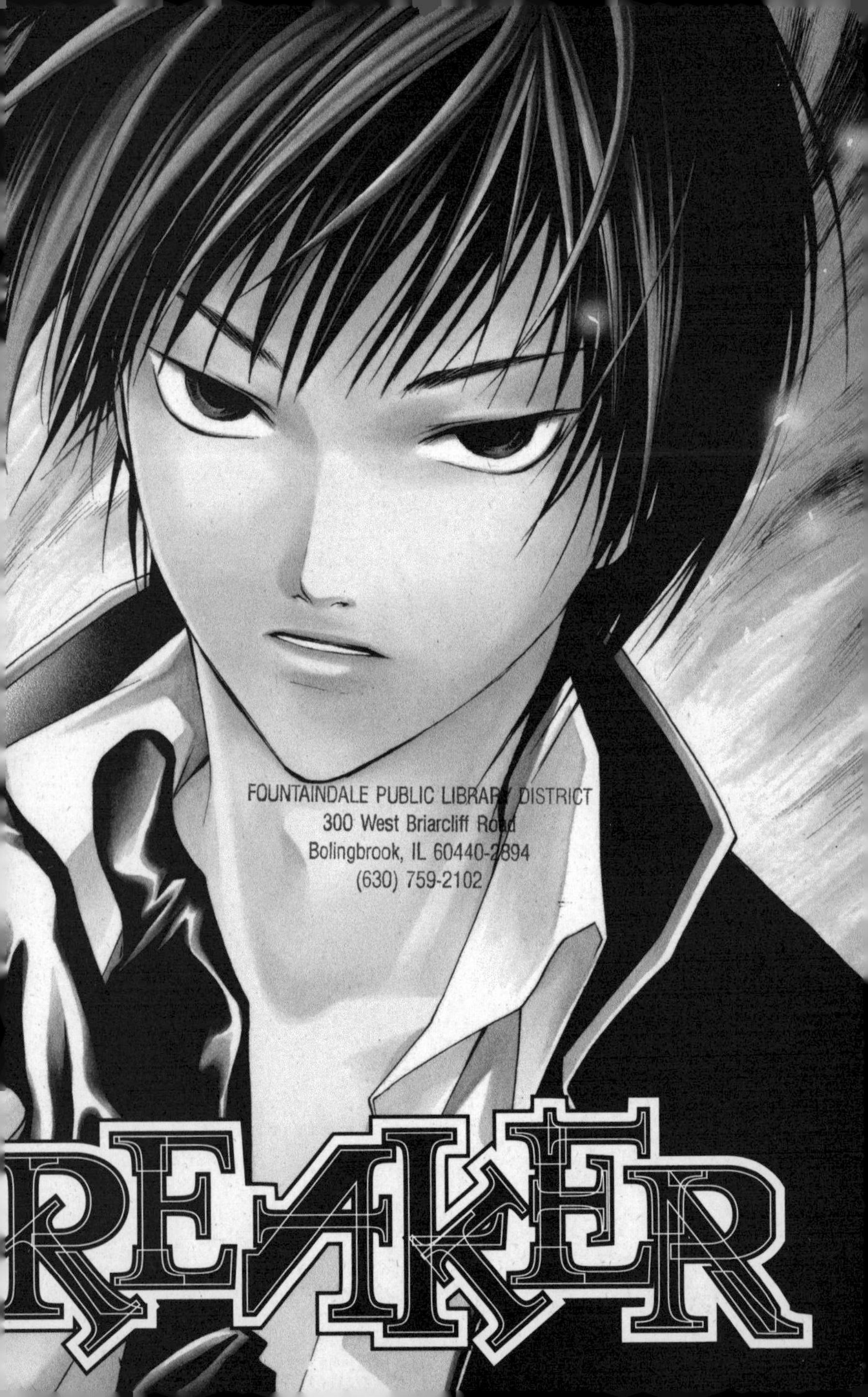
REAKER

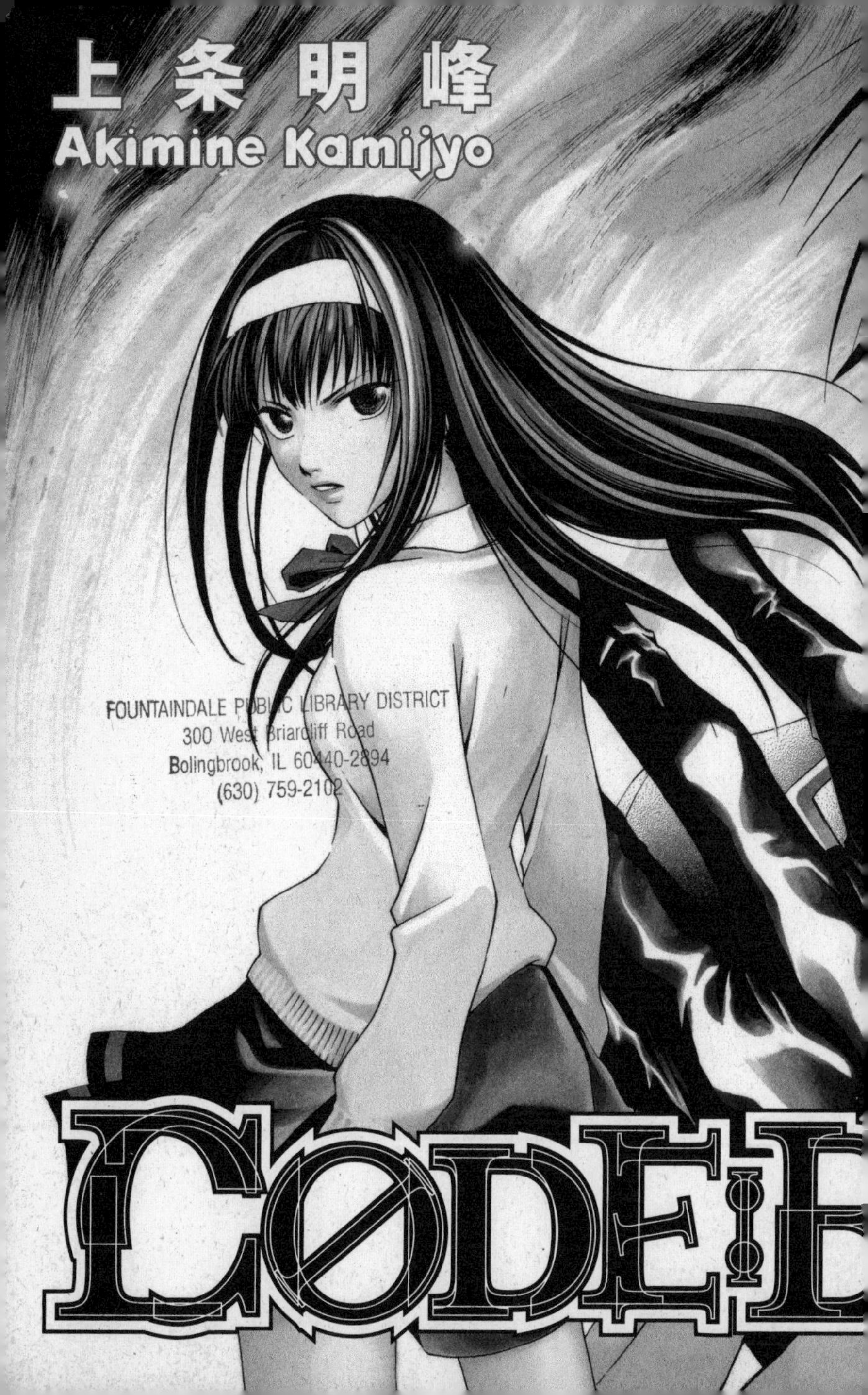
上条明峰
Akimine Kamijyo
CODE

Contents

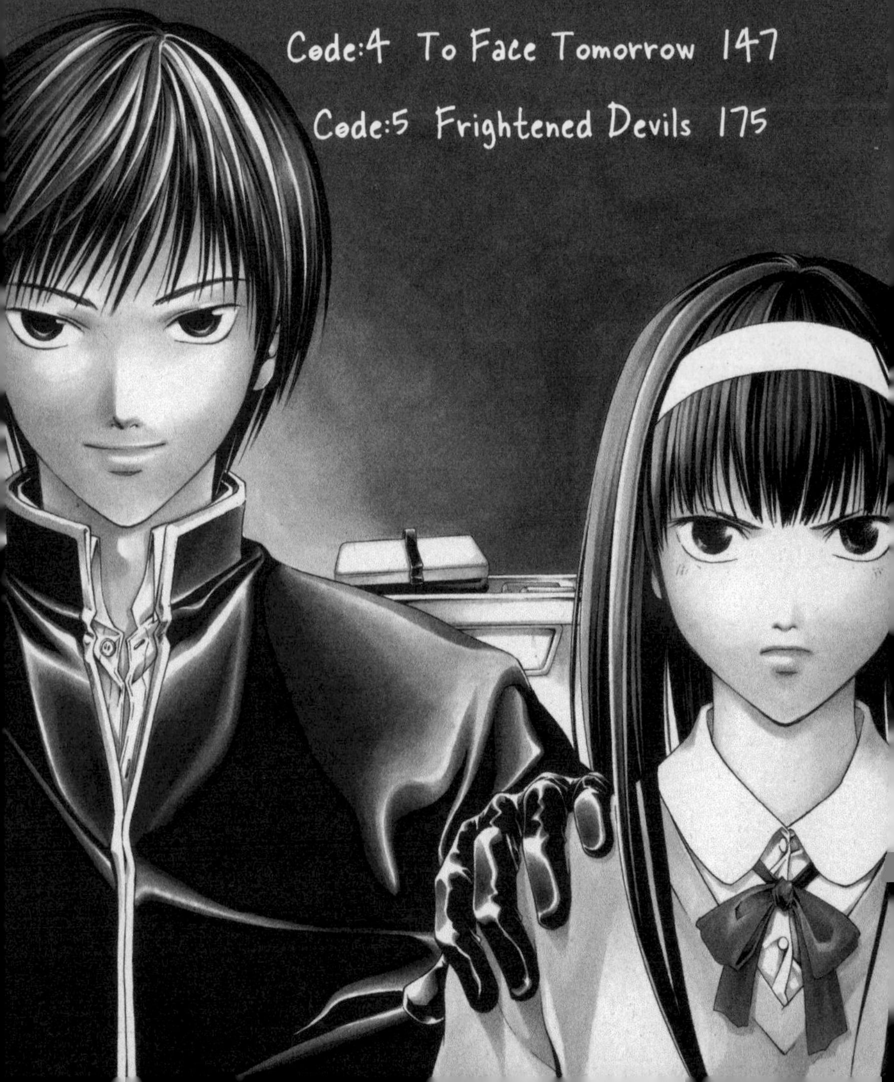

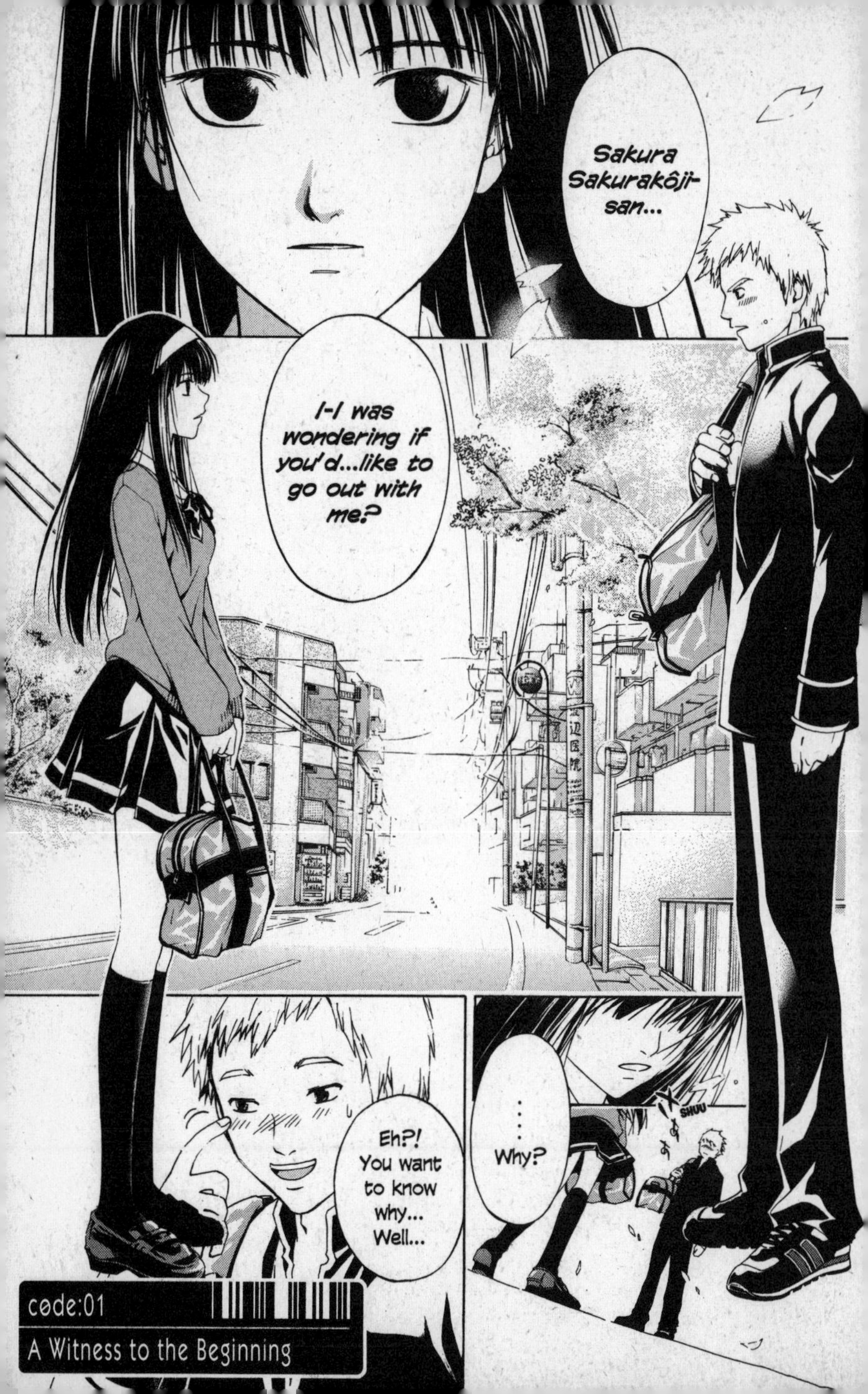
Sakura Sakurakôji-san...
I-I was wondering if you'd...like to go out with me?
SHUU
...Why?
Eh?! You want to know why... Well...

code:01

A Witness to the Beginning

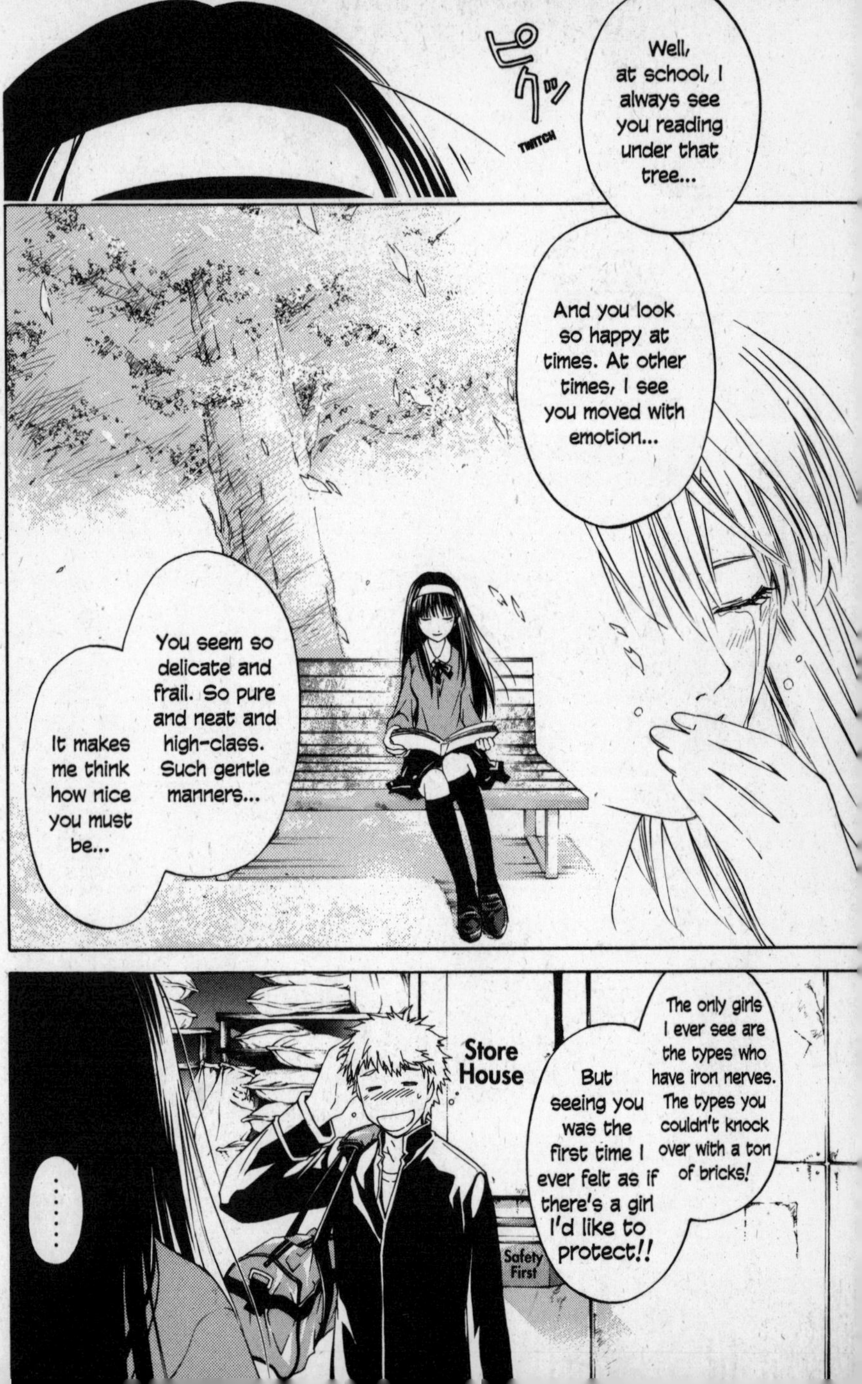
Well, at school, I always see you reading under that tree...
ピクッ
TWITCH
And you look so happy at times. At other times, I see you moved with emotion...
You seem so delicate and frail. So pure and neat and high-class. Such gentle manners...
It makes me think how nice you must be...
The only girls I ever see are the types who have iron nerves. The types you couldn't knock over with a ton of bricks!
But seeing you was the first time I ever felt as if there's a girl I'd like to protect!!
Store House
Safety First
......

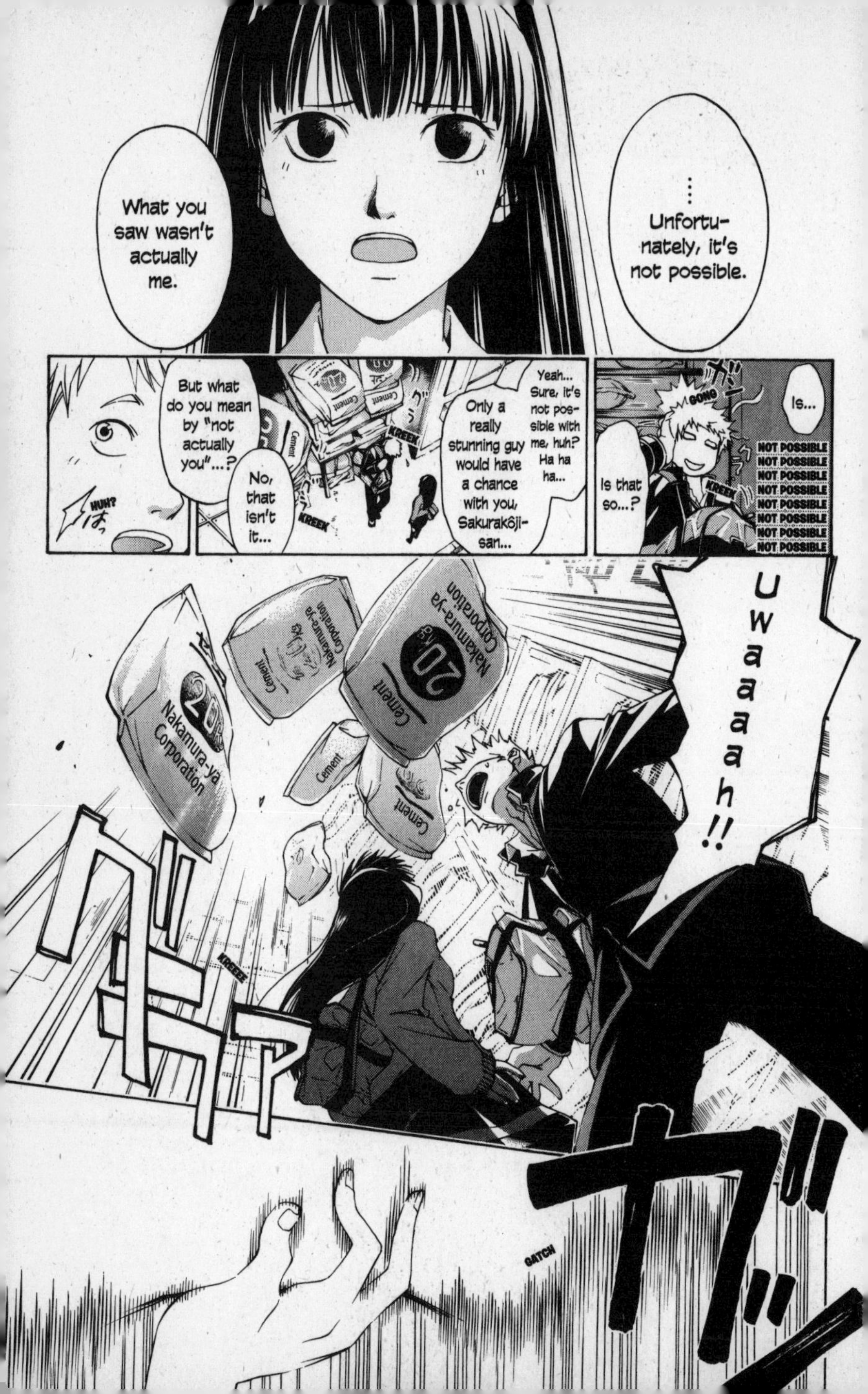
...
Unfortu-nately, it's not possible.
What you saw wasn't actually me.
Is...
GONG
NOT POSSIBLE
NOT POSSIBLE
NOT POSSIBLE
NOT POSSIBLE
NOT POSSIBLE
NOT POSSIBLE
NOT POSSIBLE
NOT POSSIBLE
KREEK
Is that so...?
Yeah... Sure, it's not pos-sible with me, huh? Ha ha ha...
Only a really stunning guy would have a chance with you, Sakurakôji-san...
KREEK
Cement
Cement
No, that isn't it...
KREEK
But what do you mean by "not actually you"...?
HUH?
Uwaaaaah!!
Nakamura-ya Corporation
Cement
Nakamura-ya Corporation
Cement
Nakamura-ya Corporation
Cement
Cement
KREEEE
GATCH

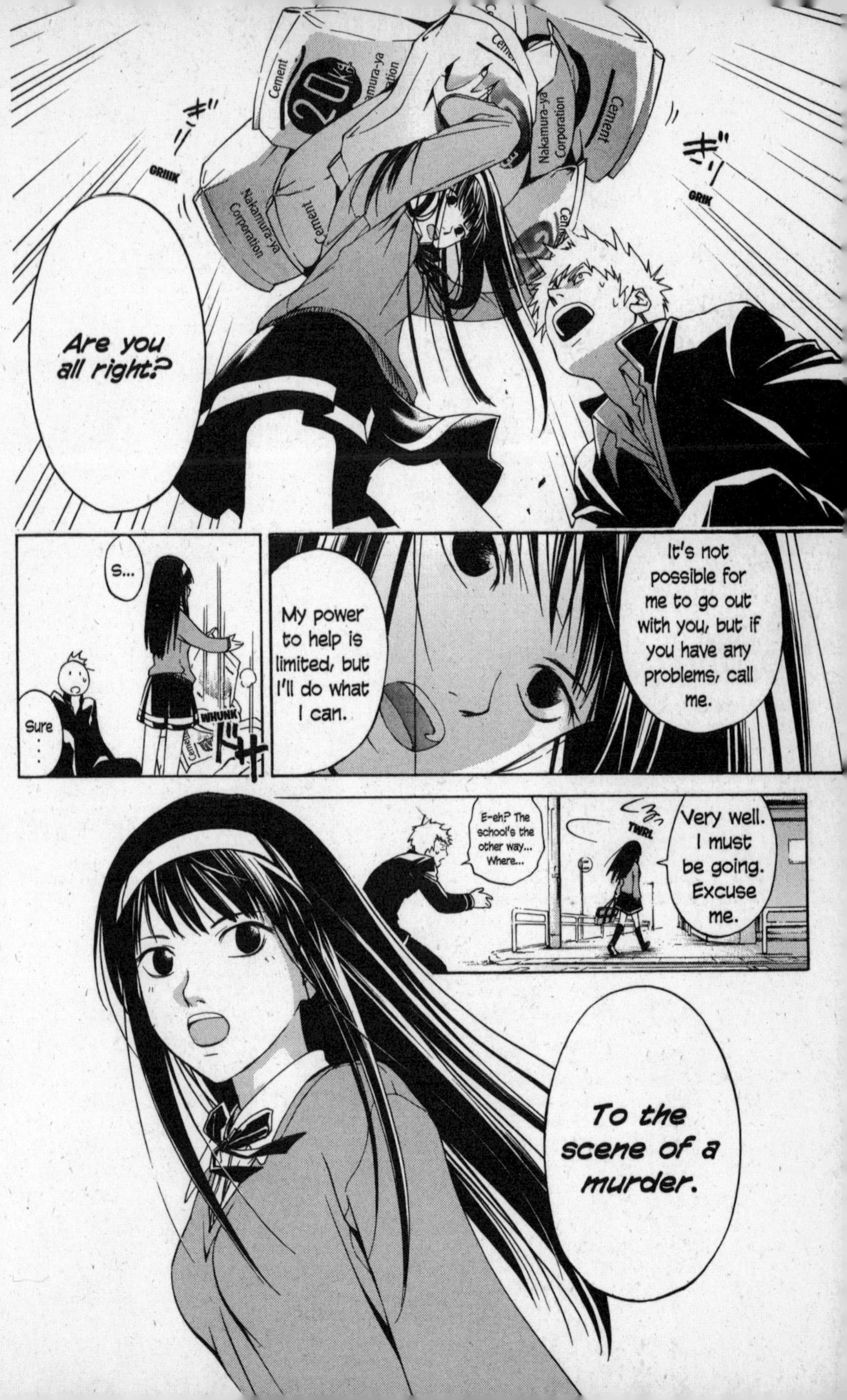
GRIK
GRIIK
Cement
Nakamura-ya Corporation
20kg
Are you all right?
It's not possible for me to go out with you, but if you have any problems, call me.
My power to help is limited, but I'll do what I can.
S...
WHUNK
Sure...
Very well. I must be going. Excuse me.
TWRL
E-eh? The school's the other way... Where...
To the scene of a murder.

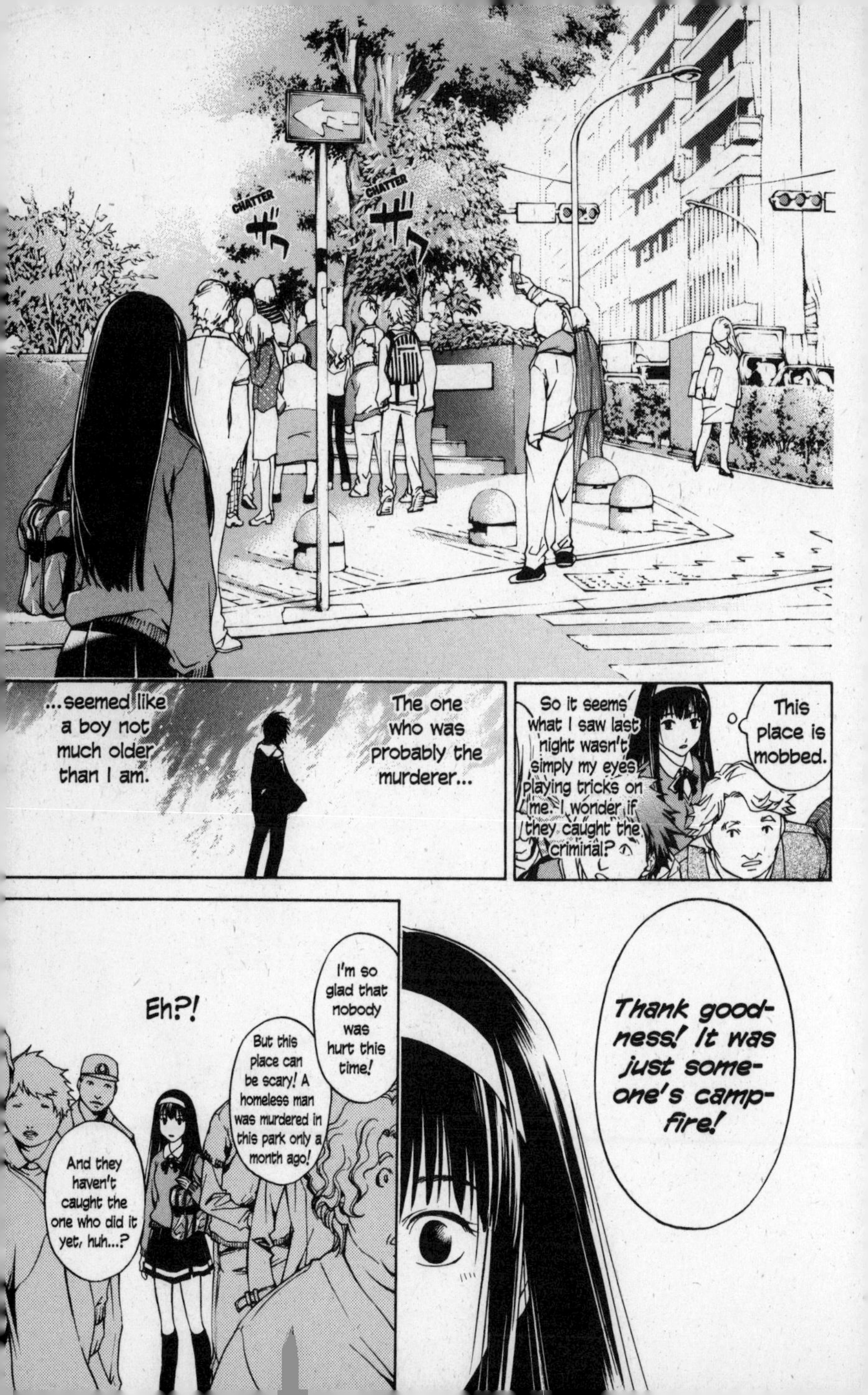
CHATTER
CHATTER
This place is mobbed.
So it seems what I saw last night wasn't simply my eyes playing tricks on me. I wonder if they caught the criminal?
The one who was probably the murderer...
...seemed like a boy not much older than I am.
Thank goodness! It was just someone's campfire!
I'm so glad that nobody was hurt this time!
But this place can be scary! A homeless man was murdered in this park only a month ago!
And they haven't caught the one who did it yet, huh...?
Eh?!

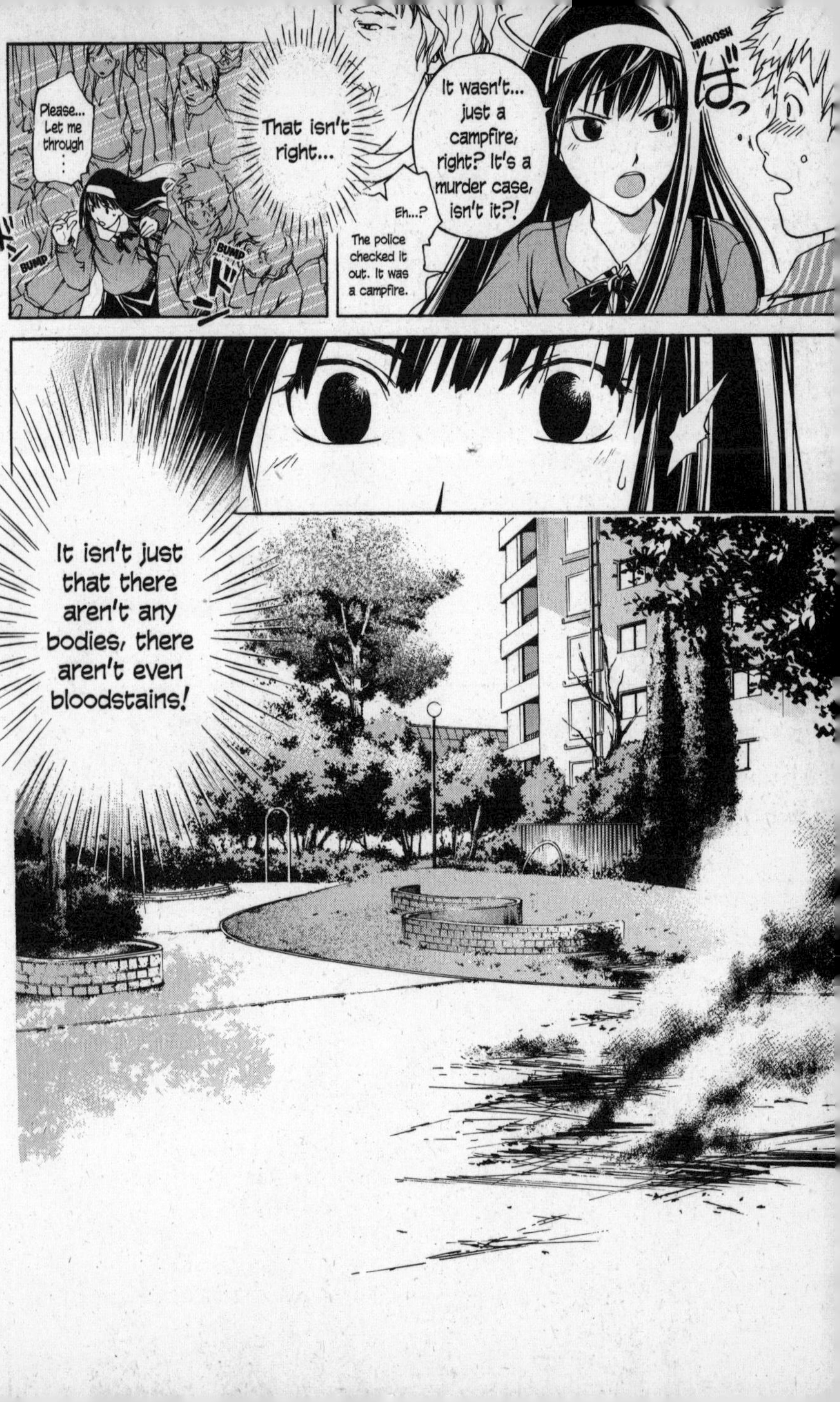
WHOOSH
ばっ
It wasn't... just a campfire, right? It's a murder case, isn't it?!
Eh...?
The police checked it out. It was a campfire.
That isn't right...
Please... Let me through...
BUMP
ド
BUMP
ド
It isn't just that there aren't any bodies, there aren't even bloodstains!

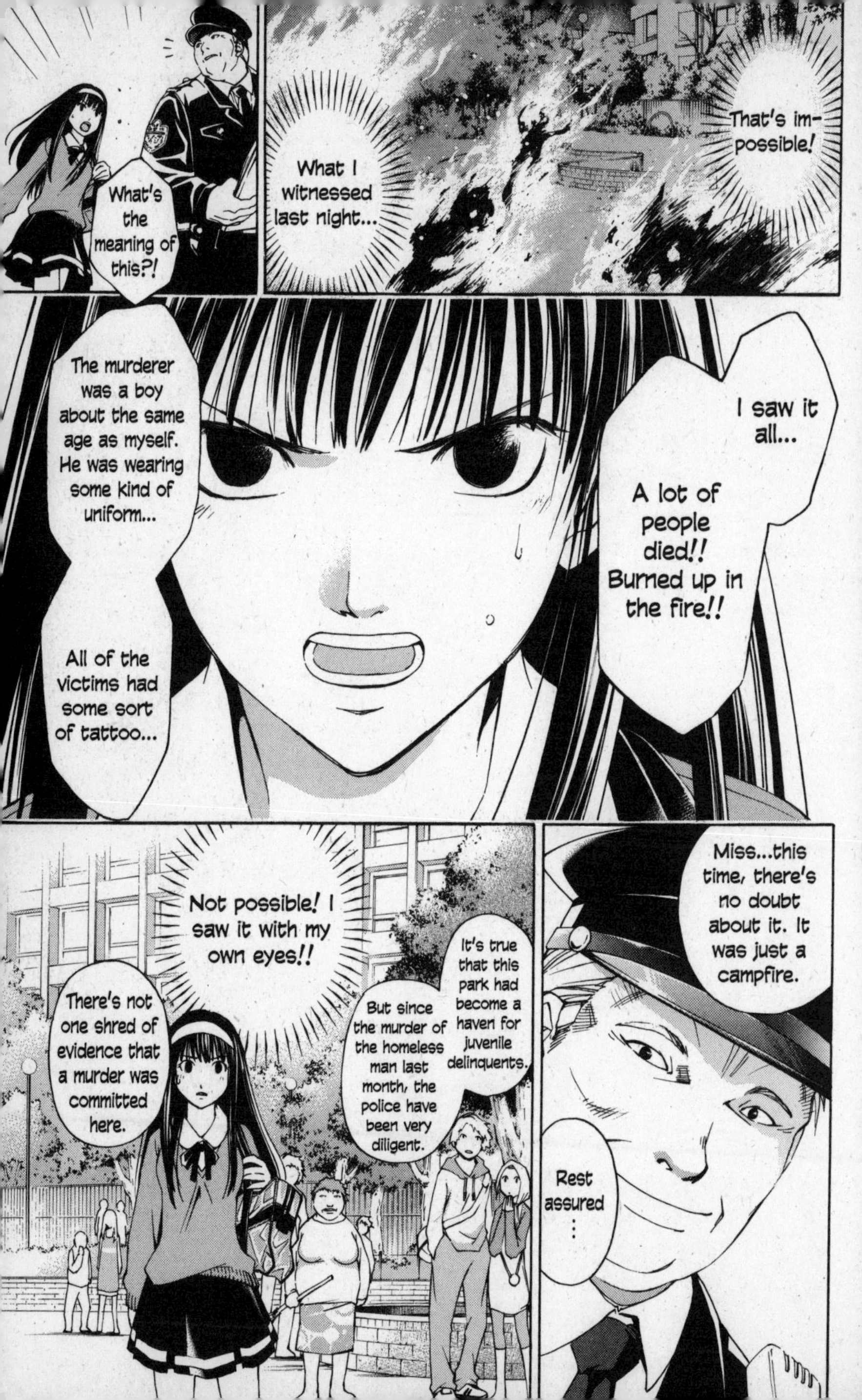
That's impossible!
What I witnessed last night...
What's the meaning of this?!
I saw it all...
A lot of people died!! Burned up in the fire!!
The murderer was a boy about the same age as myself. He was wearing some kind of uniform...
All of the victims had some sort of tattoo...
Miss...this time, there's no doubt about it. It was just a campfire.
Rest assured...
Not possible! I saw it with my own eyes!!
It's true that this park had become a haven for juvenile delinquents.
But since the murder of the homeless man last month, the police have been very diligent.
There's not one shred of evidence that a murder was committed here.

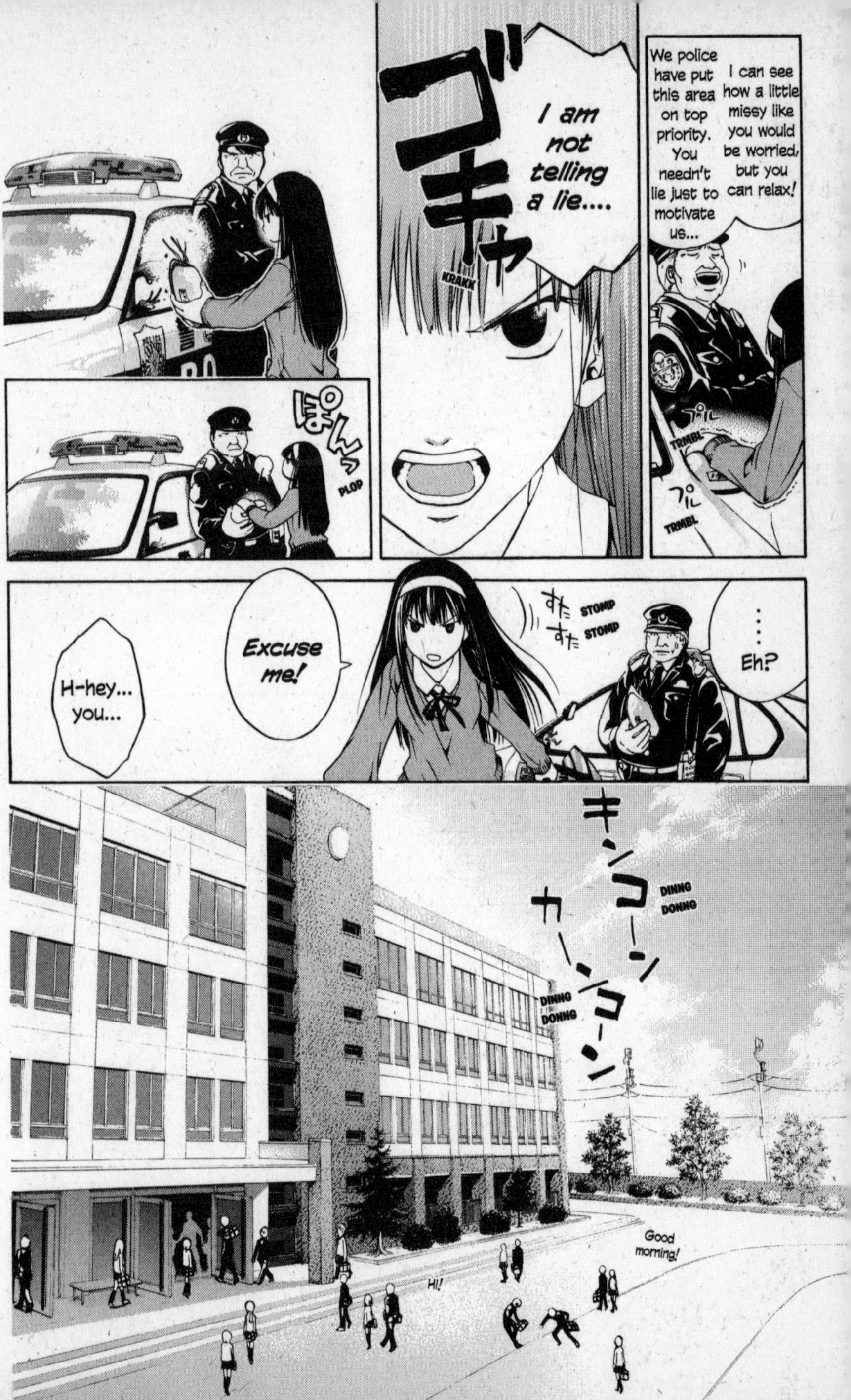
I can see how a little missy like you would be worried, but you can relax!
We police have put this area on top priority. You needn't lie just to motivate us...
プル
TRMBL
プル
TRMBL
ゴキャ
KRAKK
I am not telling a lie....
ぽんっ
PLOP
. . . Eh?
すた すた
STOMP STOMP
Excuse me!
H-hey... you...
キンコーン
DINNG DONNG
カーンコーン
DINNG DONNG
Good morning!
Hi!

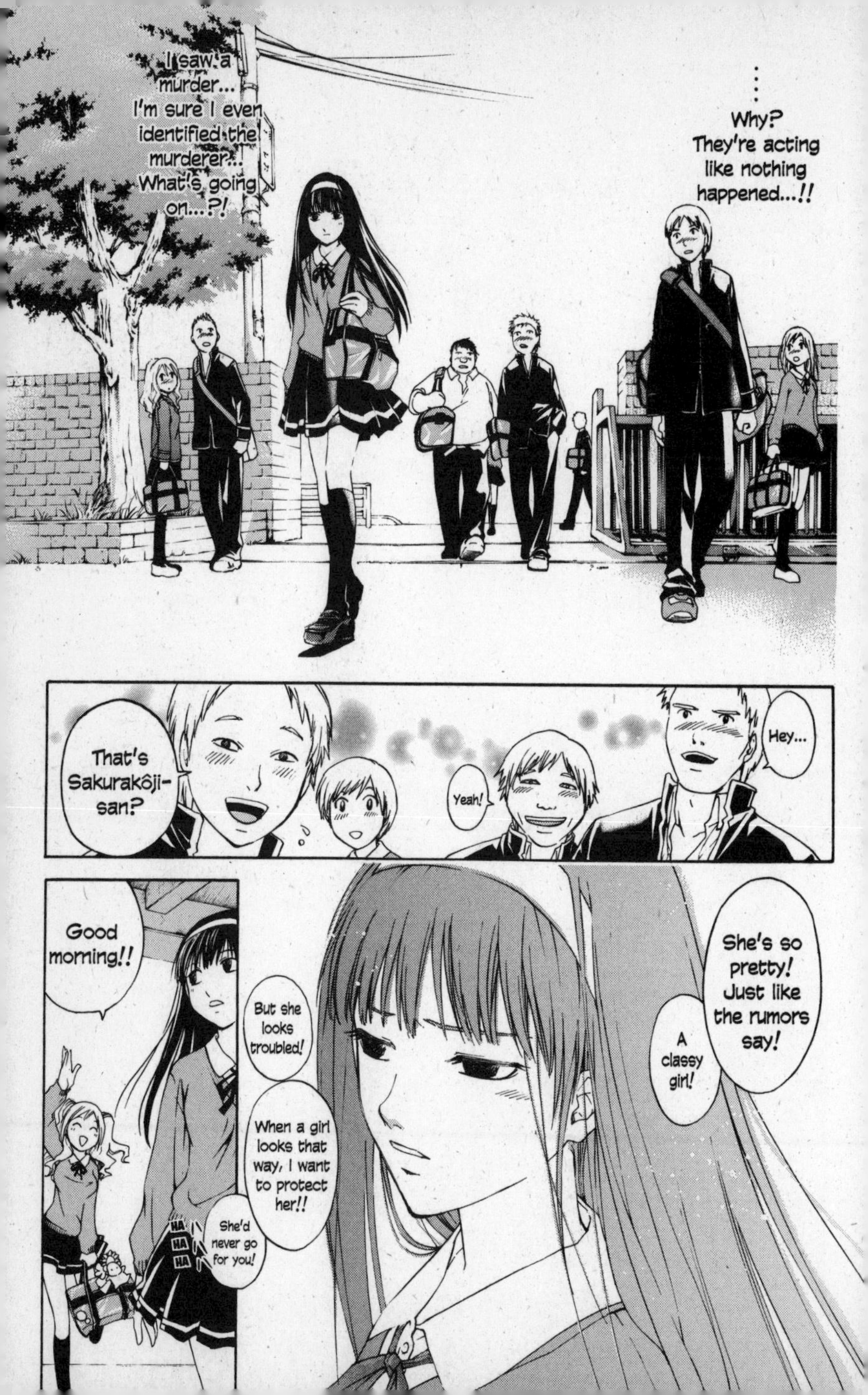
. . . . .
Why? They're acting like nothing happened...!!
I saw a murder... I'm sure I even identified the murderer... What's going on...?!
Hey...
Yeah!
That's Sakurakôji-san?
She's so pretty! Just like the rumors say!
A classy girl!
But she looks troubled!
When a girl looks that way, I want to protect her!!
She'd never go for you!
HA HA HA
Good morning!!

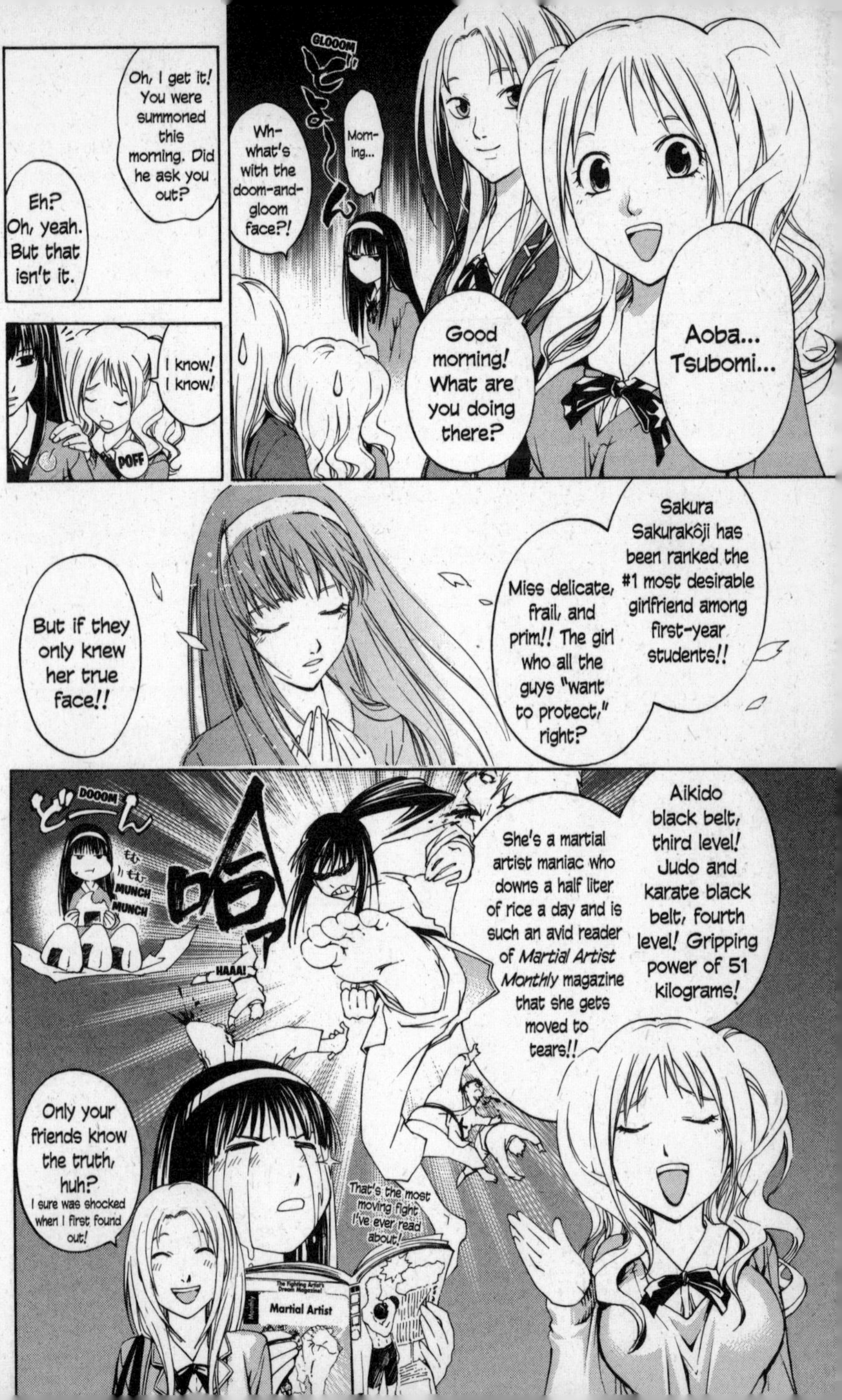
Aoba... Tsubomi...
Good morning! What are you doing there?
Morning...
GLOOOM
Wh-what's with the doom-and-gloom face?!
Oh, I get it! You were summoned this morning. Did he ask you out?
Eh? Oh, yeah. But that isn't it.
I know! I know!
POFF
Sakura Sakurakôji has been ranked the #1 most desirable girlfriend among first-year students!!
Miss delicate, frail, and prim!! The girl who all the guys "want to protect," right?
But if they only knew her true face!!
Aikido black belt, third level! Judo and karate black belt, fourth level! Gripping power of 51 kilograms!
She's a martial artist maniac who downs a half liter of rice a day and is such an avid reader of *Martial Artist Monthly* magazine that she gets moved to tears!!
DOOOM
MUNCH MUNCH
HAAA!
That's the most moving fight I've ever read about!
Only your friends know the truth, huh?
I sure was shocked when I first found out!
Martial Artist

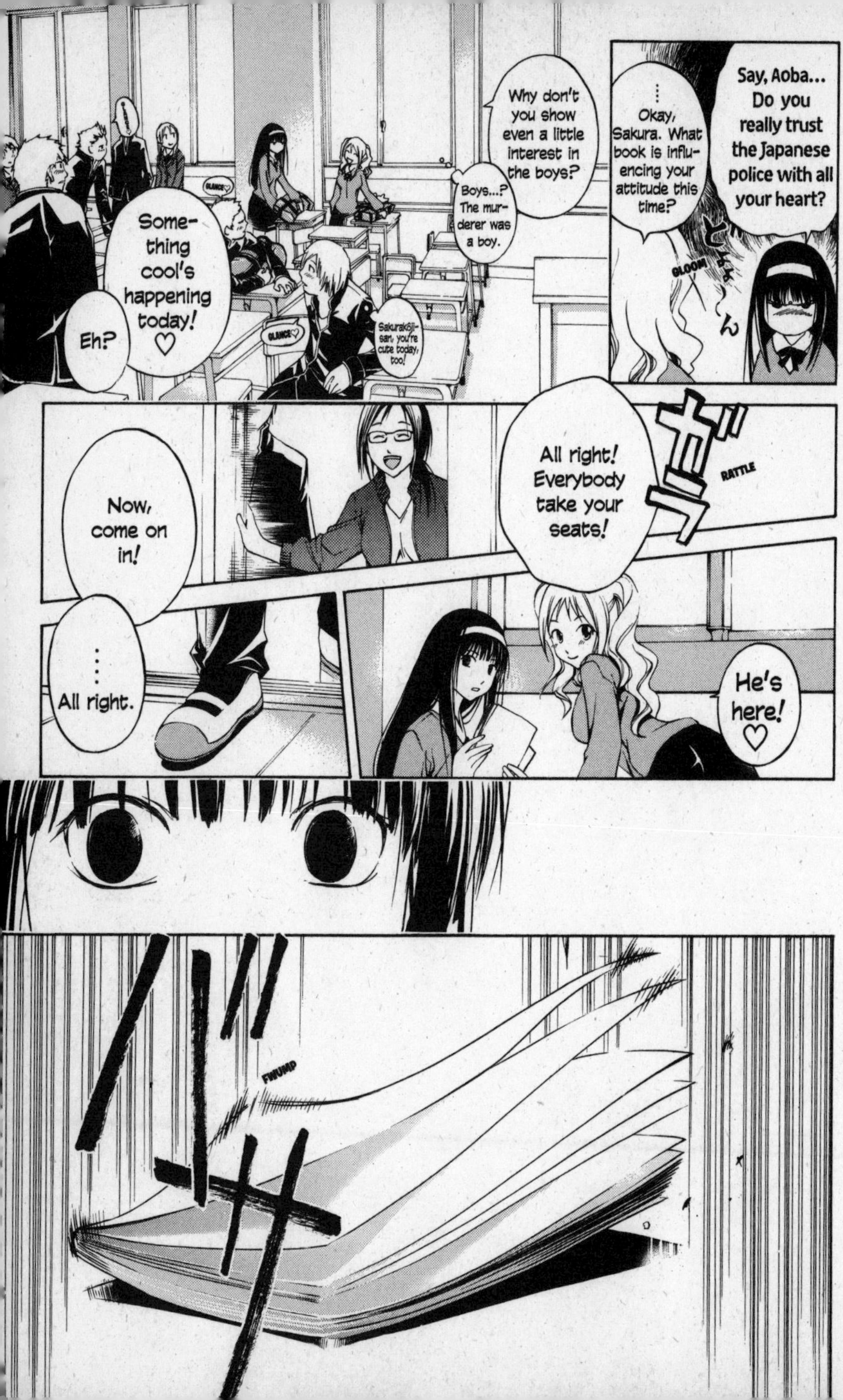
Say, Aoba... Do you really trust the Japanese police with all your heart?
... Okay, Sakura. What book is influencing your attitude this time?
GLOOM
Why don't you show even a little interest in the boys?
Boys...? The murderer was a boy.
Sakurakōji-san, you're cute today, too!
GLANCE♡
GLANCE♡
Something cool's happening today! ♡
Eh?
RATTLE
All right! Everybody take your seats!
Now, come on in!
He's here! ♡
.... All right.
FWUMP

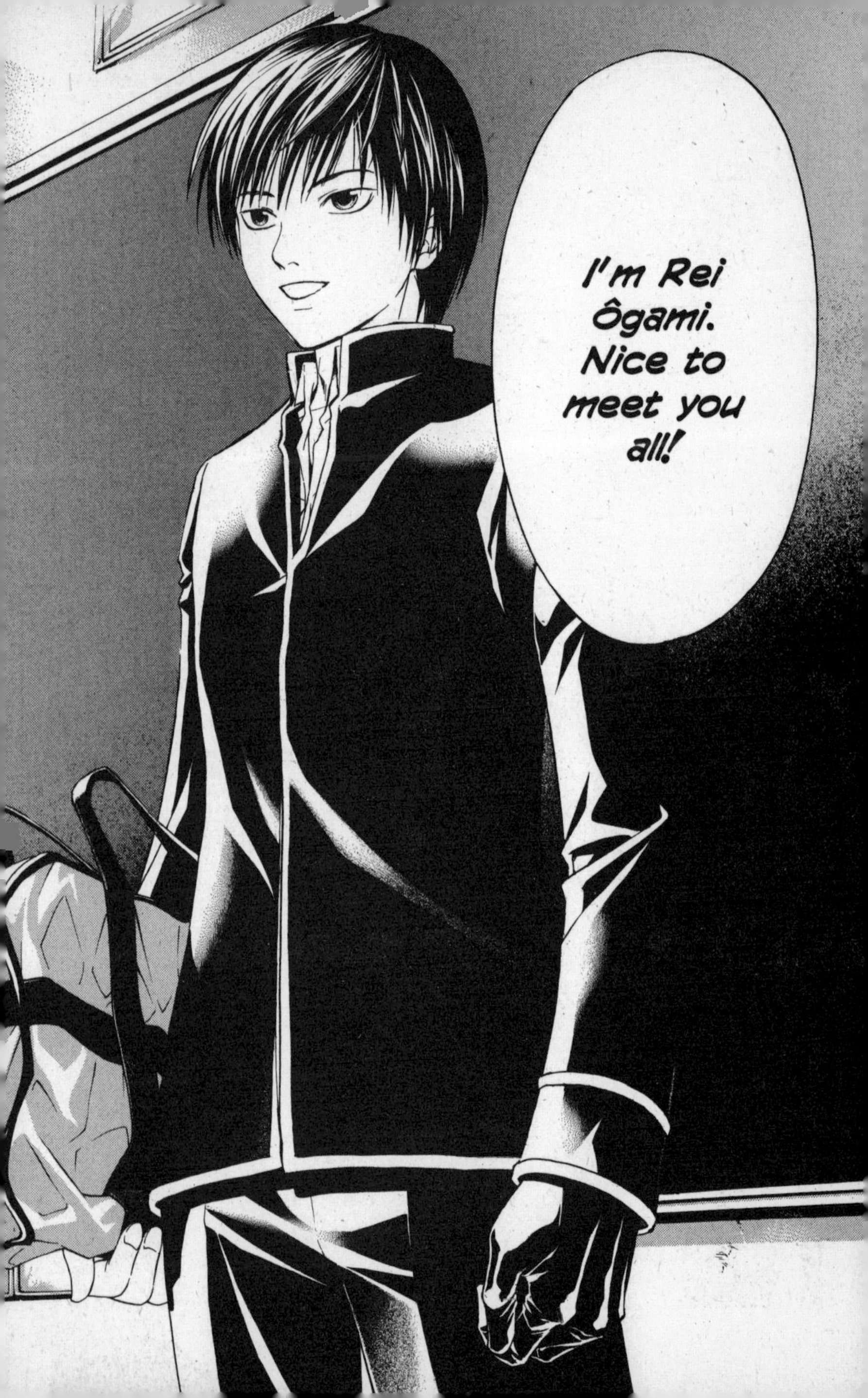
I'm Rei Ôgami. Nice to meet you all!

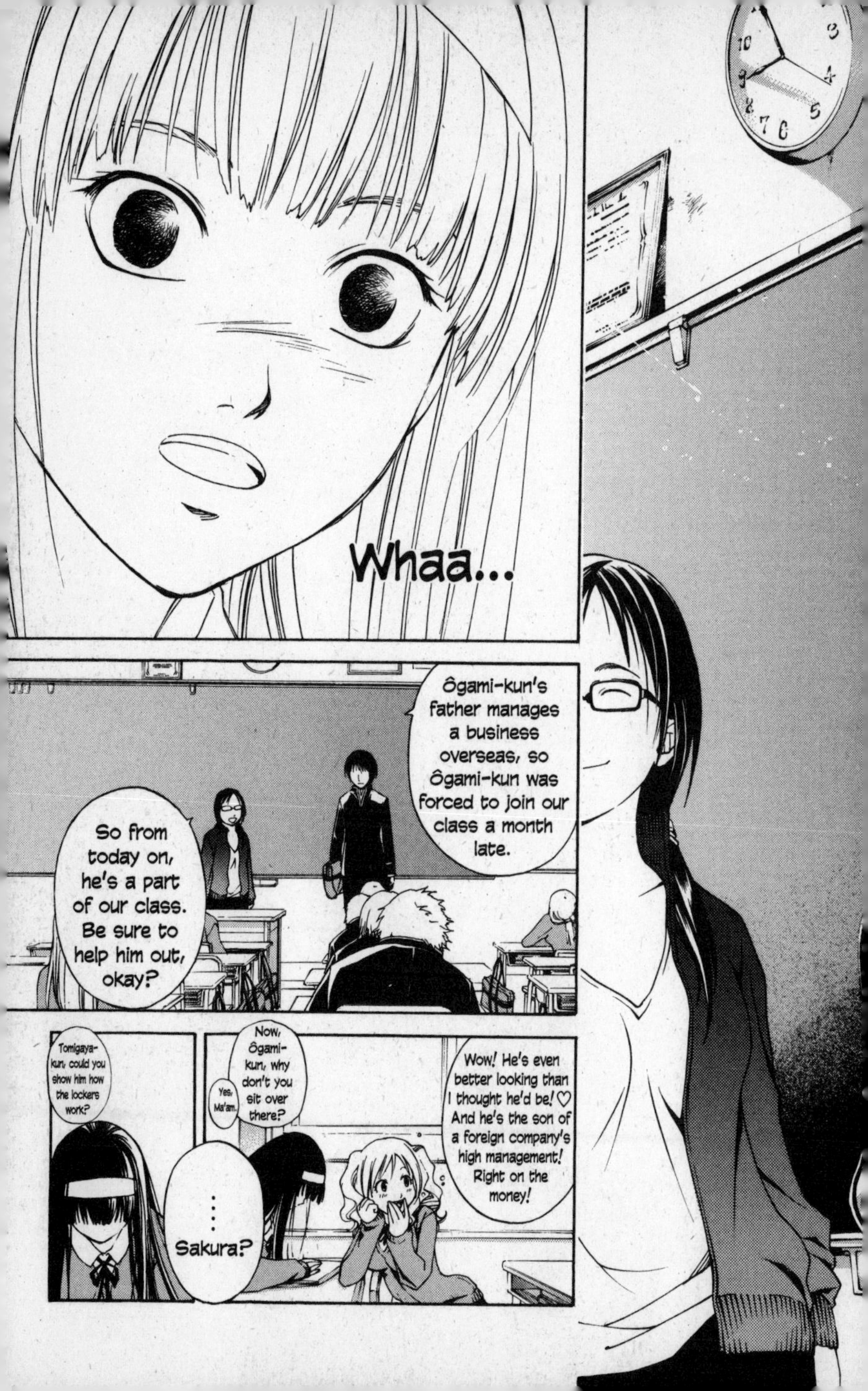

Whaa...
Ôgami-kun's father manages a business overseas, so Ôgami-kun was forced to join our class a month late.
So from today on, he's a part of our class. Be sure to help him out, okay?
Now, Ôgami-kun, why don't you sit over there?
Yes, Ma'am.
Wow! He's even better looking than I thought he'd be! ♡ And he's the son of a foreign company's high management! Right on the money!
.... Sakura?
Tomigaya-kun, could you show him how the lockers work?

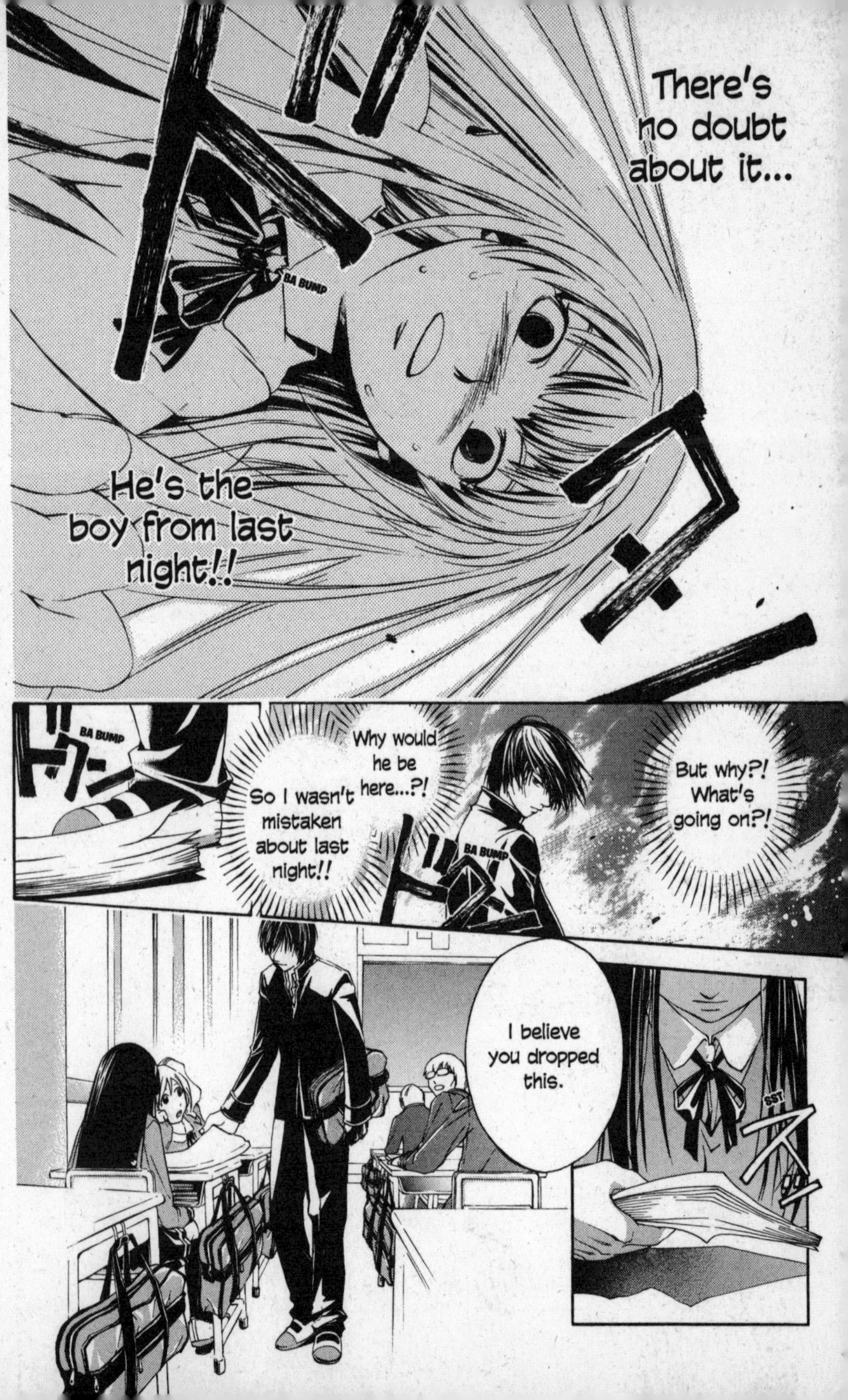
There's no doubt about it...
BA BUMP
He's the boy from last night!!
But why?! What's going on?!
BA BUMP
Why would he be here...?!
So I wasn't mistaken about last night!!
BA BUMP
SST
I believe you dropped this.

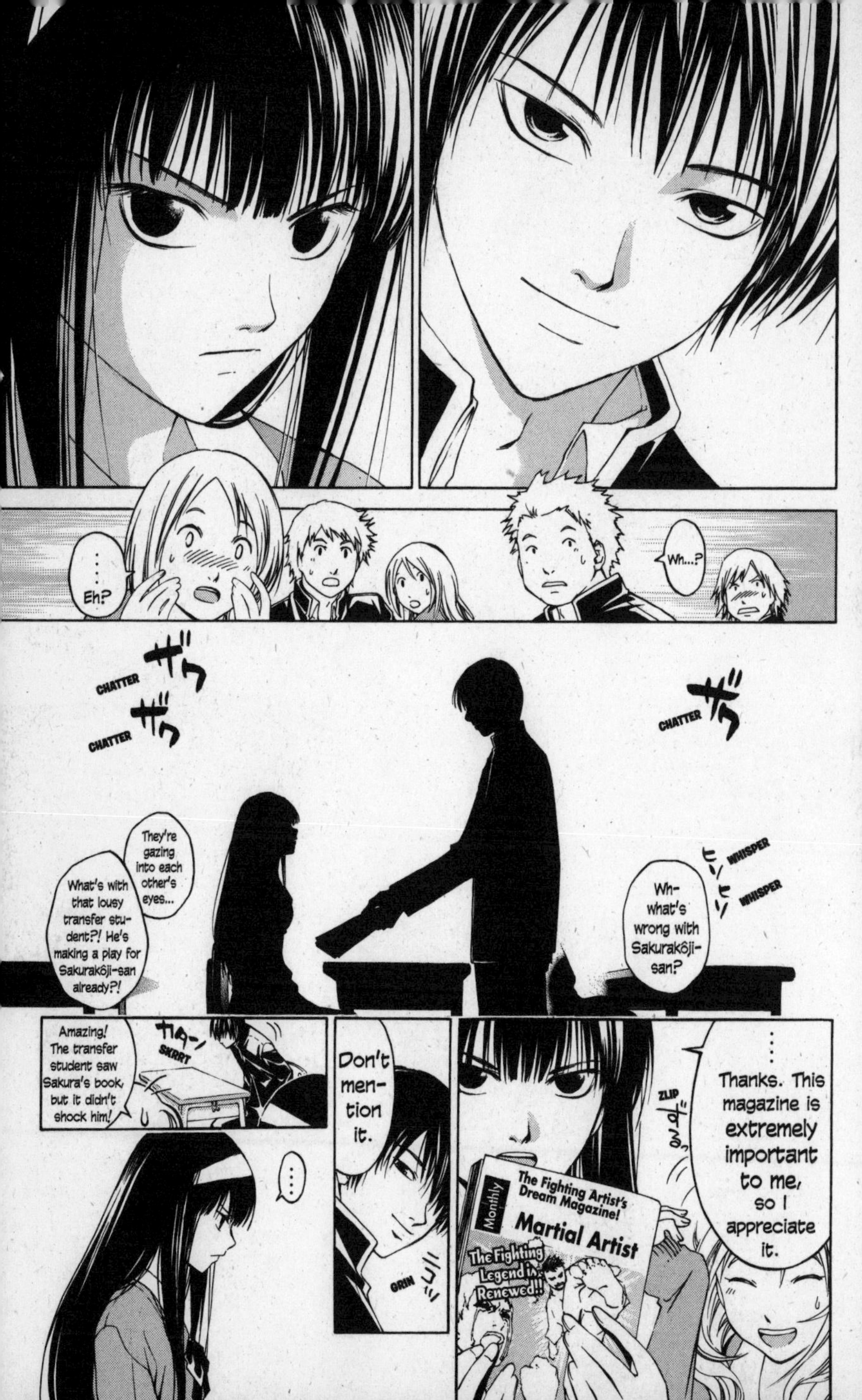
Wh...?
......
Eh?
CHATTER
WHISPER
WHISPER
Wh-what's wrong with Sakurakôji-san?
CHATTER
CHATTER
They're gazing into each other's eyes...
What's with that lousy transfer student?! He's making a play for Sakurakôji-san already?!
......
Thanks. This magazine is extremely important to me, so I appreciate it.
ZLIP
Monthly
The Fighting Artist's Dream Magazine!
Martial Artist
The Fighting Legend is Renewed!!
Don't mention it.
GRIN
Amazing! The transfer student saw Sakura's book, but it didn't shock him!
SKRRT
....

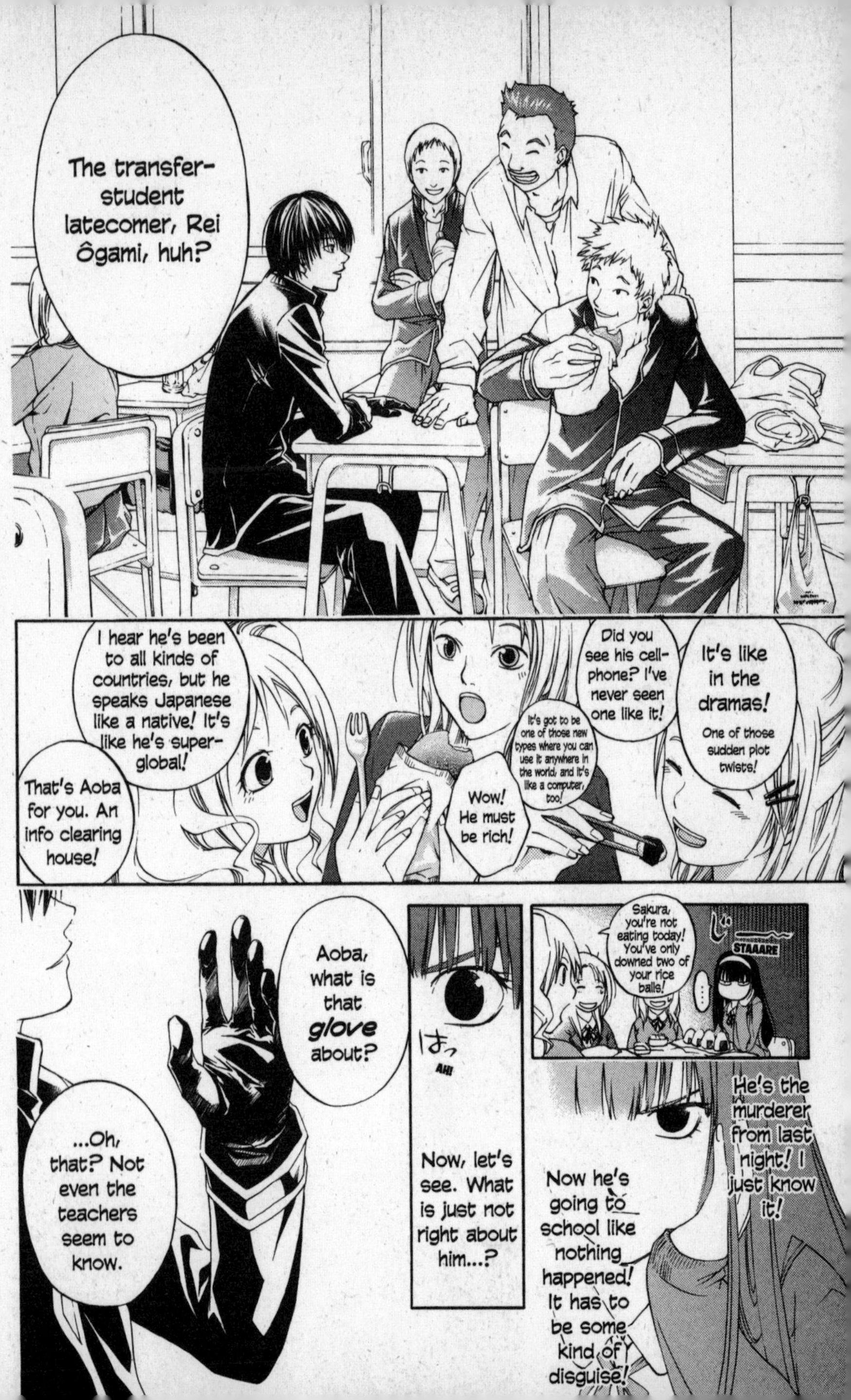
The transfer-student latecomer, Rei Ôgami, huh?
It's like in the dramas!
One of those sudden plot twists!
Did you see his cell-phone? I've never seen one like it!
It's got to be one of those new types where you can use it anywhere in the world, and it's like a computer, too!
Wow! He must be rich!
I hear he's been to all kinds of countries, but he speaks Japanese like a native! It's like he's super-global!
That's Aoba for you. An info clearing house!
じー
STAAARE
Sakura, you're not eating today! You've only downed two of your rice balls!
...
He's the murderer from last night! I just know it!
Now he's going to school like nothing happened! It has to be some kind of disguise!
はっ
AH!
Now, let's see. What is just not right about him...?
Aoba, what is that glove about?
...Oh, that? Not even the teachers seem to know.

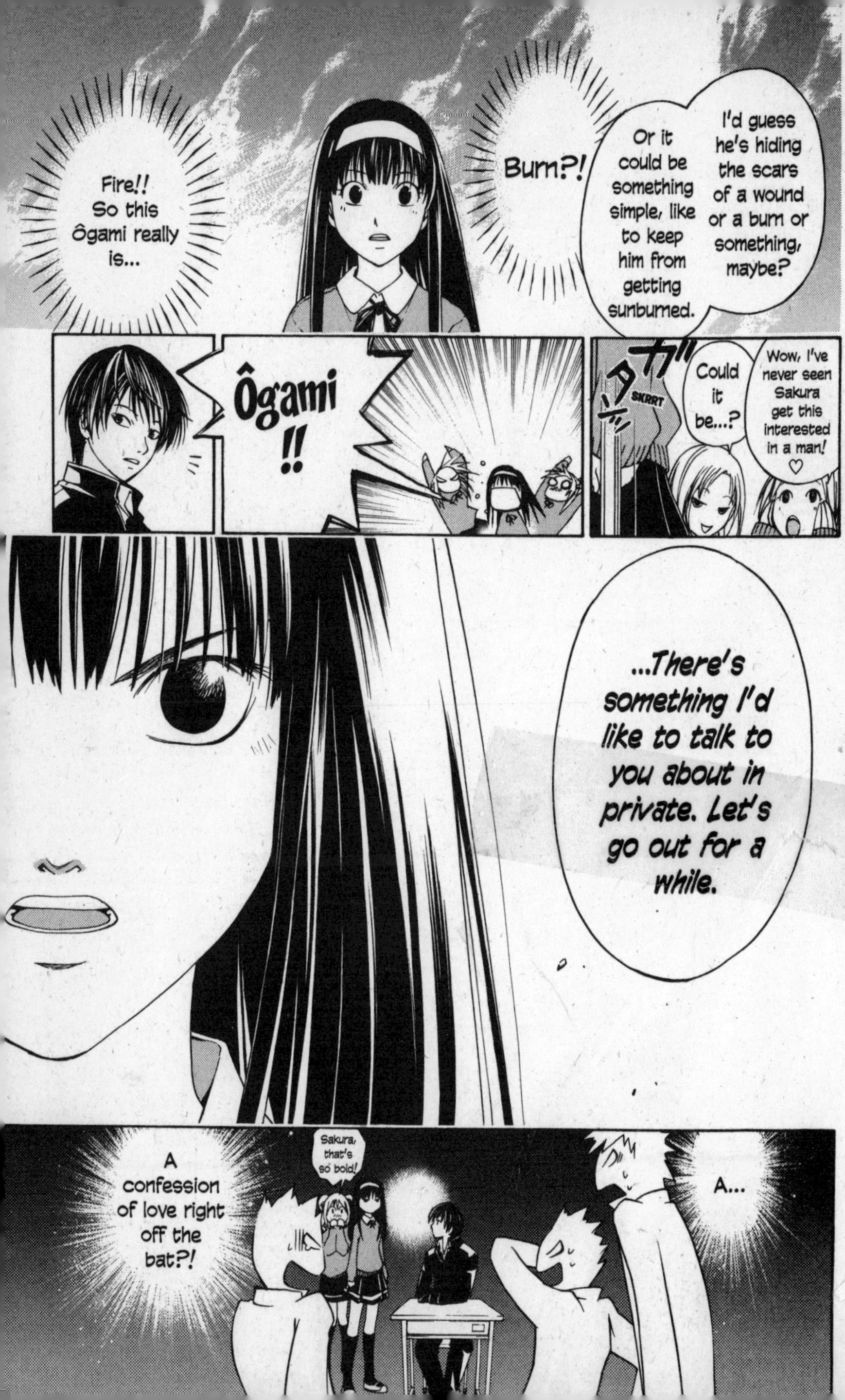
I'd guess he's hiding the scars of a wound or a burn or something, maybe?
Or it could be something simple, like to keep him from getting sunburned.
Burn?!
Fire!! So this Ôgami really is...
Wow, I've never seen Sakura get this interested in a man! ♡
Could it be...?
SKRRT
Ôgami!!
...There's something I'd like to talk to you about in private. Let's go out for a while.
A...
Sakura, that's so bold!
A confession of love right off the bat?!

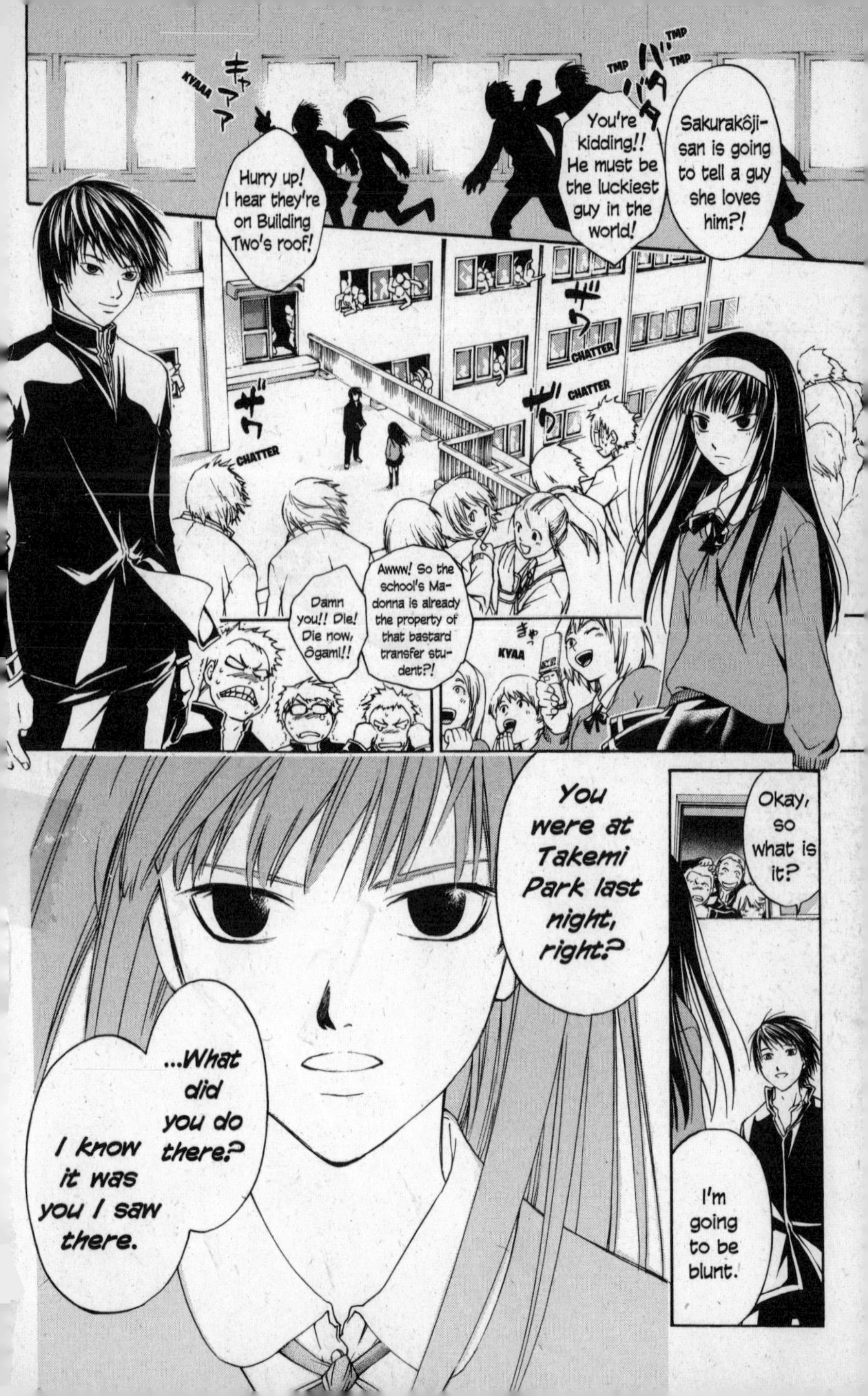
TMP TMP TMP
バタバタ
Sakurakôji-san is going to tell a guy she loves him?!
You're kidding!! He must be the luckiest guy in the world!
キャアア
KYAAA
Hurry up! I hear they're on Building Two's roof!
ザワ
CHATTER
ザワ
CHATTER
ザワ
CHATTER
きゃっ
KYAA
Awww! So the school's Madonna is already the property of that bastard transfer student?!
Damn you!! Die! Die now, Ôgami!!
Okay, so what is it?
I'm going to be blunt.
You were at Takemi Park last night, right?
...What did you do there?
I know it was you I saw there.

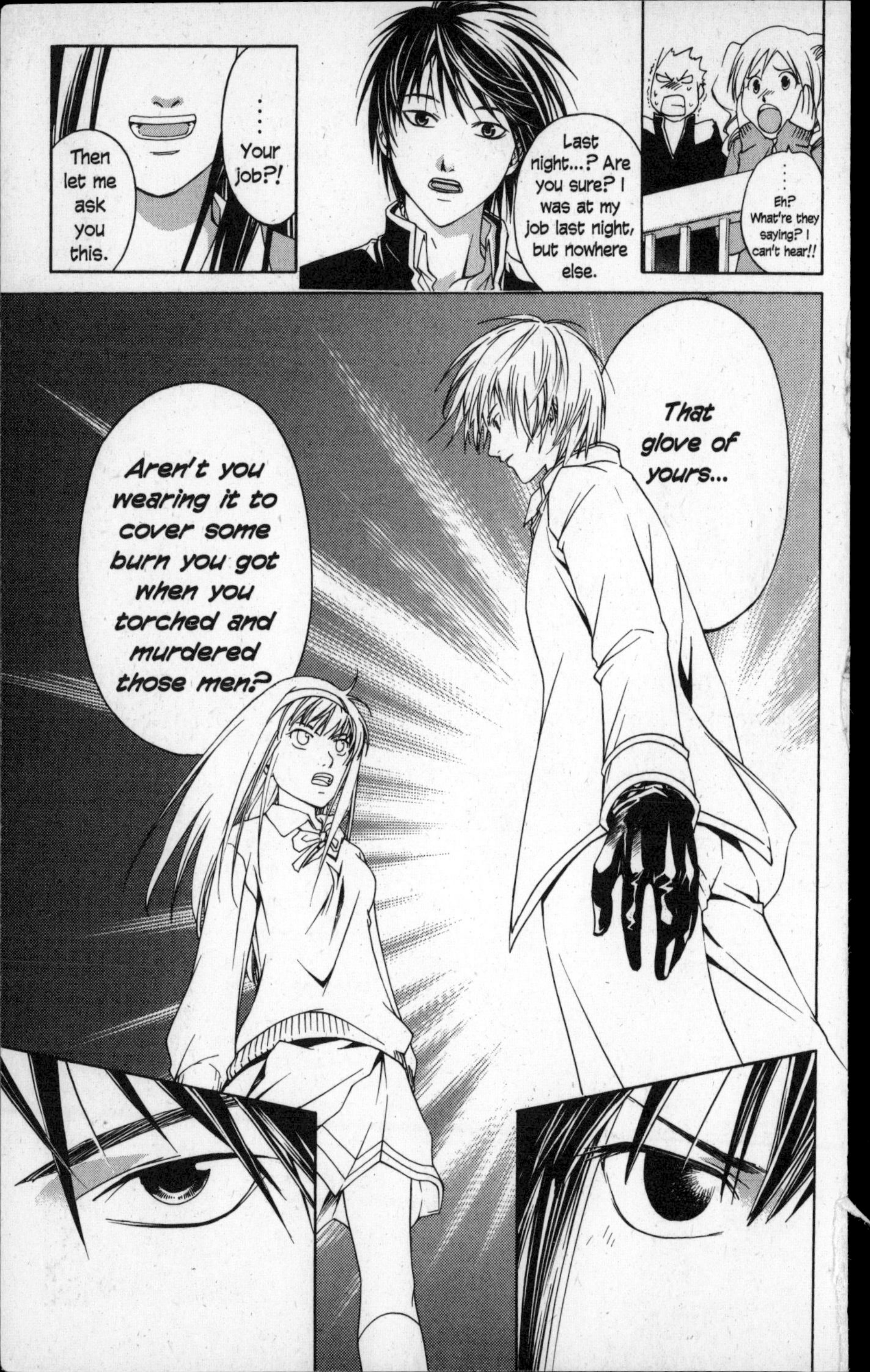
......
Eh? What're they saying? I can't hear!!
Last night...? Are you sure? I was at my job last night, but nowhere else.
.... Your job?!
Then let me ask you this.
That glove of yours...
Aren't you wearing it to cover some burn you got when you torched and murdered those men?

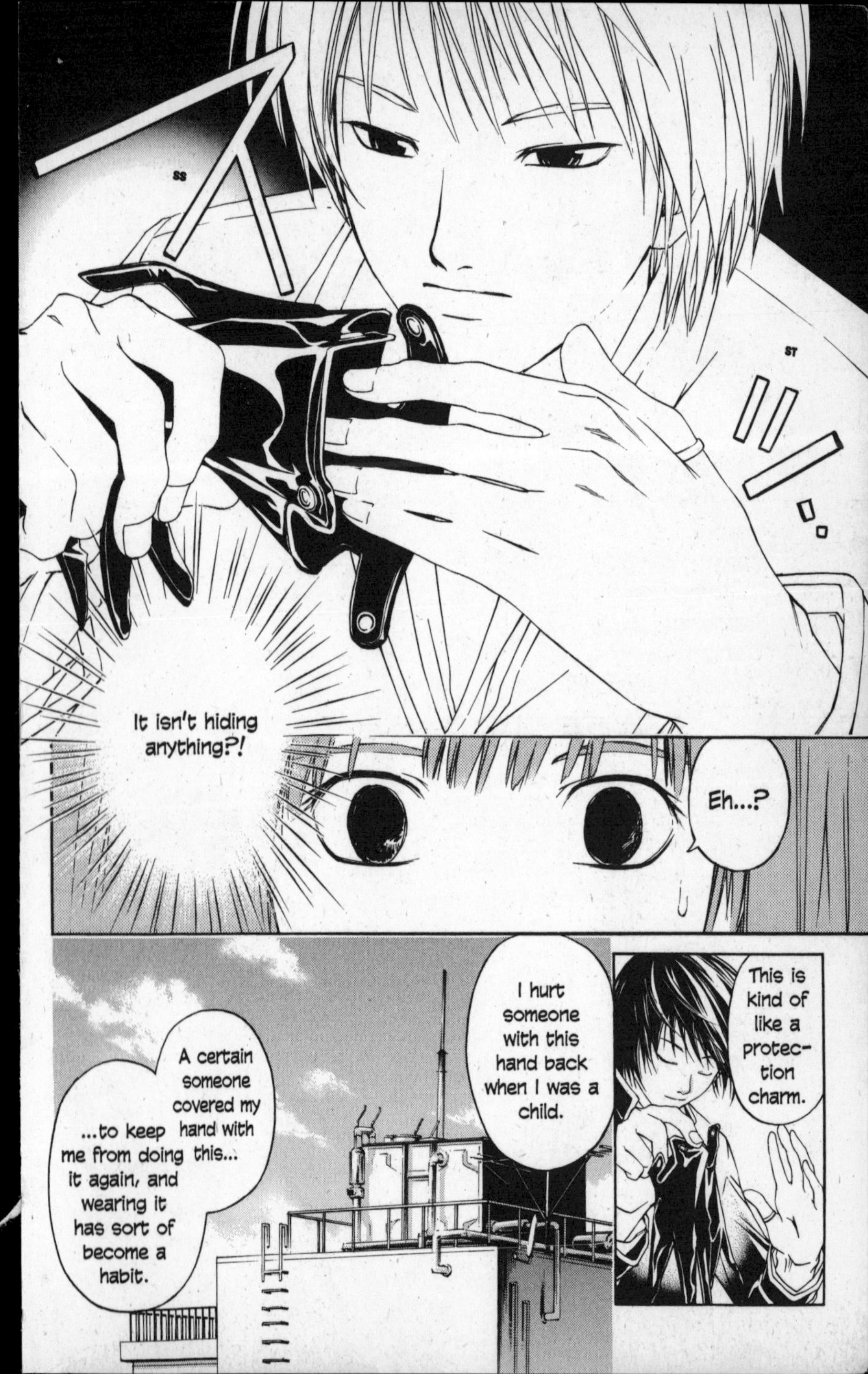
ST
SS
Eh...?
It isn't hiding anything?!
This is kind of like a protection charm.
I hurt someone with this hand back when I was a child.
A certain someone covered my hand with this...
...to keep me from doing it again, and wearing it has sort of become a habit.

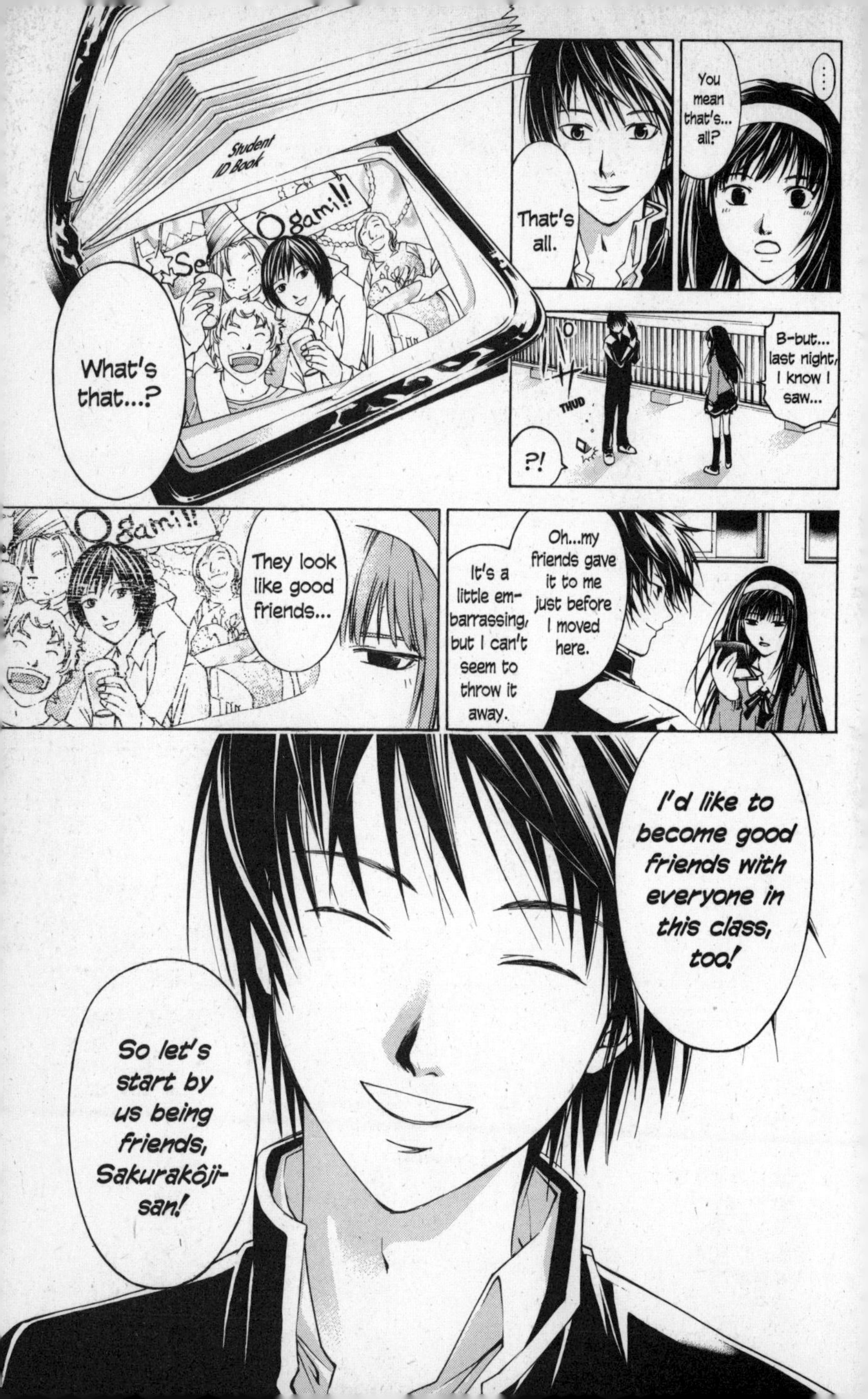
...
You mean that's... all?
That's all.
B-but... last night, I know I saw...
THUD
?!
Student ID Book
Ôgami!!
Se
What's that...?
Oh...my friends gave it to me just before I moved here.
It's a little embarrassing, but I can't seem to throw it away.
Ôgami!!
They look like good friends...
I'd like to become good friends with everyone in this class, too!
So let's start by us being friends, Sakurakôji-san!

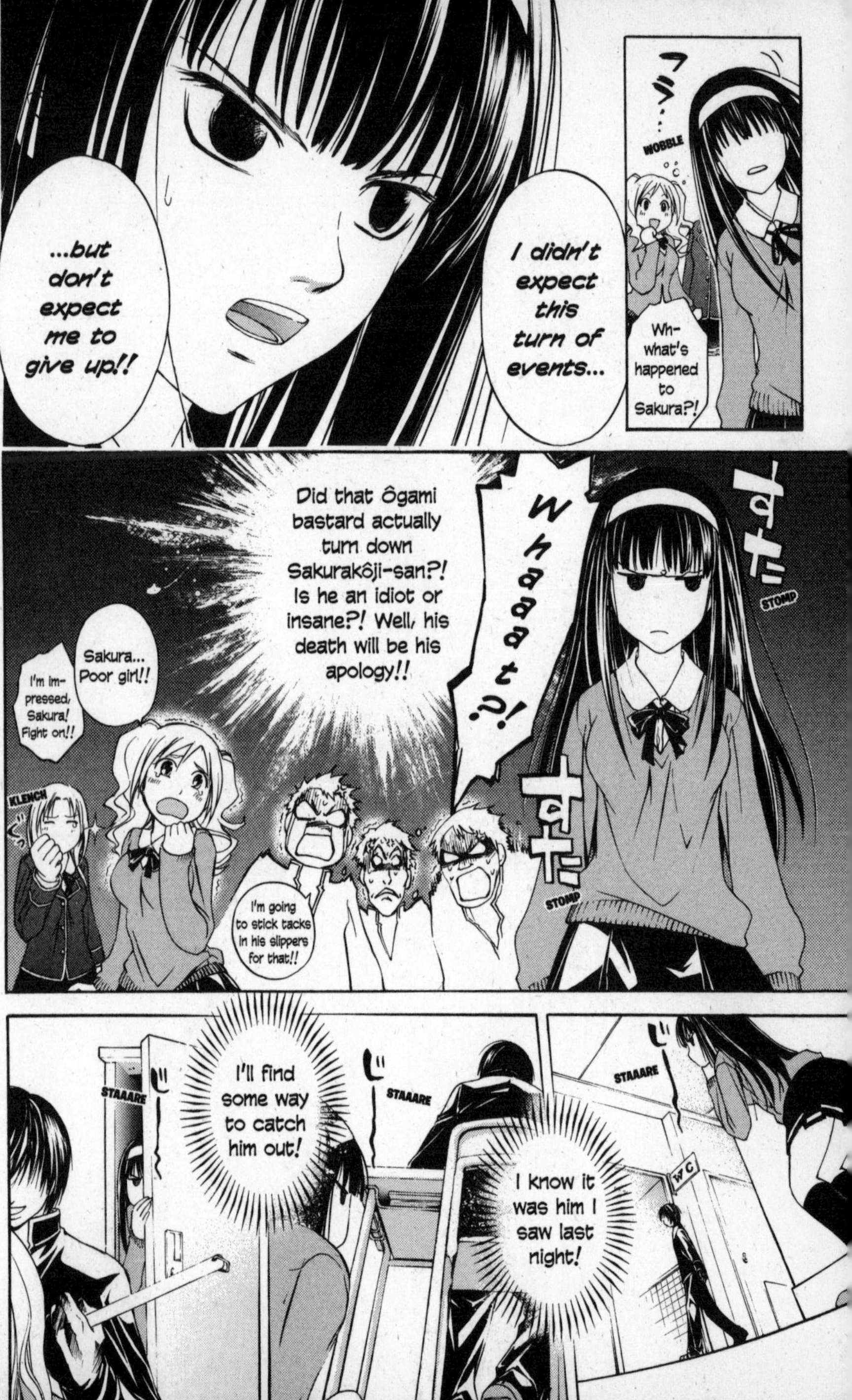
フラ…
WOBBLE
Wh-what's happened to Sakura?!
I didn't expect this turn of events...
...but don't expect me to give up!!
すた
STOMP
Whaaaat?!
Did that Ôgami bastard actually turn down Sakurakôji-san?! Is he an idiot or insane?! Well, his death will be his apology!!
Sakura... Poor girl!!
I'm impressed, Sakura! Fight on!!
KLENCH
I'm going to stick tacks in his slippers for that!!
すた
STOMP
じ
STAAARE
WC
I know it was him I saw last night!
じ
STAAARE
I'll find some way to catch him out!
じ
STAAARE

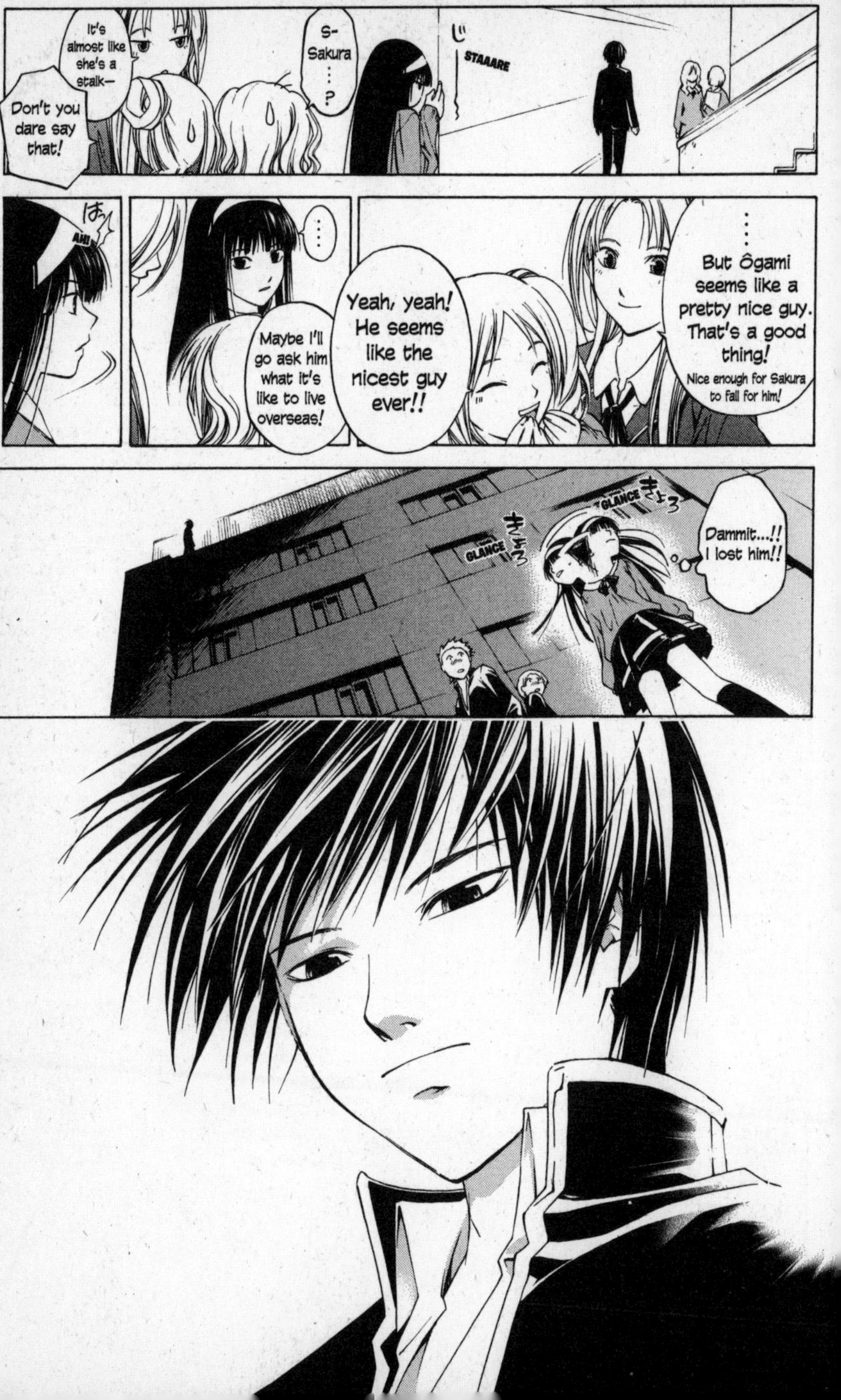
じ
STAAARE
S-Sakura...?
It's almost like she's a stalk—
Don't you dare say that!
......
But Ôgami seems like a pretty nice guy. That's a good thing!
Nice enough for Sakura to fall for him!
Yeah, yeah! He seems like the nicest guy ever!!
......
Maybe I'll go ask him what it's like to live overseas!
は
AH!
Dammit...!! I lost him!!
GLANCE
きょろ
GLANCE
きょろ

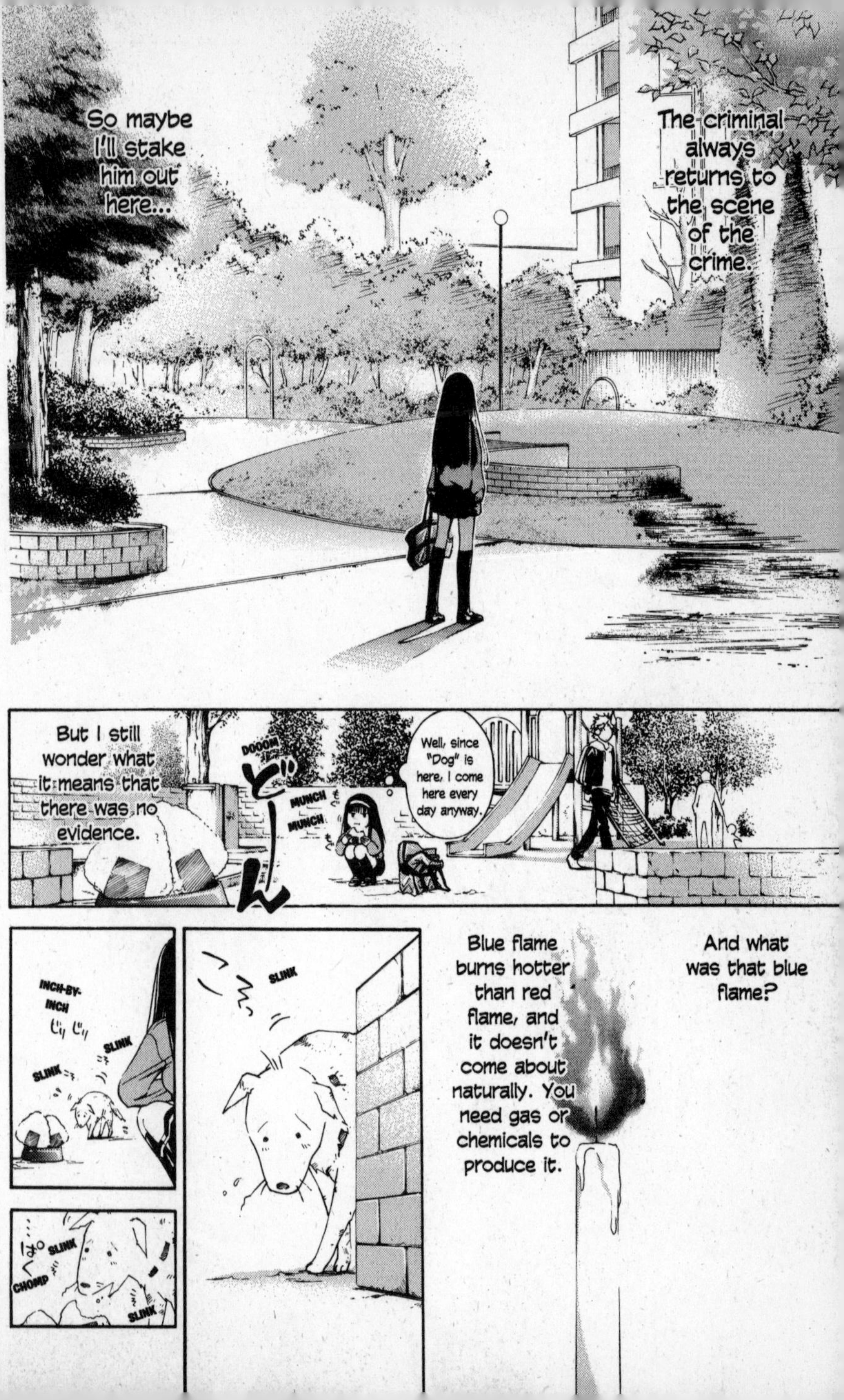

The criminal always returns to the scene of the crime.
So maybe I'll stake him out here...
Well, since "Dog" is here, I come here every day anyway.
MUNCH MUNCH
DOOOM
But I still wonder what it means that there was no evidence.
And what was that blue flame?
Blue flame burns hotter than red flame, and it doesn't come about naturally. You need gas or chemicals to produce it.
SLINK
INCH-BY-INCH
SLINK
SLINK
SLINK
CHOMP
SLINK

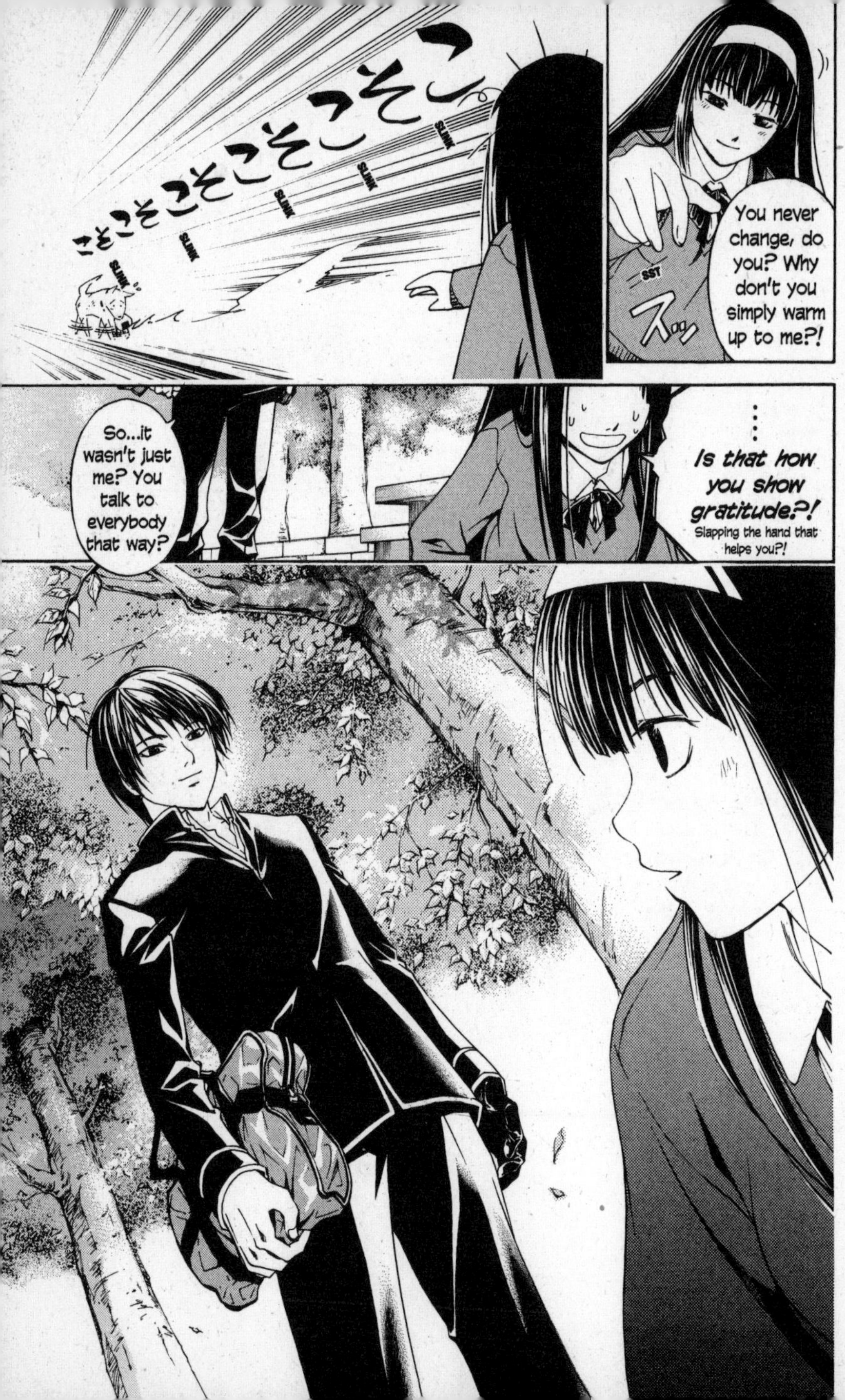
You never change, do you? Why don't you simply warm up to me?!
SST
SLINK
SLINK
SLINK
SLINK
SLINK
...
Is that how you show gratitude?!
Slapping the hand that helps you?!
So...it wasn't just me? You talk to everybody that way?

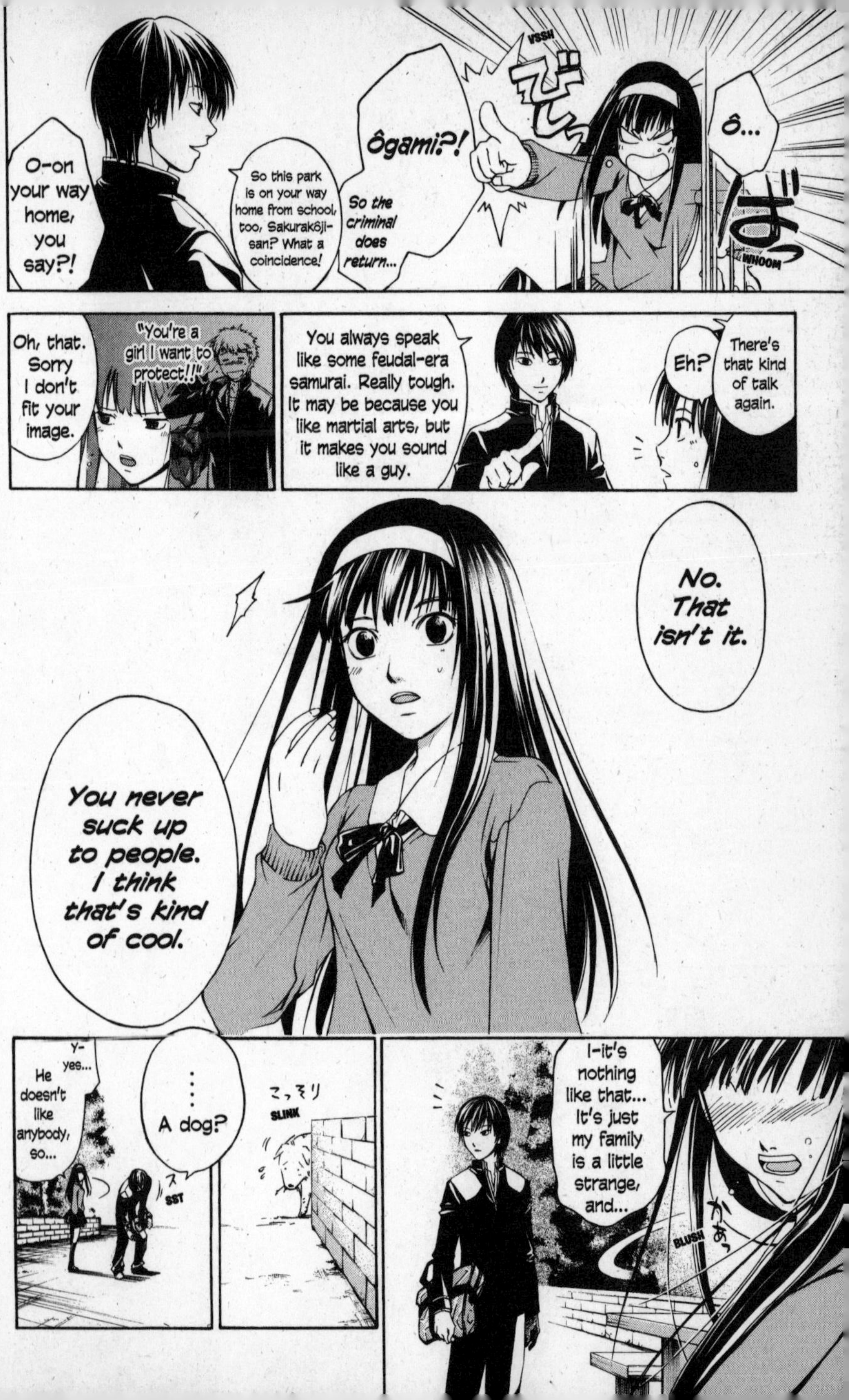
Ô...
VSSH
WHOOM
Ôgami?!
So the criminal does return...
So this park is on your way home from school, too, Sakurakōji-san? What a coincidence!
O-on your way home, you say?!
There's that kind of talk again.
Eh?
You always speak like some feudal-era samurai. Really tough. It may be because you like martial arts, but it makes you sound like a guy.
Oh, that. Sorry I don't fit your image.
"You're a girl I want to protect!!"
No. That isn't it.
You never suck up to people. I think that's kind of cool.
I-it's nothing like that... It's just my family is a little strange, and...
BLUSH
SLINK
... A dog?
SST
Y-yes... He doesn't like anybody, so...

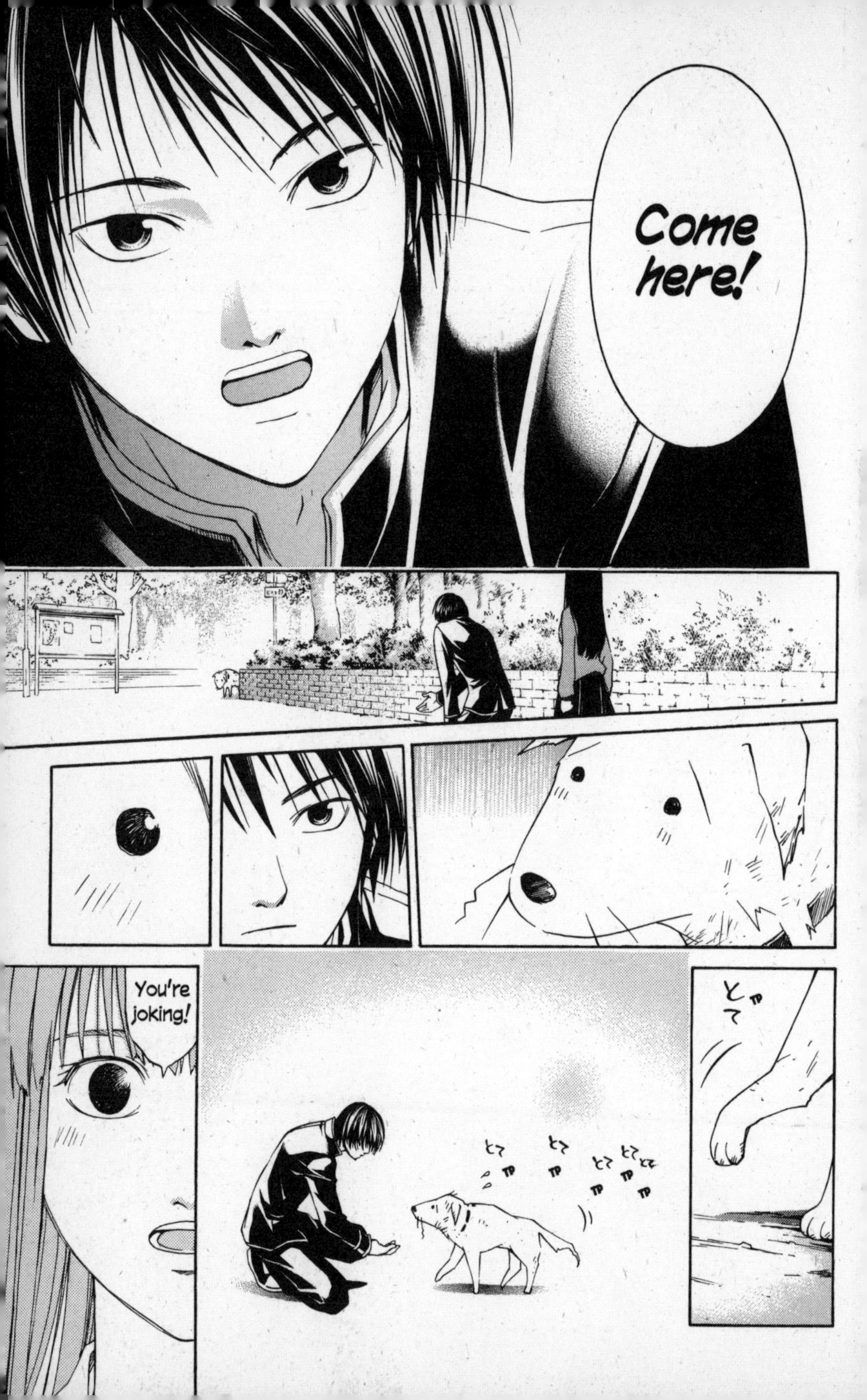
Come here!
とて TP
とて TP とて TP とて TP とて TP とて TP
You're joking!

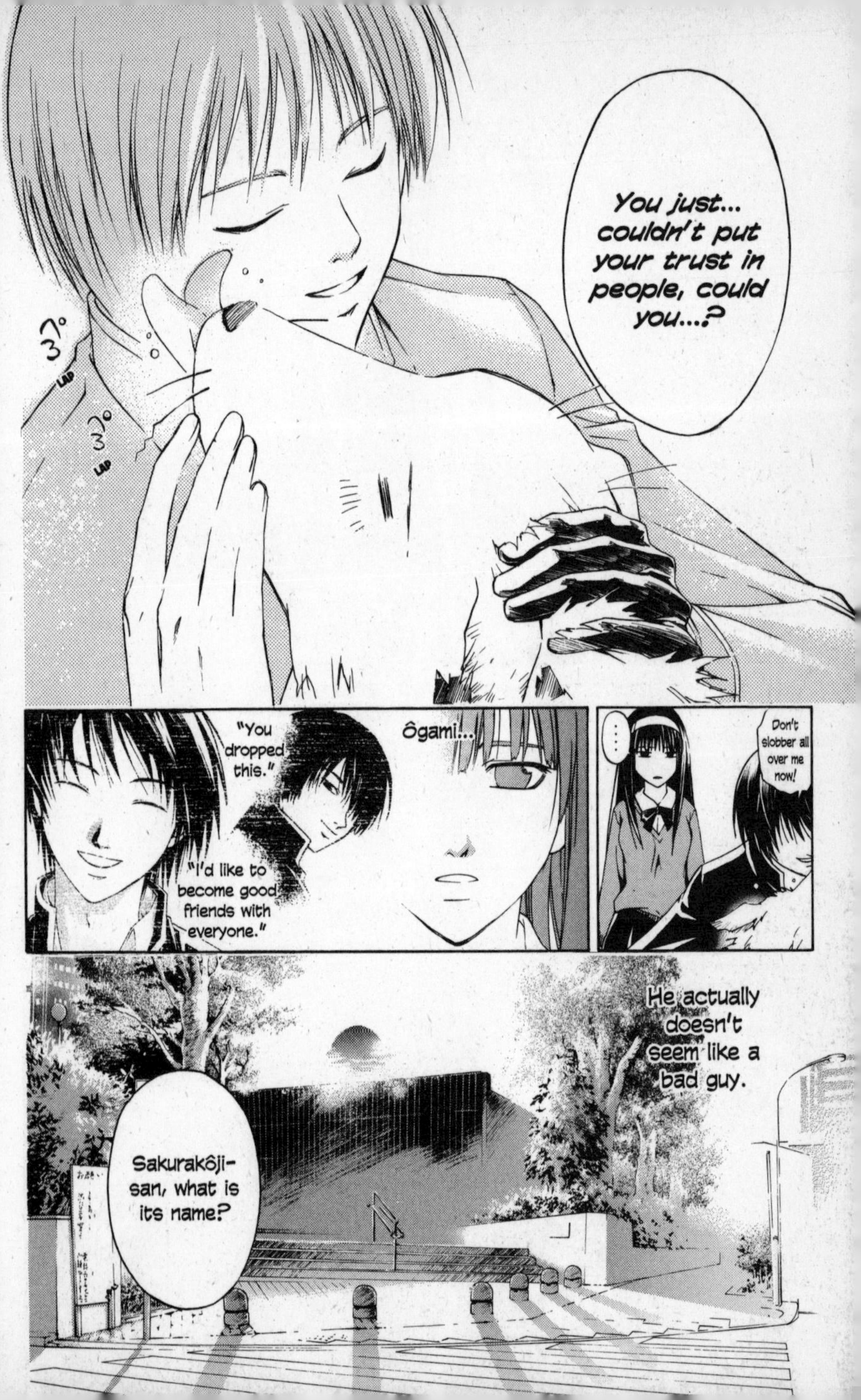
You just... couldn't put your trust in people, could you...?
LAP
LAP
...
Don't slobber all over me now!
Ôgami...
"You dropped this."
"I'd like to become good friends with everyone."
He actually doesn't seem like a bad guy.
Sakurakôji-san, what is its name?

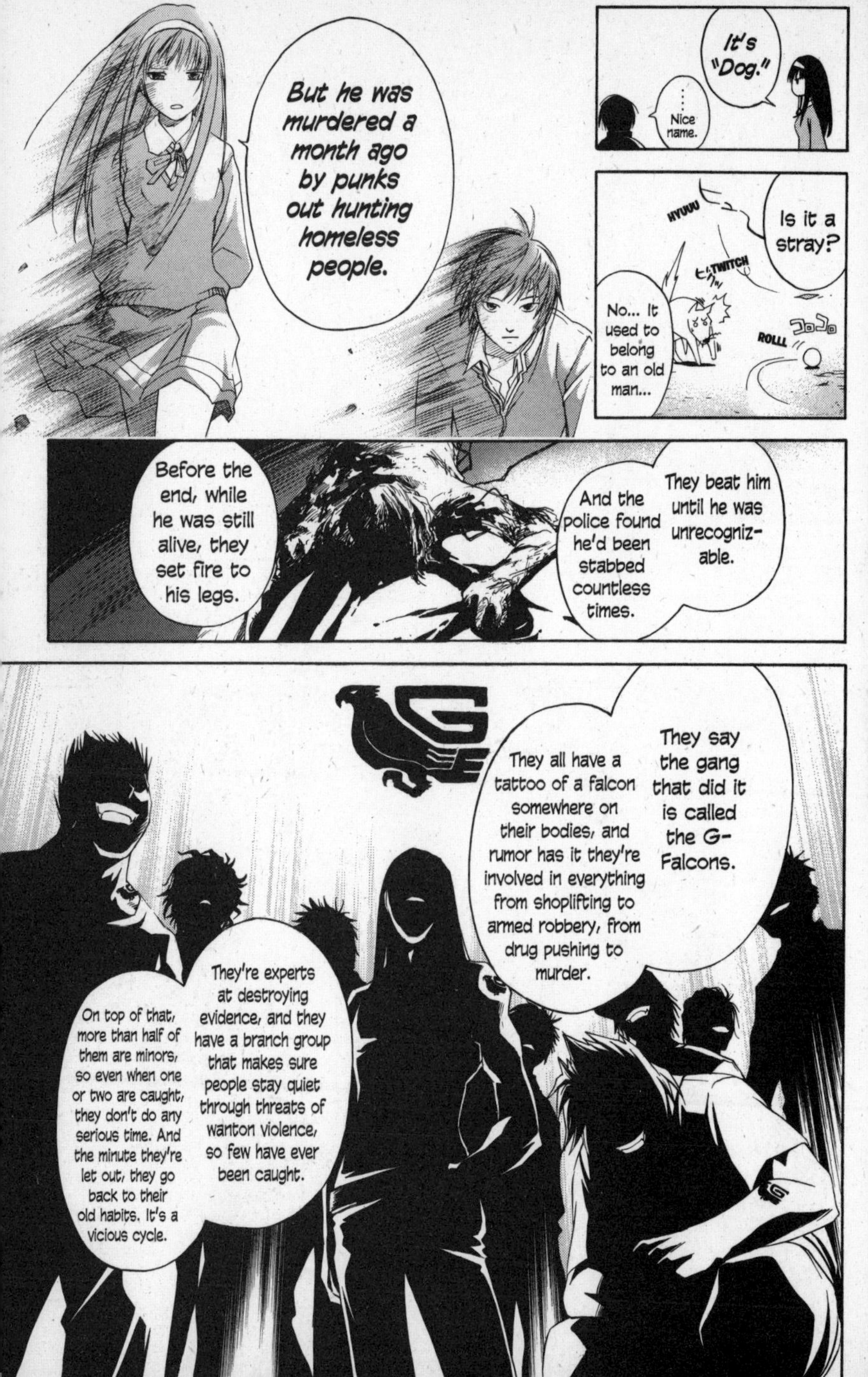
It's "Dog."
... Nice name.
Is it a stray?
HYUUU
TWITCH
No... It used to belong to an old man...
ROLLL
But he was murdered a month ago by punks out hunting homeless people.
They beat him until he was unrecognizable.
And the police found he'd been stabbed countless times.
Before the end, while he was still alive, they set fire to his legs.
They say the gang that did it is called the G-Falcons.
They all have a tattoo of a falcon somewhere on their bodies, and rumor has it they're involved in everything from shoplifting to armed robbery, from drug pushing to murder.
They're experts at destroying evidence, and they have a branch group that makes sure people stay quiet through threats of wanton violence, so few have ever been caught.
On top of that, more than half of them are minors, so even when one or two are caught, they don't do any serious time. And the minute they're let out, they go back to their old habits. It's a vicious cycle.

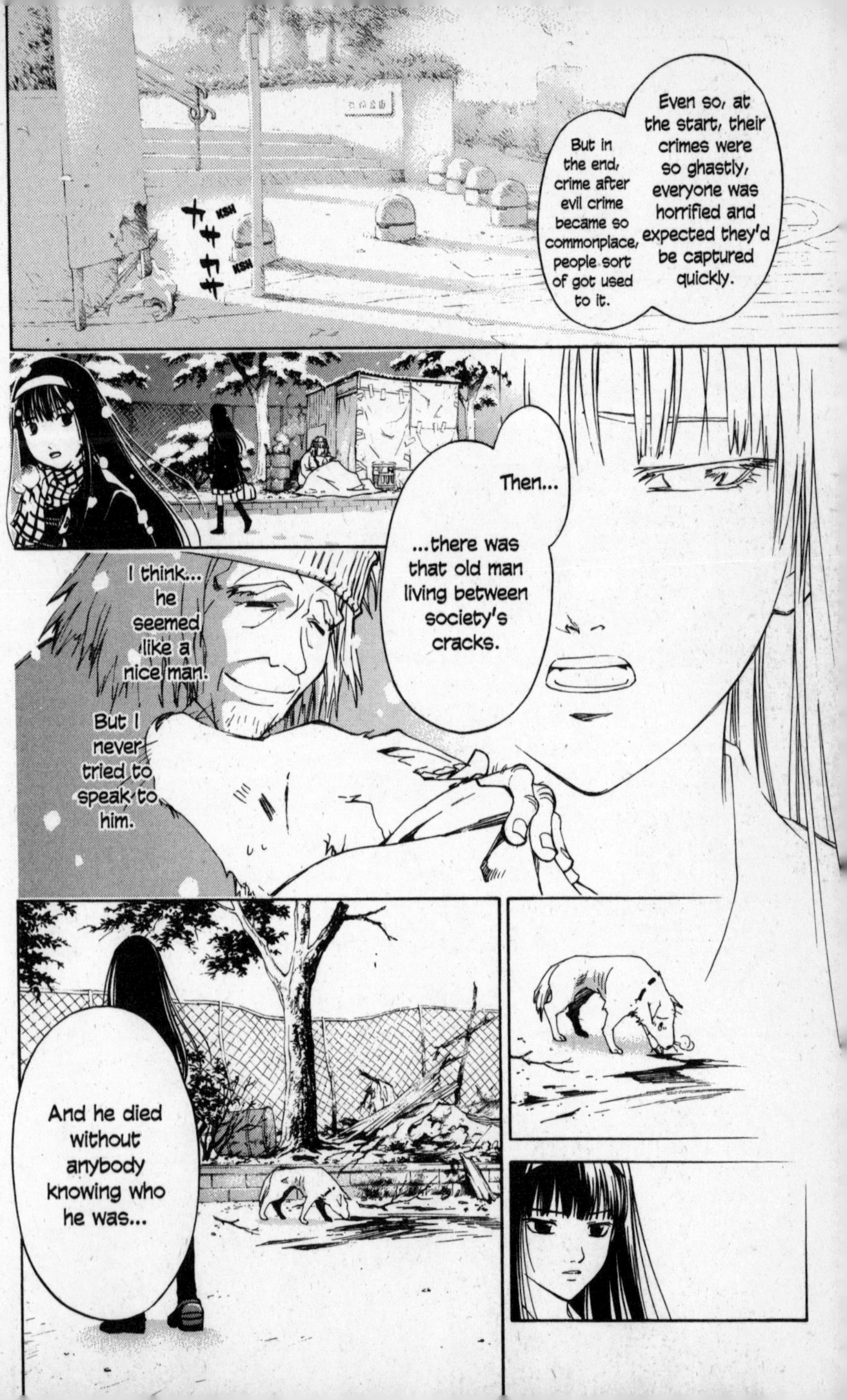
Even so, at the start, their crimes were so ghastly, everyone was horrified and expected they'd be captured quickly.
But in the end, crime after evil crime became so commonplace, people sort of got used to it.
KSH
KSH
Then...
...there was that old man living between society's cracks.
I think... he seemed like a nice man.
But I never tried to speak to him.
And he died without anybody knowing who he was...

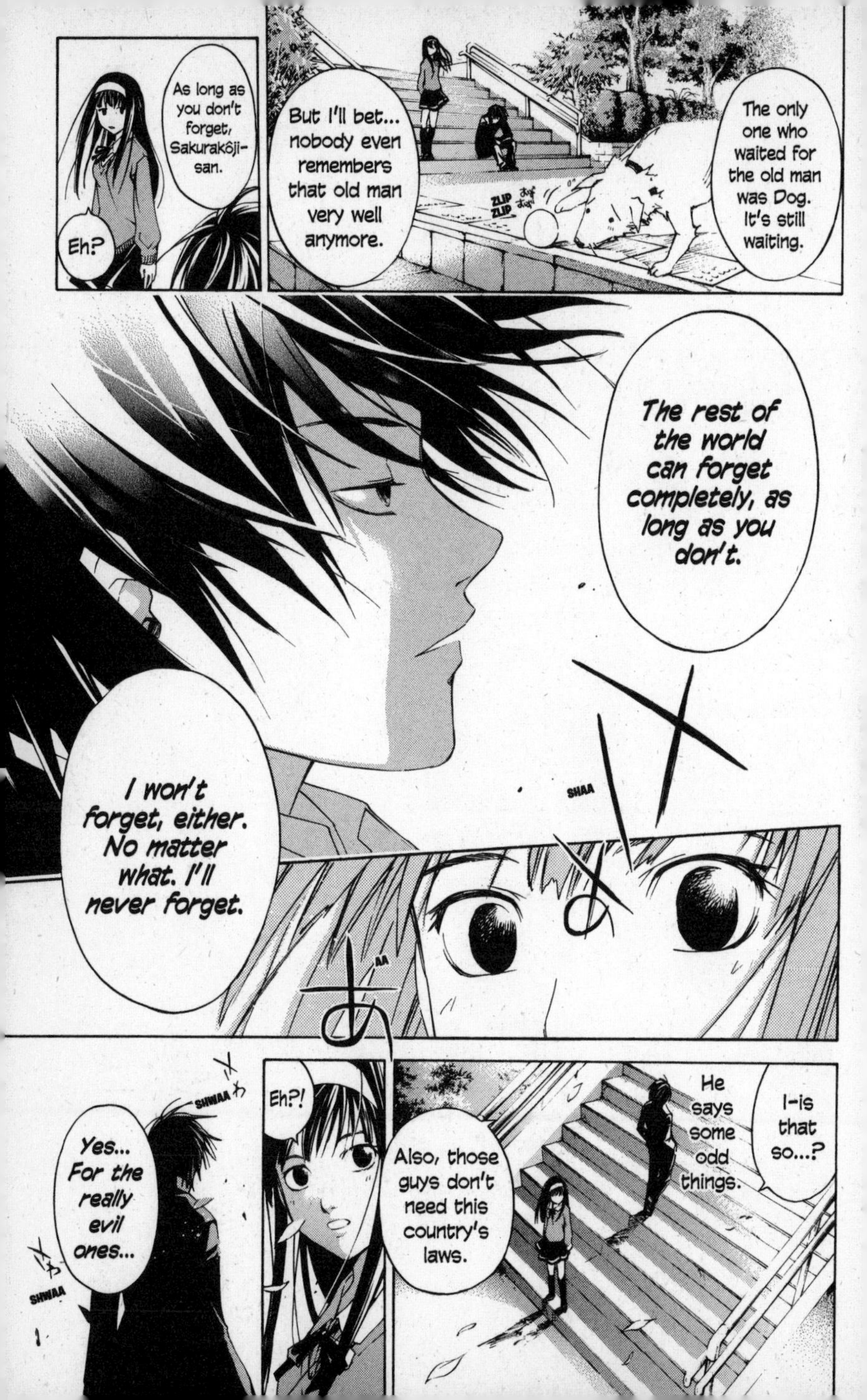
The only one who waited for the old man was Dog. It's still waiting.
ZLIP ZLIP
But I'll bet... nobody even remembers that old man very well anymore.
As long as you don't forget, Sakurakôji-san.
Eh?
The rest of the world can forget completely, as long as you don't.
SHAA
I won't forget, either. No matter what. I'll never forget.
AA
I-is that so...?
He says some odd things.
Eh?!
Also, those guys don't need this country's laws.
SHWAA
Yes... For the really evil ones...
SHWAA

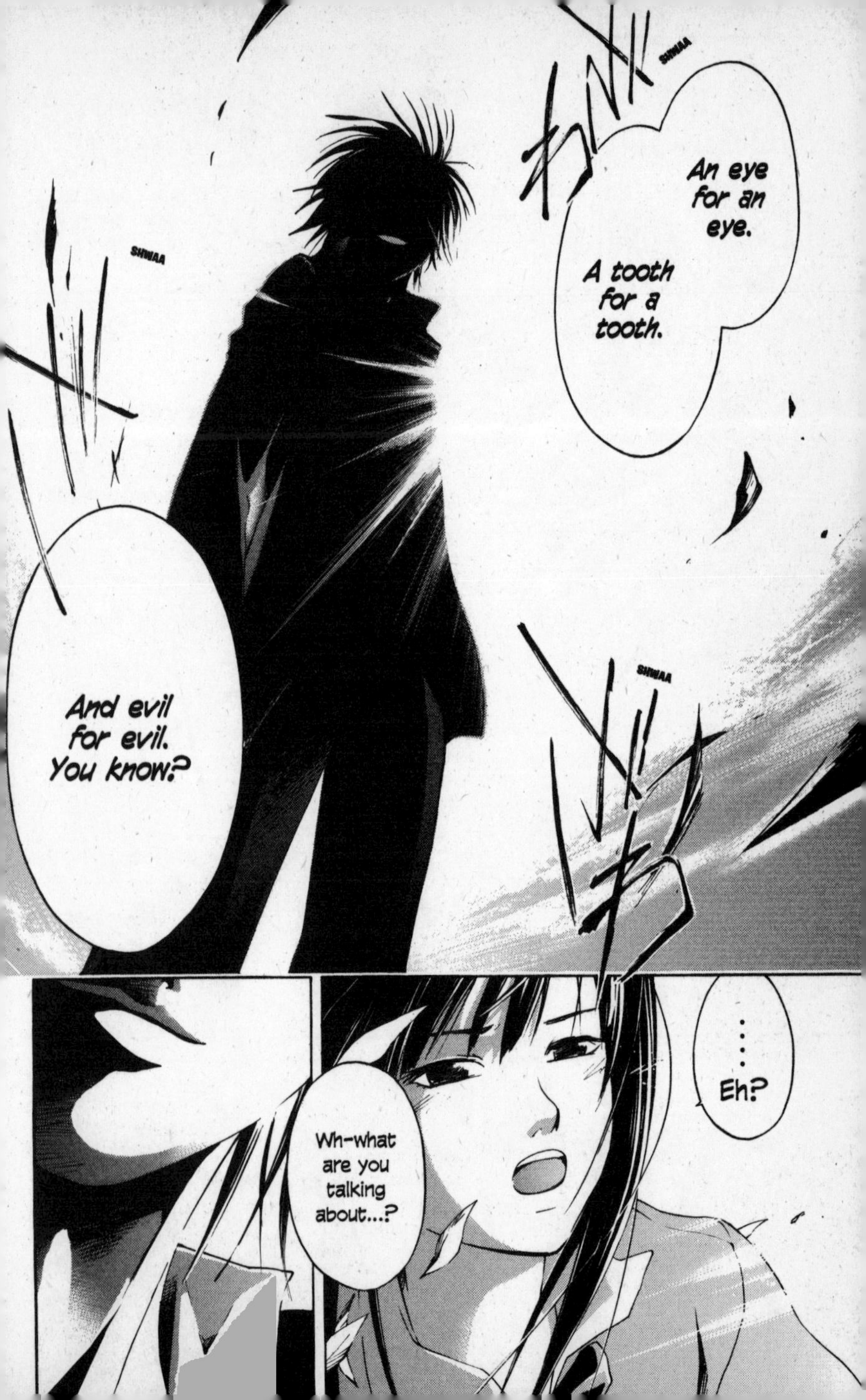
SHWAA
An eye for an eye.
A tooth for a tooth.
SHWAA
SHWAA
And evil for evil. You know?
....Eh?
Wh-what are you talking about...?

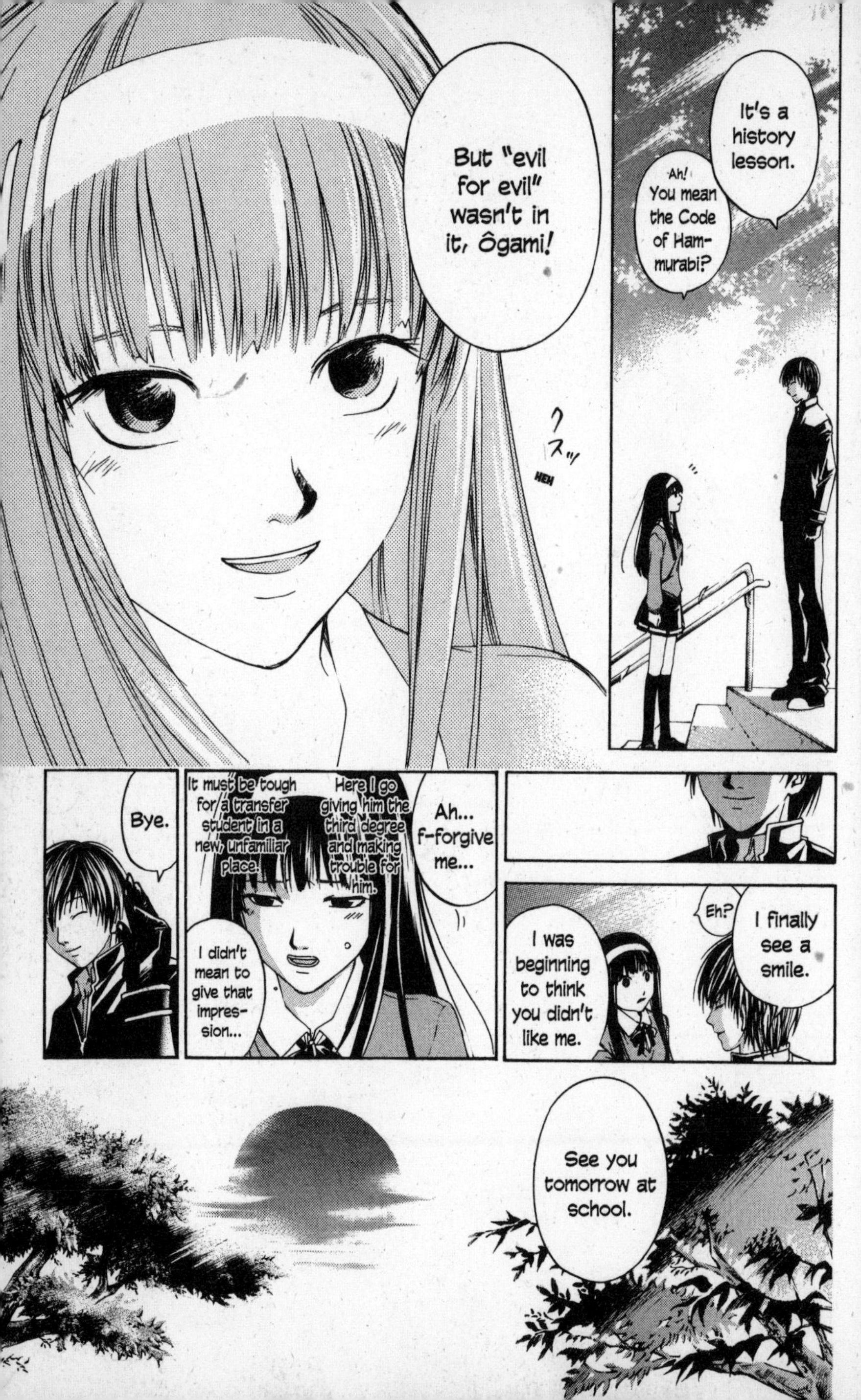
It's a history lesson.
Ah! You mean the Code of Ham-murabi?
But "evil for evil" wasn't in it, Ôgami!
クスッ
HEH
I finally see a smile.
Eh?
I was beginning to think you didn't like me.
Ah... f-forgive me...
Here I go giving him the third degree and making trouble for him.
It must be tough for a transfer student in a new, unfamiliar place.
I didn't mean to give that impression...
Bye.
See you tomorrow at school.

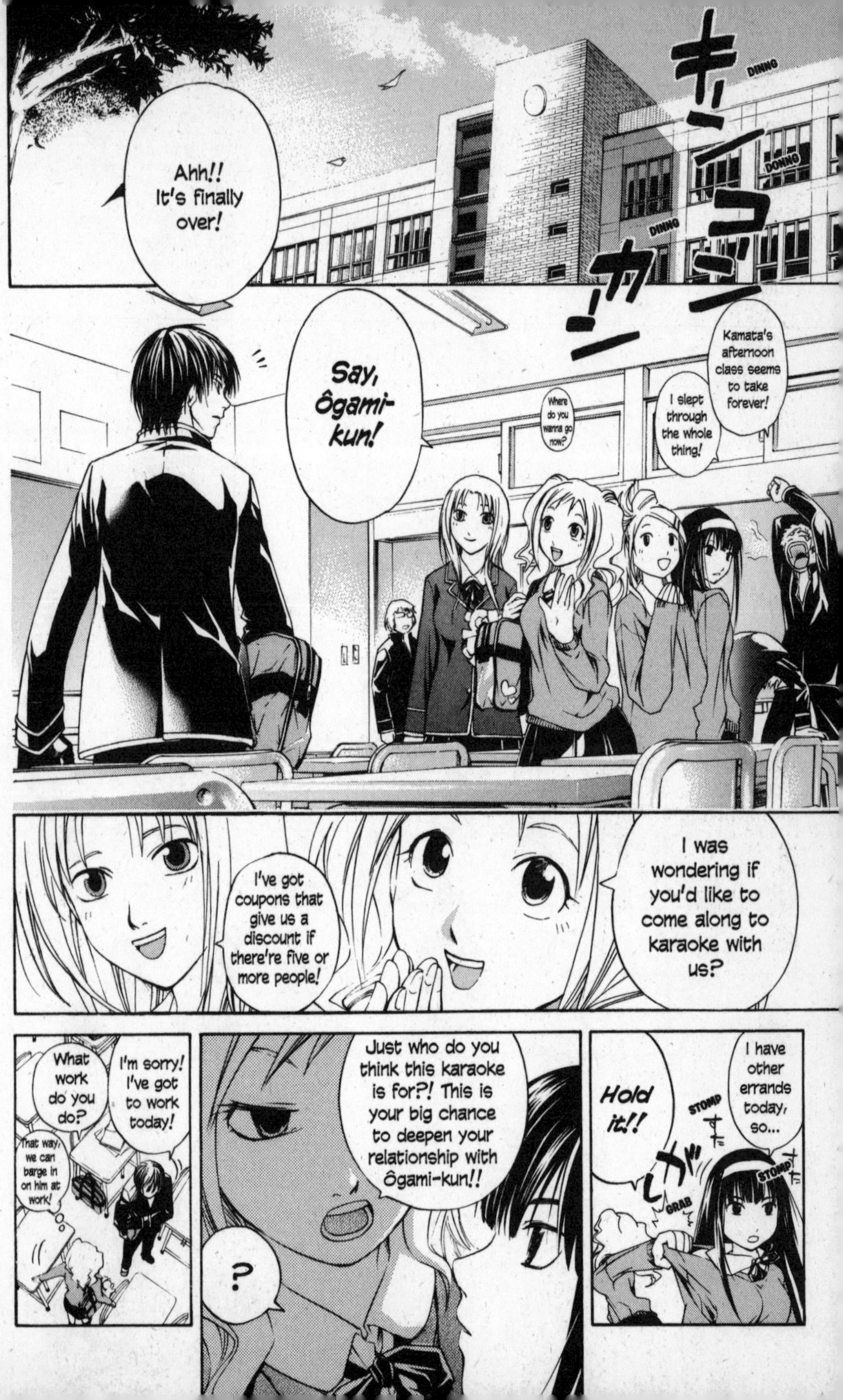
DINNG
DONNG
DINNG
Ahh!! It's finally over!
Kamata's afternoon class seems to take forever!
I slept through the whole thing!
Where do you wanna go now?
Say, Ôgami-kun!
I was wondering if you'd like to come along to karaoke with us?
I've got coupons that give us a discount if there're five or more people!
I have other errands today, so...
STOMP
STOMP
GRAB
Hold it!!
Just who do you think this karaoke is for?! This is your big chance to deepen your relationship with Ôgami-kun!!
?
I'm sorry! I've got to work today!
What work do you do?
That way, we can barge in on him at work!

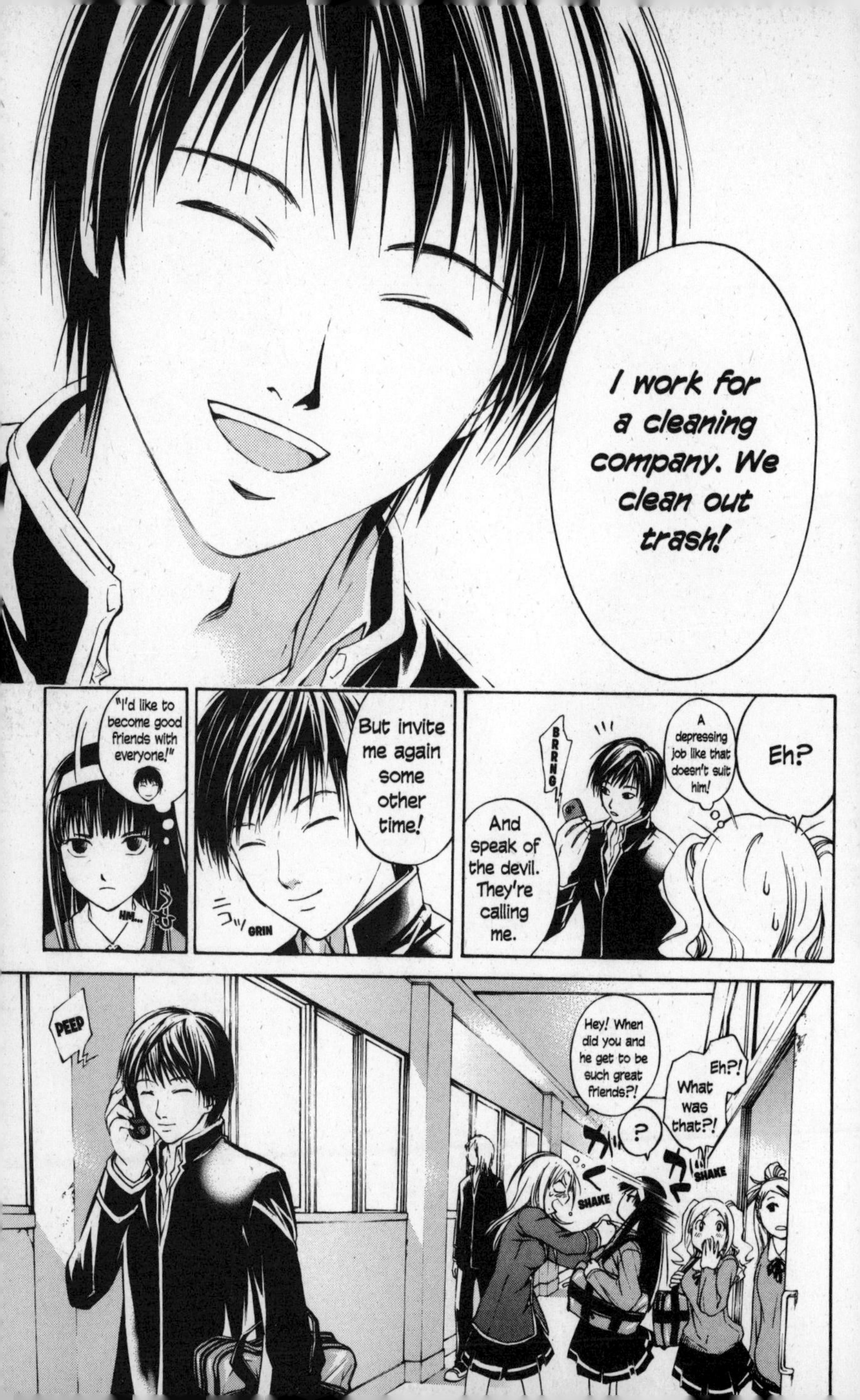
I work for a cleaning company. We clean out trash!
Eh?
A depressing job like that doesn't suit him!
BRRNG
And speak of the devil. They're calling me.
But invite me again some other time!
GRIN
"I'd like to become good friends with everyone!"
HM...
Eh?! What was that?!
SHAKE
Hey! When did you and he get to be such great friends?!
?
SHAKE
PEEP

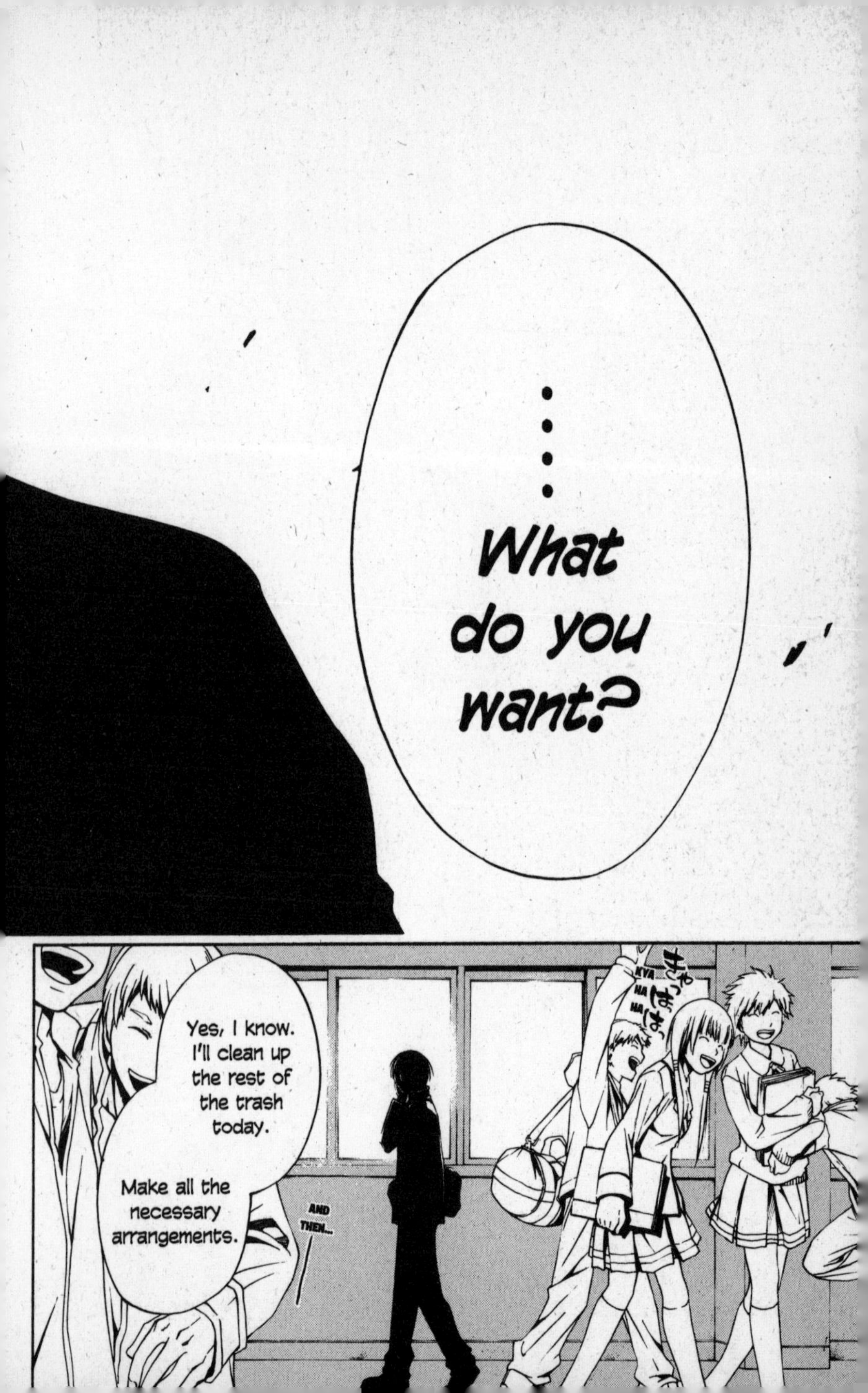
. . . . What do you want?
KYA HA HA
Yes, I know. I'll clean up the rest of the trash today.
Make all the necessary arrangements.
AND THEN...

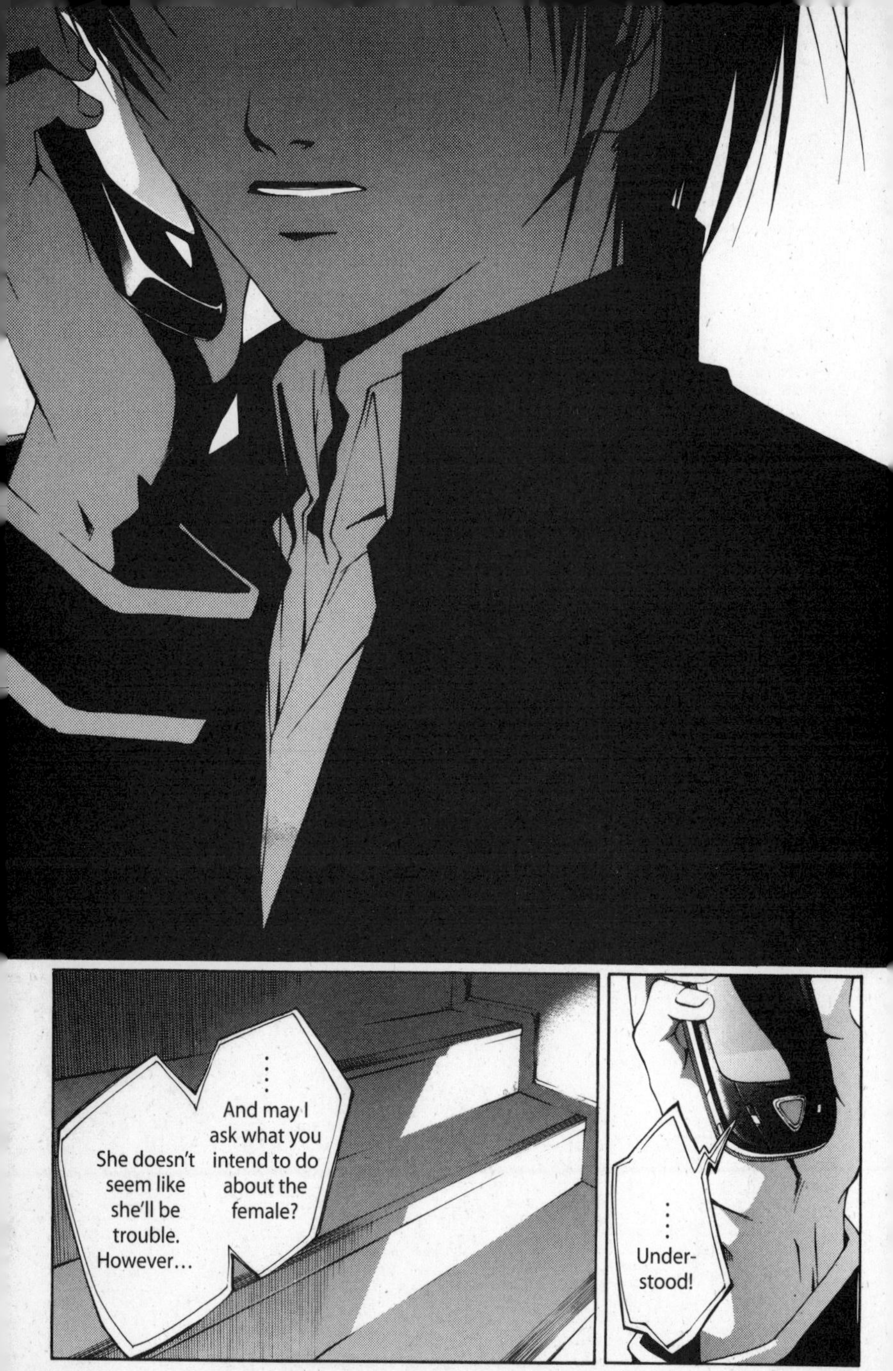
…
Understood!
…
And may I ask what you intend to do about the female?
She doesn't seem like she'll be trouble. However…

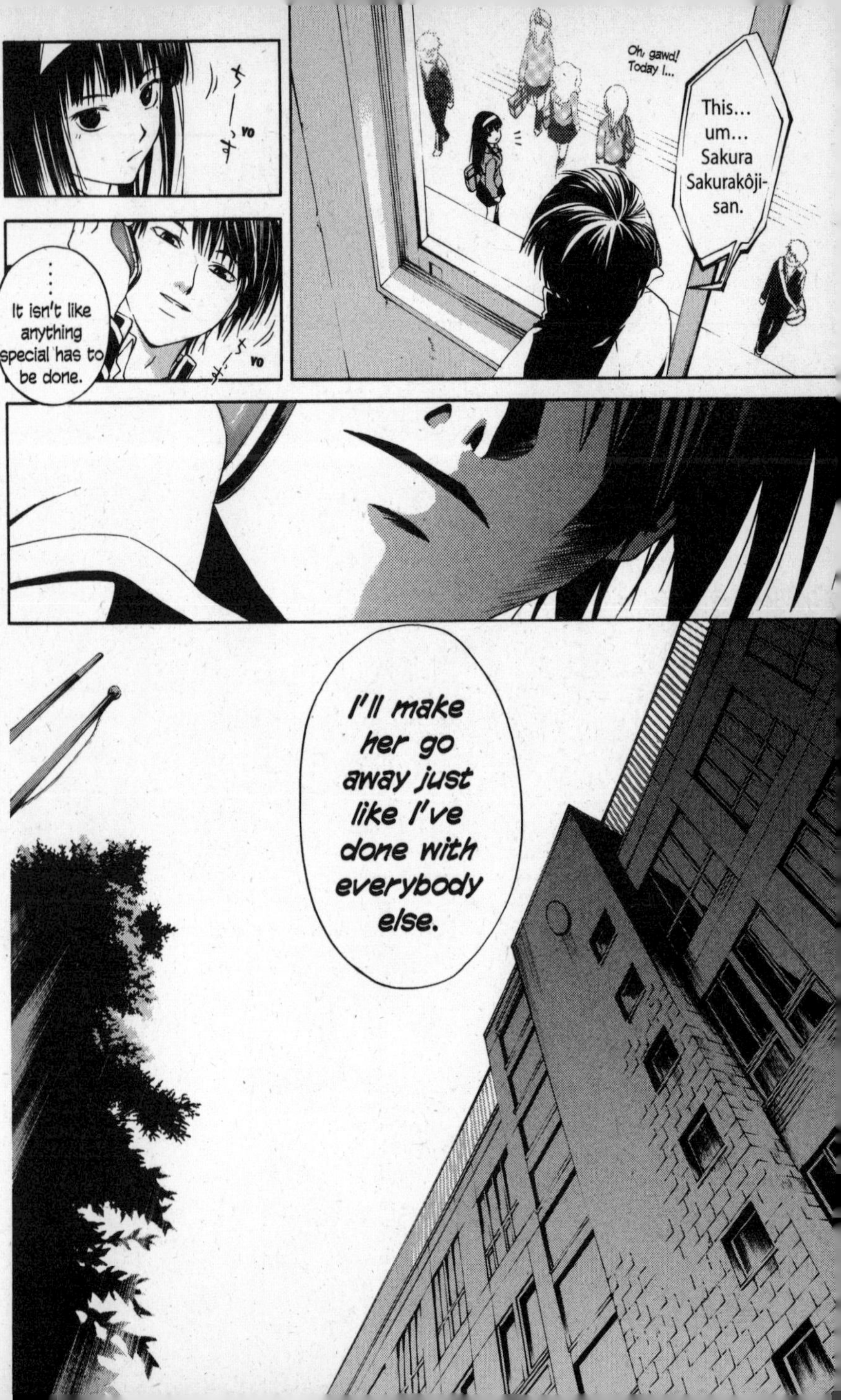
This… um… Sakura Sakurakôji-san.
Oh, gawd! Today I…
ちーっす
YO
…It isn't like anything special has to be done.
YO
I'll make her go away just like I've done with everybody else.

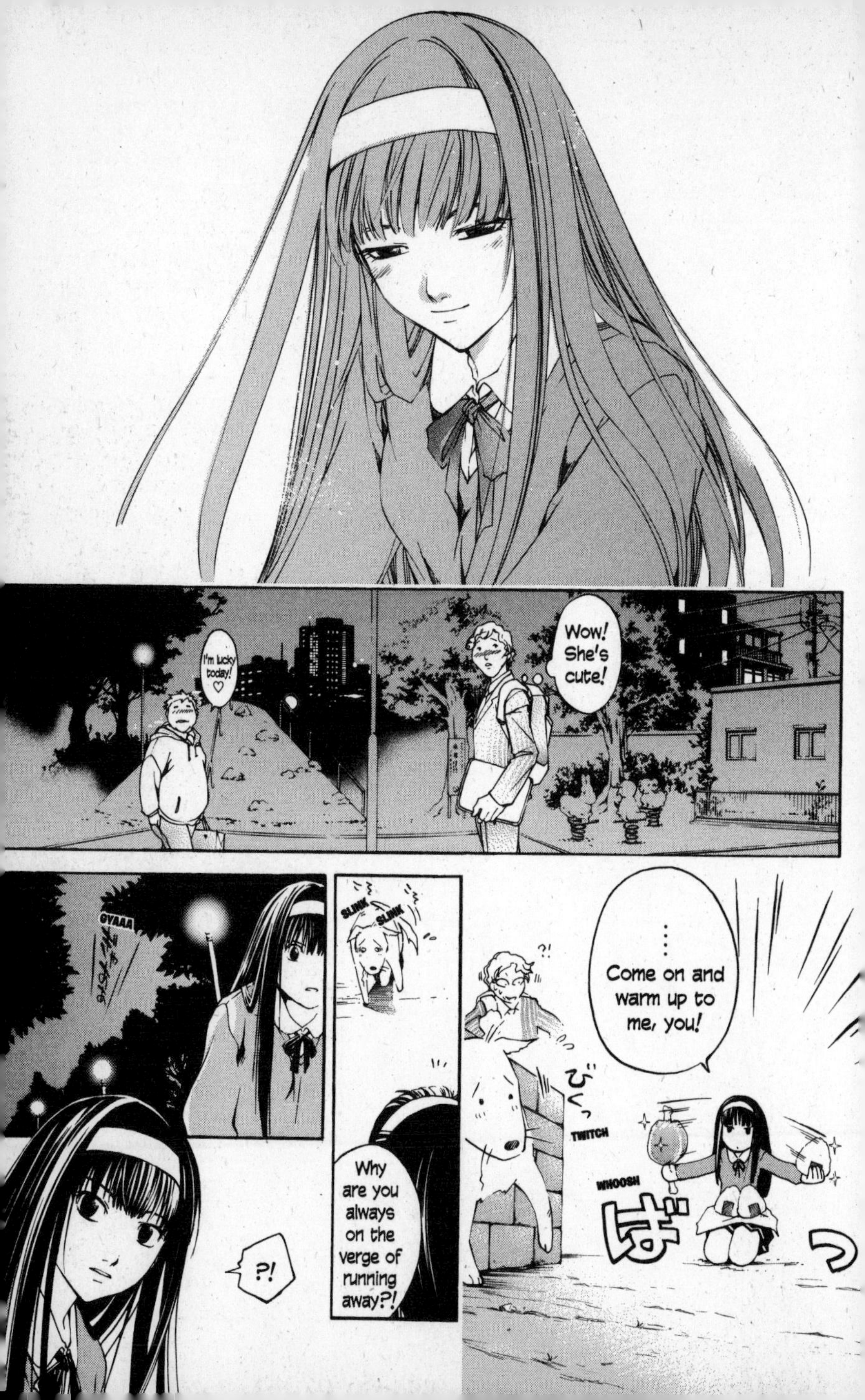
Wow! She's cute!
I'm lucky today! ♡
... Come on and warm up to me, you!
?!
びくっ
TWITCH
WHOOSH
ばっ
SLINK
SLINK
Why are you always on the verge of running away?!
GYAAA
?!

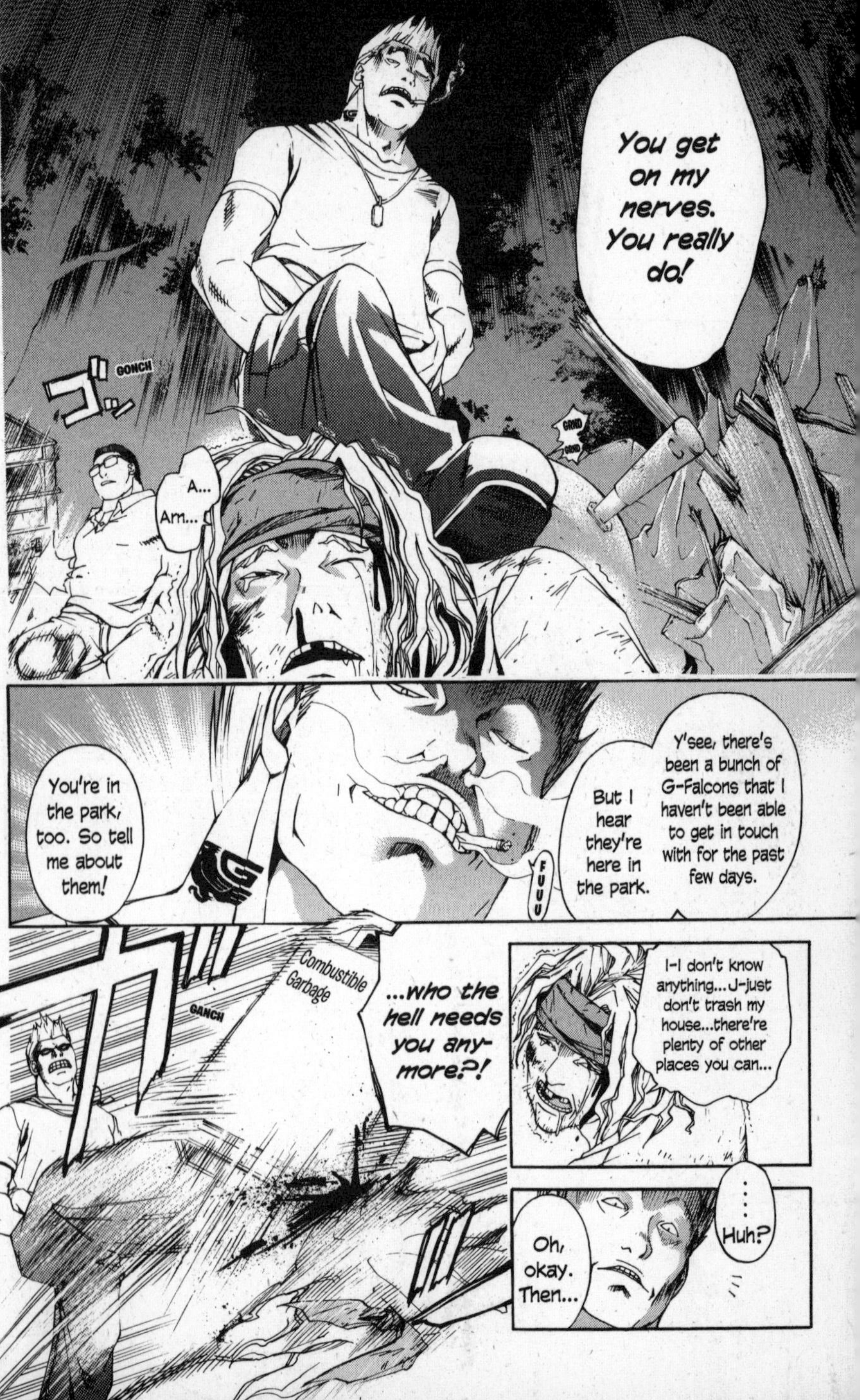
You get on my nerves. You really do!
GRIND GRIND
GONCH
A... Am...
Y'see, there's been a bunch of G-Falcons that I haven't been able to get in touch with for the past few days.
But I hear they're here in the park.
FUUU
You're in the park, too. So tell me about them!
I-I don't know anything... J-just don't trash my house... there're plenty of other places you can...
.....
Huh?
Oh, okay. Then...
...who the hell needs you any-more?!
Combustible Garbage
GANCH

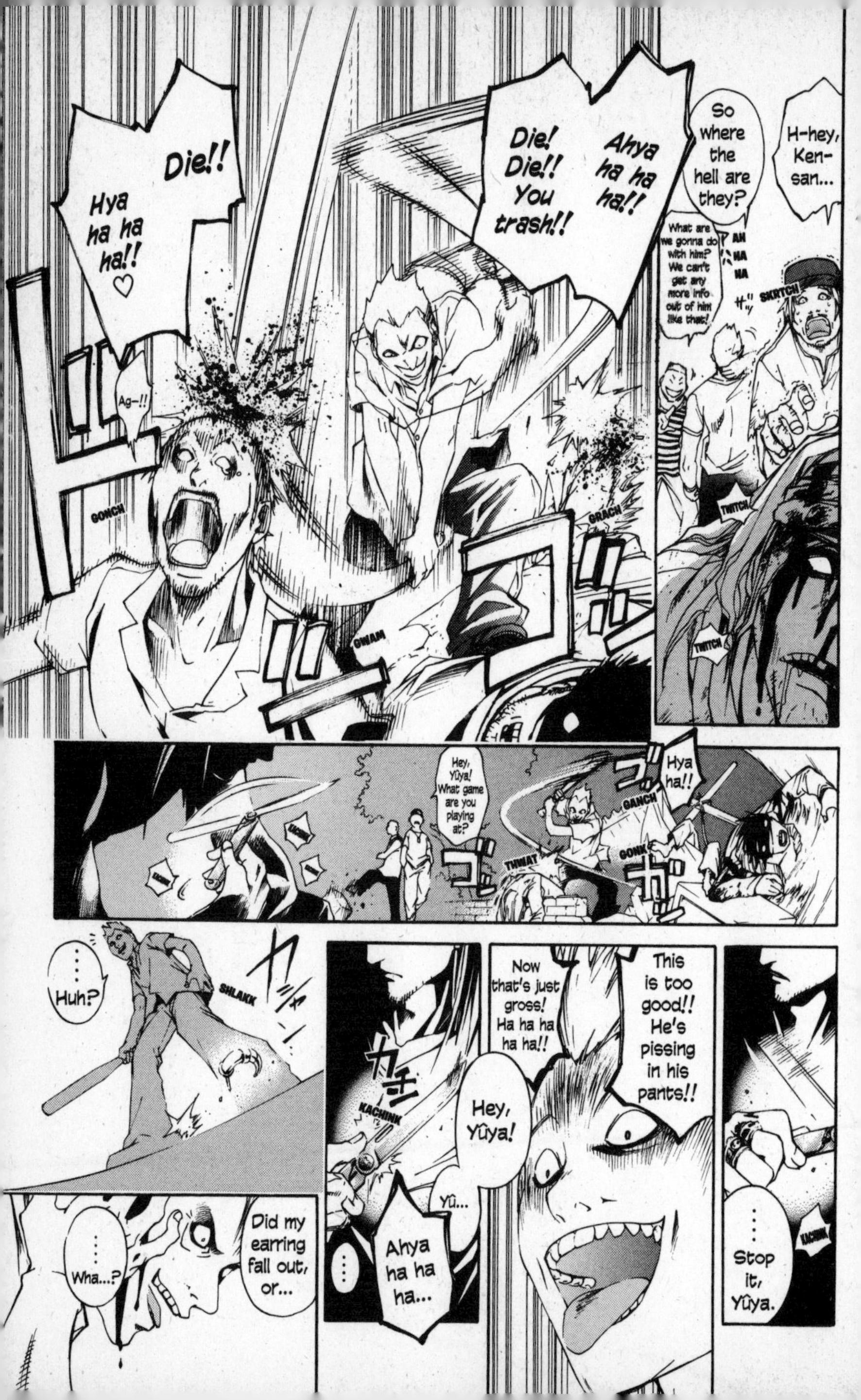
H-hey, Ken-san...
So where the hell are they?
What are we gonna do with him? We can't get any more info out of him like that!
AH HA HA
SKRTCH
TWITCH
TWITCH
Ahya ha ha ha!!
Die! Die!! You trash!!
Die!!
Hya ha ha ha!! ♡
Ag—!!
GONCH
GRACH
GWAM
Hya ha!!
GANCH
GONK
THWAT
Hey, Yûya! What game are you playing at?
KACHINK
... Stop it, Yûya.
This is too good!! He's pissing in his pants!!
Now that's just gross! Ha ha ha ha ha!!
Hey, Yûya!
KACHINK
Yû...
Ahya ha ha ha...
...
... Huh?
SHLAKK
Did my earring fall out, or...
... Wha...?

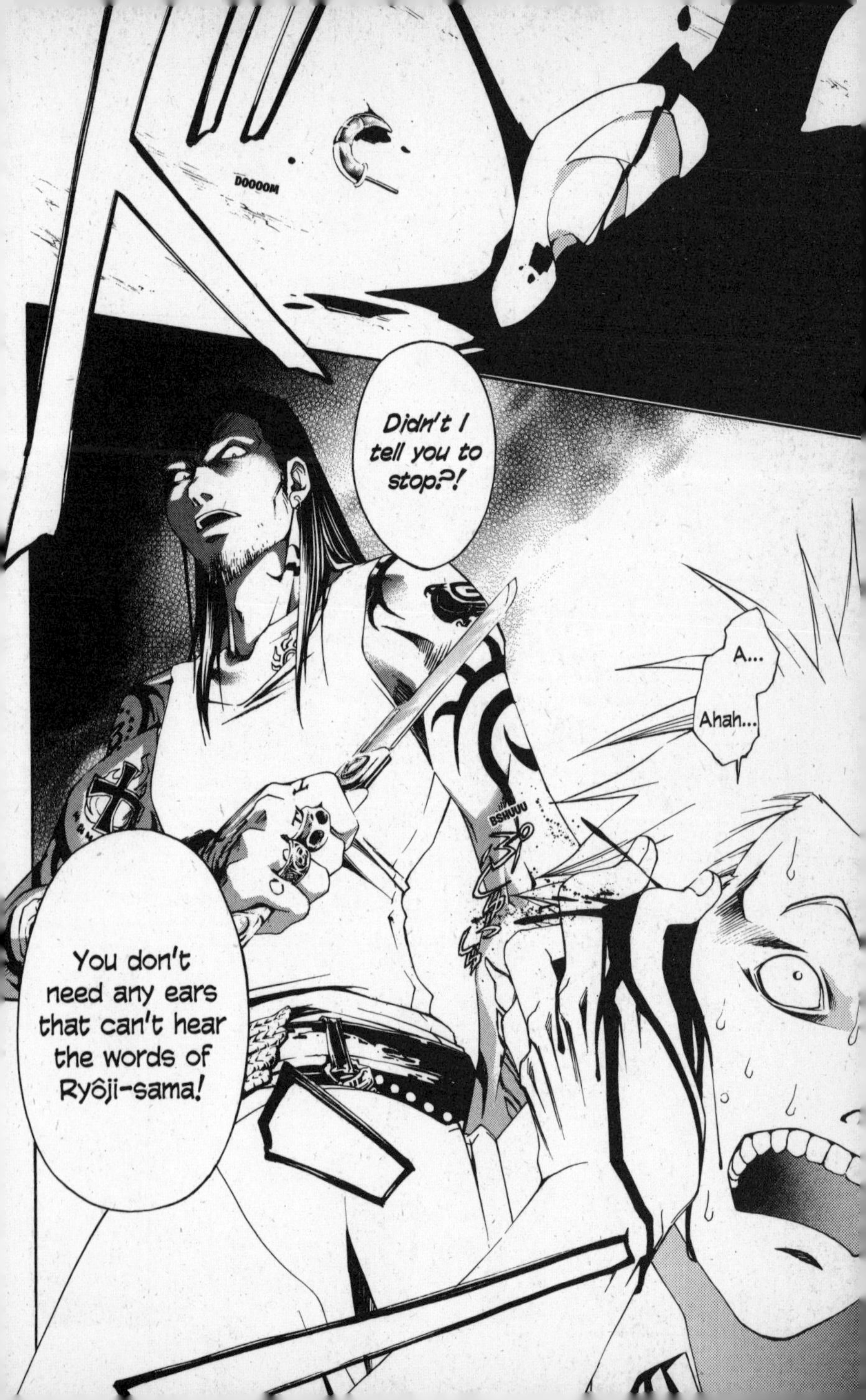
DOOOOM
Didn't I tell you to stop?!
A...
Ahah...
BSHUUU
You don't need any ears that can't hear the words of Ryôji-sama!

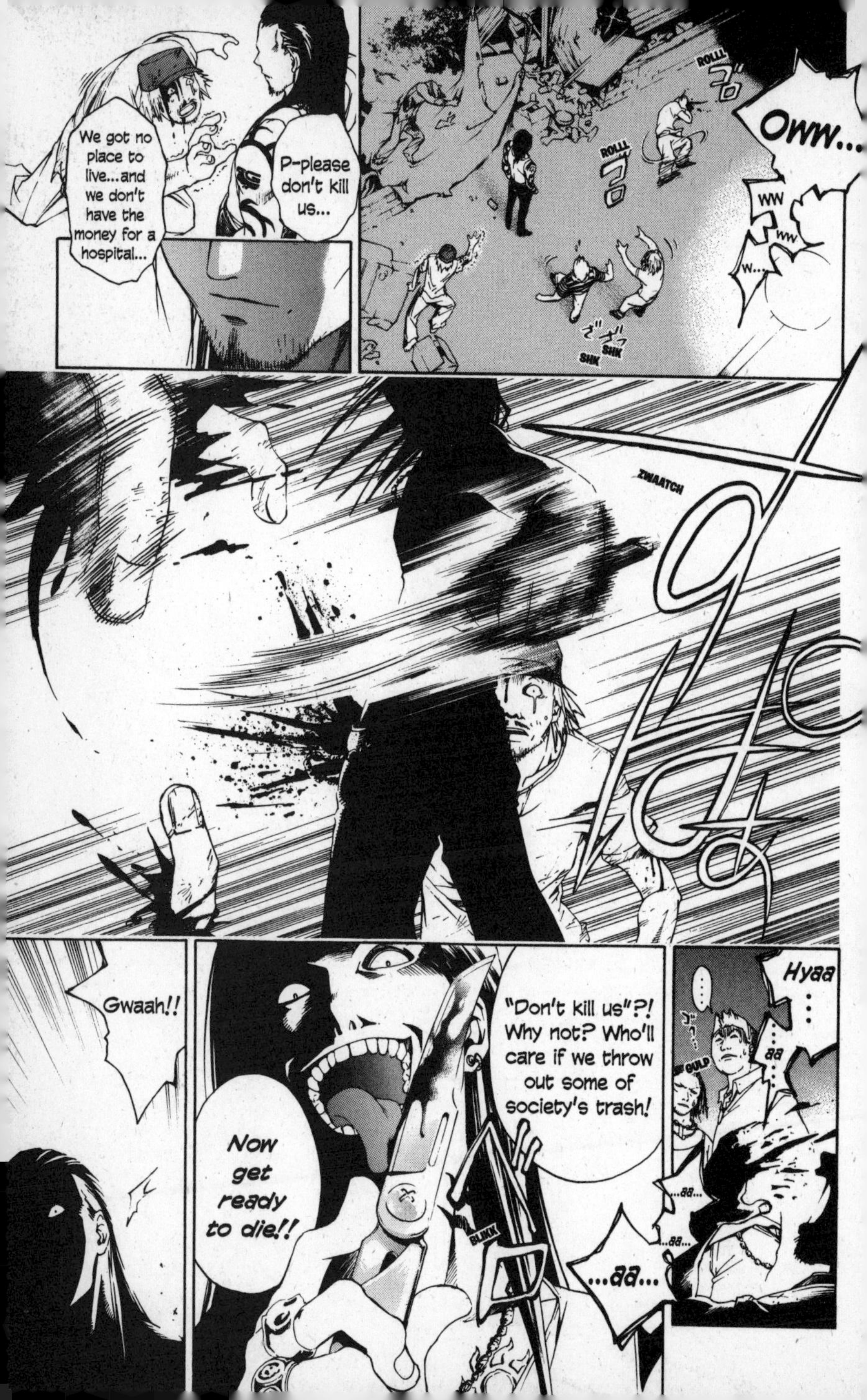
ROLLL
Oww...
ww
ww
w...
ROLLL
SHK
SHK
P-please don't kill us...
We got no place to live...and we don't have the money for a hospital...
ZWAATCH
Hyaa
...
...aa
GULP
...aa...
...aa...
...aa...
"Don't kill us"?! Why not? Who'll care if we throw out some of society's trash!
Now get ready to die!!
BLIKK
Gwaah!!

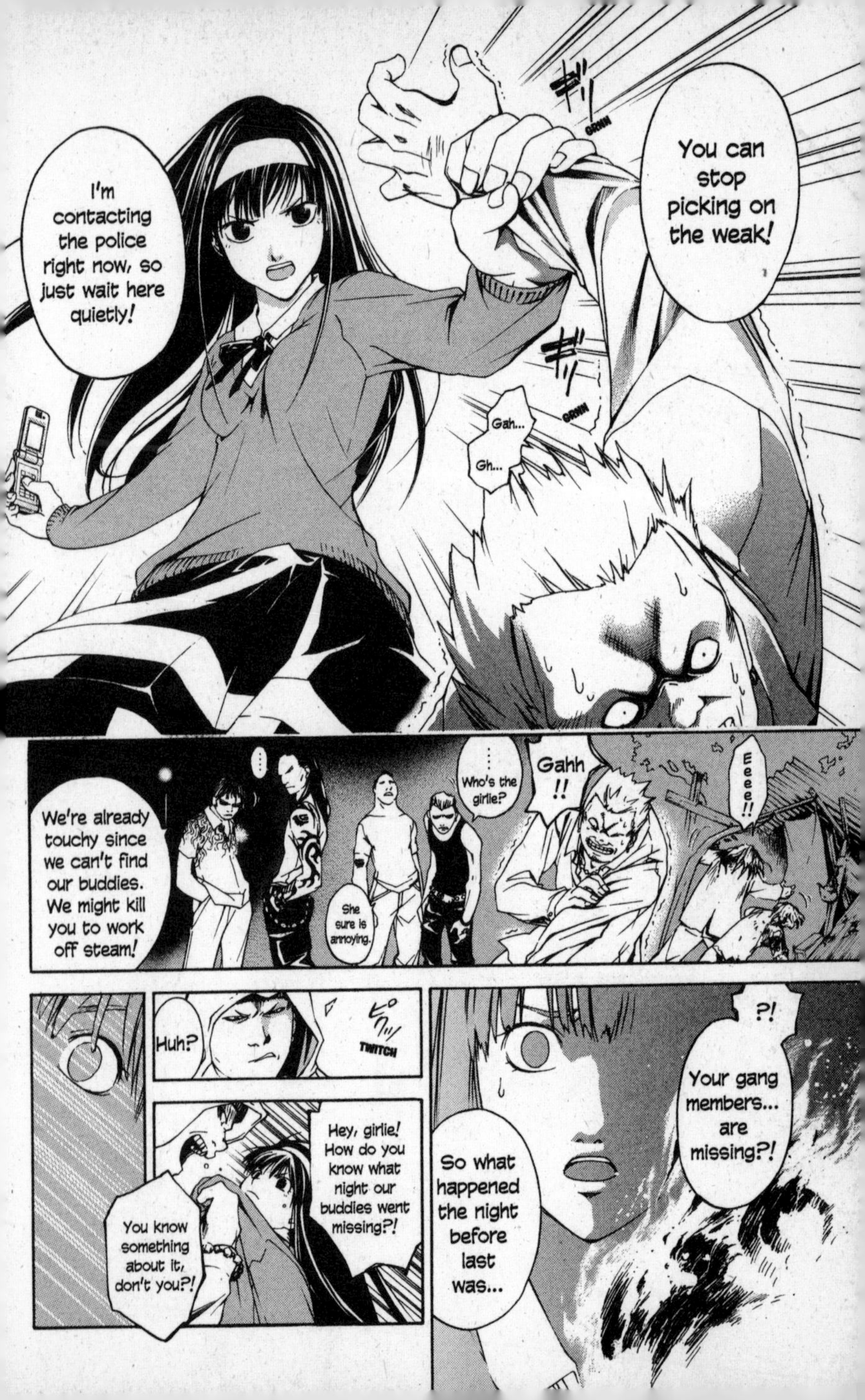
You can stop picking on the weak!
GRNN
I'm contacting the police right now, so just wait here quietly!
GRNN
Gah...
Gh...
Eeee!!
Gahh!!
... Who's the girlie?
...
We're already touchy since we can't find our buddies. We might kill you to work off steam!
She sure is annoying.
?!
Your gang members... are missing?!
So what happened the night before last was...
TWITCH
Huh?
Hey, girlie! How do you know what night our buddies went missing?!
You know something about it, don't you?!

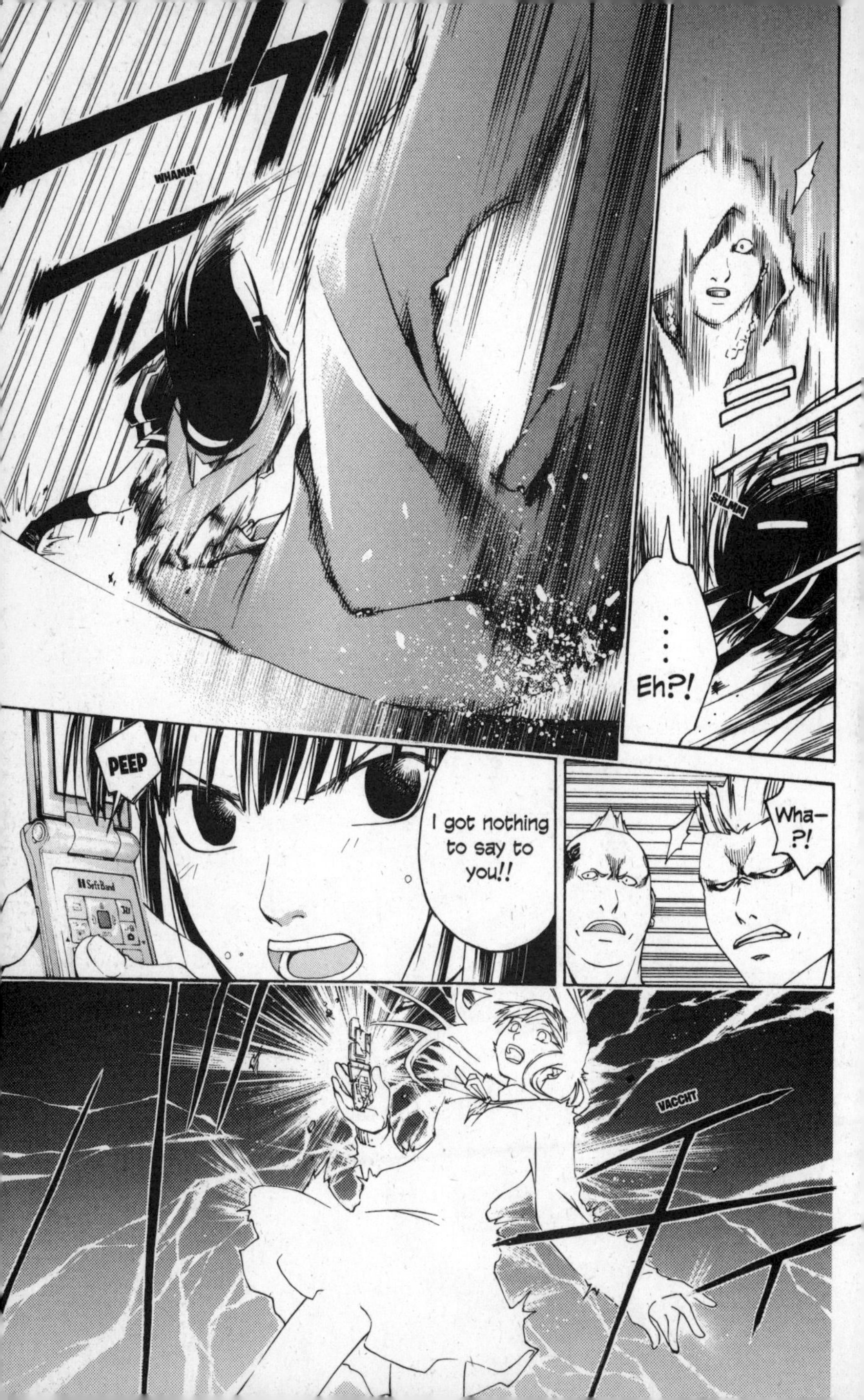
SHLMM
... Eh?!
WHAMM
Wha- ?!
PEEP
I got nothing to say to you!!
VACCHT

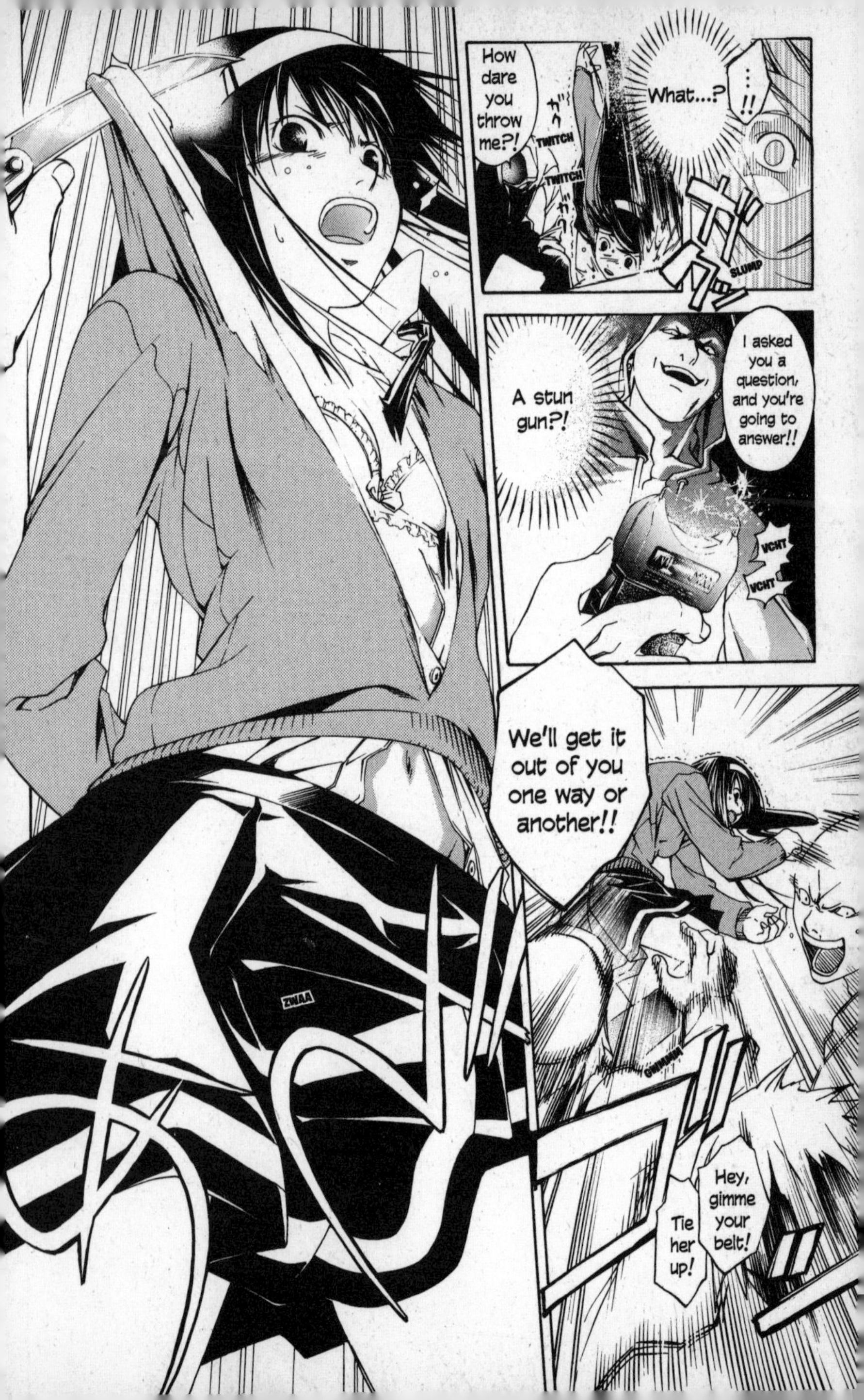
…!!
What…?
SLUMP
How dare you throw me?!
TWITCH
TWITCH
I asked you a question, and you're going to answer!!
A stun gun?!
VCHT
VCHT
We'll get it out of you one way or another!!
Hey, gimme your belt!
Tie her up!
ZWAA

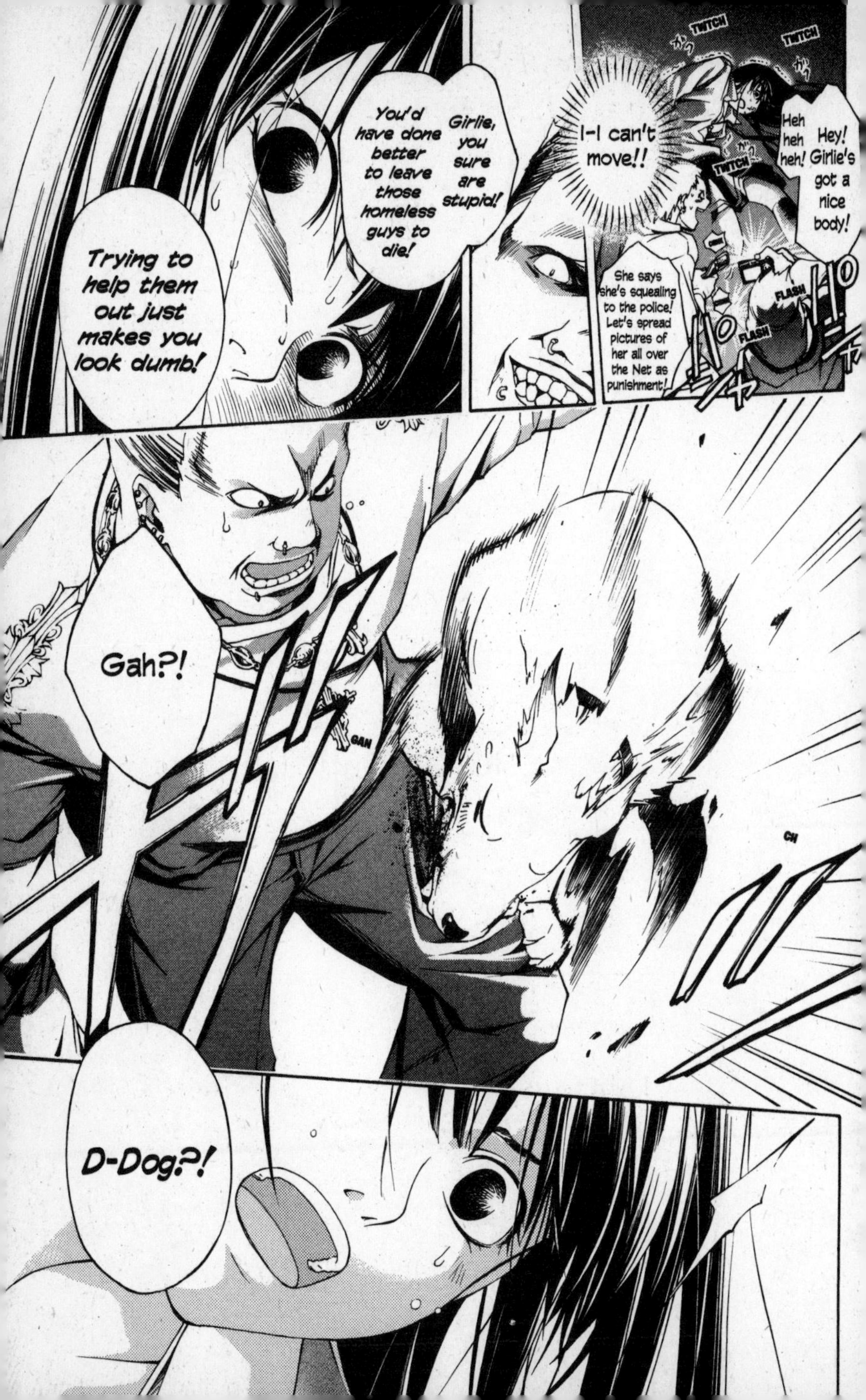

TWITCH
TWITCH
Hey! Girlie's got a nice body!
Heh heh heh!
TWITCH
I-I can't move!!
FLASH
FLASH
She says she's squealing to the police! Let's spread pictures of her all over the Net as punishment!
Girlie, you sure are stupid!
You'd have done better to leave those homeless guys to die!
Trying to help them out just makes you look dumb!
CH
GAN
Gah?!
D-Dog?!

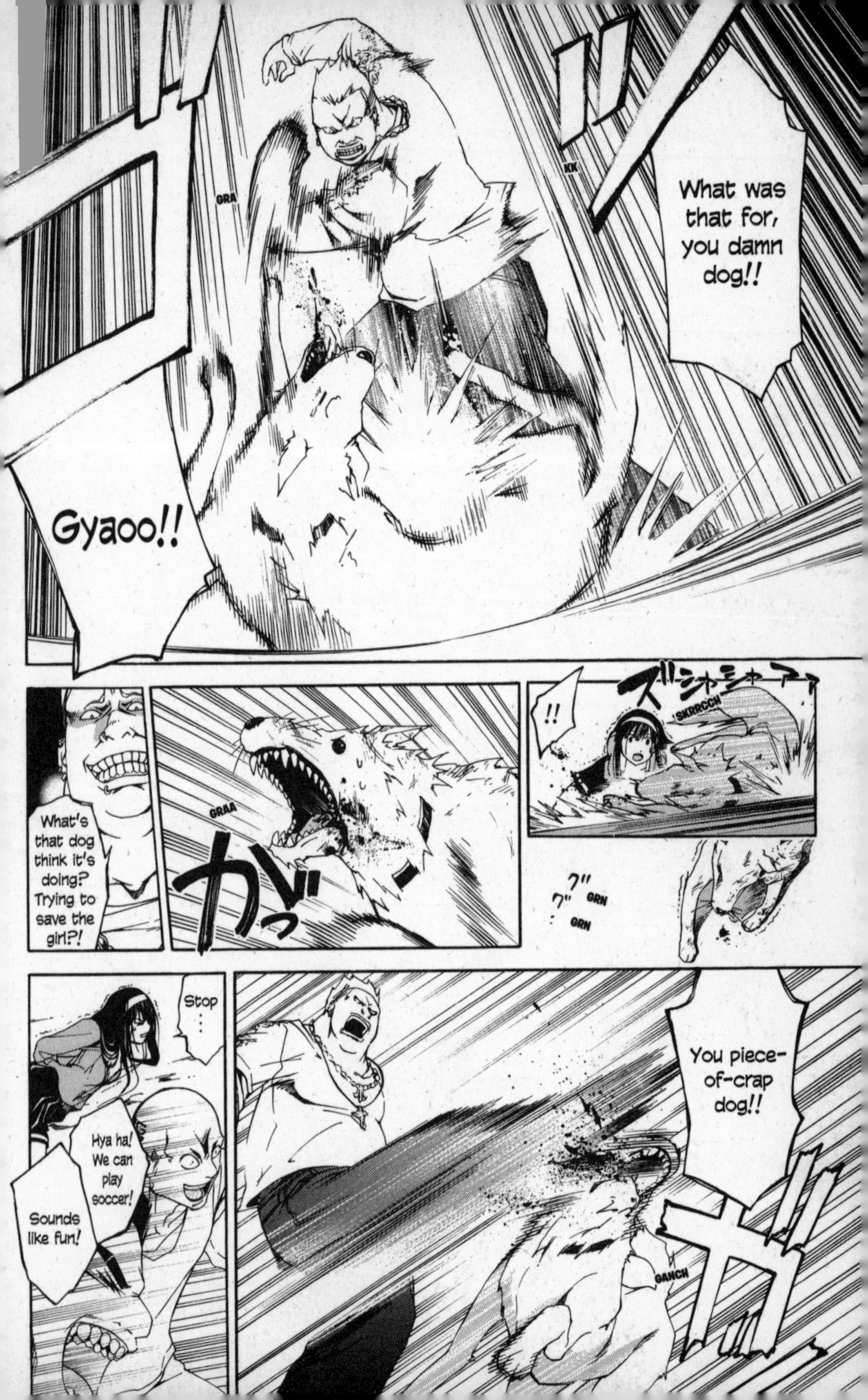
What was that for, you damn dog!!
KK
GRA
Gyaoo!!
!!
SKRRCCH
GRN
GRN
GRAA
What's that dog think it's doing? Trying to save the girl?!
You piece-of-crap dog!!
GANCH
Stop...
Hya ha! We can play soccer!
Sounds like fun!

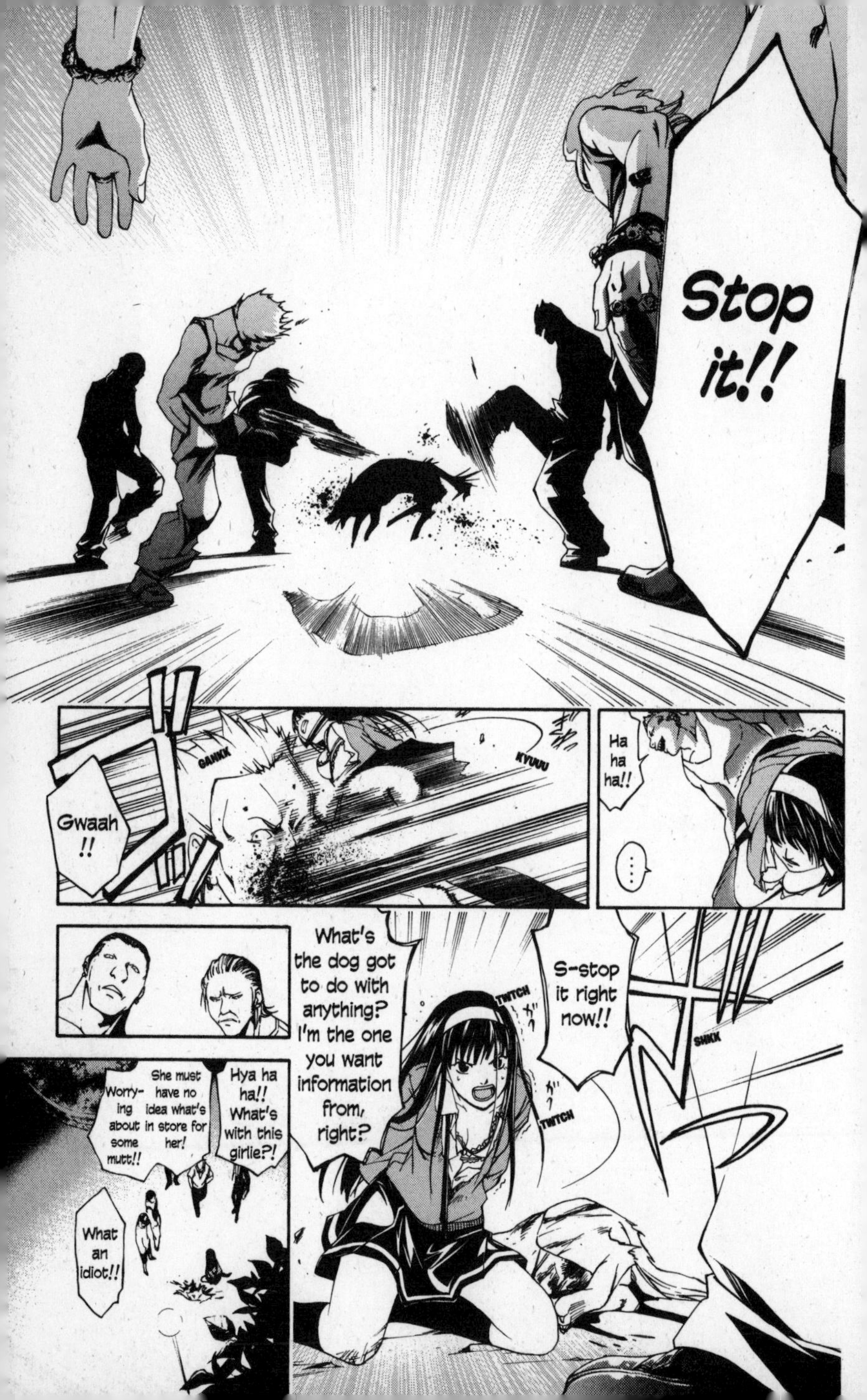
Stop it!!
Ha ha ha!!
...
KYUUU
GANKK
Gwaah!!
S-stop it right now!!
TWITCH
SHKK
TWITCH
What's the dog got to do with anything? I'm the one you want information from, right?
Hya ha ha!! What's with this girlie?!
She must have no idea what's in store for her!
Worry-ing about some mutt!!
What an idiot!!

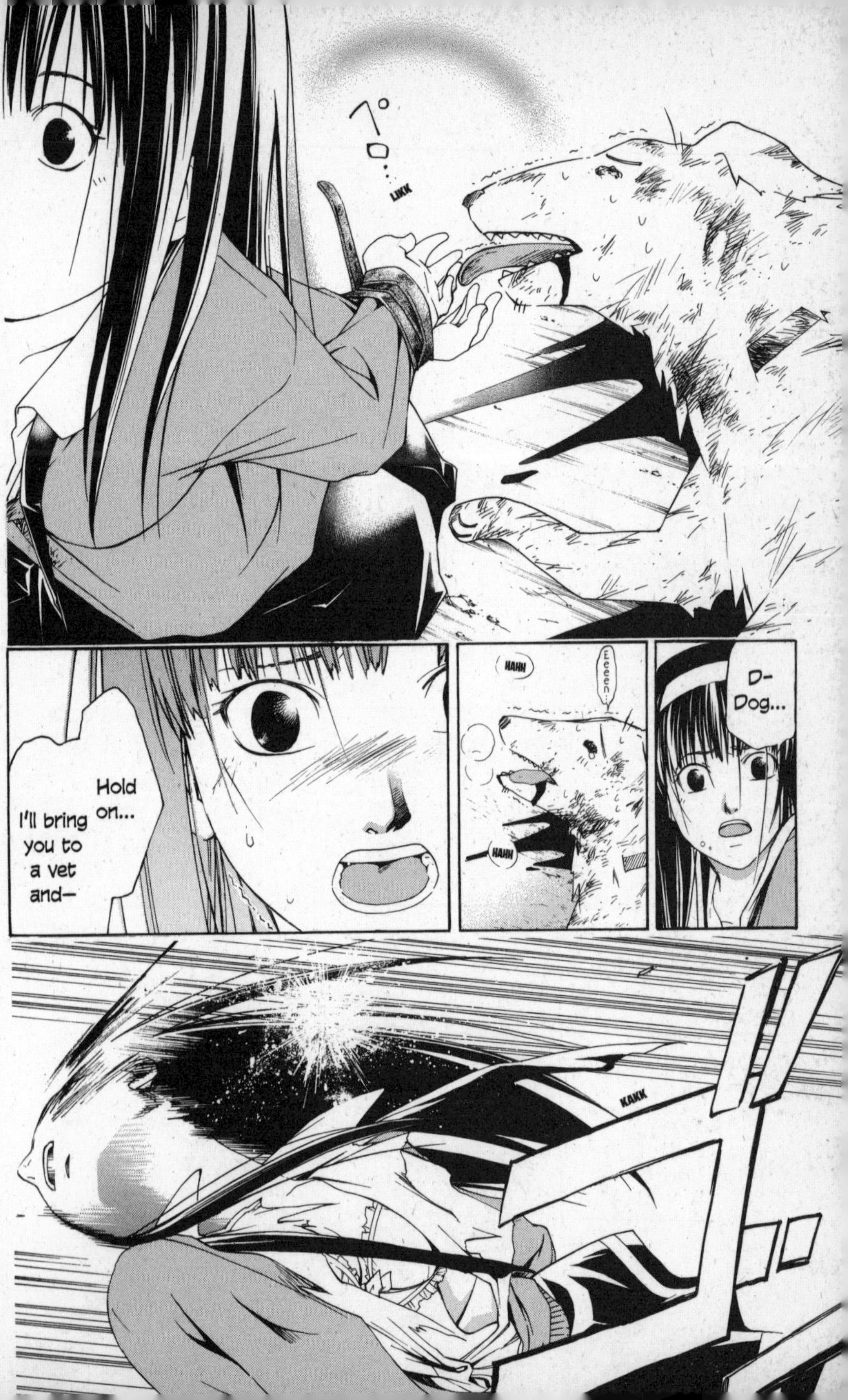
ペロ...
LIKK
D-Dog...
HAHH
Eeeen...
HAHH
Hold on...
I'll bring you to a vet and—
KAKK

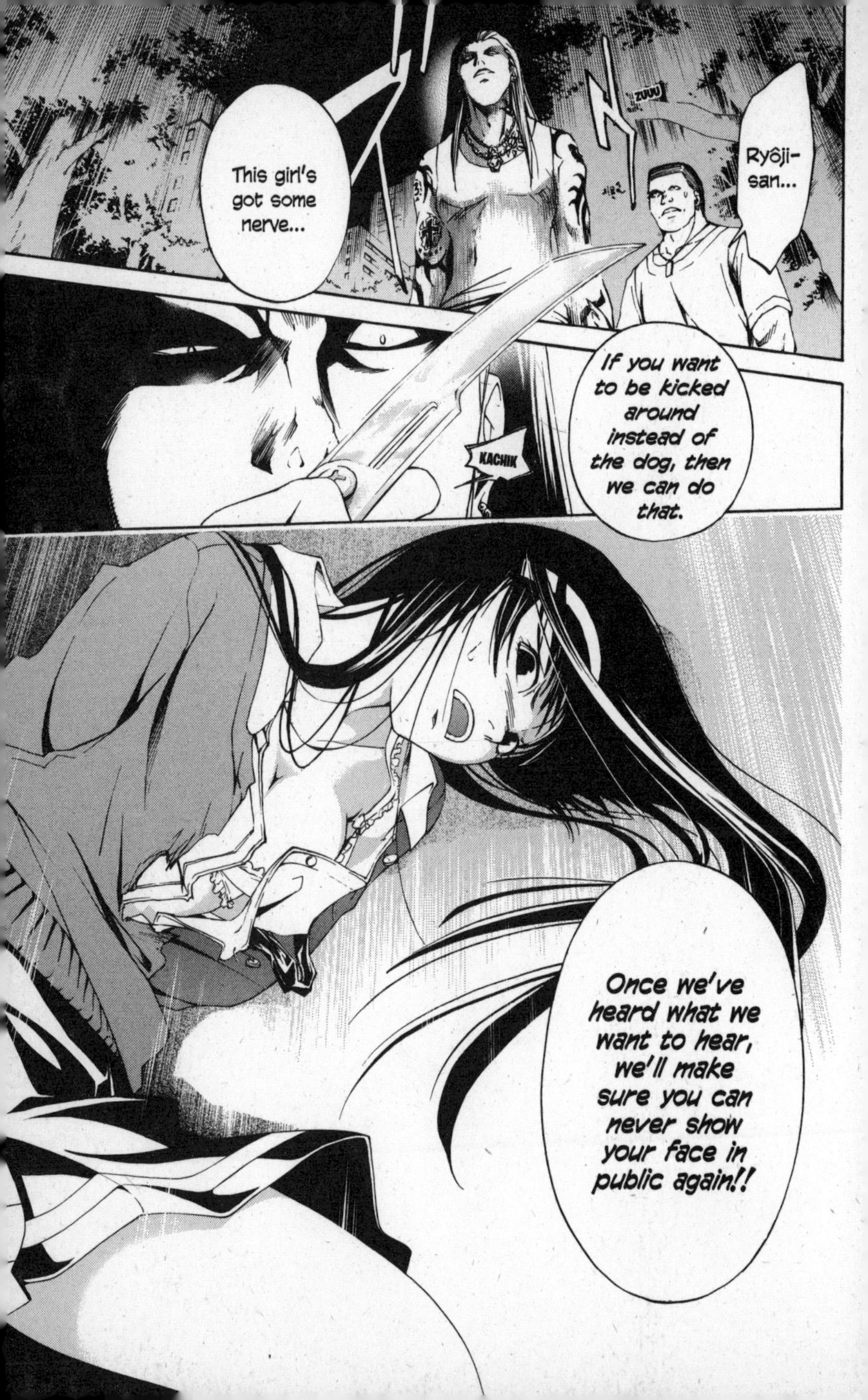
Ryôji-san...
ZUUU
This girl's got some nerve...
If you want to be kicked around instead of the dog, then we can do that.
KACHIK
Once we've heard what we want to hear, we'll make sure you can never show your face in public again!!

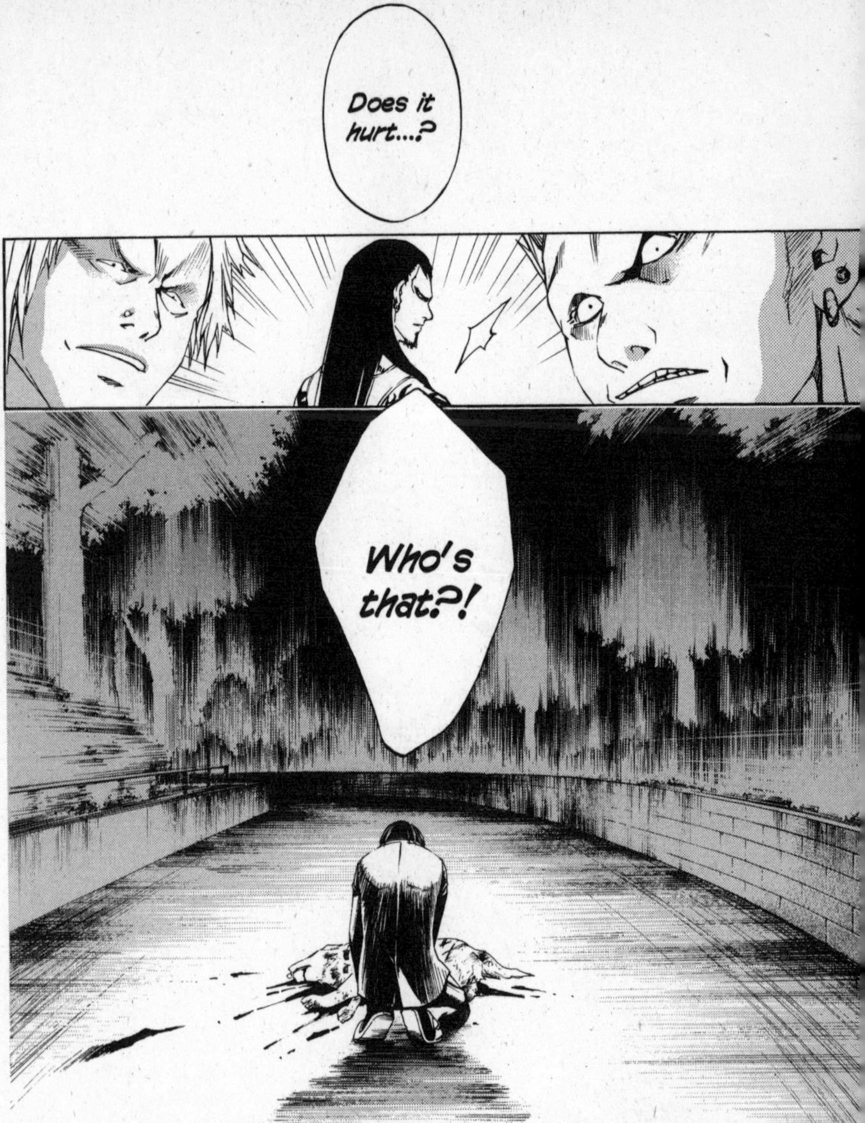
Does it hurt...?
Who's that?!

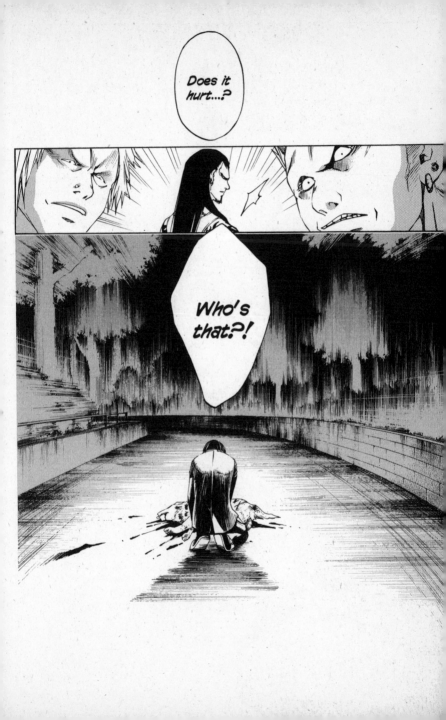

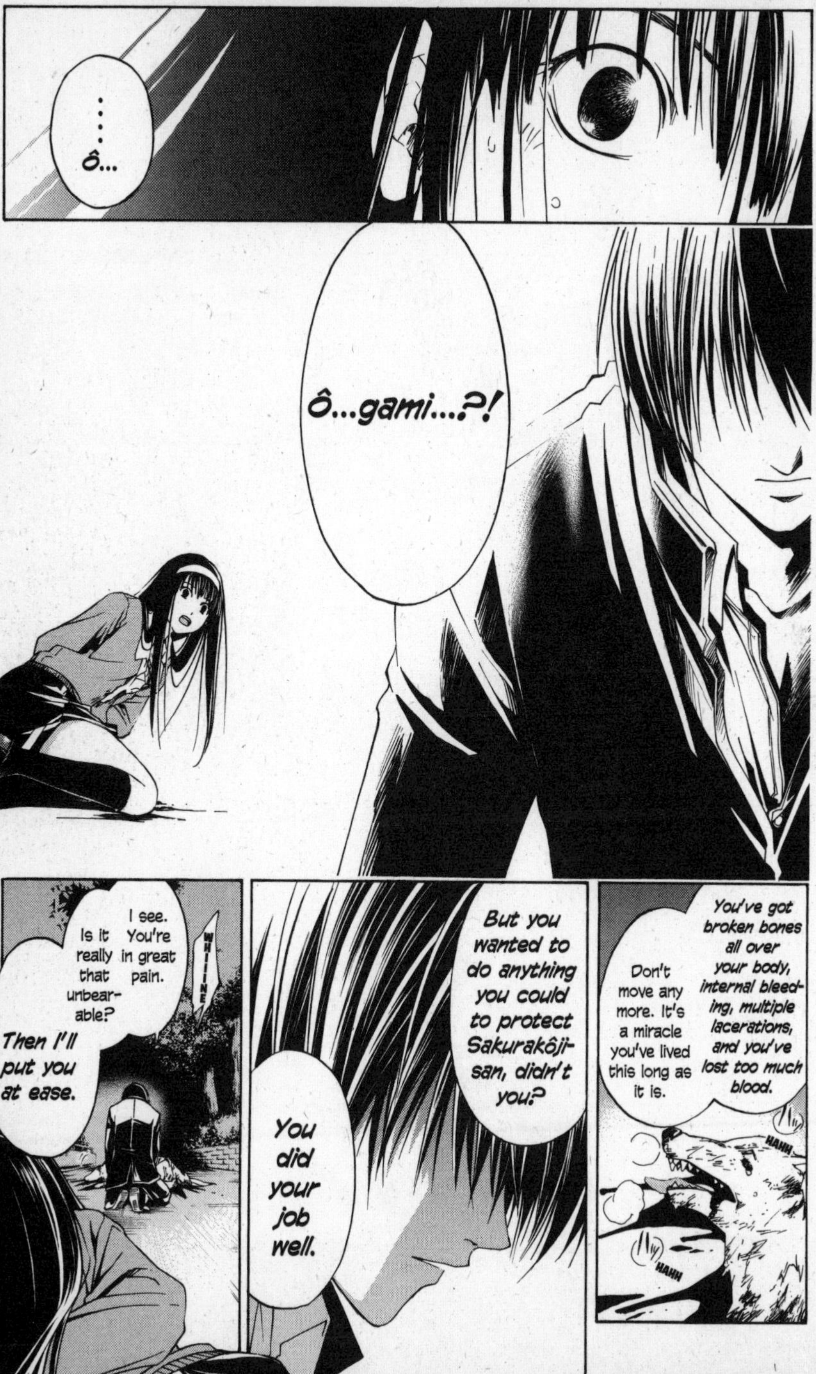

....ô...
ô...gami...?!
You've got broken bones all over your body, internal bleeding, multiple lacerations, and you've lost too much blood.
Don't move any more. It's a miracle you've lived this long as it is.
HAHH
HAHH
But you wanted to do anything you could to protect Sakurakôji-san, didn't you?
You did your job well.
I see. You're in great pain.
Is it really that unbearable?
WHIIINE
Then I'll put you at ease.

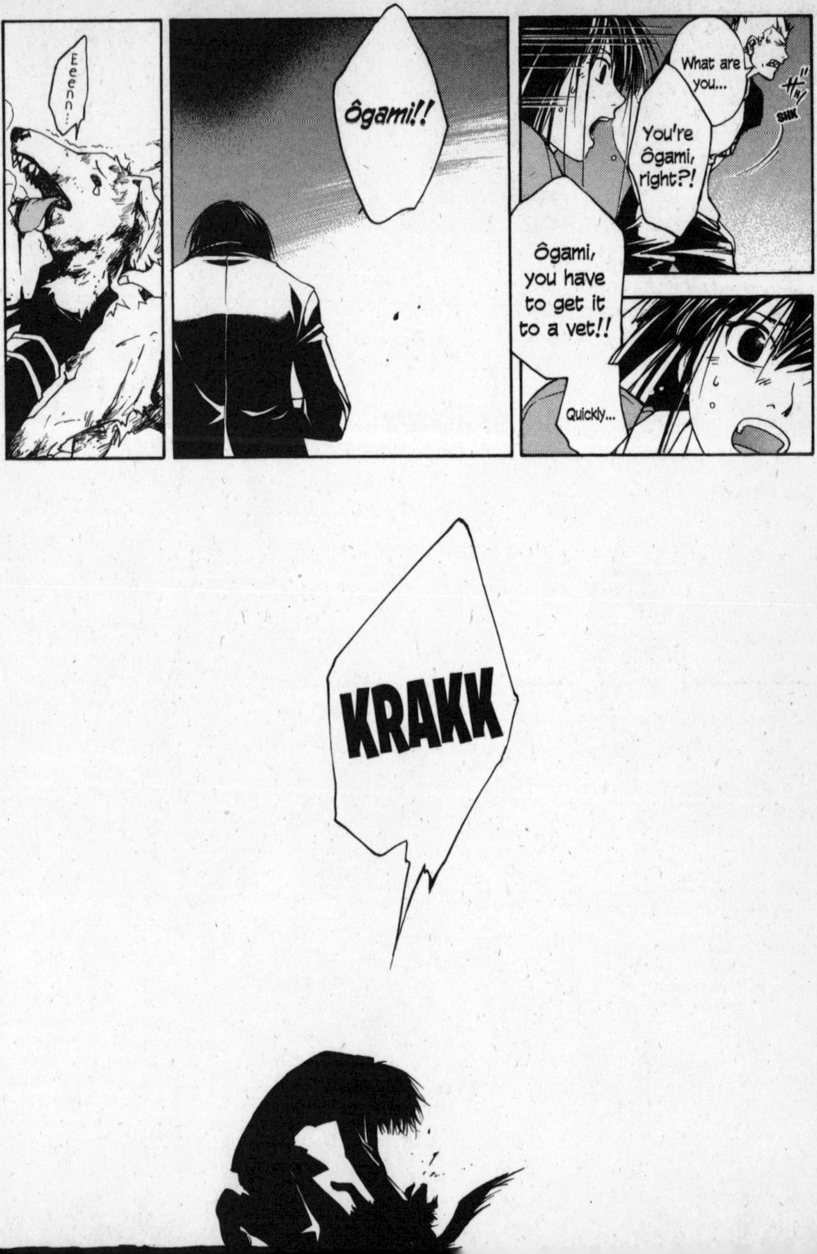
SHK
What are you...
You're Ôgami, right?!
Ôgami, you have to get it to a vet!!
Quickly...
Ôgami!!
Eeenn...
KRAKK

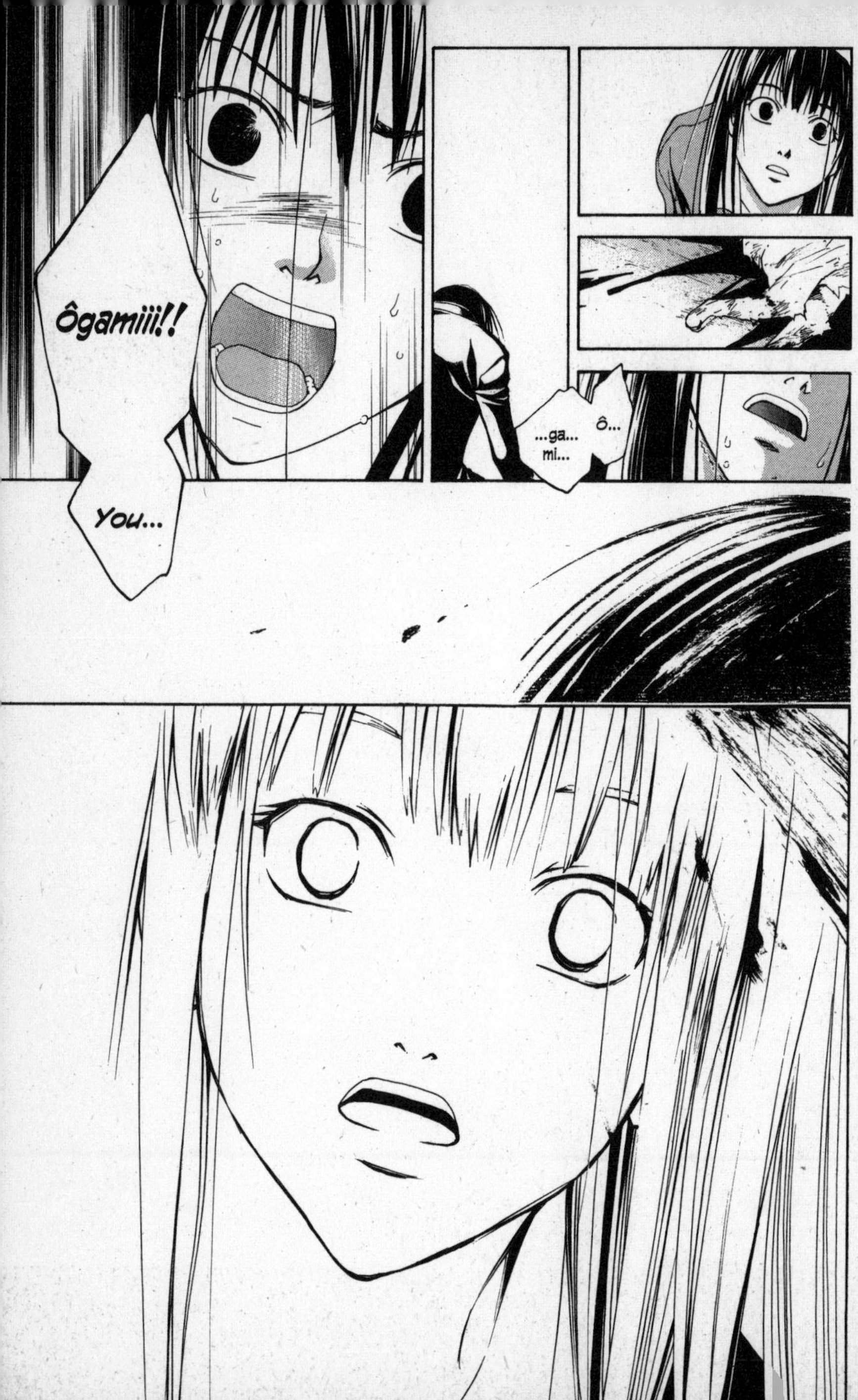
Ô... ...ga... mi...
Ôgamiii!!
You...

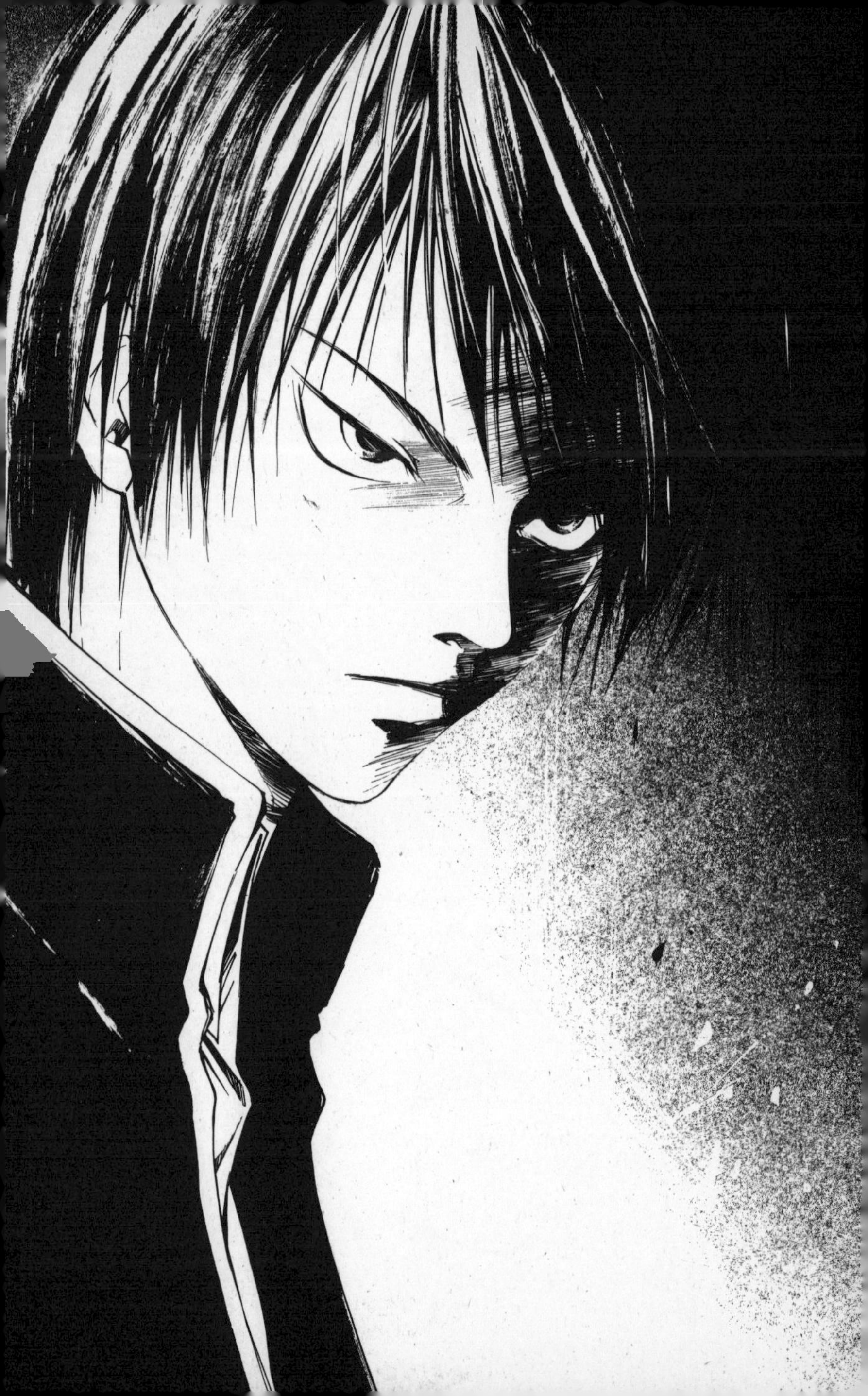

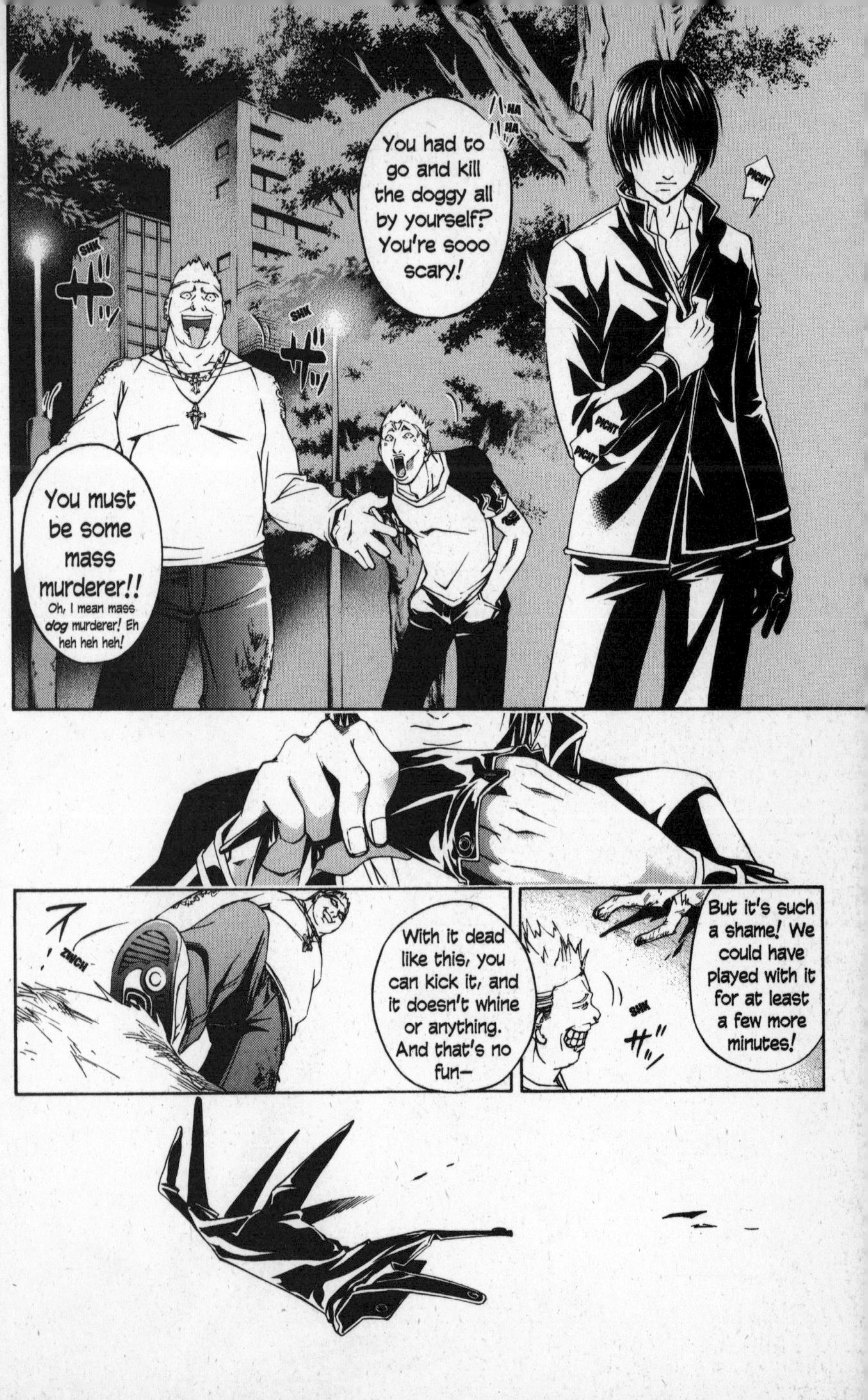
PICHT
HA
HA
You had to go and kill the doggy all by yourself? You're sooo scary!
SHK
SHK
PICHT
PICHT
You must be some mass murderer!! Oh, I mean mass *dog* murderer! Eh heh heh heh!
But it's such a shame! We could have played with it for at least a few more minutes!
SHK
With it dead like this, you can kick it, and it doesn't whine or anything. And that's no fun—
ZINCH

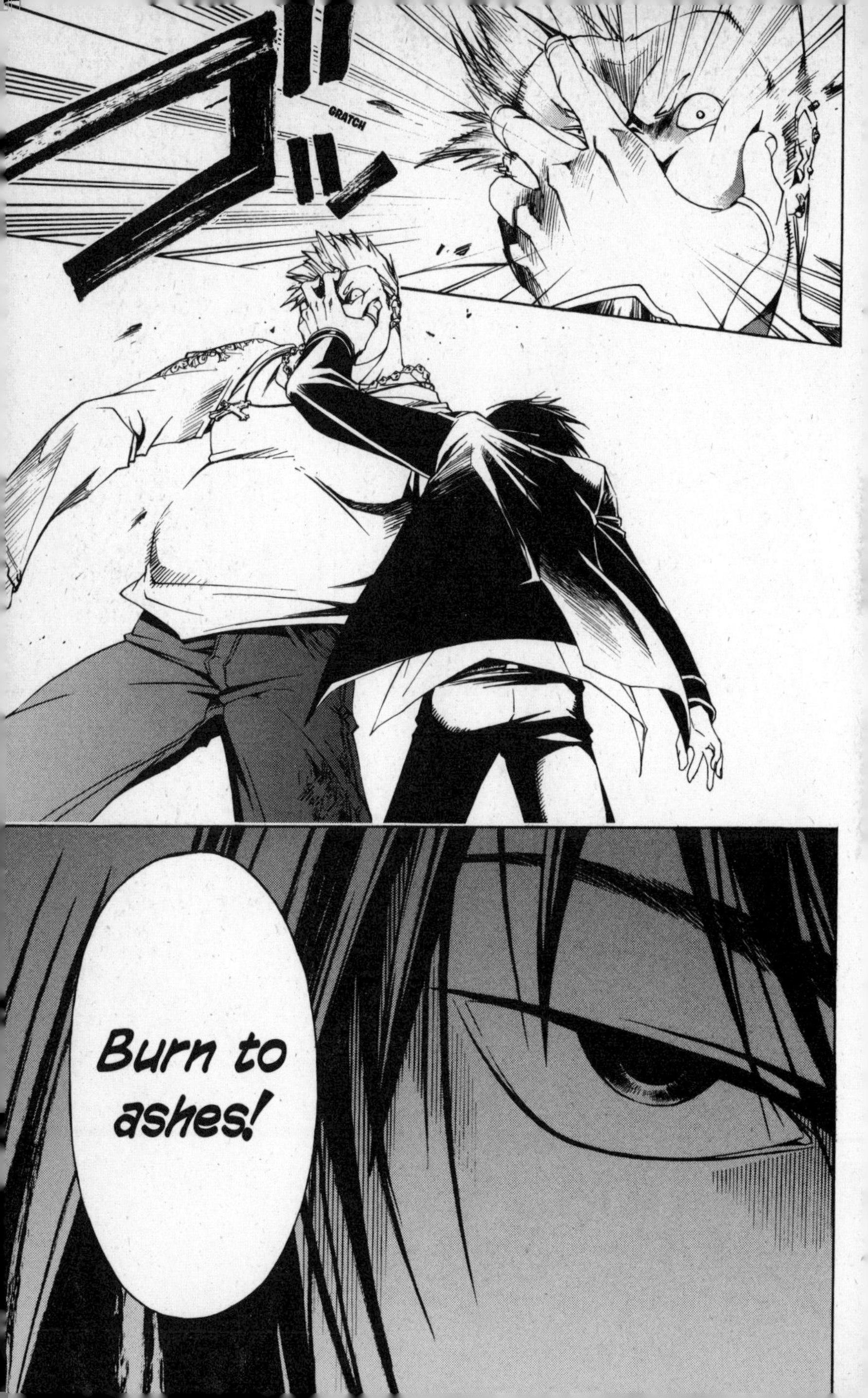
GRATCH
Burn to ashes!

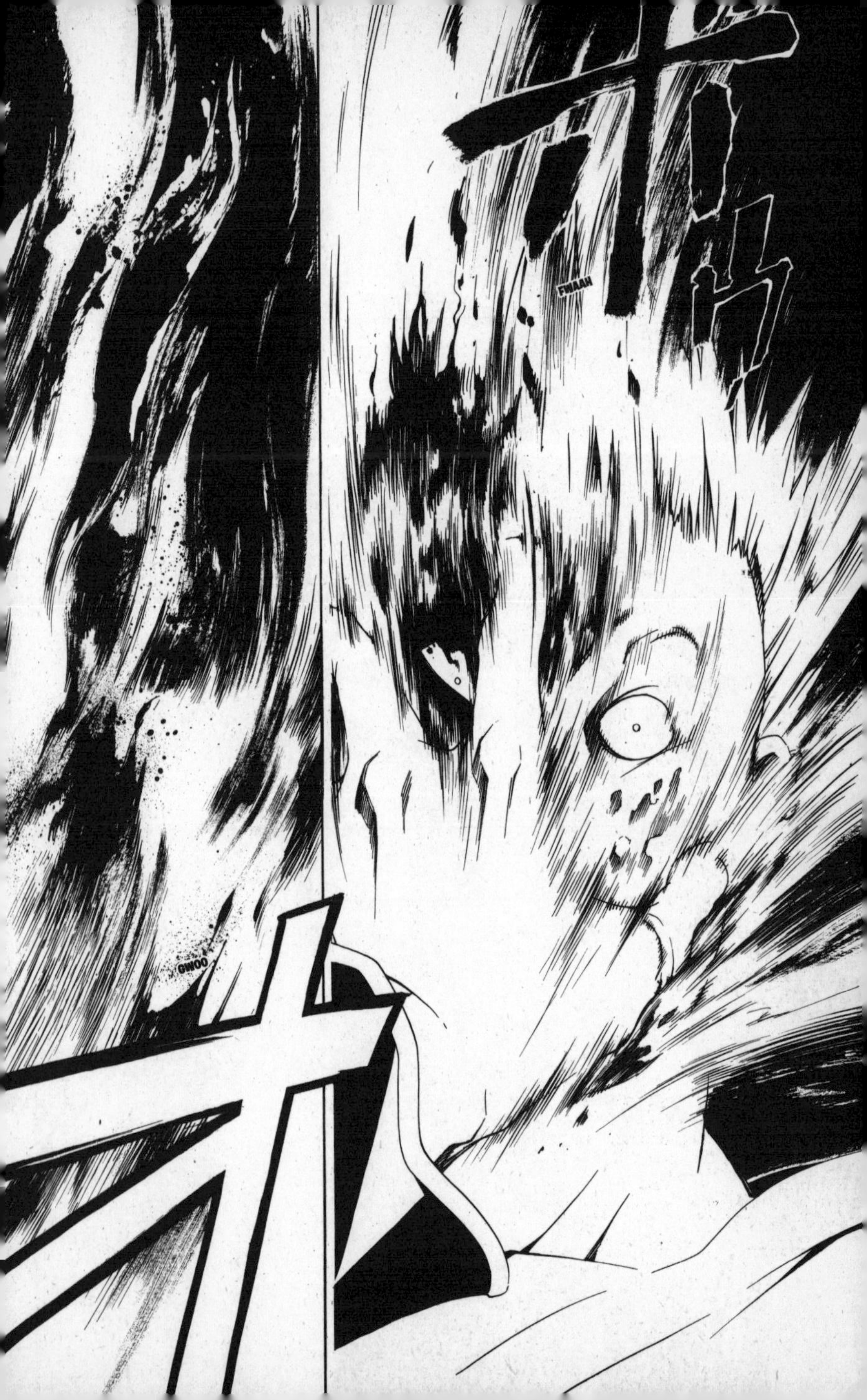
FWAAH
GWOO

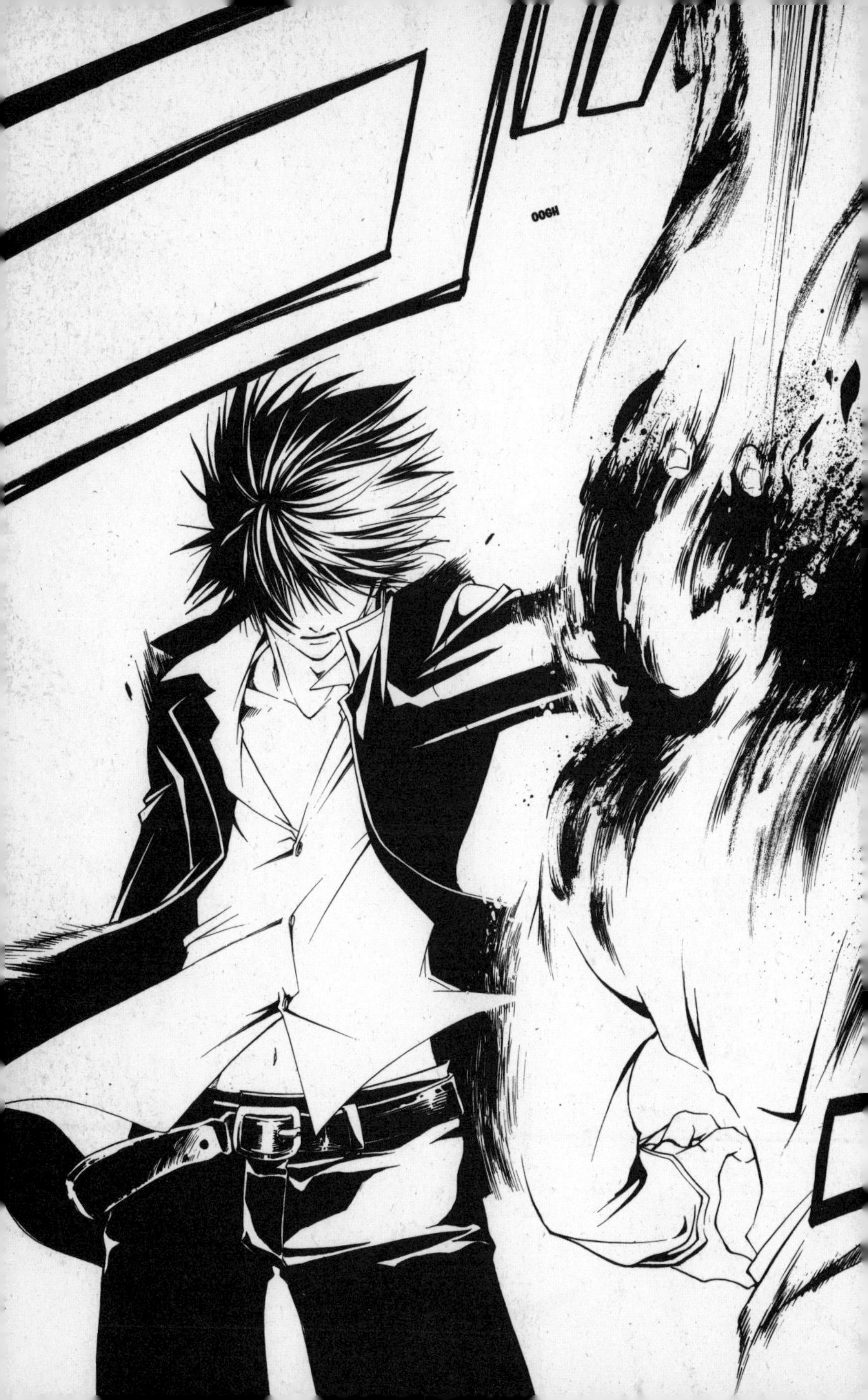
OOGH

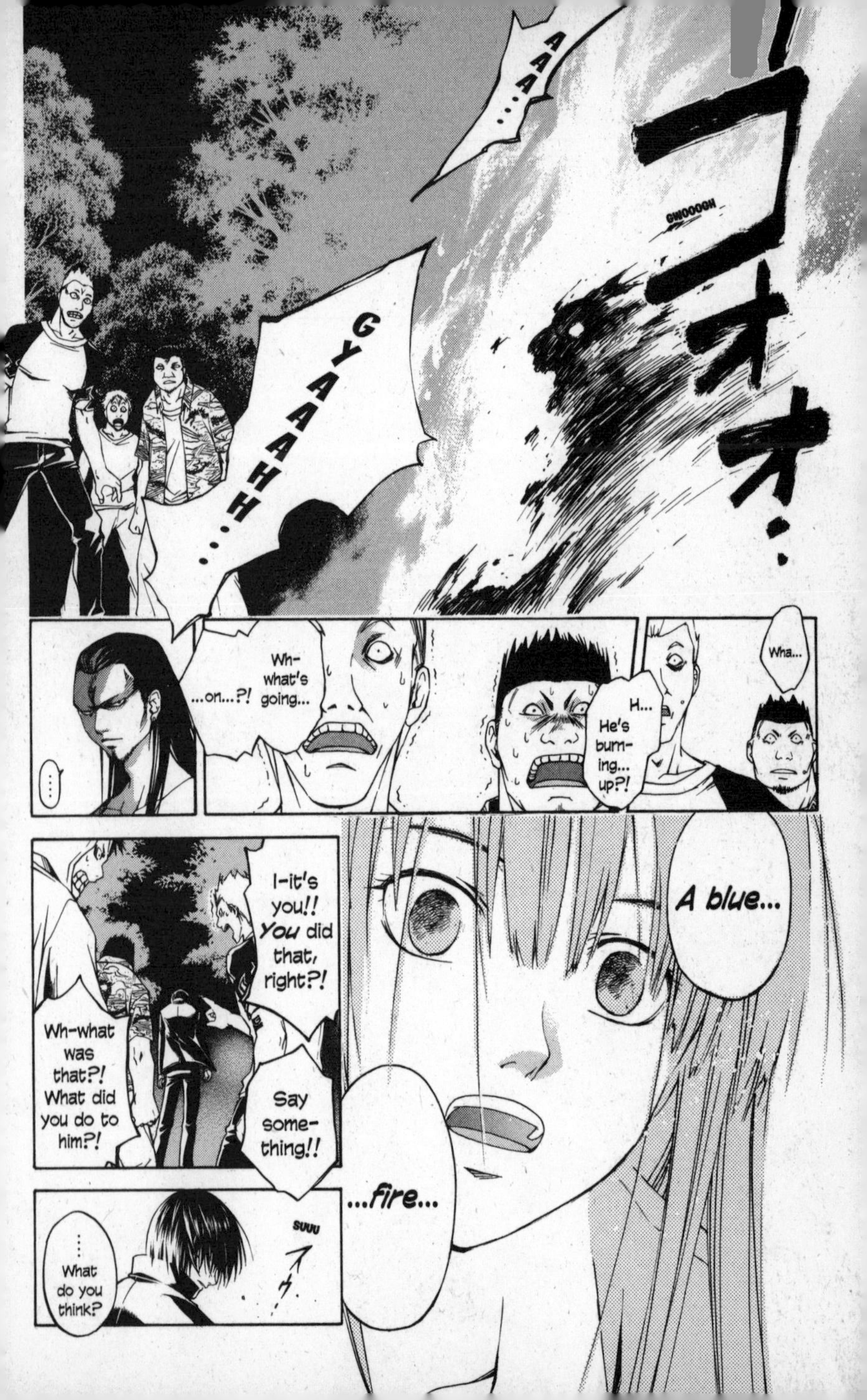
ゴオオオ!
GWOOOOGH
AAAA...
GYAAAAHH...
Wha...
H... He's burn-ing... up?!
Wh- what's going... ...on...?!
......
A blue...
...fire...
I-it's you!! You did that, right?!
Wh-what was that?! What did you do to him?!
Say some-thing!!
SUUU
...... What do you think?

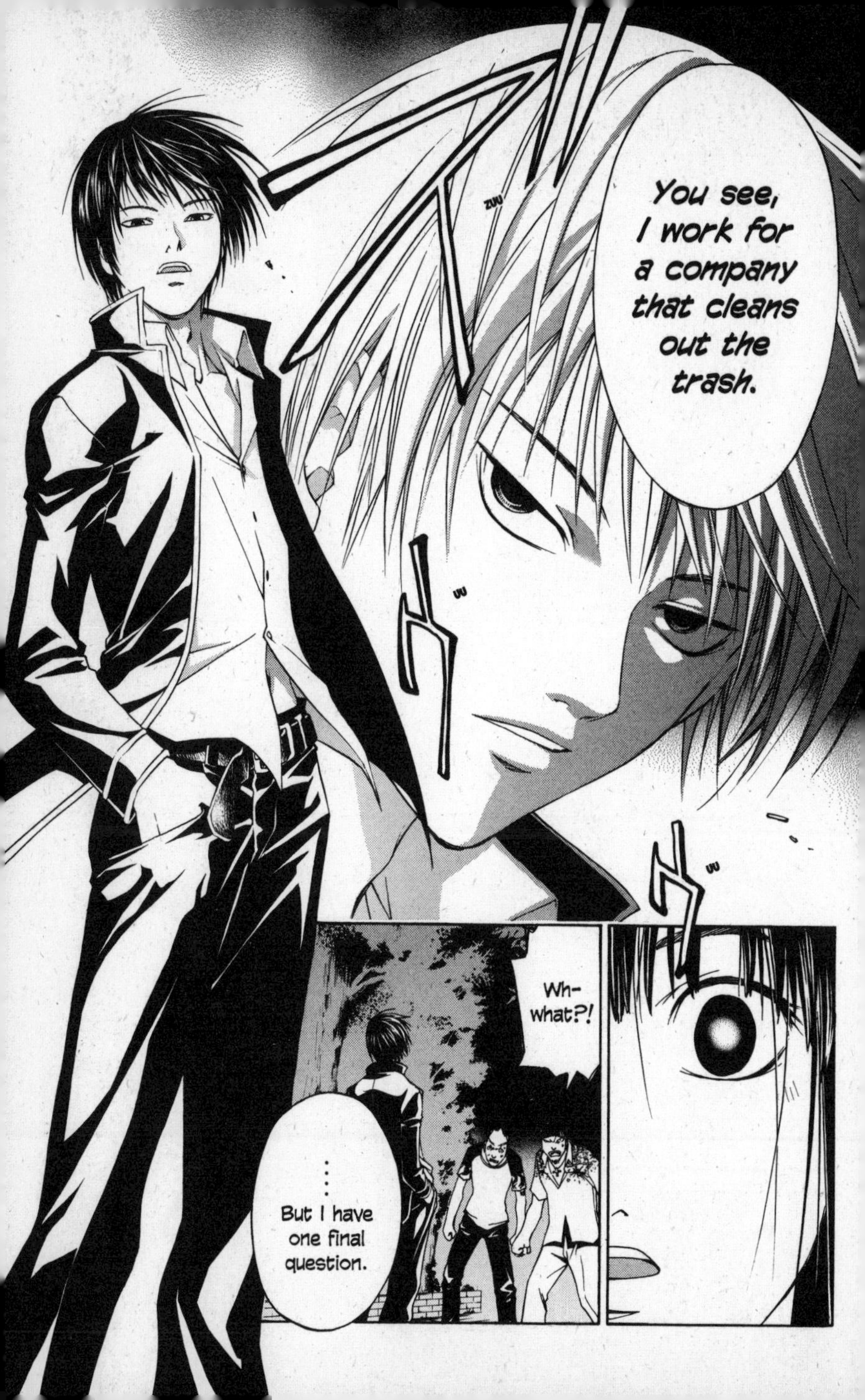
ZUU
You see, I work for a company that cleans out the trash.
UU
UU
Wh- what?!
...
But I have one final question.

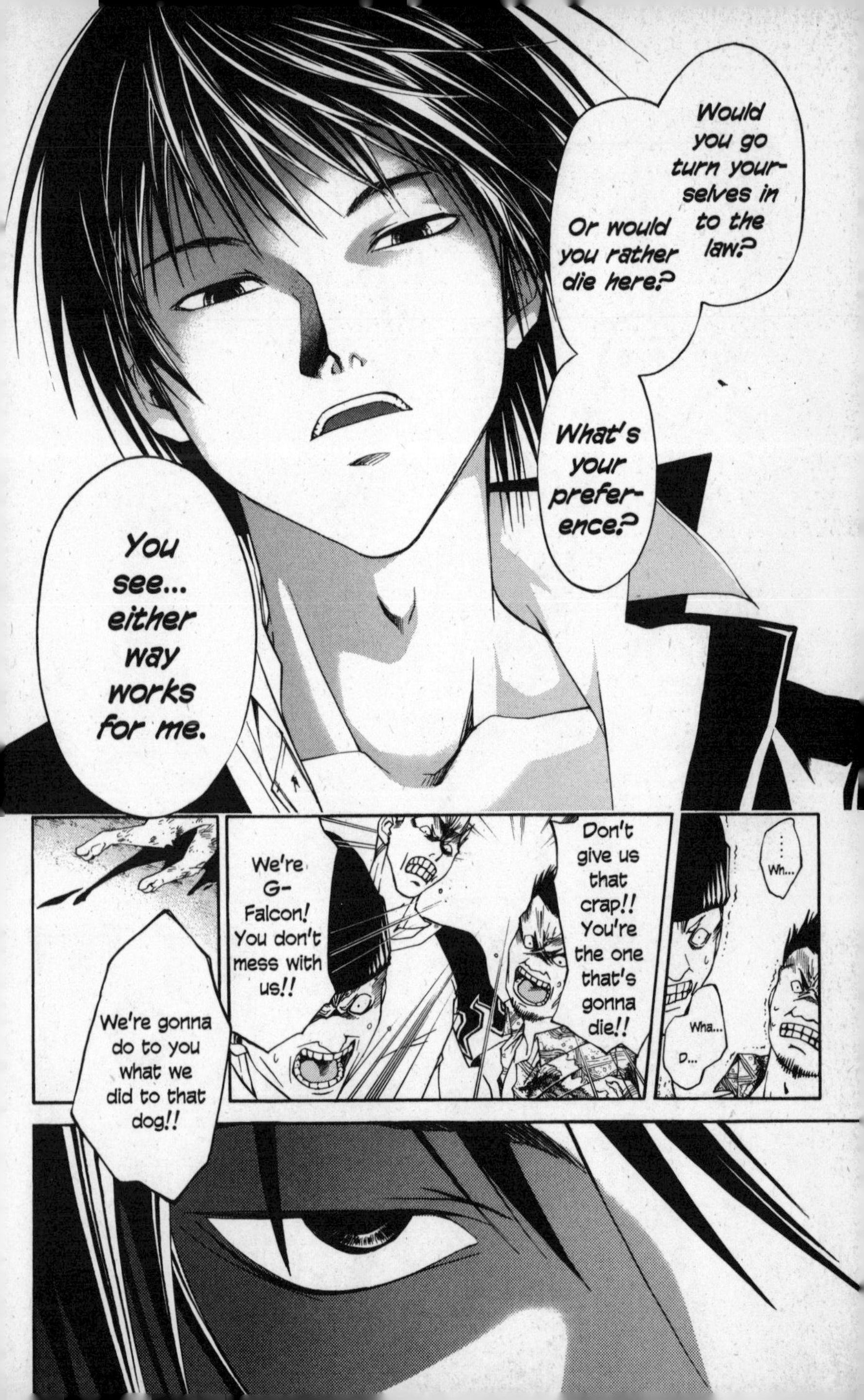
Would you go turn yourselves in to the law?
Or would you rather die here?
What's your preference?
You see... either way works for me.
...... Wh...
Wha...
D...
Don't give us that crap!! You're the one that's gonna die!!
We're G-Falcon! You don't mess with us!!
We're gonna do to you what we did to that dog!!

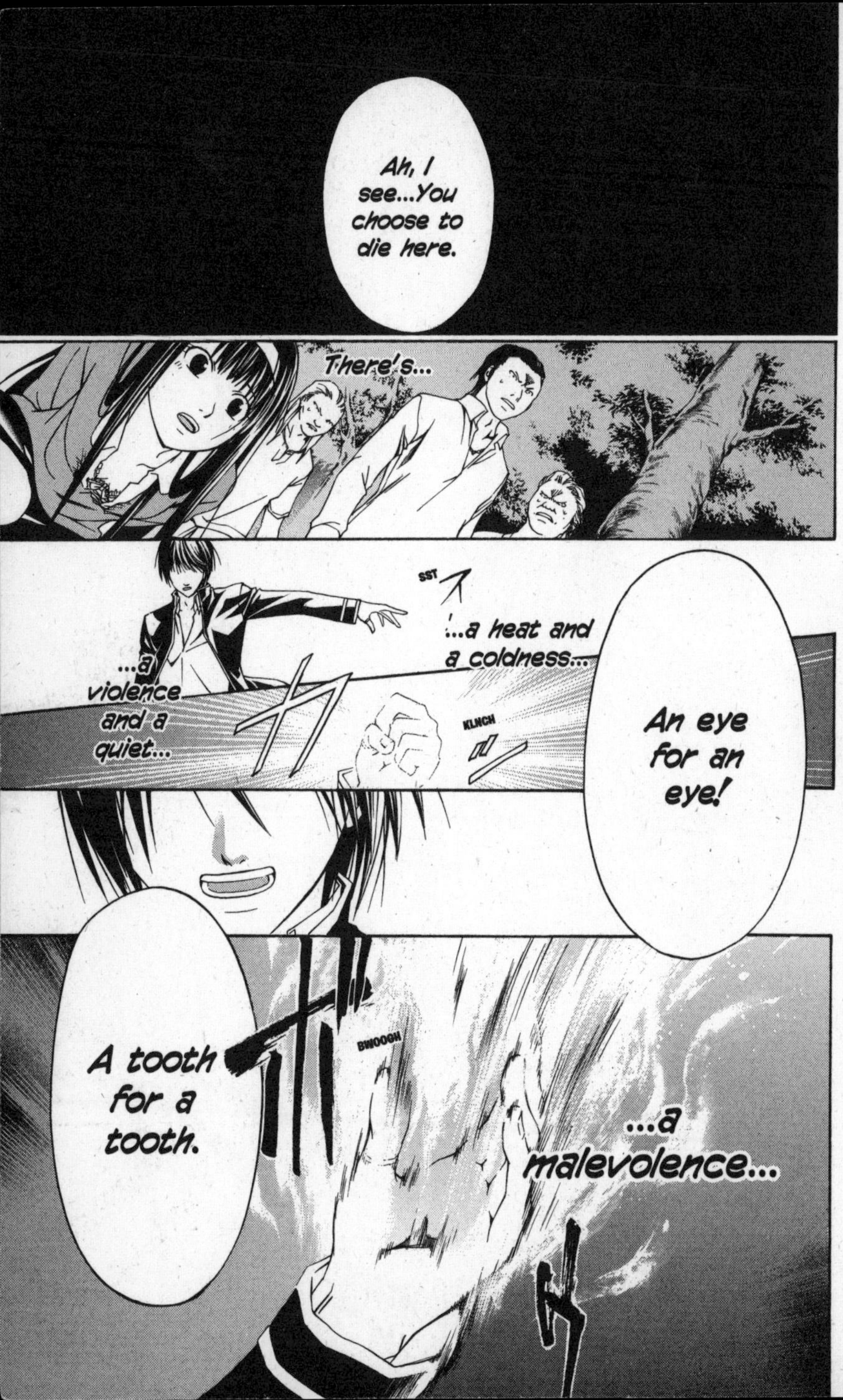
Ah, I see...You choose to die here.
There's...
An eye for an eye!
SST
...a heat and a coldness...
KLNCH
...a violence and a quiet...
...a malevolence...
BWOOGH
A tooth for a tooth.

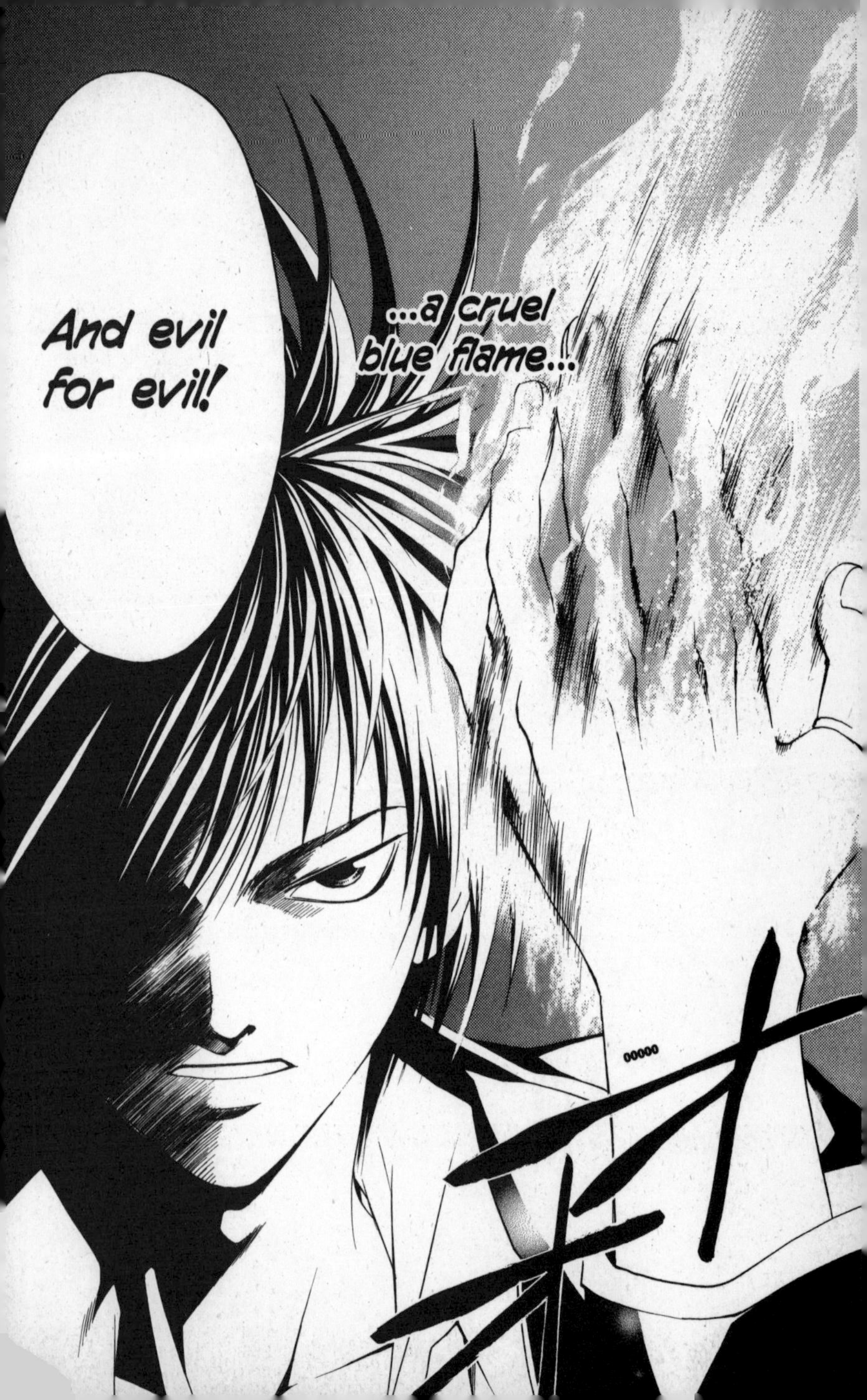
...a cruel blue flame...
.....
And evil for evil!

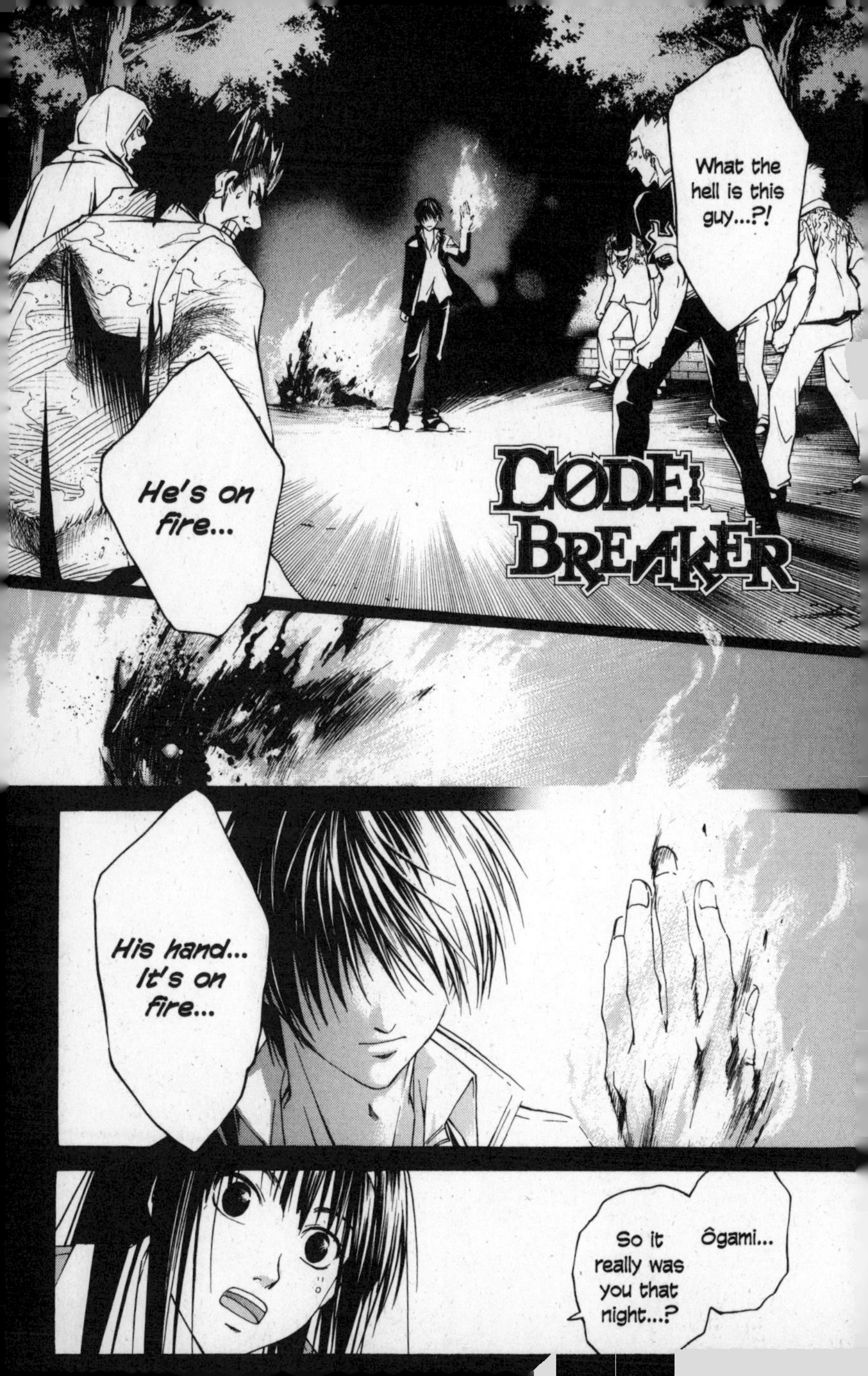
What the hell is this guy...?!
He's on fire...
CODE:BREAKER
His hand... It's on fire...
Ôgami...
So it really was you that night...?

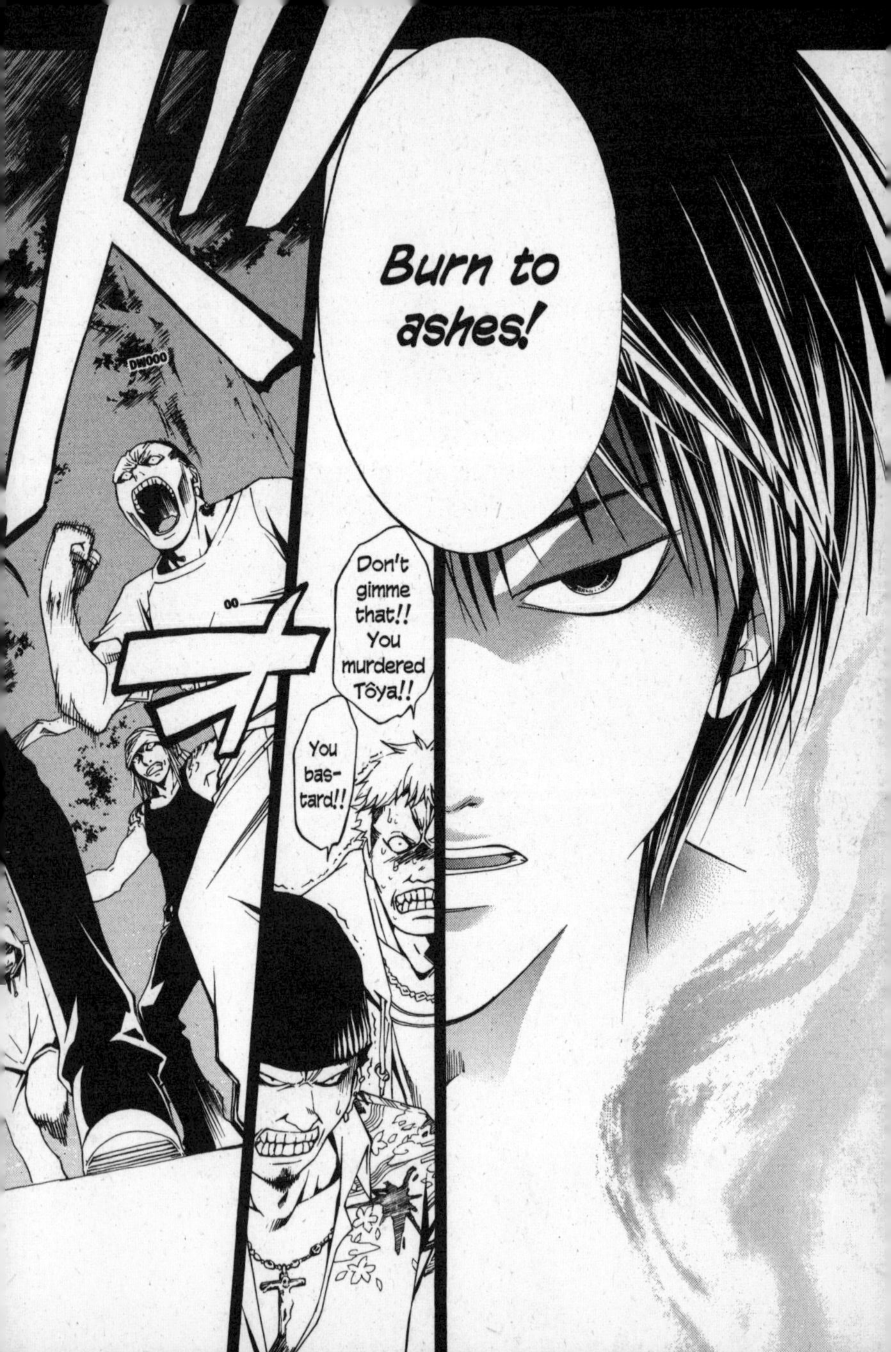
Burn to ashes!
Don't gimme that!! You murdered Tôya!!
You bastard!!
DWOOO

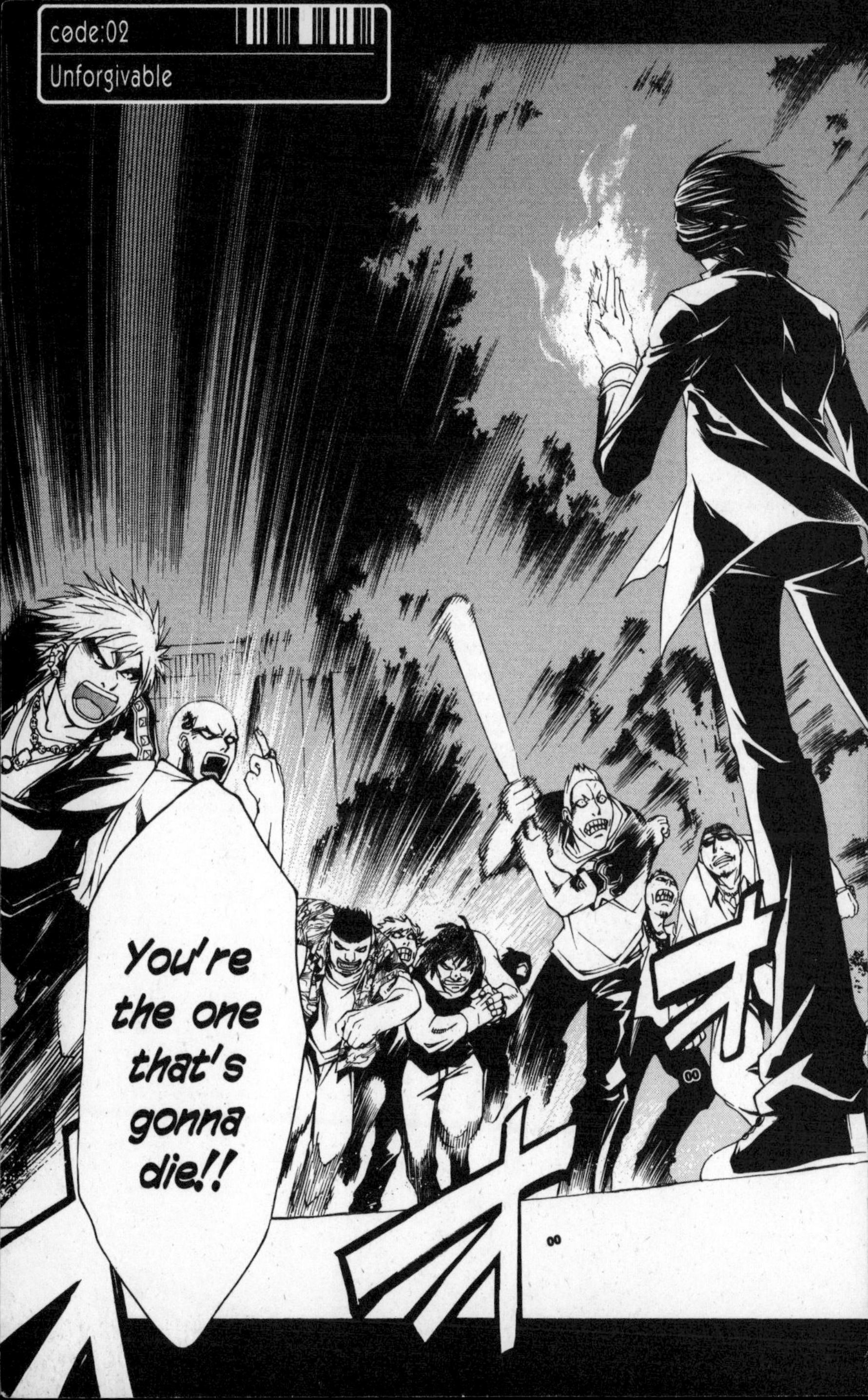
code:02
Unforgivable
You're the one that's gonna die!!

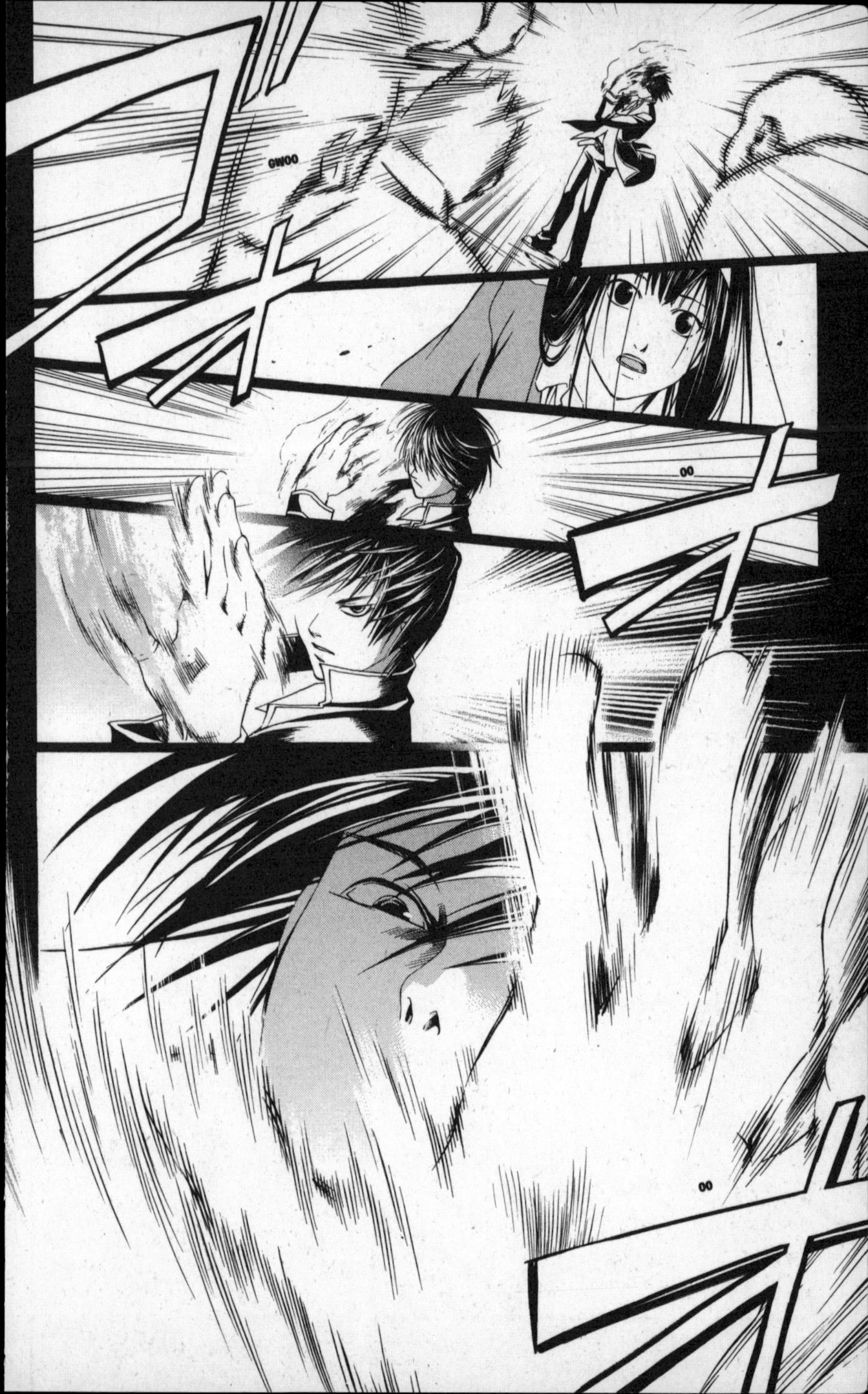
GWOO
OO
OO

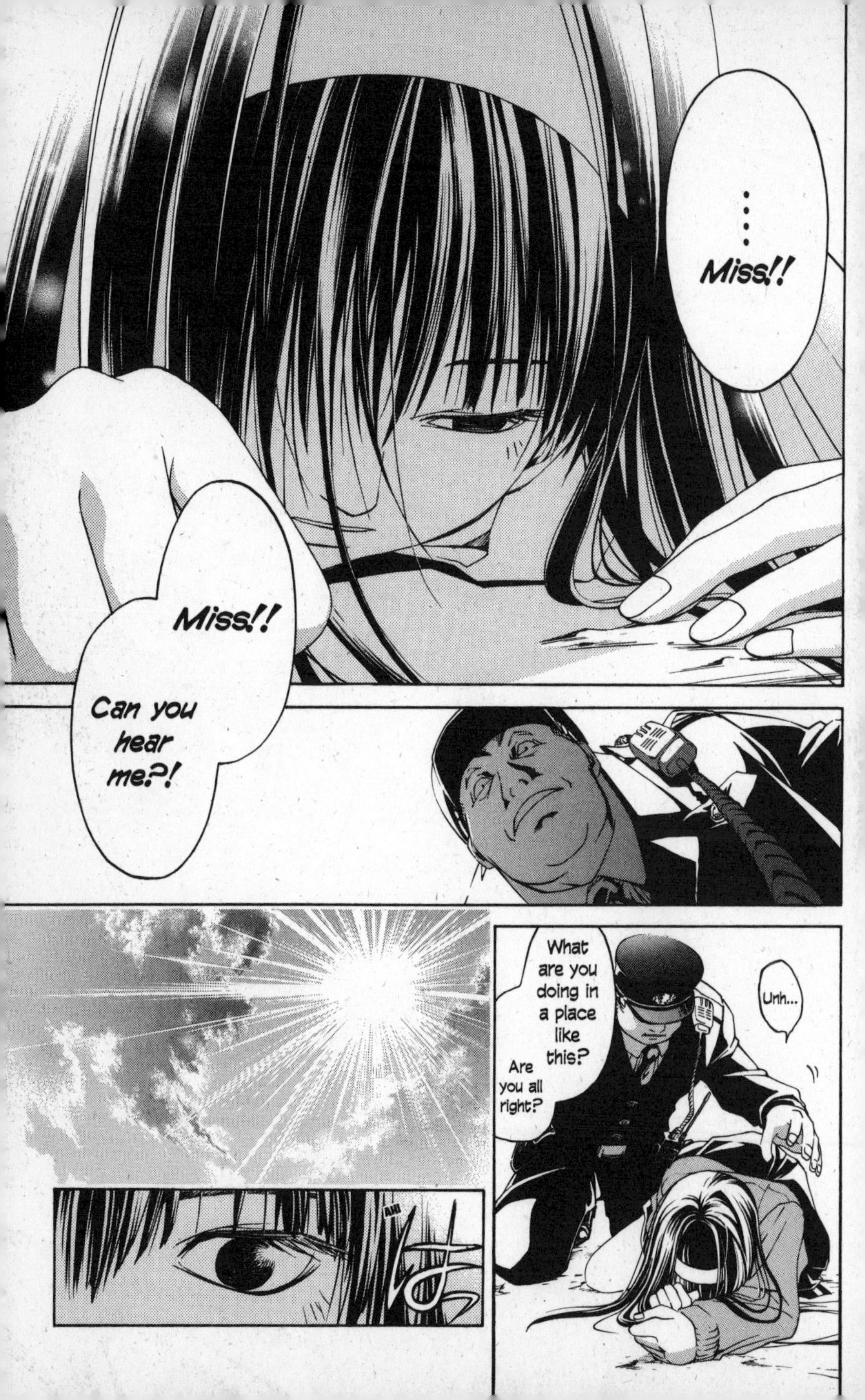
...... Miss!!
Miss!! Can you hear me?!
What are you doing in a place like this?
Are you all right?
Unh...
AH!

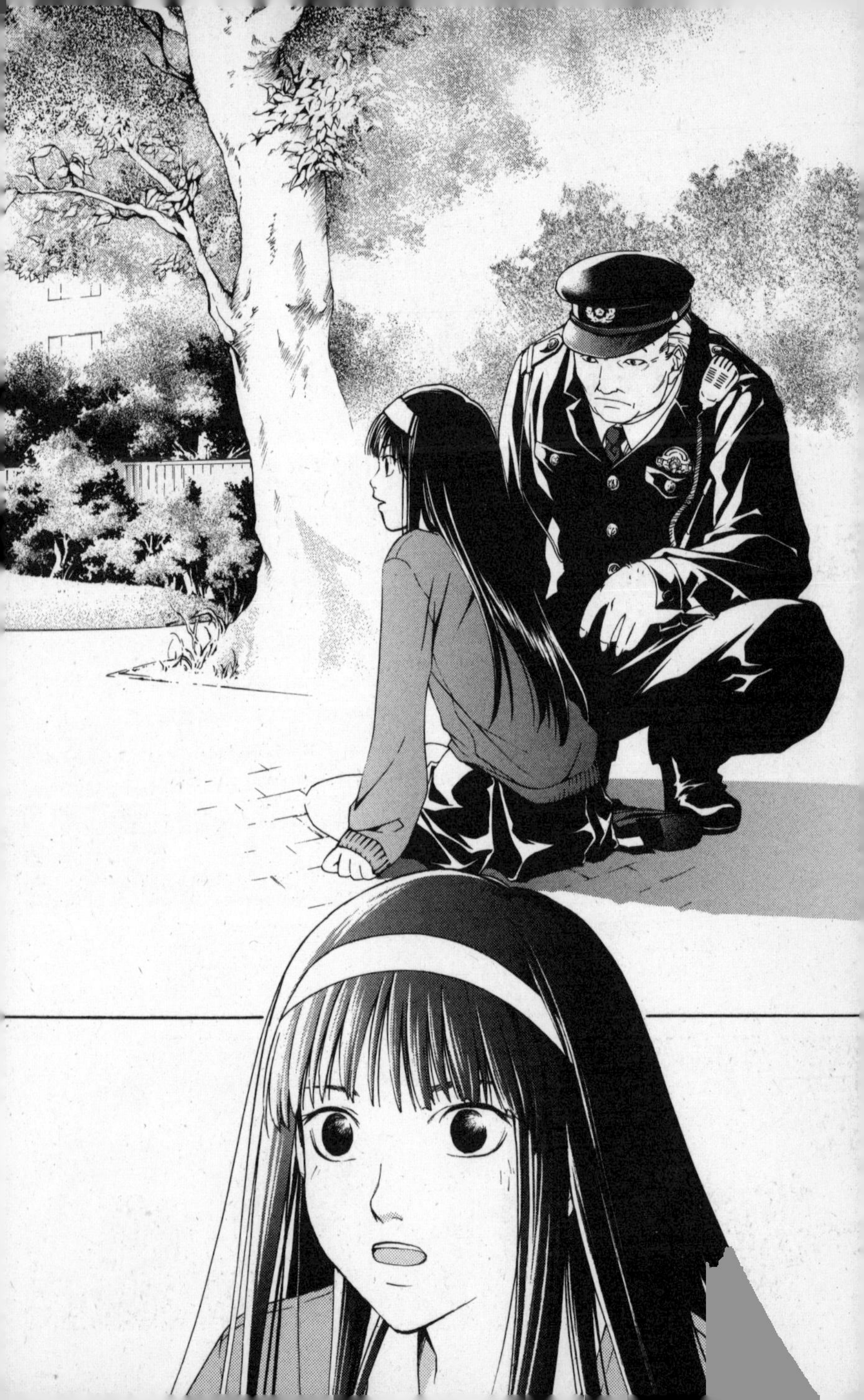

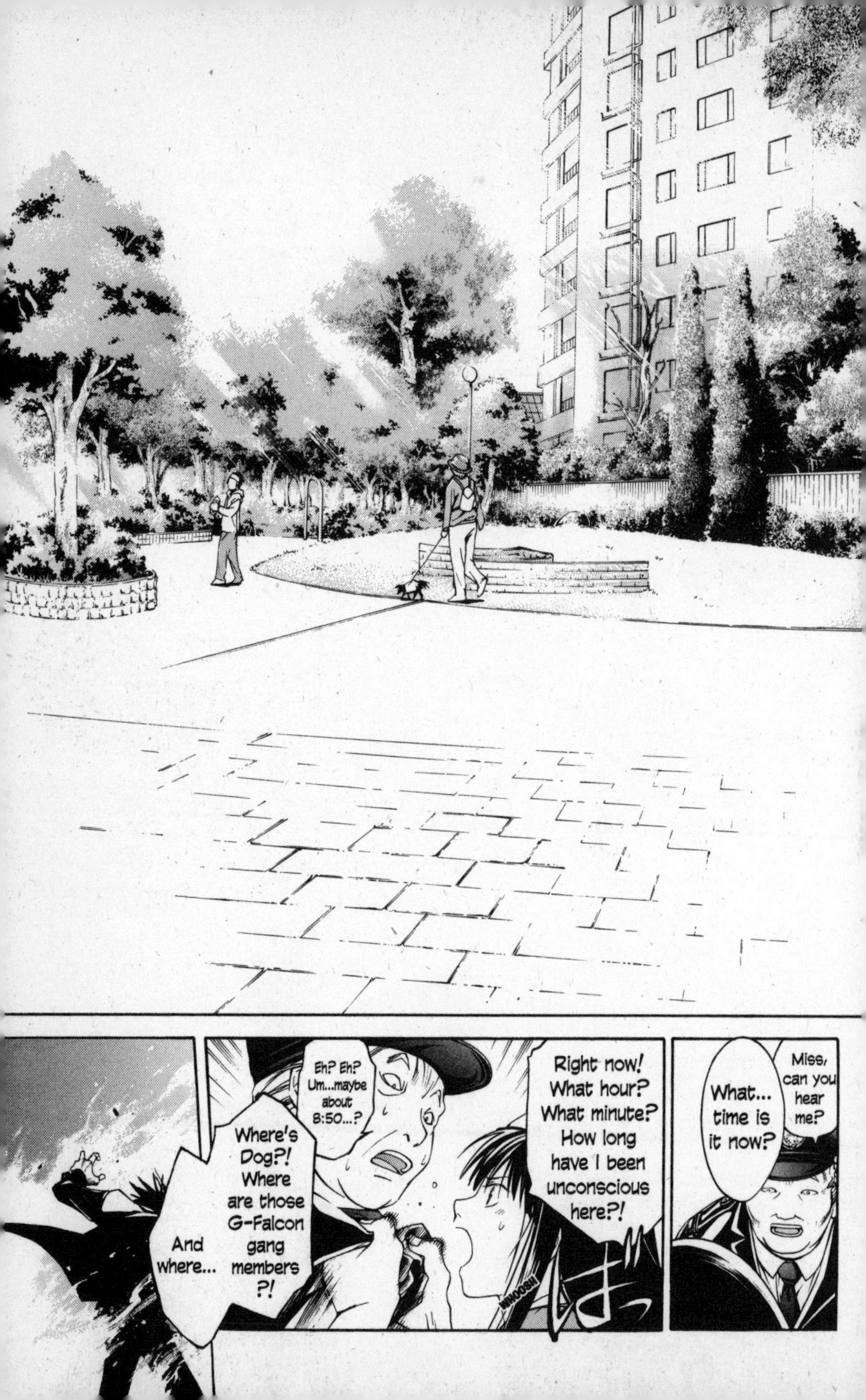
Miss, can you hear me?
What... time is it now?
Right now! What hour? What minute? How long have I been unconscious here?!
Eh? Eh? Um...maybe about 8:50...?
WHOOSH
Where's Dog?! Where are those G-Falcon gang members?!
And where...

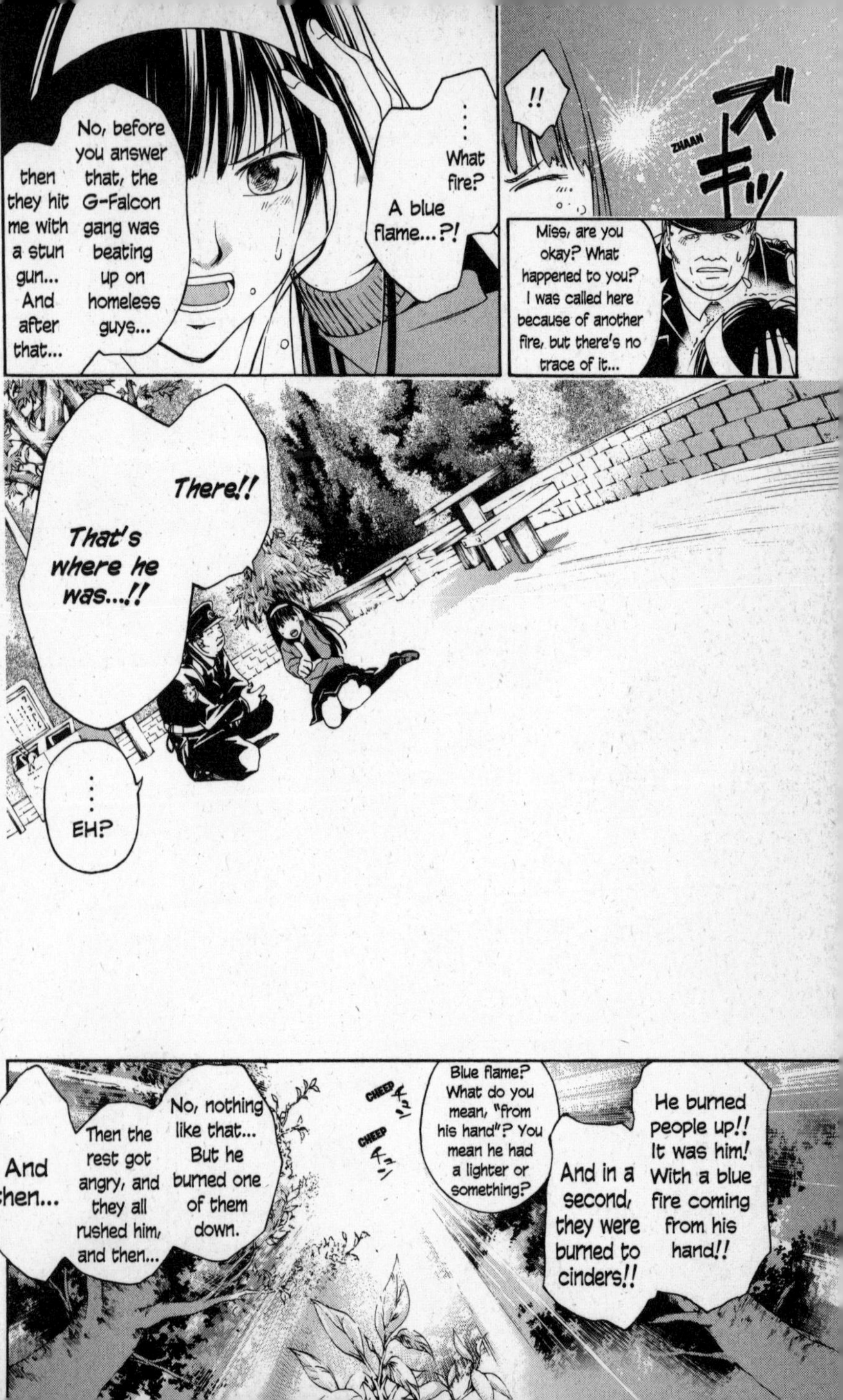
!!
ZHAAN
Miss, are you okay? What happened to you? I was called here because of another fire, but there's no trace of it...
... What fire?
A blue flame...?!
No, before you answer that, the G-Falcon gang was beating up on homeless guys...
then they hit me with a stun gun... And after that...
There!!
That's where he was...!!
... EH?
He burned people up!! It was him! With a blue fire coming from his hand!!
And in a second, they were burned to cinders!!
Blue flame? What do you mean, "from his hand"? You mean he had a lighter or something?
CHEEP
CHEEP
No, nothing like that... But he burned one of them down.
Then the rest got angry, and they all rushed him, and then...
And then...

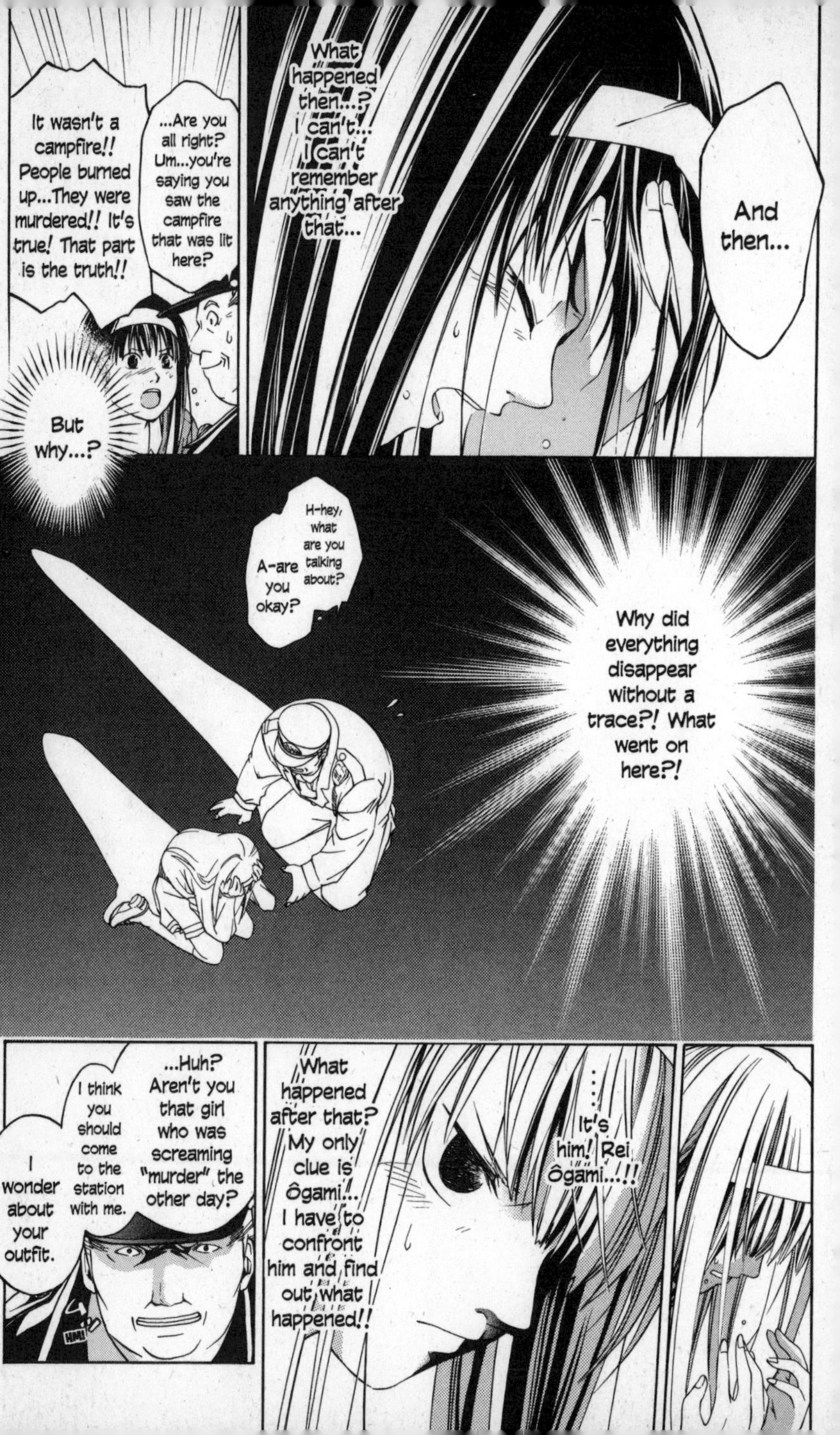
And then...
What happened then...? I can't... I can't remember anything after that...
...Are you all right? Um...you're saying you saw the campfire that was lit here?
It wasn't a campfire!! People burned up...They were murdered!! It's true! That part is the truth!!
But why...?
Why did everything disappear without a trace?! What went on here?!
H-hey, what are you talking about?
A-are you okay?
......
It's him! Rei Ôgami...!!!
What happened after that? My only clue is Ôgami... I have to confront him and find out what happened!!
...Huh? Aren't you that girl who was screaming "murder" the other day?
I think you should come to the station with me.
I wonder about your outfit.

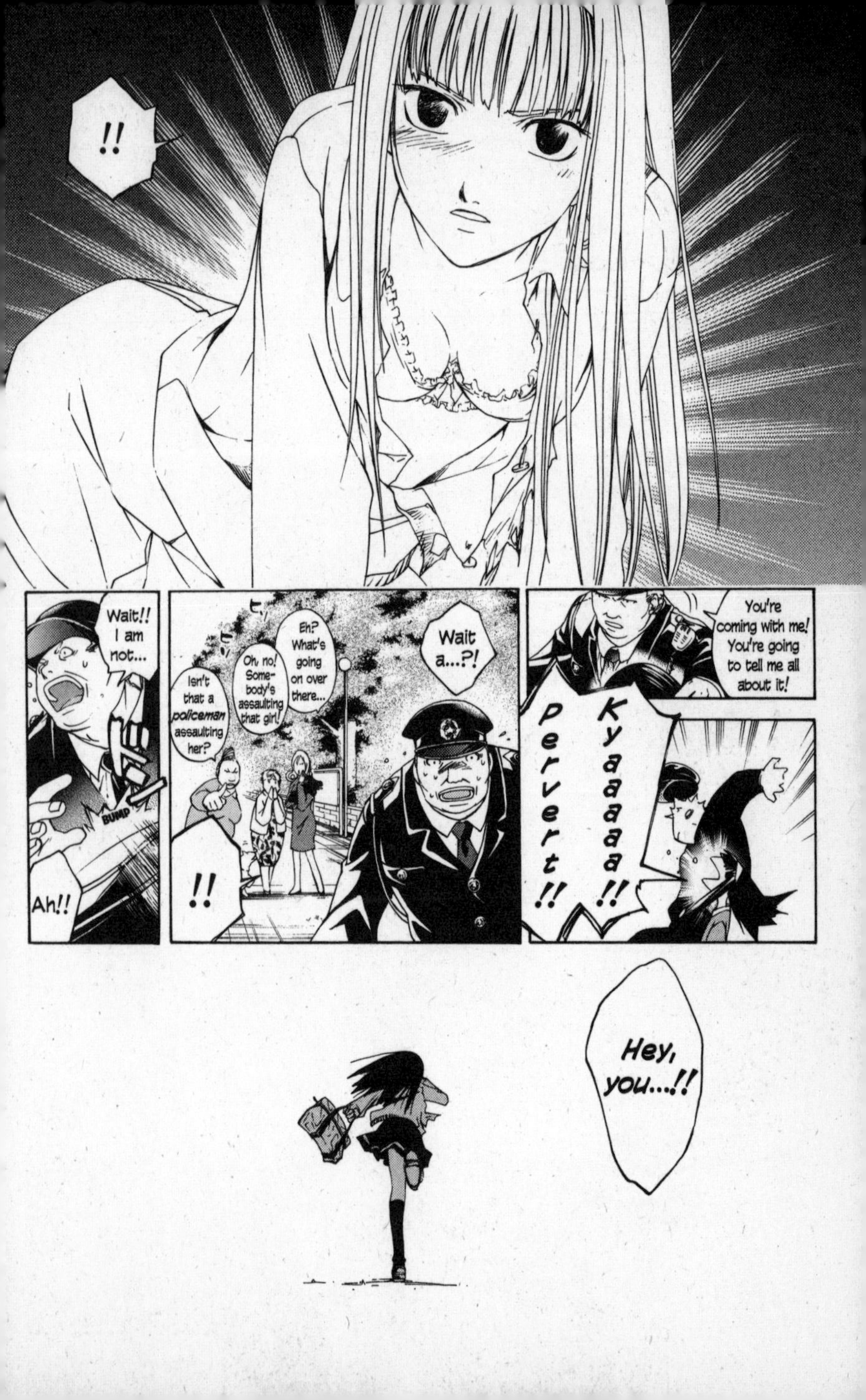
!!
You're coming with me! You're going to tell me all about it!
Kyaaaaa!!
Pervert!!
Wait a...?!
Eh? What's going on over there...
Oh, no! Somebody's assaulting that girl!
Isn't that a policeman assaulting her?
!!
Wait!! I am not...
BUMP
Ah!!
Hey, you...!!

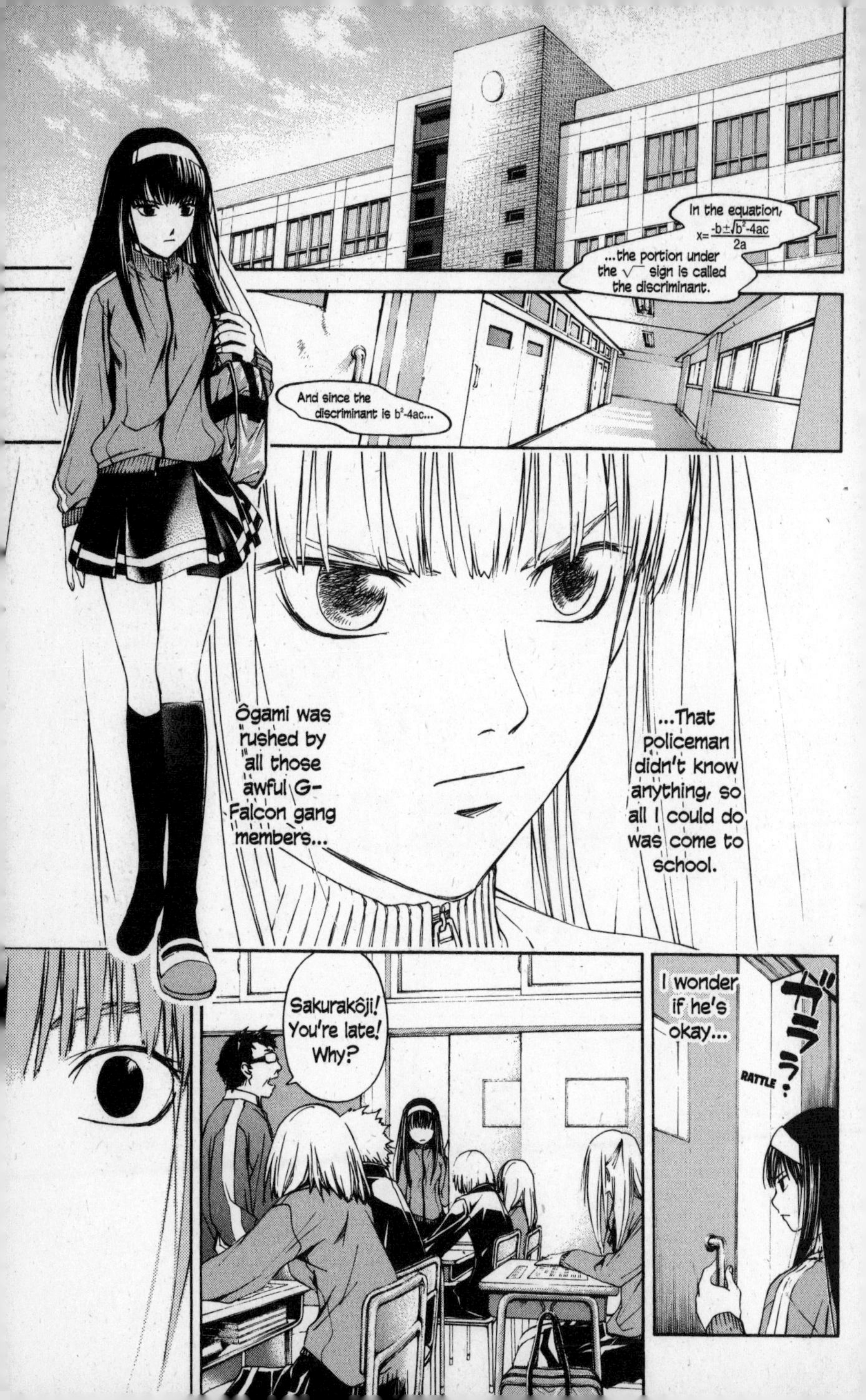
In the equation, $x=\frac{-b\pm\sqrt{b^2-4ac}}{2a}$
...the portion under the $\sqrt{\ }$ sign is called the discriminant.
And since the discriminant is b^2-4ac...
...That policeman didn't know anything, so all I could do was come to school.
Ôgami was rushed by all those awful G-Falcon gang members...
I wonder if he's okay...
ガラ
RATTLE
Sakurakôji! You're late! Why?

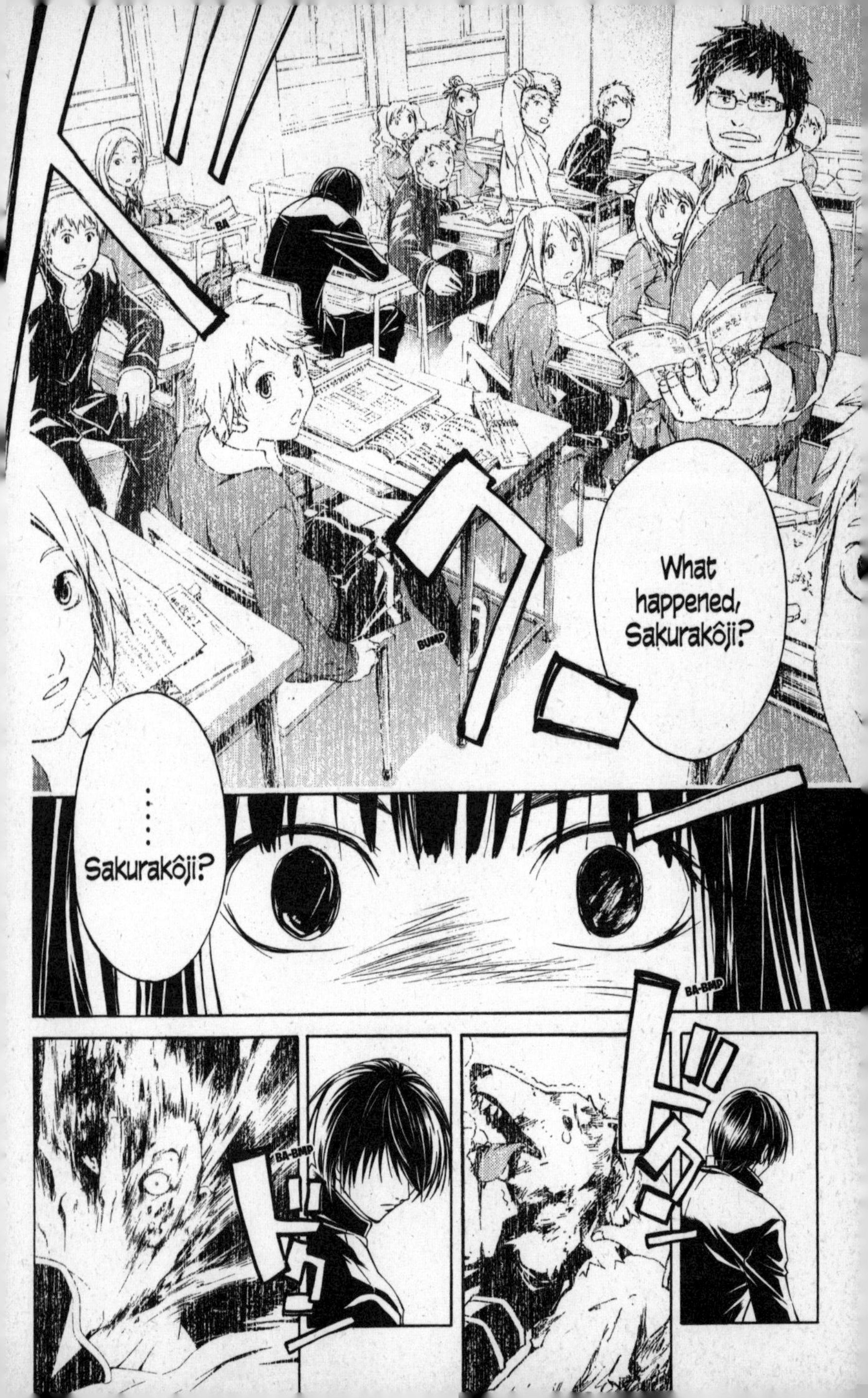
BA
BUMP
What happened, Sakurakôji?
..... Sakurakôji?
BA-BMP
BA-BMP

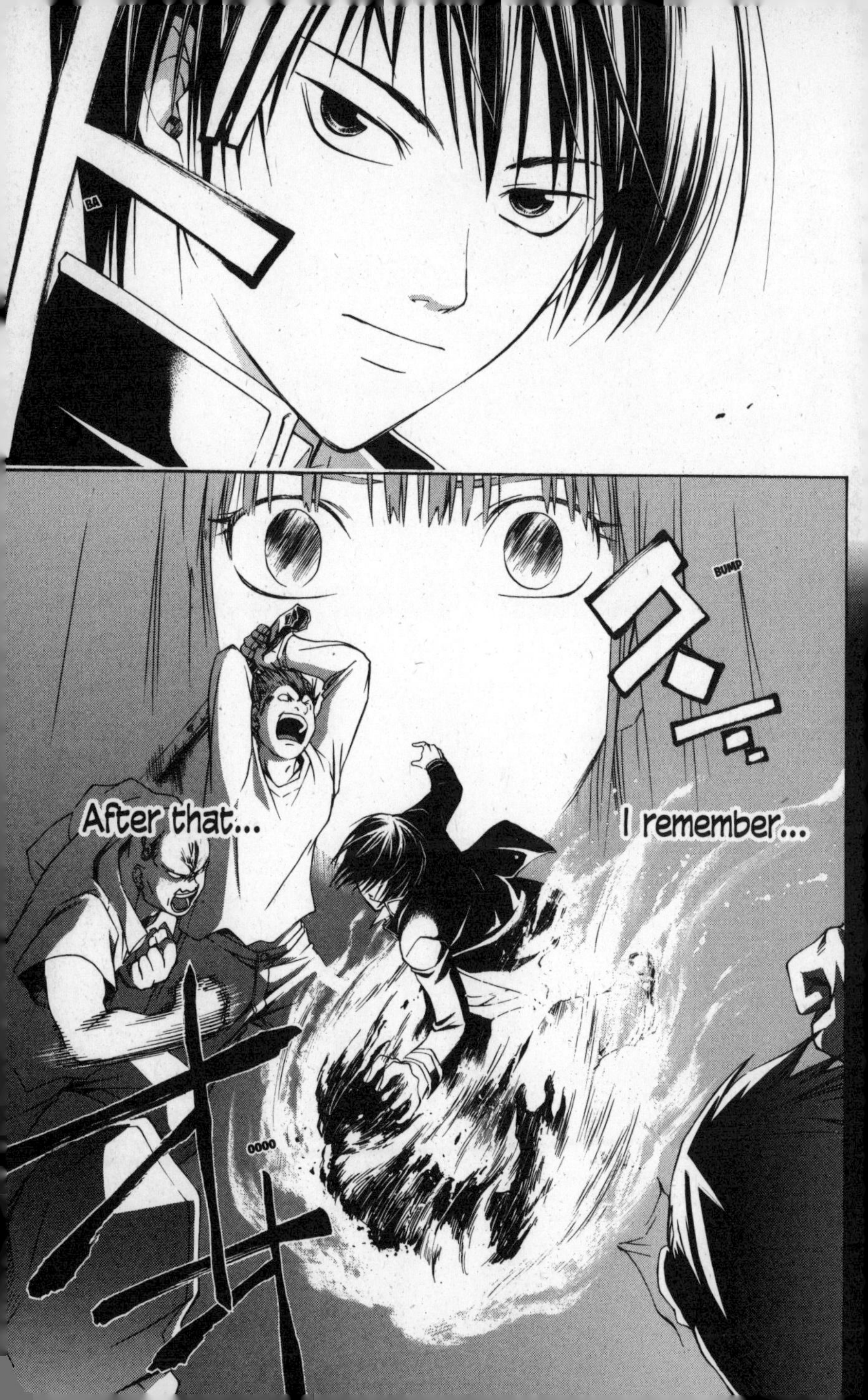
BA
BUMP
I remember...
After that...
OOOO

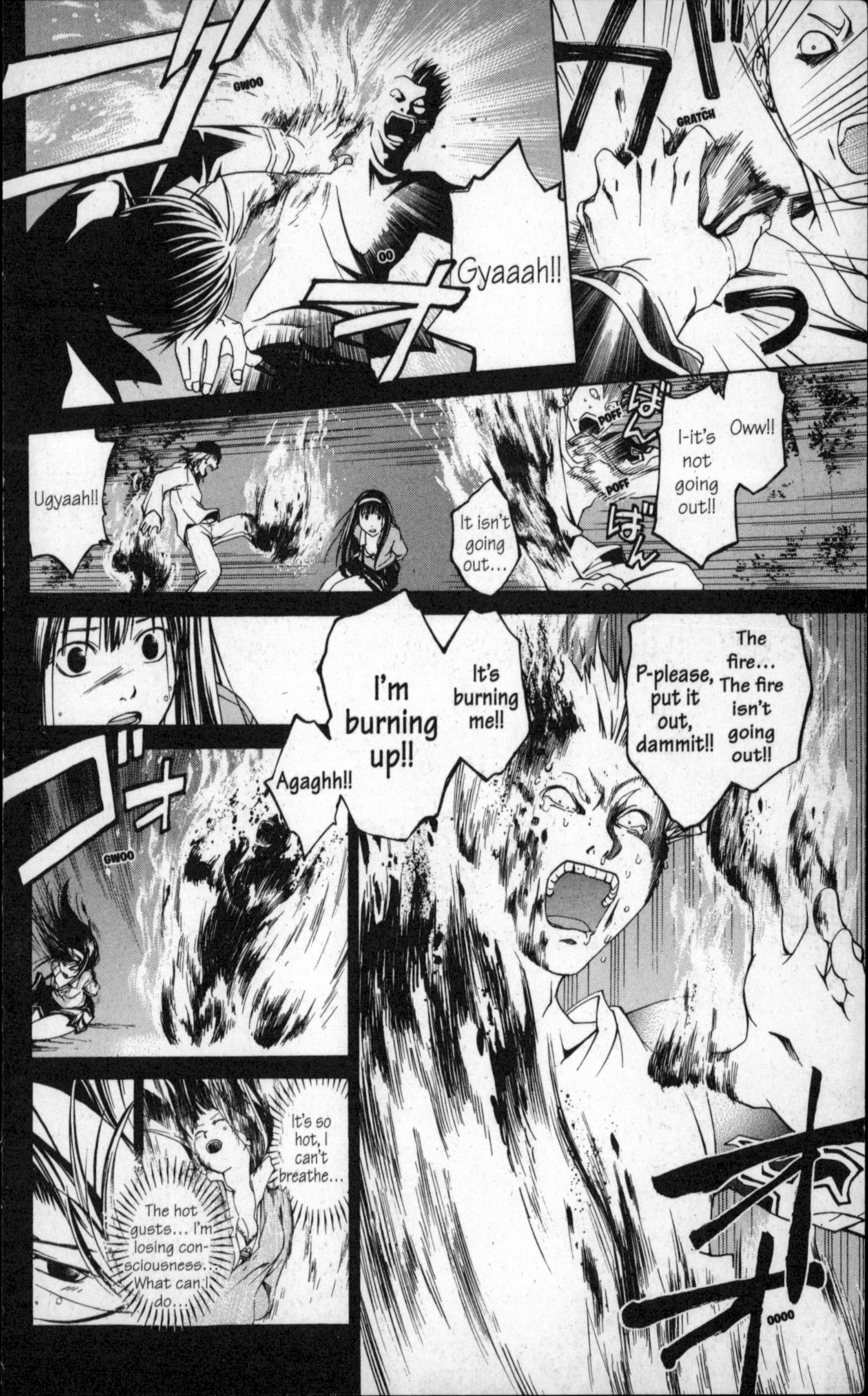
GRATCH
Gyaaah!!
GWOO
Oww!!
POFF
I-it's not going out!!
POFF
It isn't going out...
Ugyaah!!
The fire... The fire isn't going out!!
P-please, put it out, dammit!!
It's burning me!!
I'm burning up!!
Agaghh!!
OOOO
GWOO
It's so hot, I can't breathe...
The hot gusts... I'm losing consciousness... What can I do...

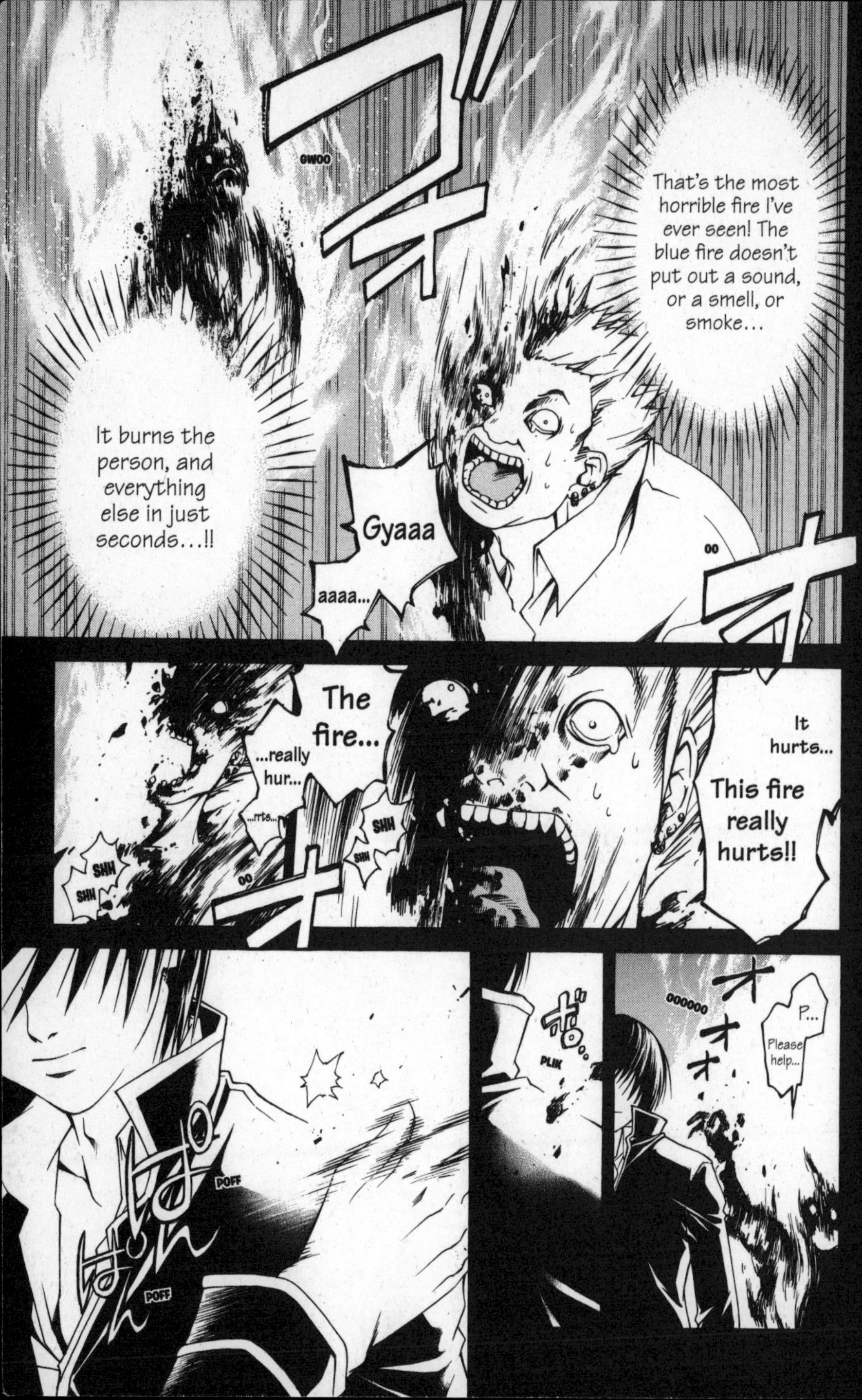

That's the most horrible fire I've ever seen! The blue fire doesn't put out a sound, or a smell, or smoke…
GWOO
It burns the person, and everything else in just seconds…!!
Gyaaa
aaaa...
OO
It hurts...
This fire really hurts!!
The fire...
...really hur...
...rts...
SHH
SHH
OO
SHH
SHH
OOOOOO
P...
Please help...
PLIK
POFF
POFF

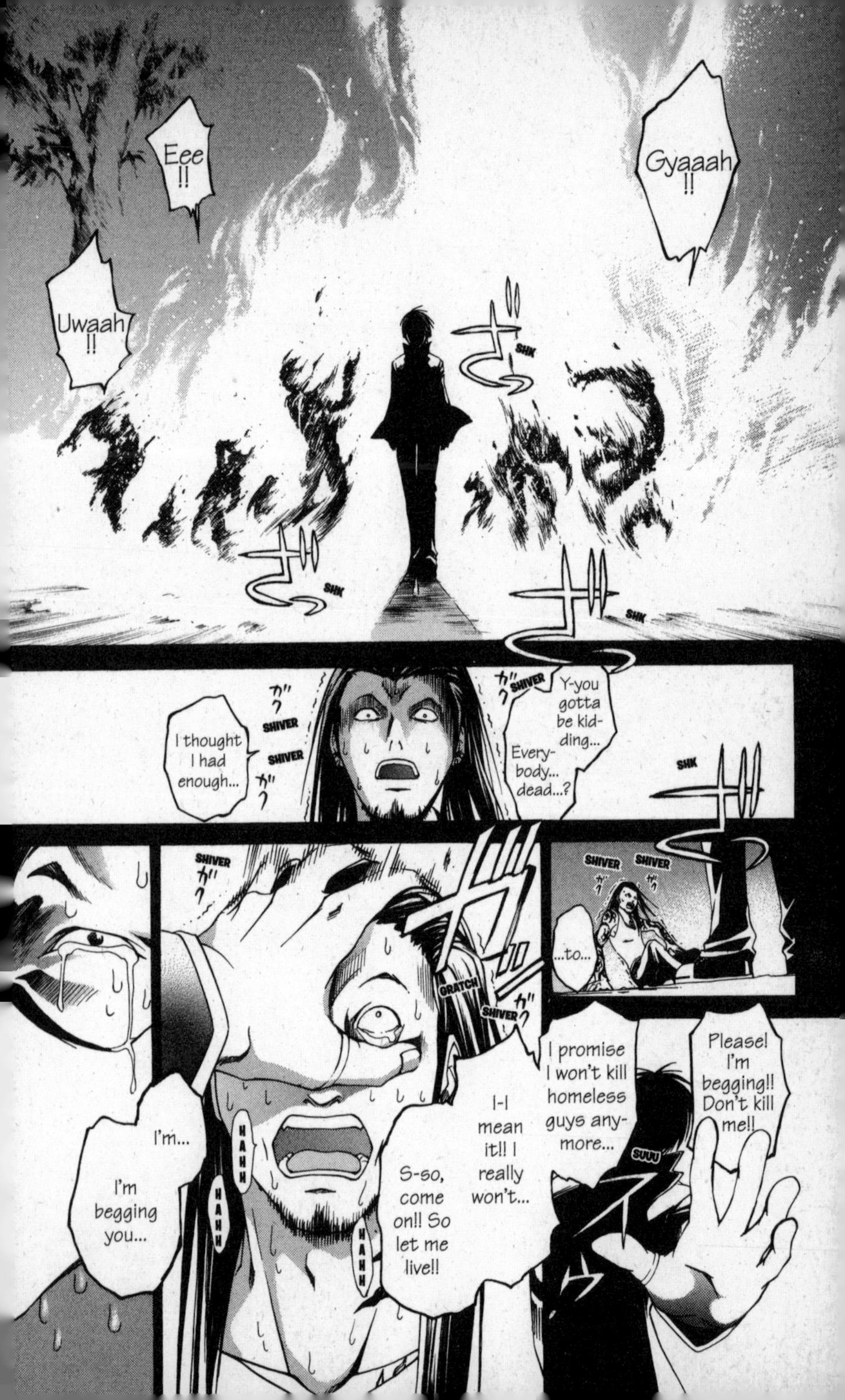
Gyaaah !!
Eee !!
SHK
Uwaah !!
SHK
SHK
Y-you gotta be kid-ding... Every-body... dead...?
SHIVER
SHK
SHIVER
I thought I had enough...
SHIVER
SHIVER SHIVER
...to...
SHIVER
GRATCH
SHIVER
Please! I'm begging!! Don't kill me!!
SUUU
I promise I won't kill homeless guys any-more...
I-I mean it!! I really won't...
S-so, come on!! So let me live!!
HAHH
HAHH
HAHH
I'm...
I'm begging you...

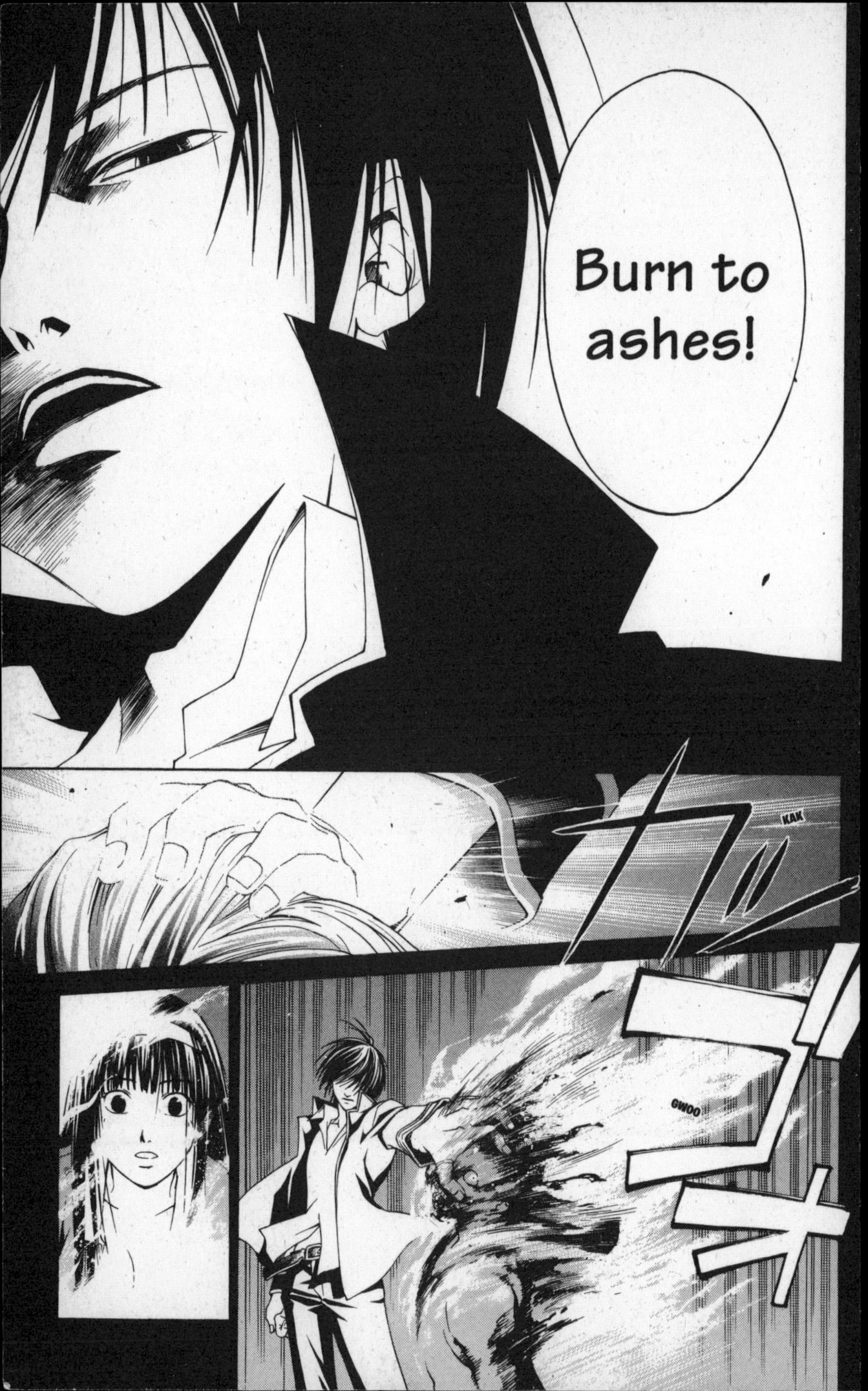
Burn to ashes!
KAK
GWOO

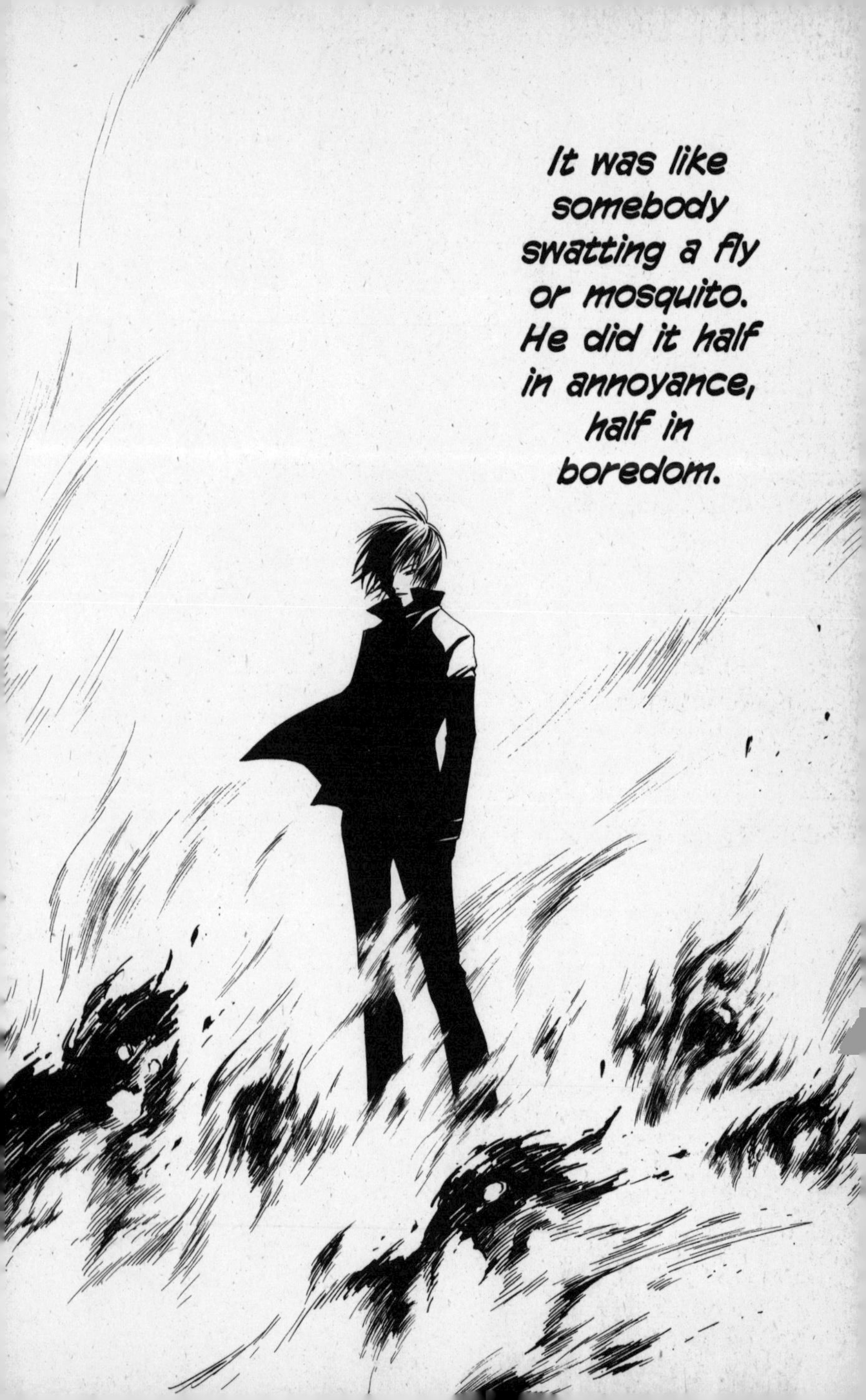
It was like somebody swatting a fly or mosquito. He did it half in annoyance, half in boredom.

Exactly the opposite of the heat of his flame.
He was cold and quiet...
...and cruel...

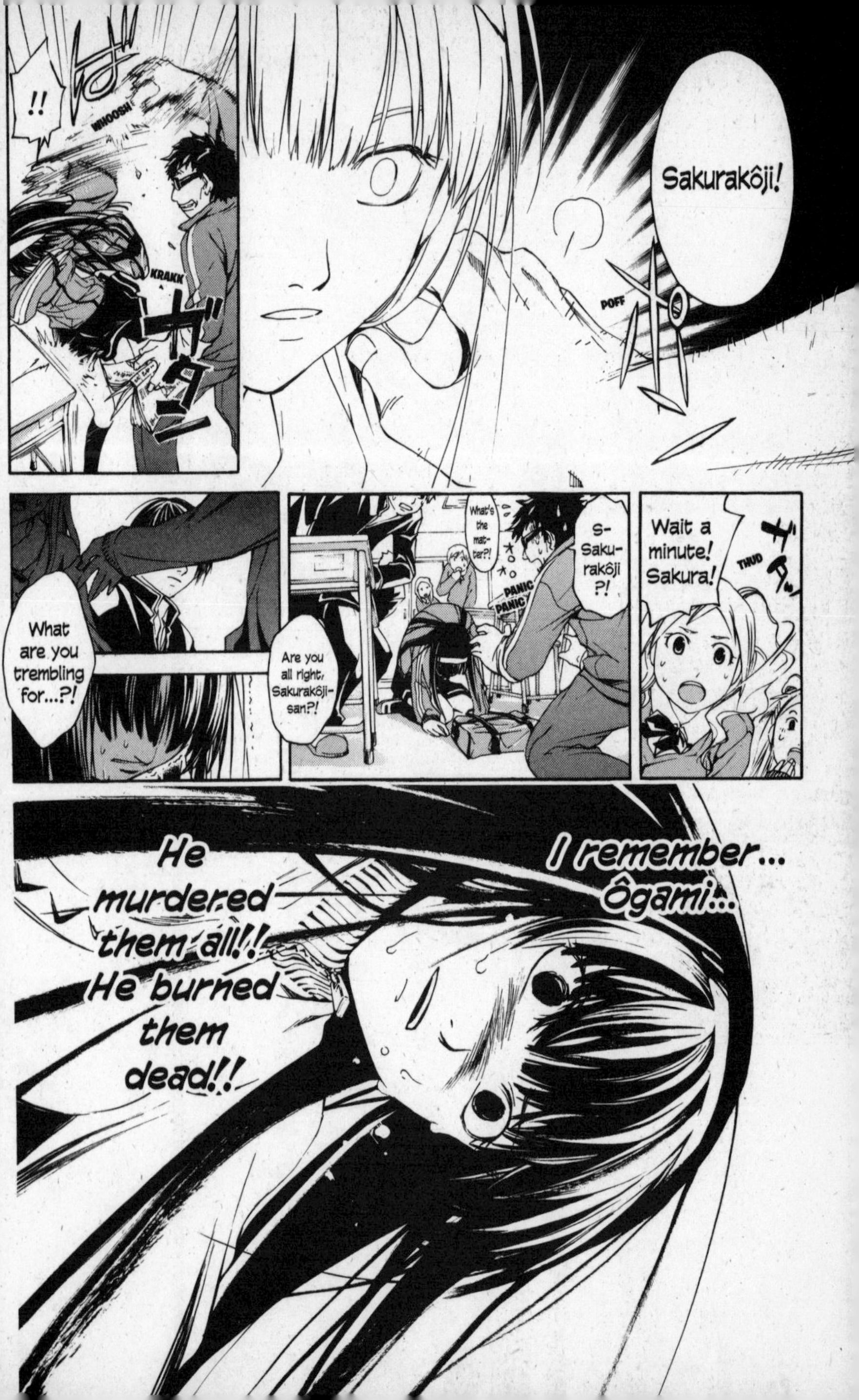
Sakurakôji!
POFF
!!
WHOOSH
KRAKK
Wait a minute! Sakura!
THUD
S-Sakurakôji?!
What's the matter?!
PANIC
PANIC
Are you all right, Sakurakôji-san?!
What are you trembling for...?!
I remember... Ôgami...
He murdered them all!! He burned them dead!!

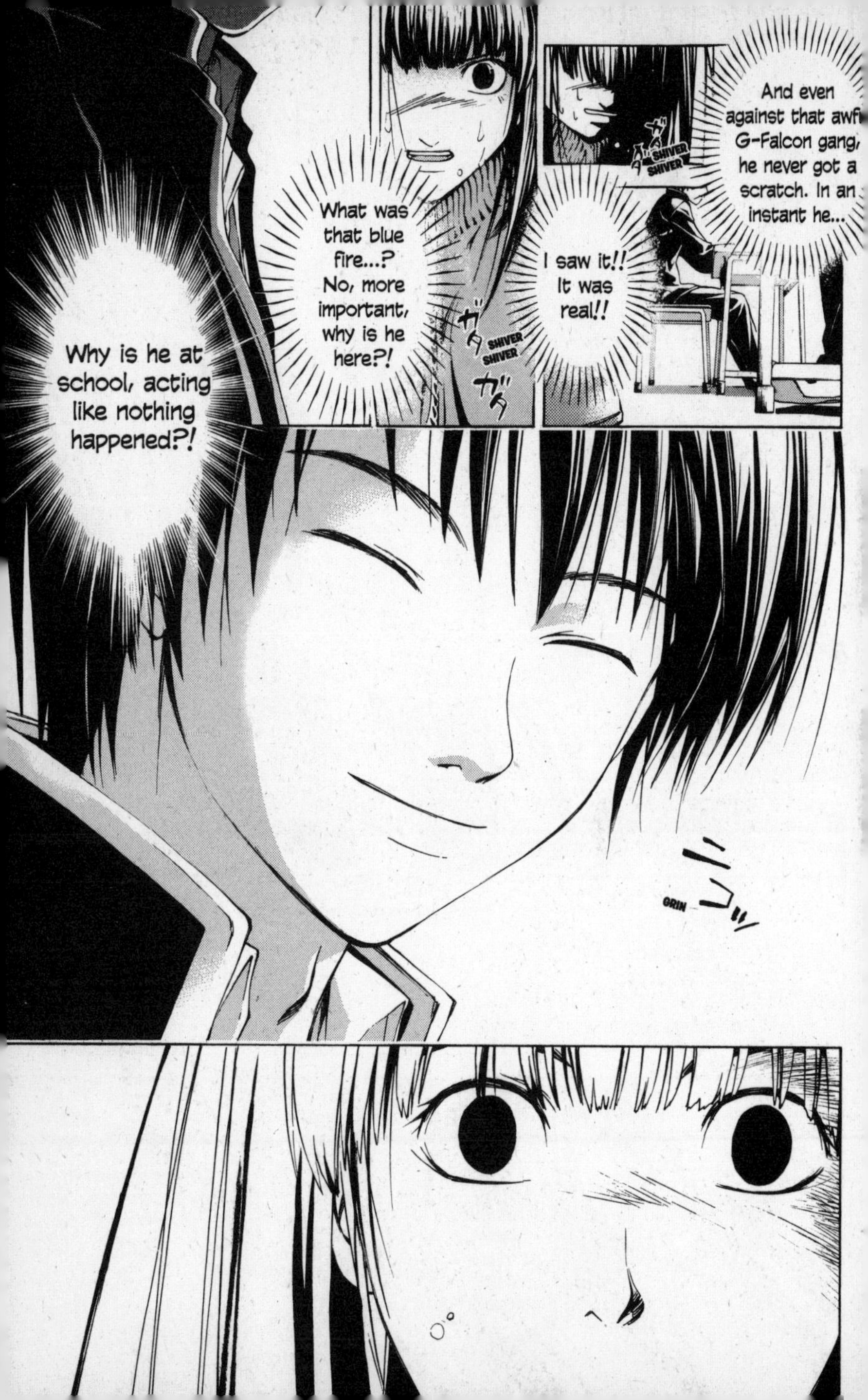

And even against that awf
G-Falcon gang, he never got a scratch. In an instant he...
SHIVER SHIVER
I saw it!! It was real!!
What was that blue fire...? No, more important, why is he here?!
SHIVER SHIVER
Why is he at school, acting like nothing happened?!
GRIN

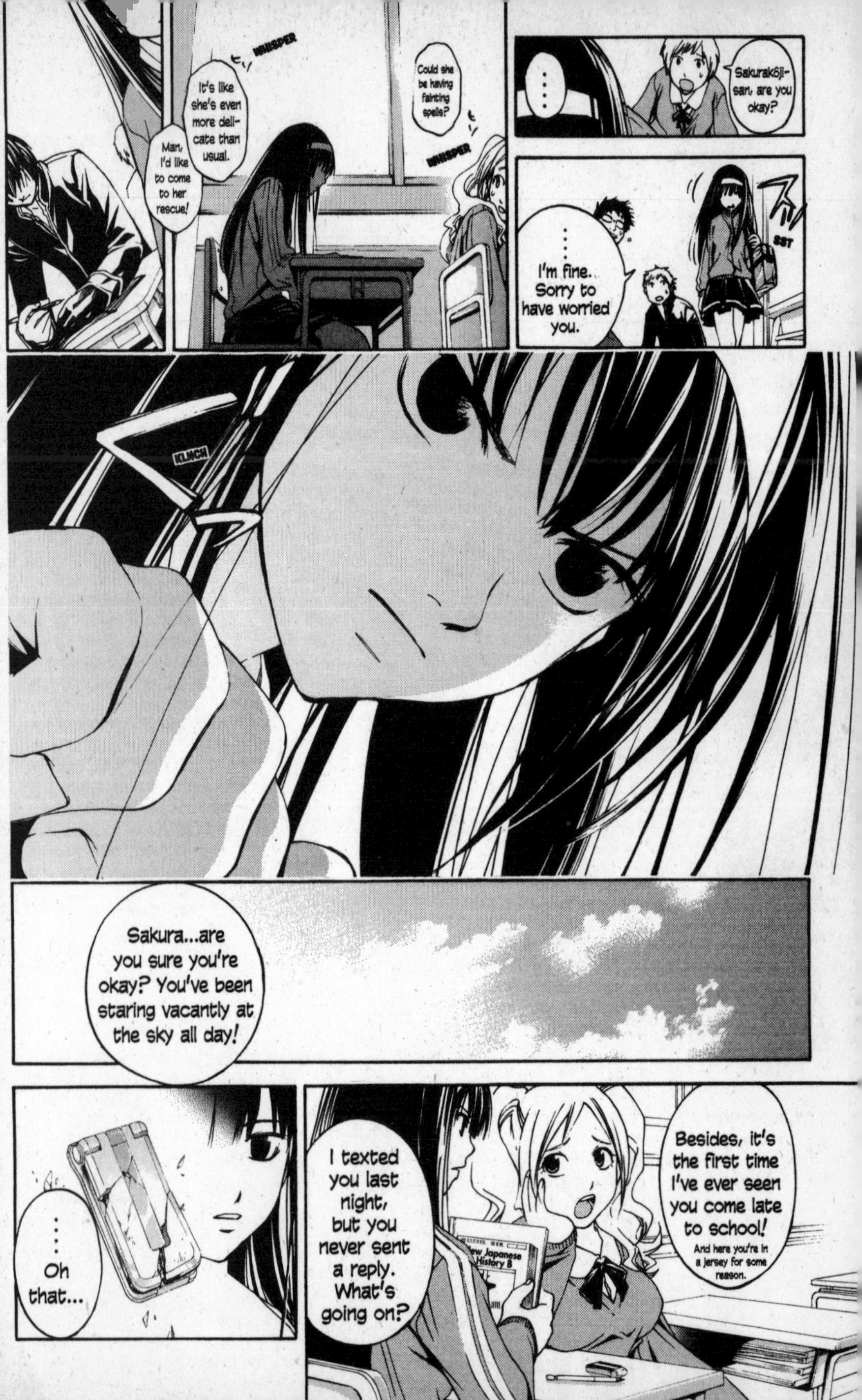
...
Sakurakôji-san, are you okay?
... I'm fine. Sorry to have worried you.
SST
Could she be having fainting spells?
WHISPER
It's like she's even more delicate than usual.
WHISPER
Man, I'd like to come to her rescue!
KLNCH
Sakura...are you sure you're okay? You've been staring vacantly at the sky all day!
Besides, it's the first time I've ever seen you come late to school!
And here you're in a jersey for some reason.
I texted you last night, but you never sent a reply. What's going on?
New Japanese History B
... Oh that...

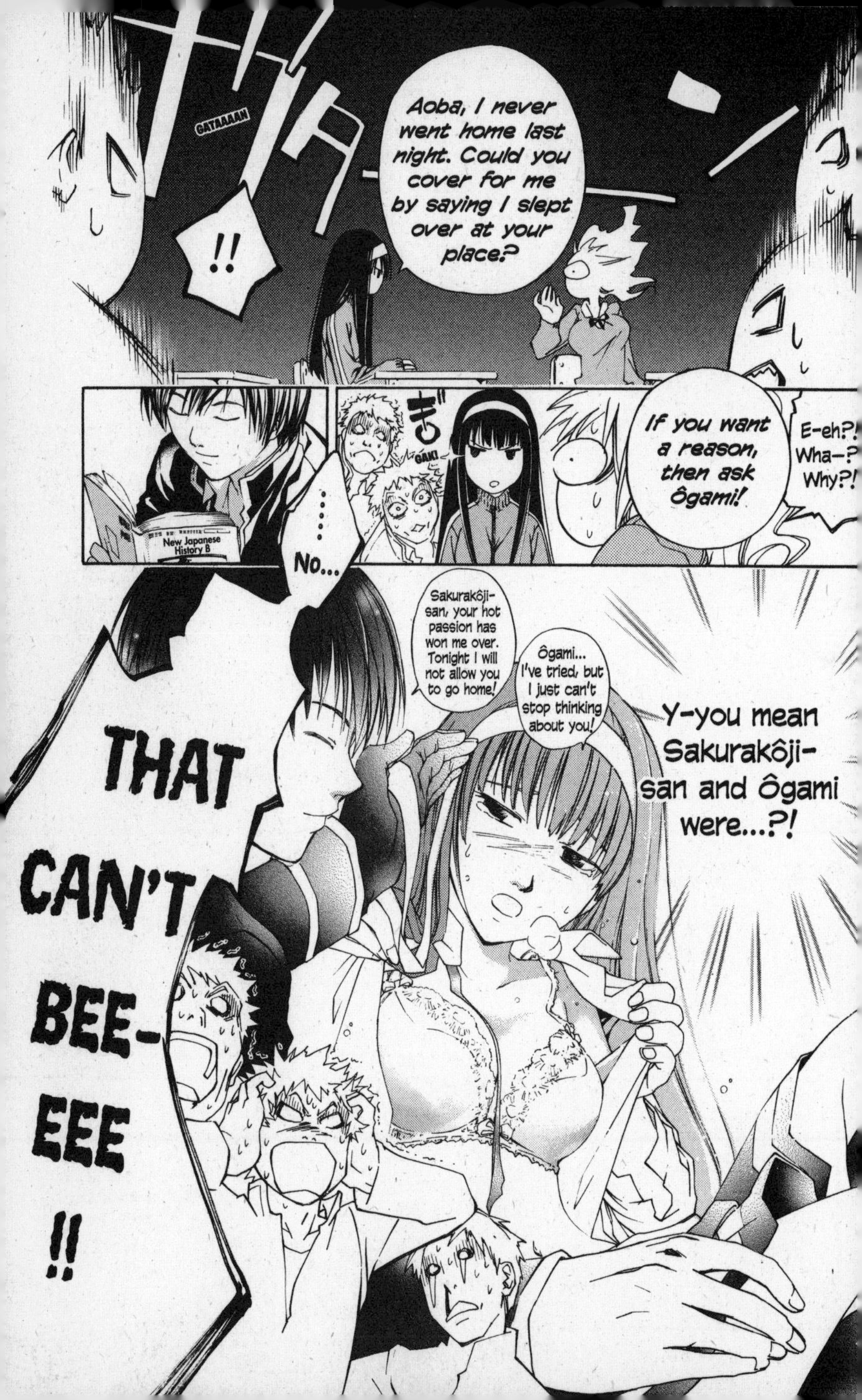
Aoba, I never went home last night. Could you cover for me by saying I slept over at your place?
!!
GATAAAAN
E-eh?! Wha–? Why?!
If you want a reason, then ask Ôgami!
GAK!
New Japanese History B
......
No...
Y-you mean Sakurakôji-san and Ôgami were...?!
Ôgami... I've tried, but I just can't stop thinking about you!
Sakurakôji-san, your hot passion has won me over. Tonight I will not allow you to go home!
THAT CAN'T BEE-EEE !!

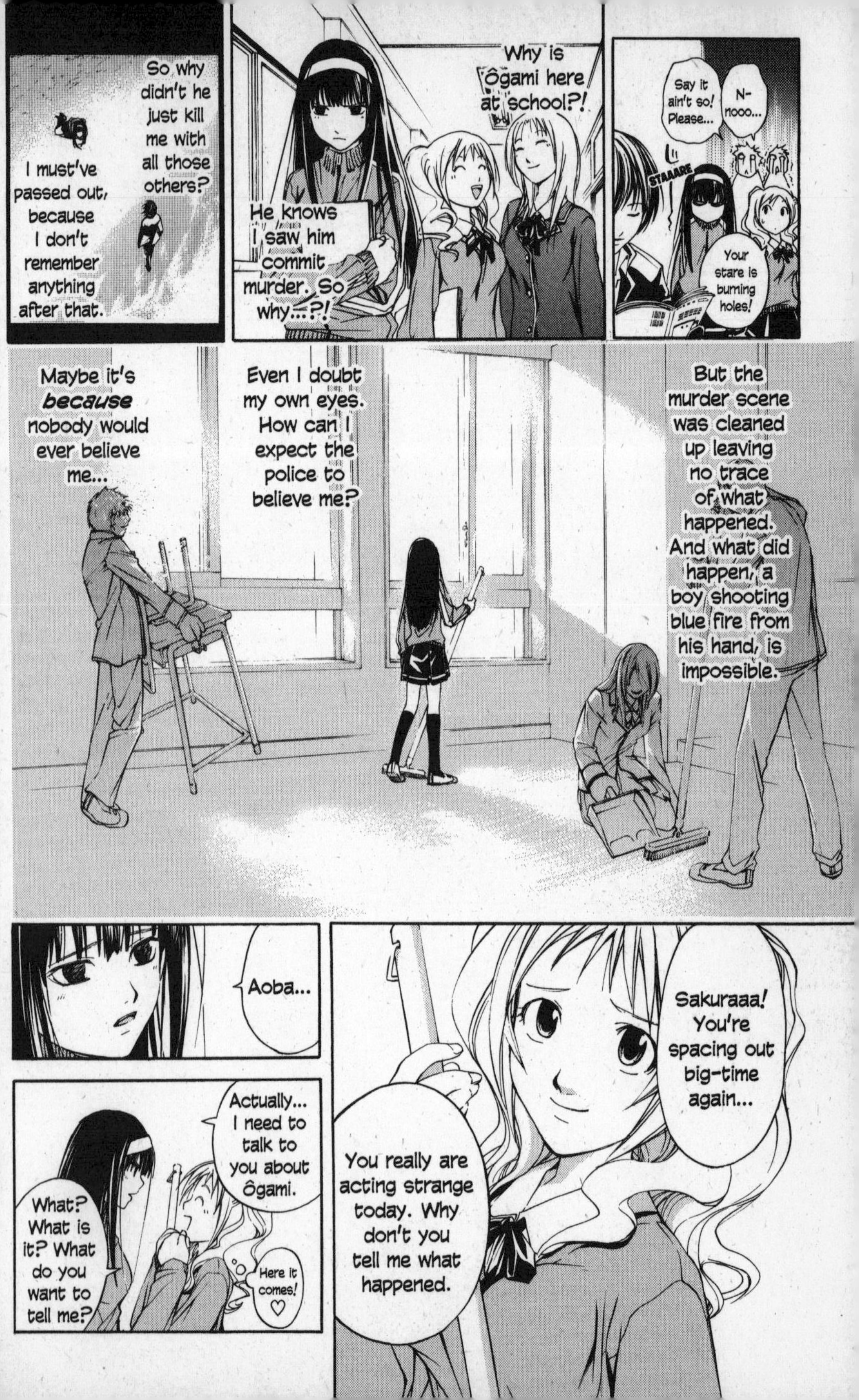
N-nooo...
Say it ain't so! Please...
STAAARE
Your stare is burning holes!
Why is Ôgami here at school?!
He knows I saw him commit murder. So why...?!
So why didn't he just kill me with all those others?
I must've passed out, because I don't remember anything after that.
But the murder scene was cleaned up leaving no trace of what happened. And what did happen, a boy shooting blue fire from his hand, is impossible.
Even I doubt my own eyes. How can I expect the police to believe me?
Maybe it's *because* nobody would ever believe me...
Sakuraaa! You're spacing out big-time again...
You really are acting strange today. Why don't you tell me what happened.
Aoba...
Actually... I need to talk to you about Ôgami.
What? What is it? What do you want to tell me?
Here it comes! ♡

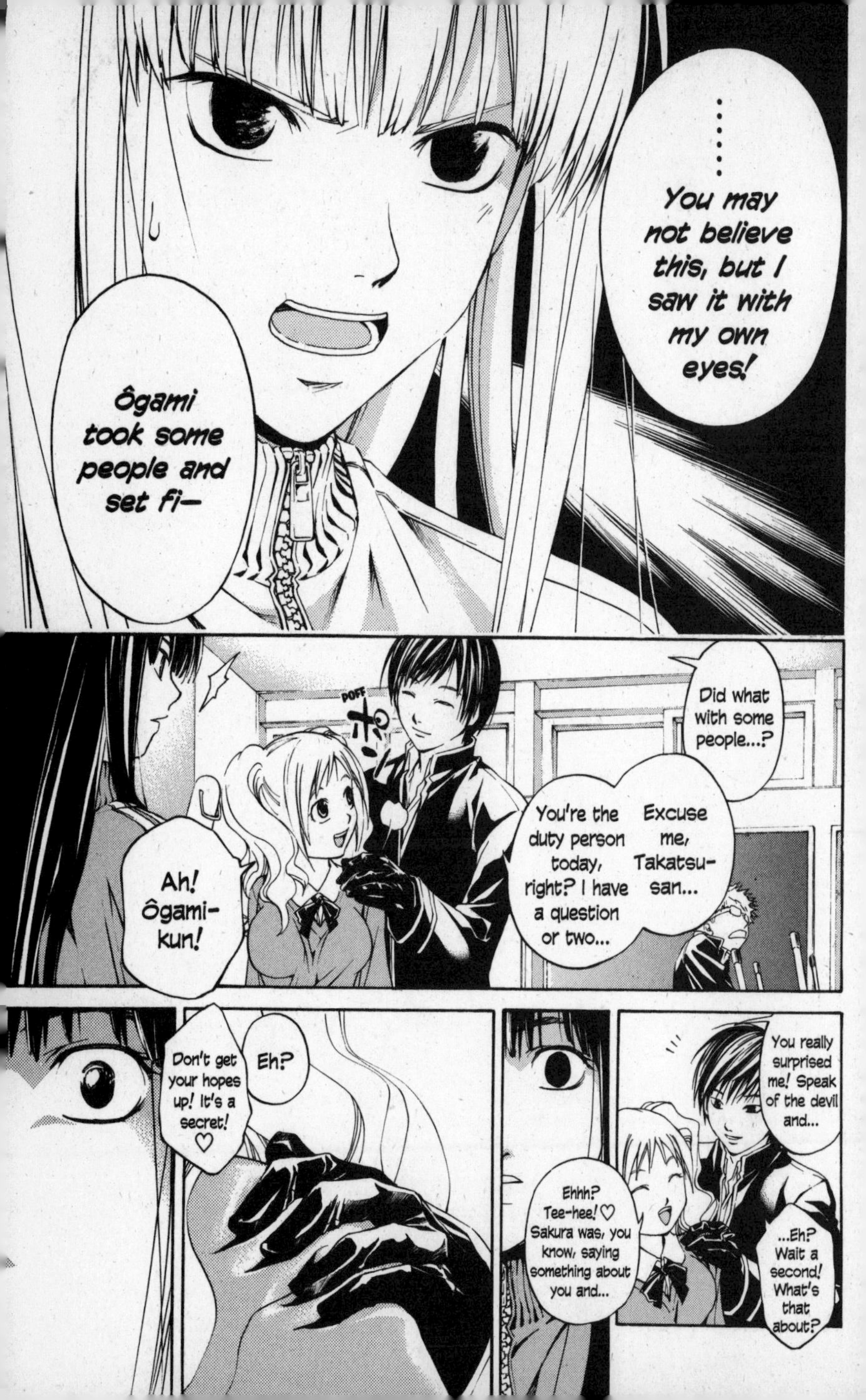

......
You may not believe this, but I saw it with my own eyes!
Ôgami took some people and set fi—
Did what with some people...?
Excuse me, Takatsu-san...
You're the duty person today, right? I have a question or two...
POFF
Ah! Ôgami-kun!
You really surprised me! Speak of the devil and...
Ehhh? Tee-hee! ♡ Sakura was, you know, saying something about you and...
...Eh? Wait a second! What's that about?
Eh?
Don't get your hopes up! It's a secret! ♡

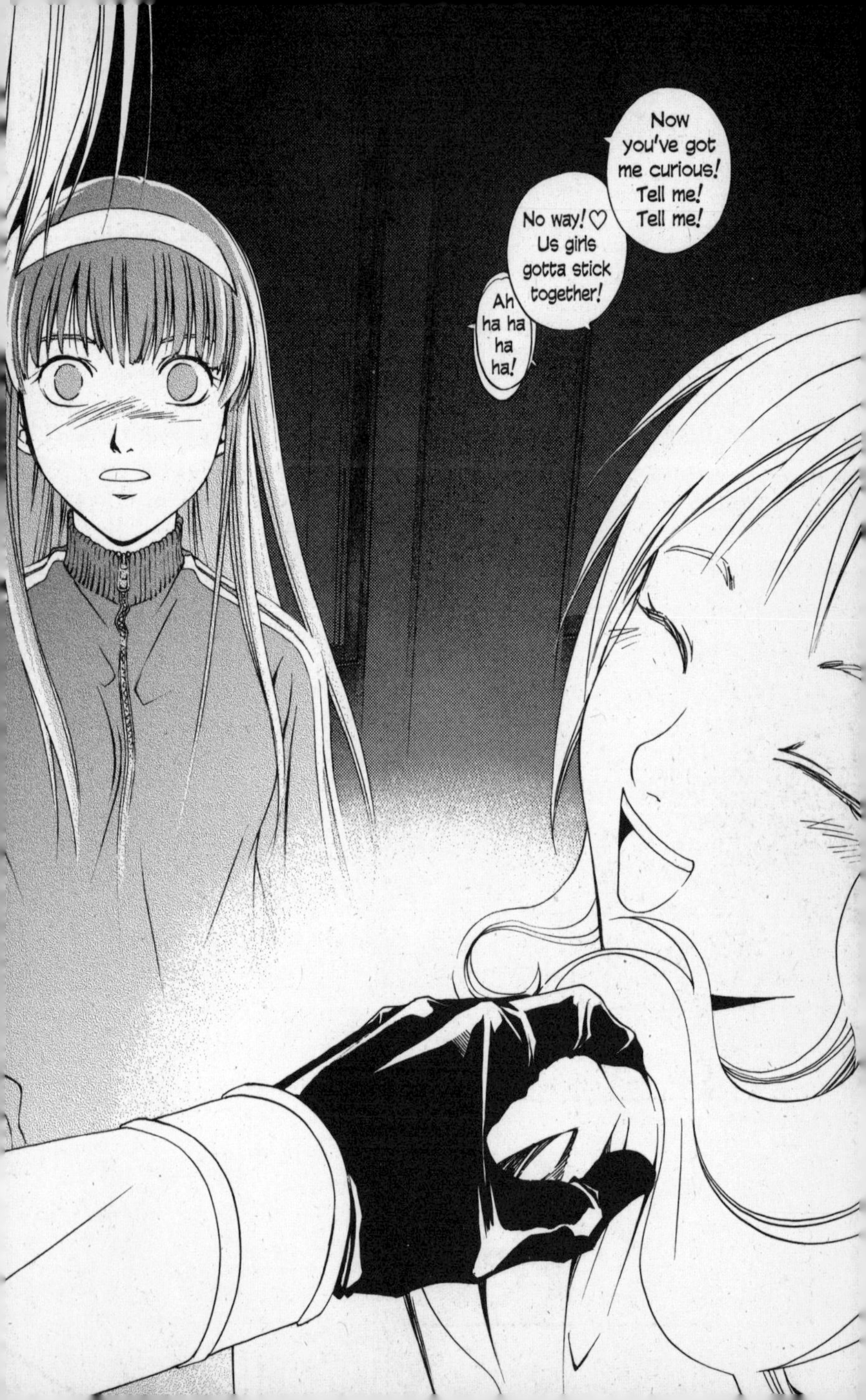
Now you've got me curious! Tell me! Tell me!
No way! ♡ Us girls gotta stick together!
Ah ha ha ha ha!

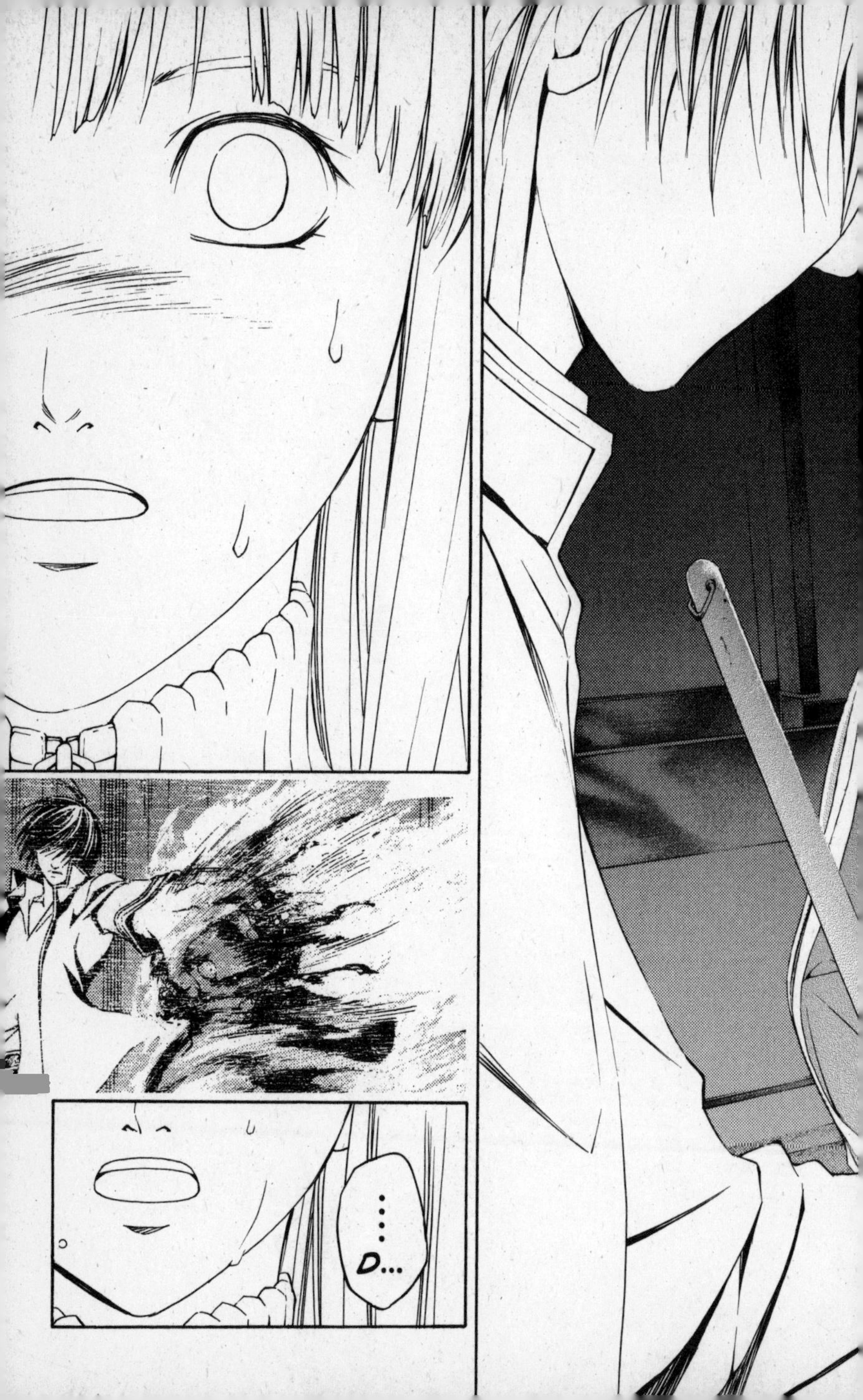

....
D...

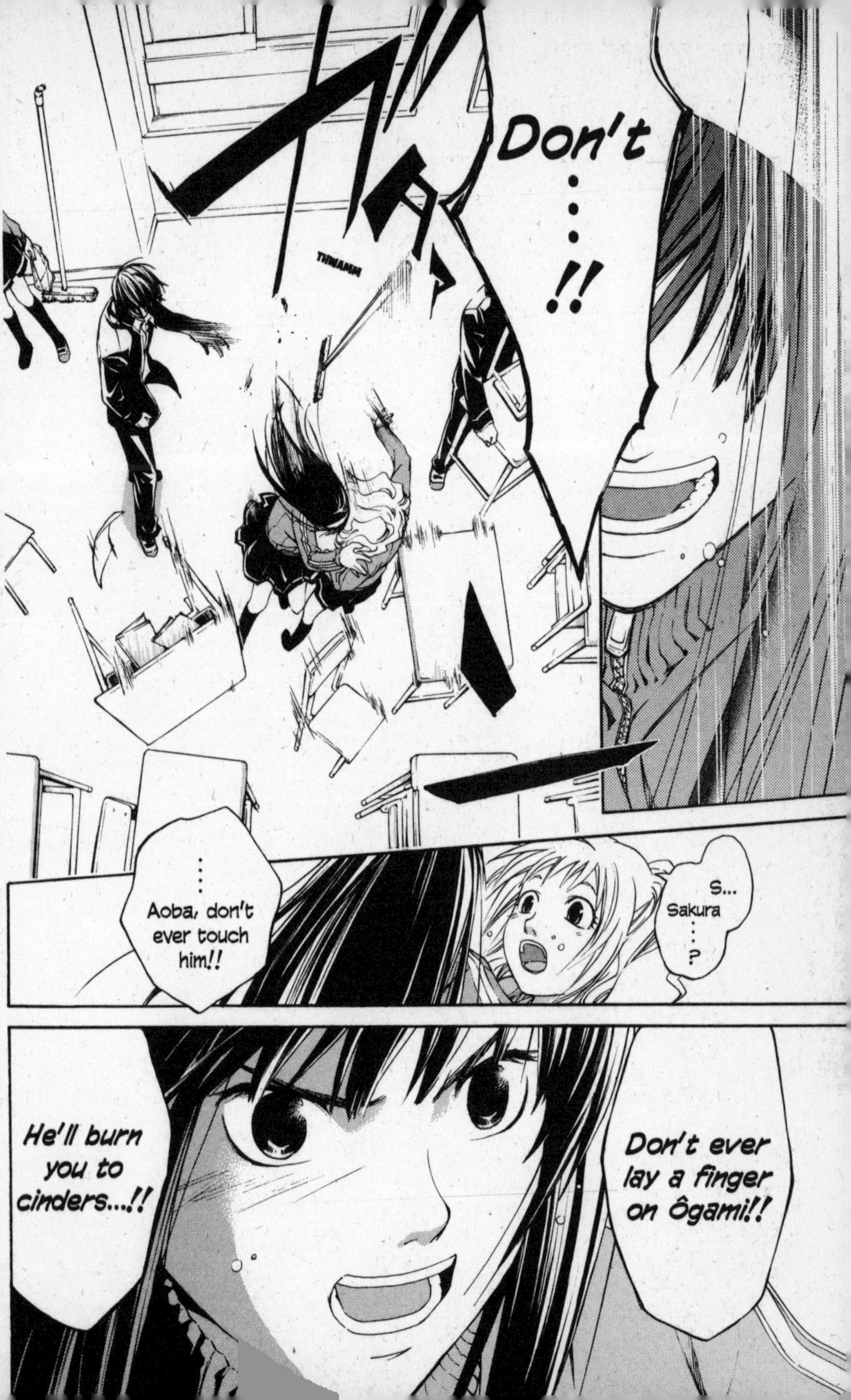
Don't ...!!
THWAMM
S... Sakura ...?
... Aoba, don't ever touch him!!
Don't ever lay a finger on Ôgami!!
He'll burn you to cinders...!!

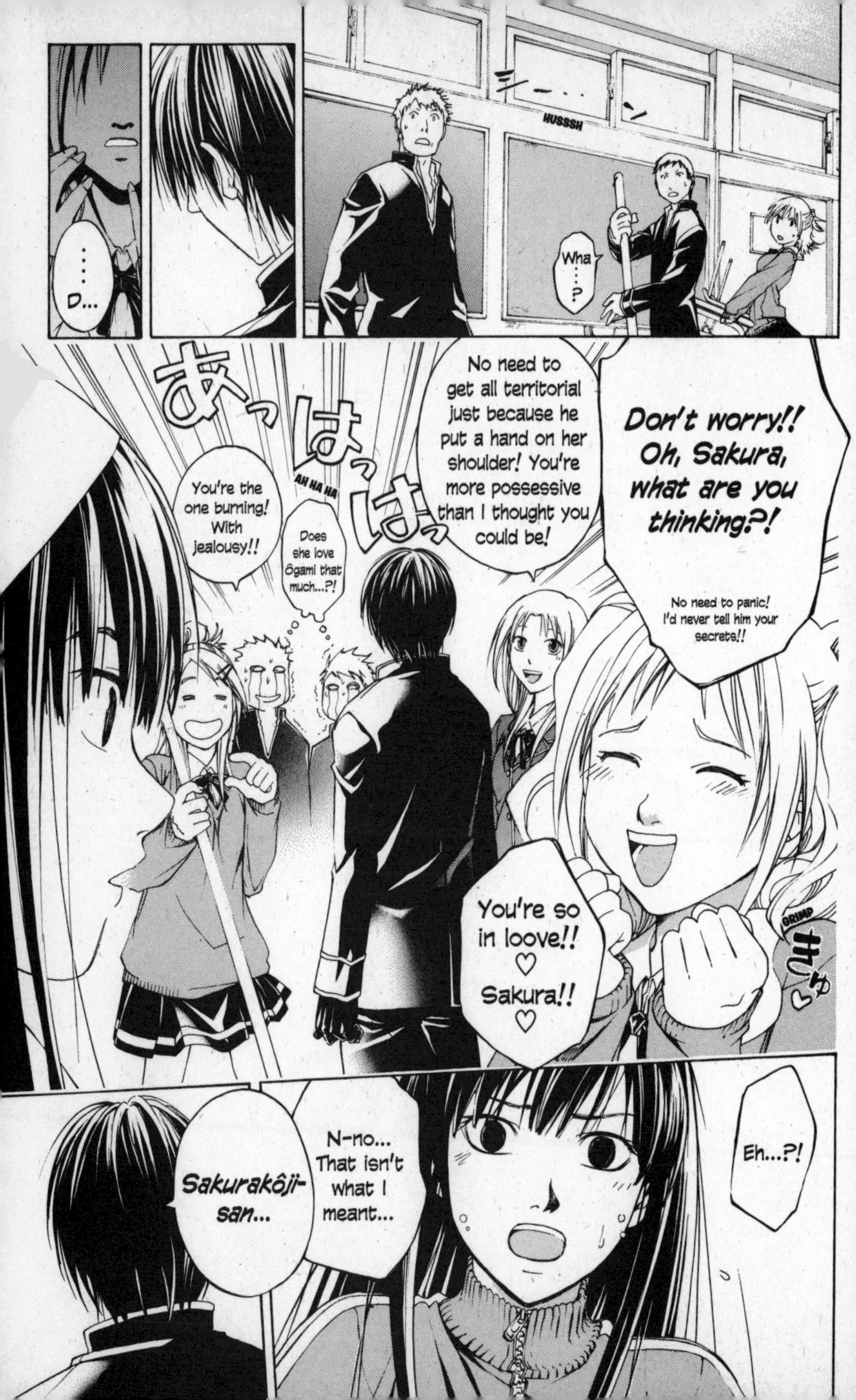
HUSSSH
Wha...?
......D...
Don't worry!! Oh, Sakura, what are you thinking?!
No need to panic! I'd never tell him your secrets!!
No need to get all territorial just because he put a hand on her shoulder! You're more possessive than I thought you could be!
AH HA HA
Does she love Ôgami that much...?!
You're the one burning! With jealousy!!
GRIMP
You're so in loove!! ♡ Sakura!! ♡
Eh...?!
N-no... That isn't what I meant...
Sakurakôji-san...

What are you talking about? Let me in on the secret, too, huh?
GRIN
Th-that little...
Was he watching me all this time to make sure I don't go talking about him?! And if I do talk...
...he'll bring flaming death to whoever I confide in! Is that his message?!

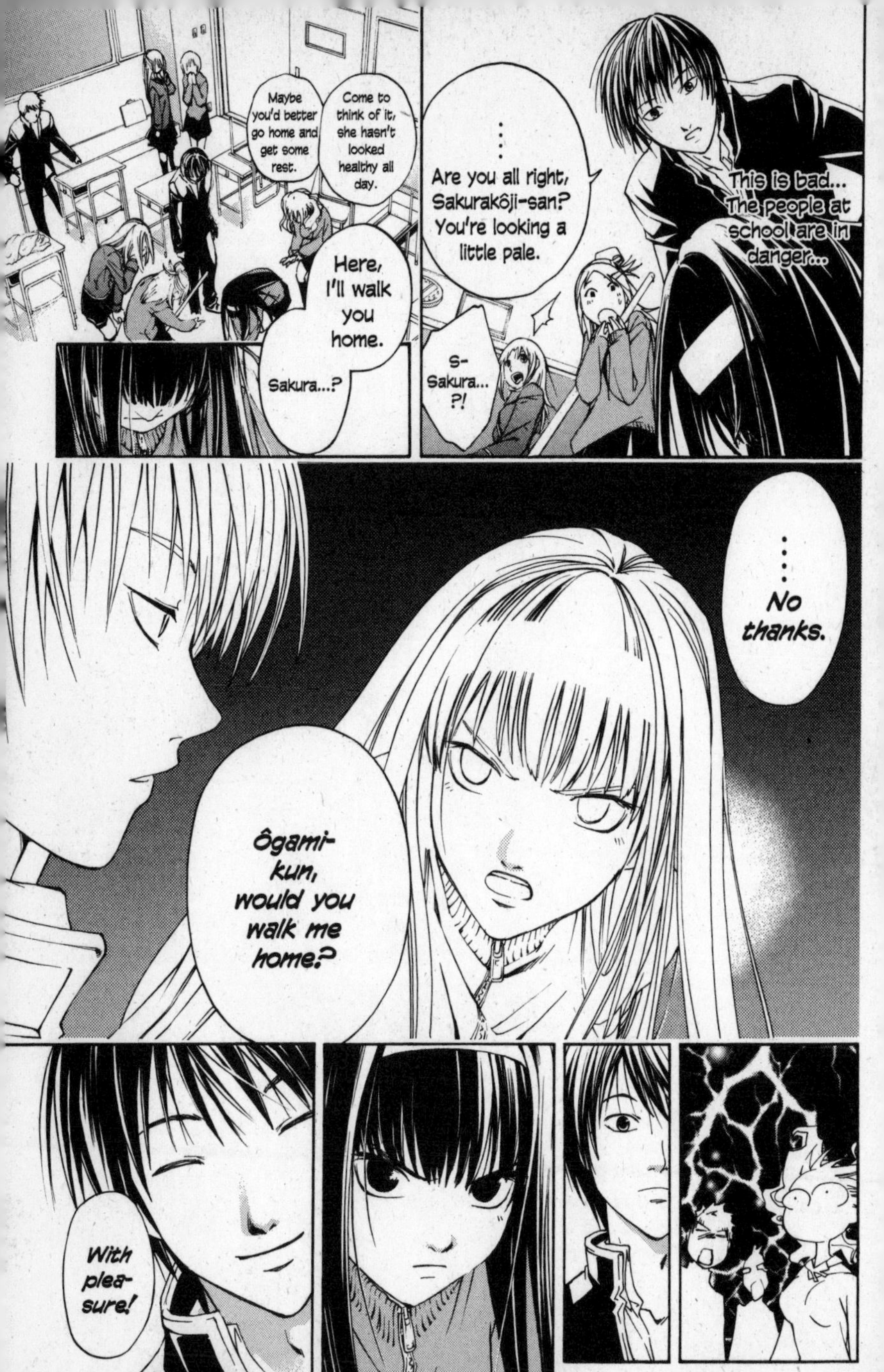
This is bad... The people at school are in danger...
... Are you all right, Sakurakôji-san? You're looking a little pale.
S-Sakura...?!
Come to think of it, she hasn't looked healthy all day.
Maybe you'd better go home and get some rest.
Here, I'll walk you home.
Sakura...?
... No thanks.
Ôgami-kun, would you walk me home?
With plea-sure!

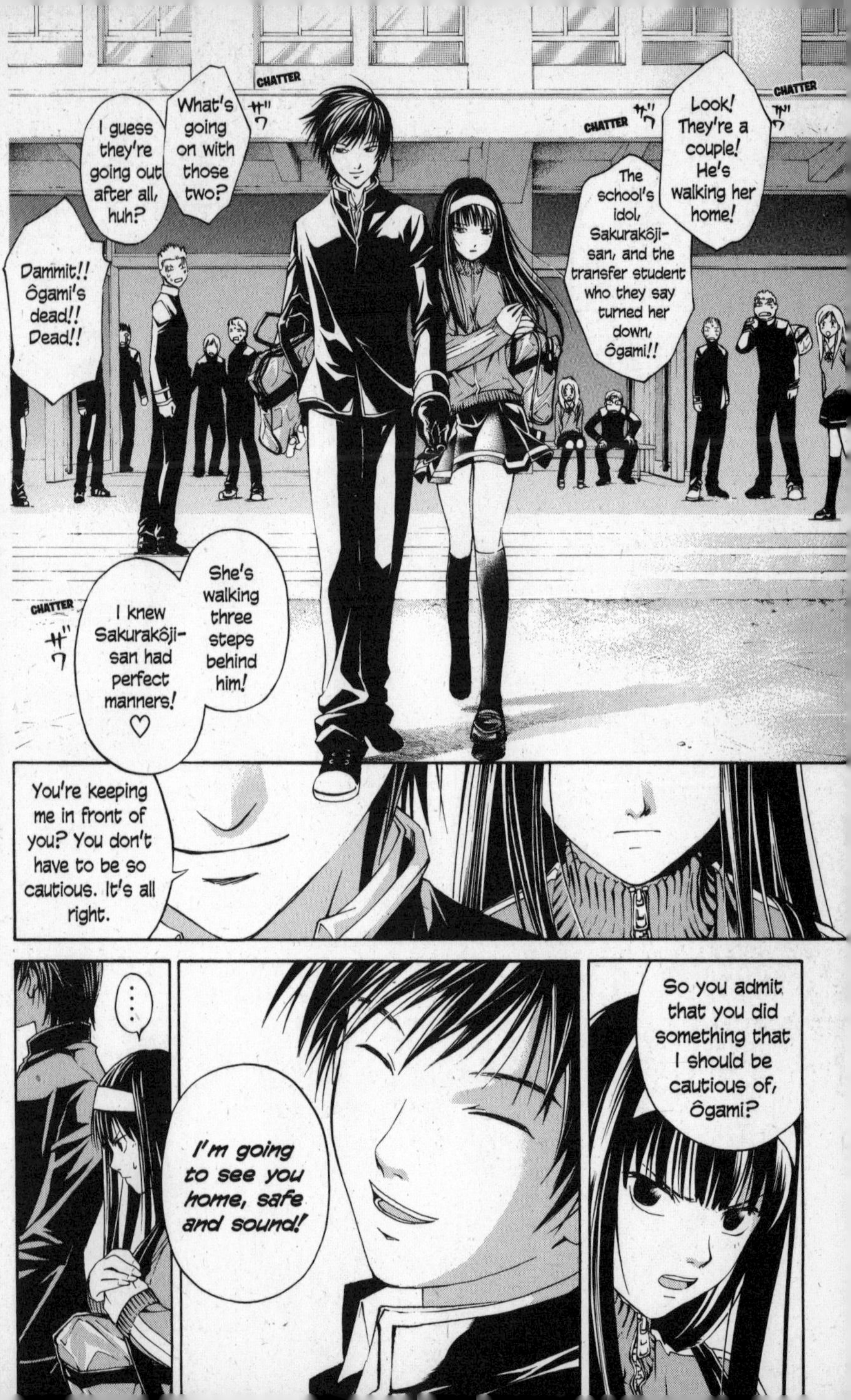
CHATTER
Look! They're a couple! He's walking her home!
CHATTER
The school's idol, Sakurakôji-san, and the transfer student who they say turned her down, Ôgami!!
CHATTER
What's going on with those two?
I guess they're going out after all, huh?
Dammit!! Ôgami's dead!! Dead!!
She's walking three steps behind him!
CHATTER
I knew Sakurakôji-san had perfect manners! ♡
You're keeping me in front of you? You don't have to be so cautious. It's all right.
So you admit that you did something that I should be cautious of, Ôgami?
I'm going to see you home, safe and sound!
....

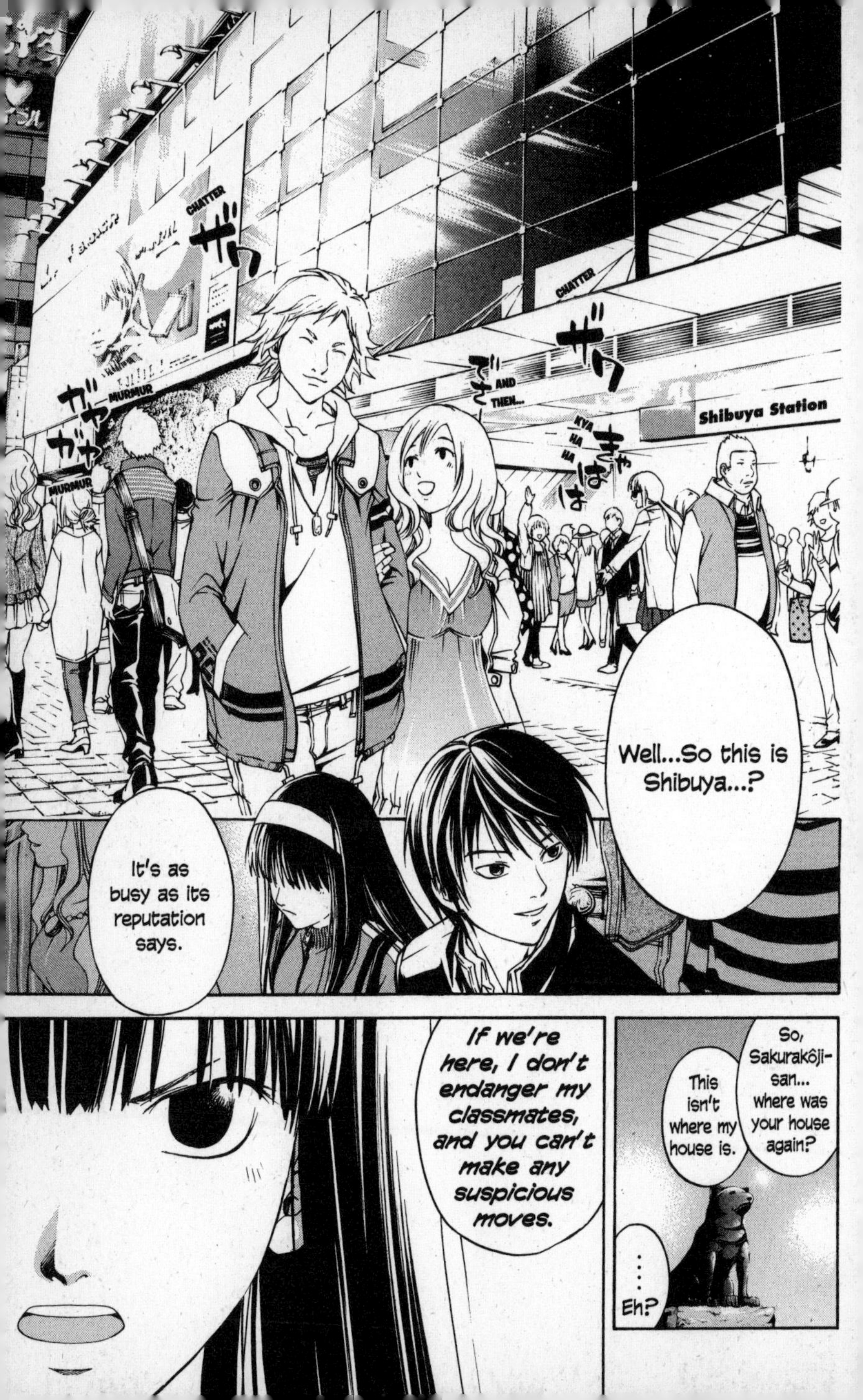
Shibuya Station
CHATTER
ザワ
きゃははは
KYA HA HA
でさ
AND THEN...
CHATTER
ザワ
ガヤガヤ
MURMUR
MURMUR
Well...So this is Shibuya...?
It's as busy as its reputation says.
So, Sakurakôji-san... where was your house again?
This isn't where my house is.
......
Eh?
If we're here, I don't endanger my classmates, and you can't make any suspicious moves.

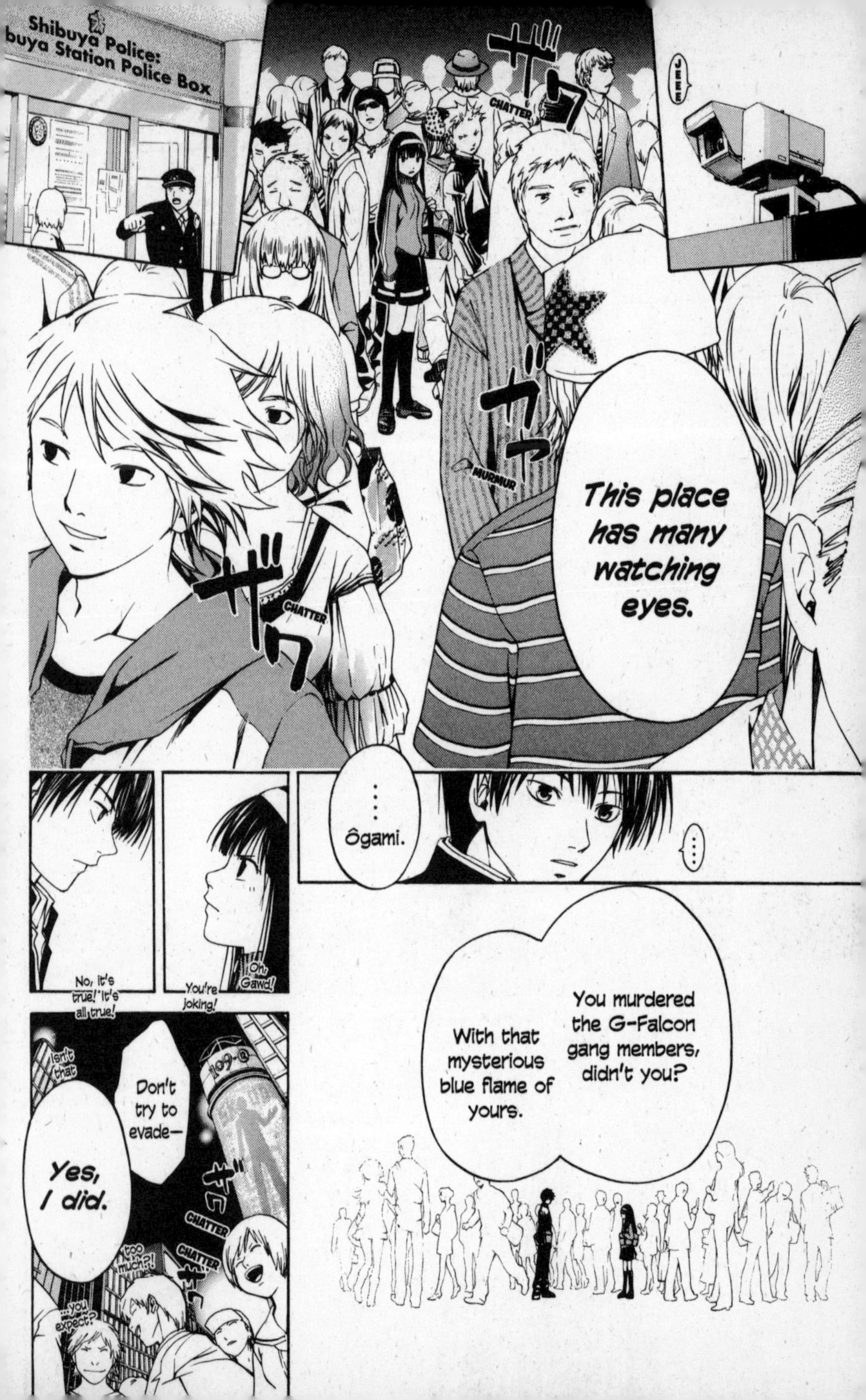
CHATTER
Shibuya Police:
buya Station Police Box
This place has many watching eyes.
MURMUR
CHATTER
....
...Ôgami.
Oh, Gawd!
You're joking!
No, it's true! It's all true!
You murdered the G-Falcon gang members, didn't you?
With that mysterious blue flame of yours.
Don't try to evade—
Yes, I did.
Isn't that
CHATTER
CHATTER
too much?!
...you expect?

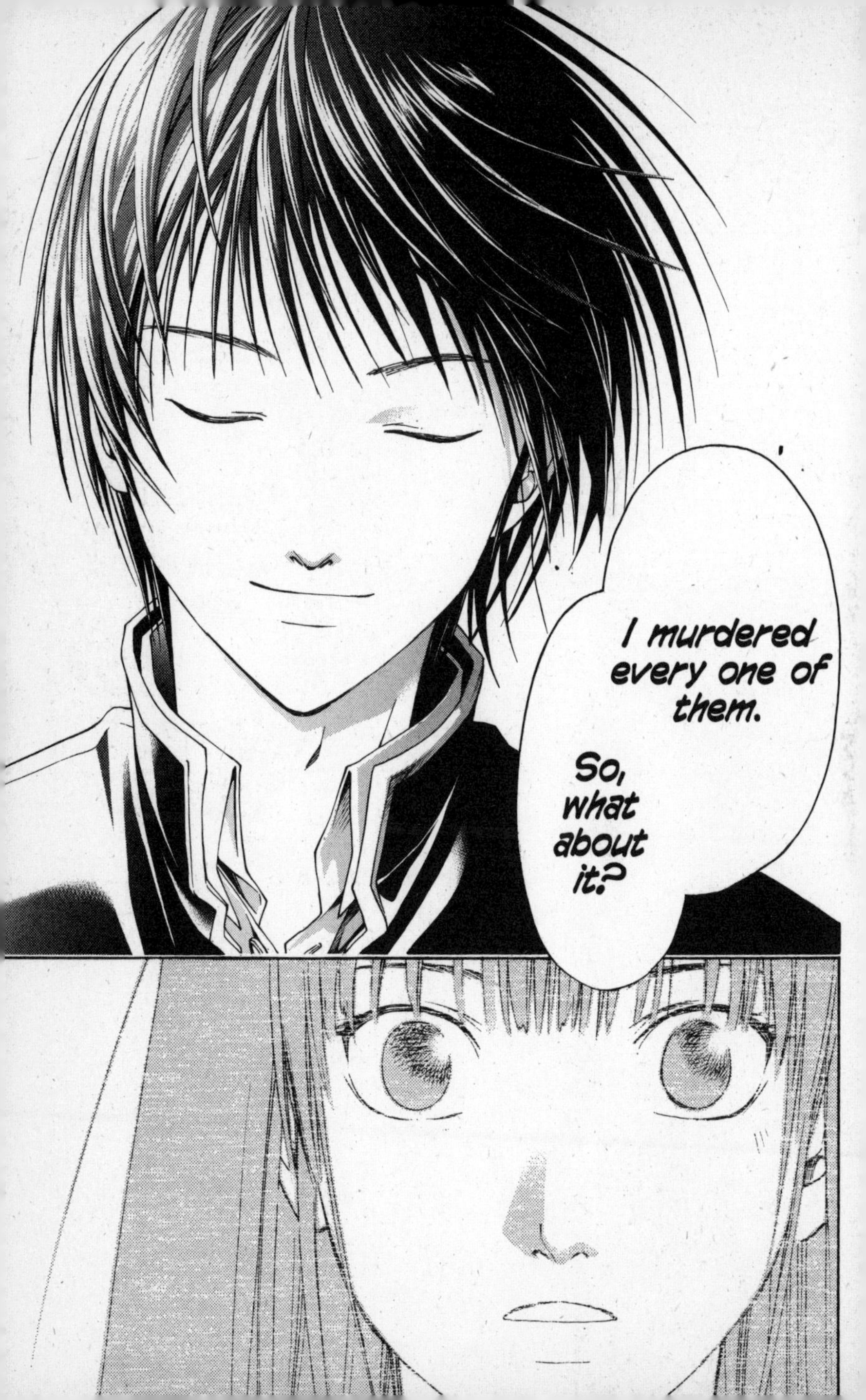
I murdered every one of them.
So, what about it?

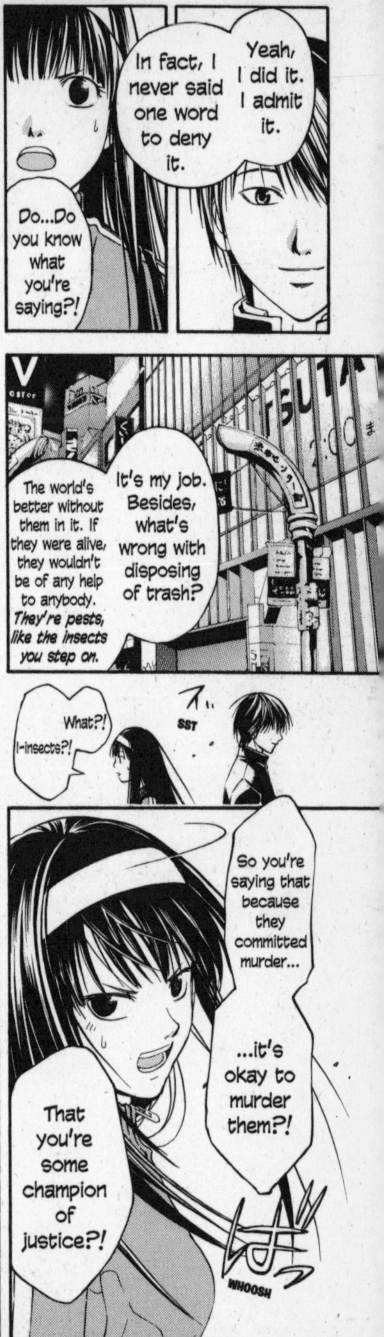

Yeah, I did it. I admit it.
In fact, I never said one word to deny it.
Do...Do you know what you're saying?!
It's my job. Besides, what's wrong with disposing of trash?
The world's better without them in it. If they were alive, they wouldn't be of any help to anybody. *They're pests, like the insects you step on.*
SST
What?! I-insects?!
So you're saying that because they committed murder...
...it's okay to murder them?!
That you're some champion of justice?!
WHOOSH

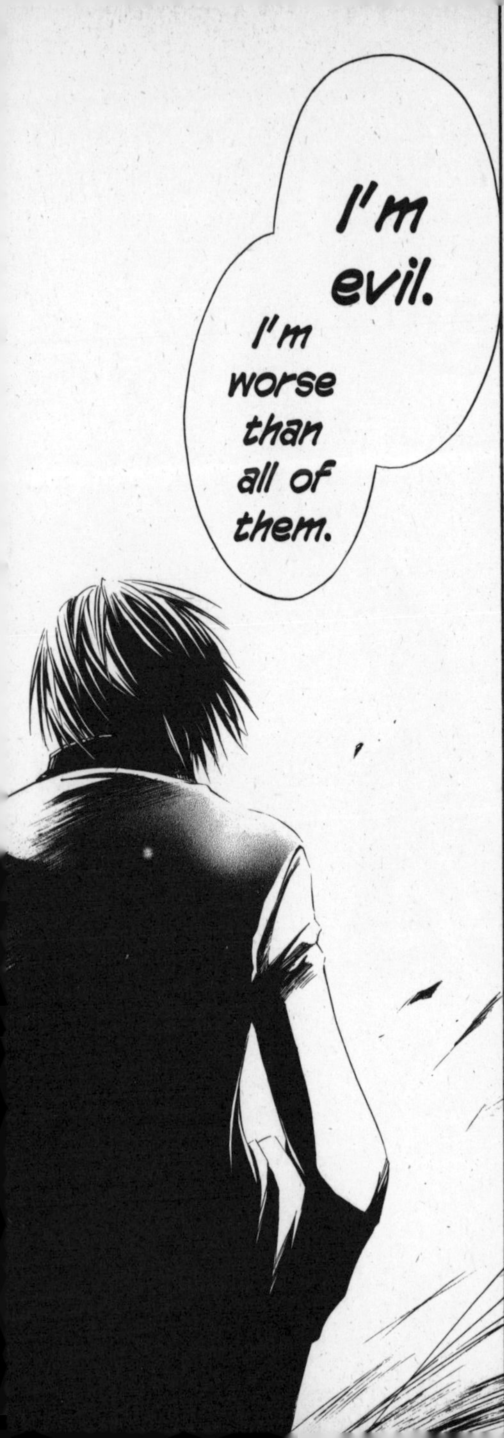

I'm evil.
I'm worse than all of them.

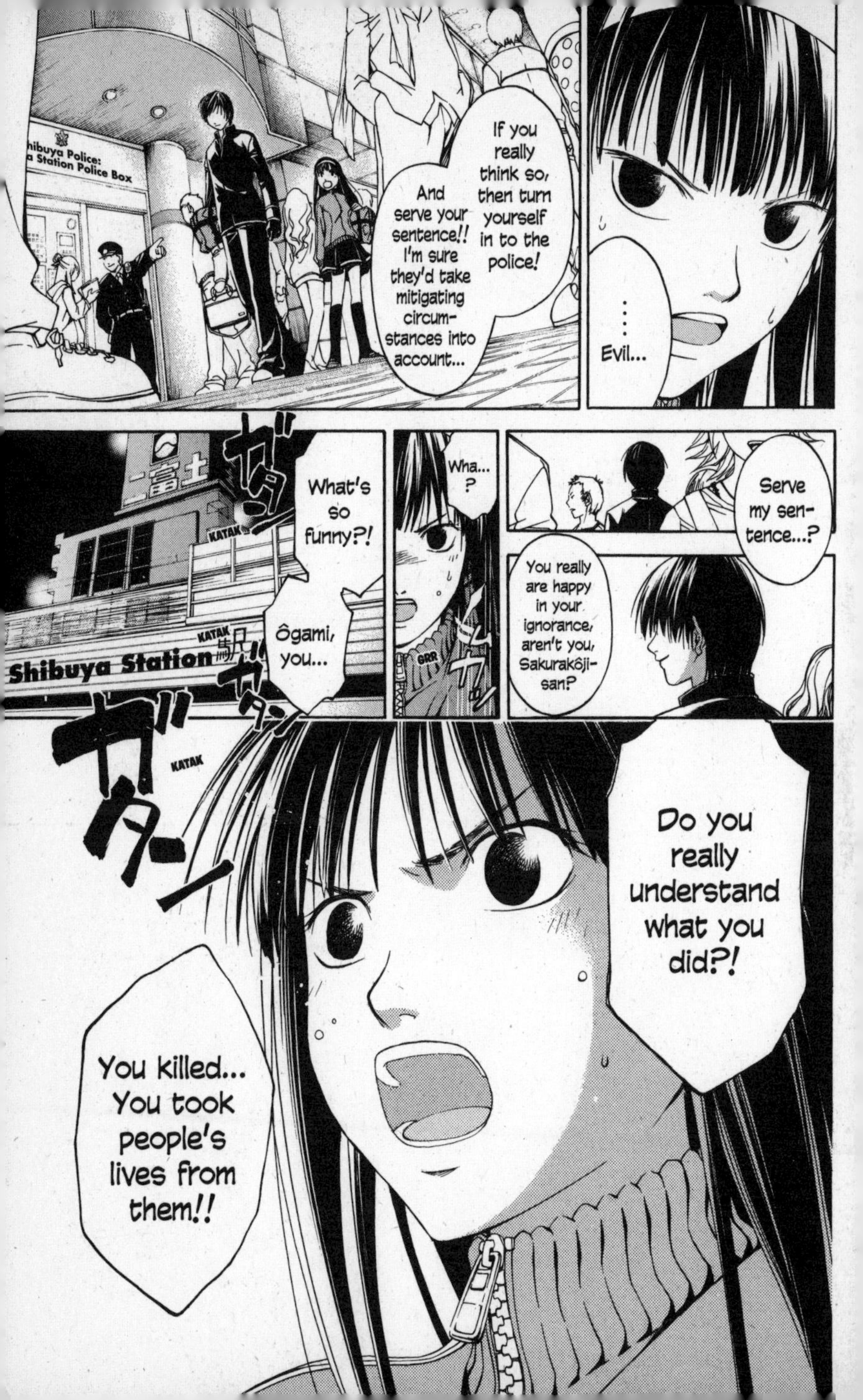

...Evil...
If you really think so, then turn yourself in to the police!
And serve your sentence!! I'm sure they'd take mitigating circumstances into account...
hibuya Police:
a Station Police Box
Serve my sentence...?
You really are happy in your ignorance, aren't you, Sakurakôji-san?
Wha...?
GRR
What's so funny?!
Ôgami, you...
KATAK
富士
Shibuya Station
KATAK
KATAK
Do you really understand what you did?!
You killed... You took people's lives from them!!

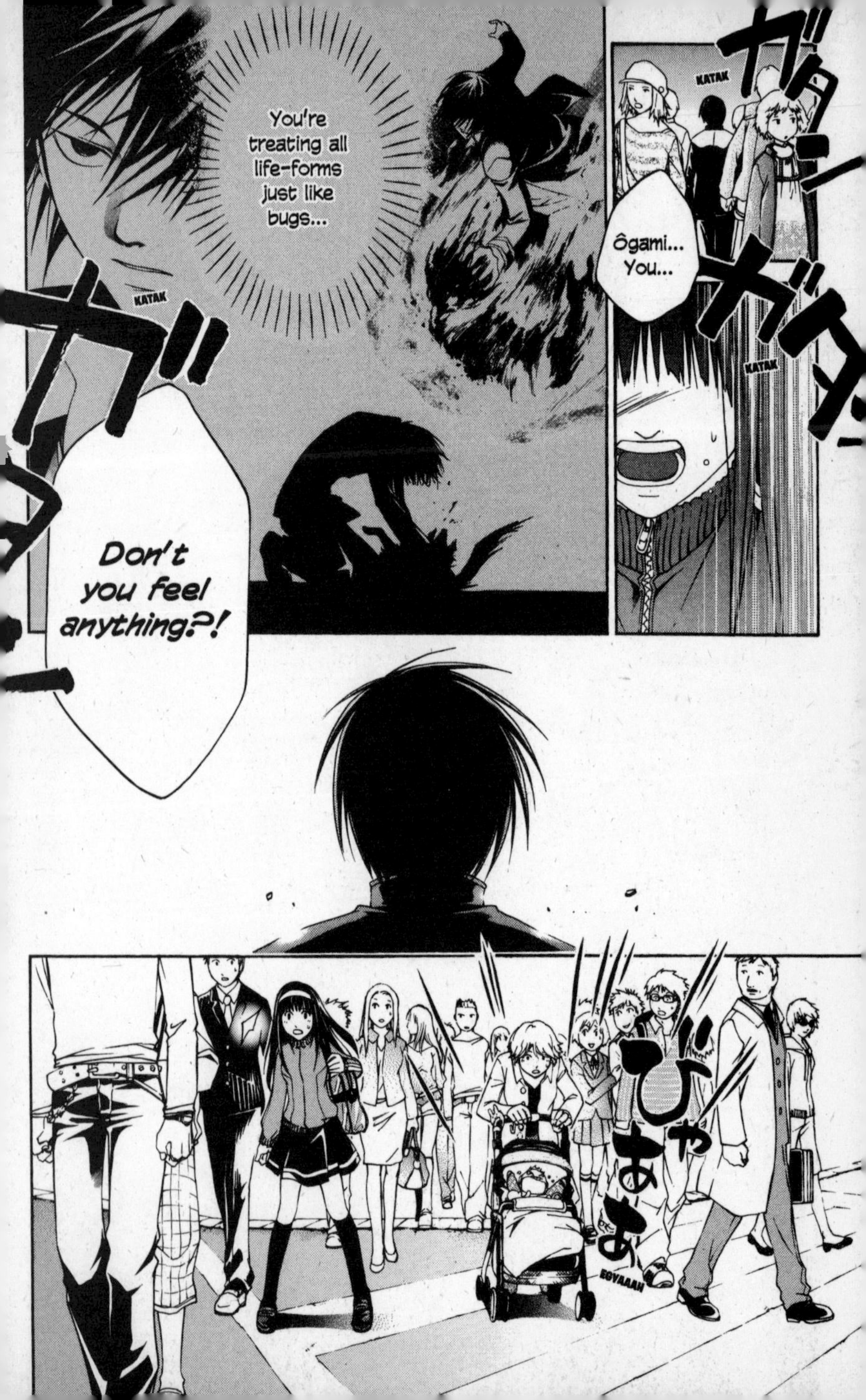
KATAK
Ôgami... You...
KATAK
You're treating all life-forms just like bugs...
KATAK
Don't you feel anything?!
EGYAAAH

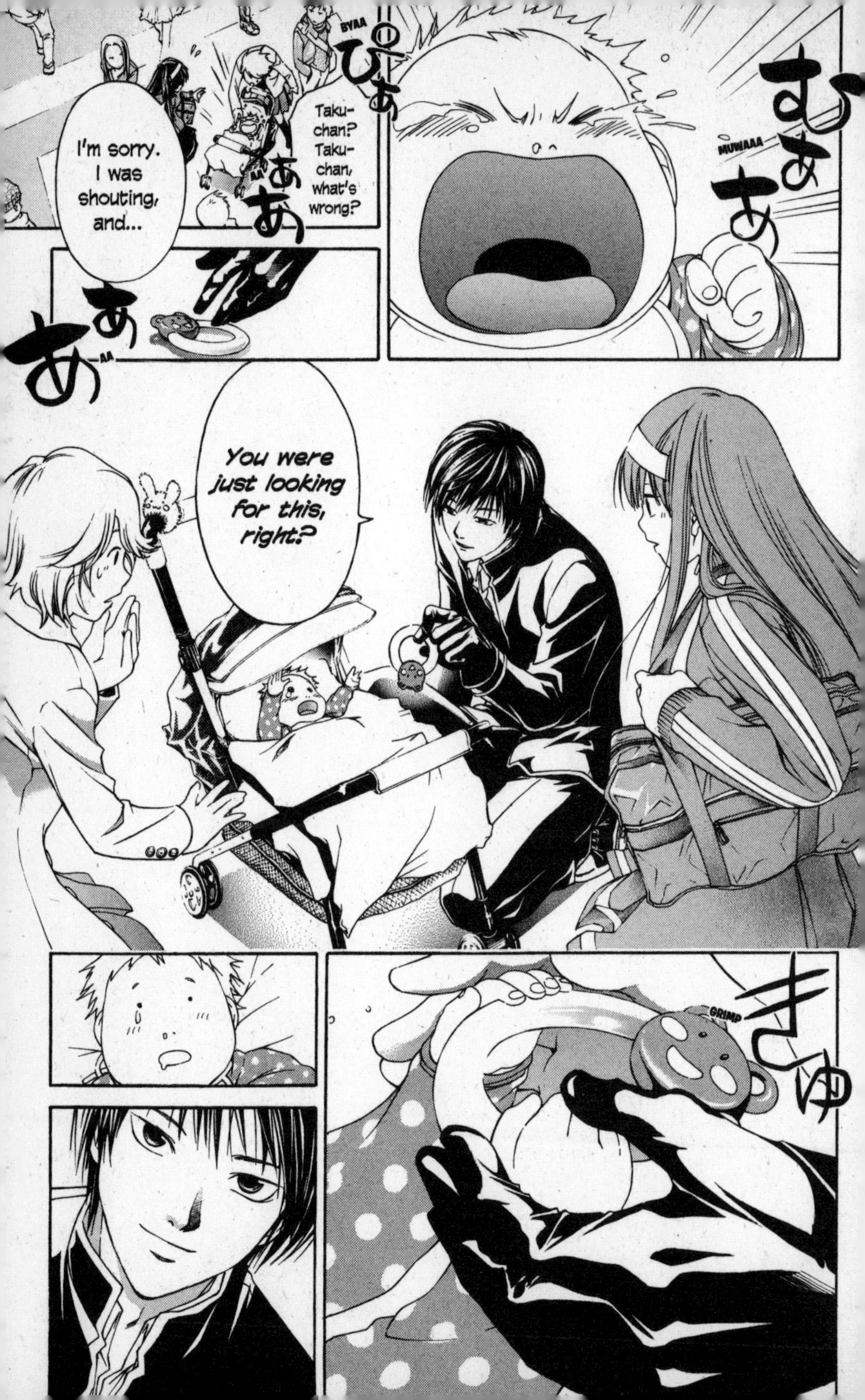
MUWAAA
BYAA
Taku-chan? Taku-chan, what's wrong?
I'm sorry. I was shouting, and...
AA
AA
You were just looking for this, right?
GRIMP

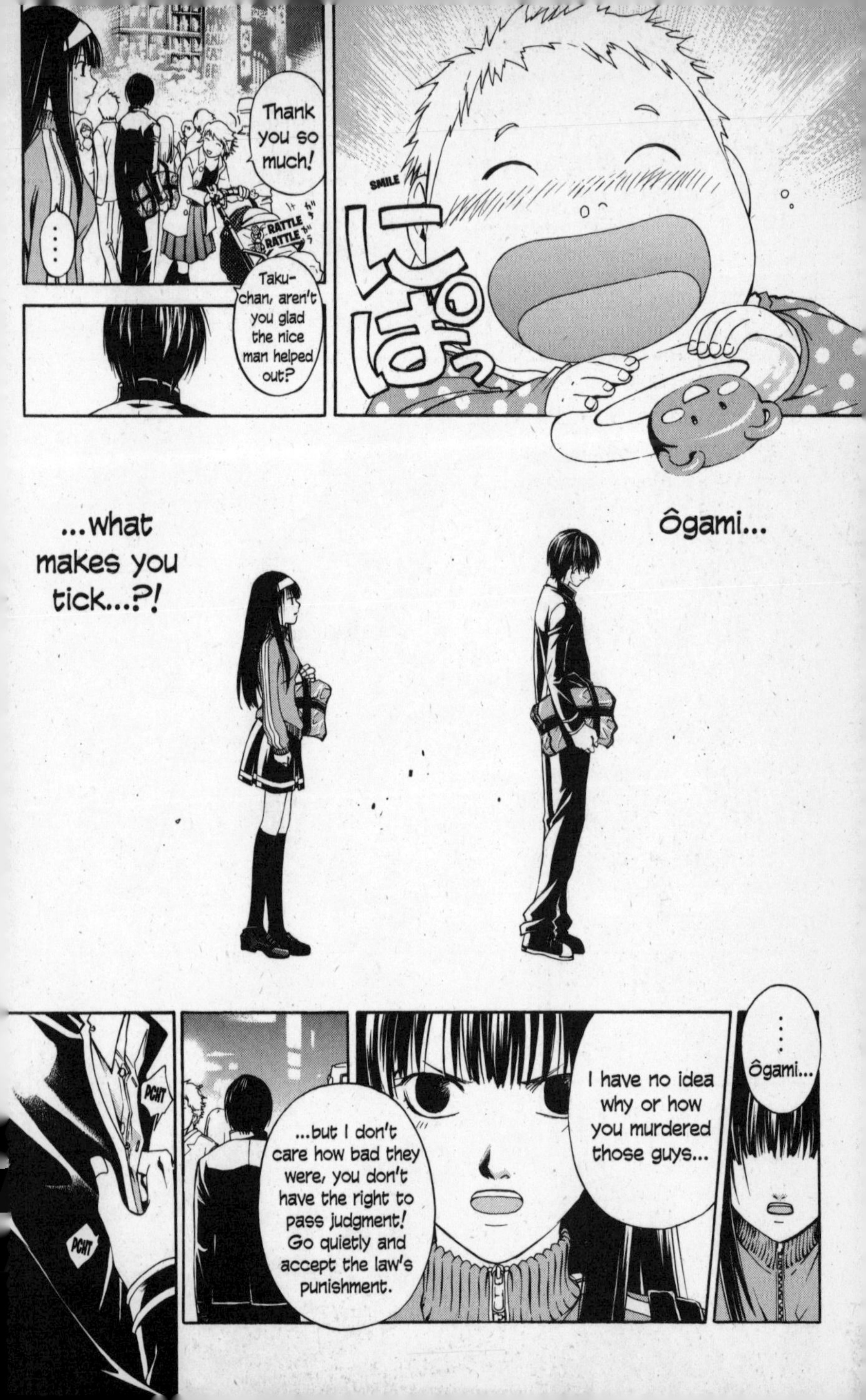
SMILE
にぱっ
Thank you so much!
RATTLE
RATTLE
....
Taku-chan, aren't you glad the nice man helped out?
Ôgami...
...what makes you tick...?!
....
Ôgami...
I have no idea why or how you murdered those guys...
...but I don't care how bad they were, you don't have the right to pass judgment! Go quietly and accept the law's punishment.
PCHT
PCHT

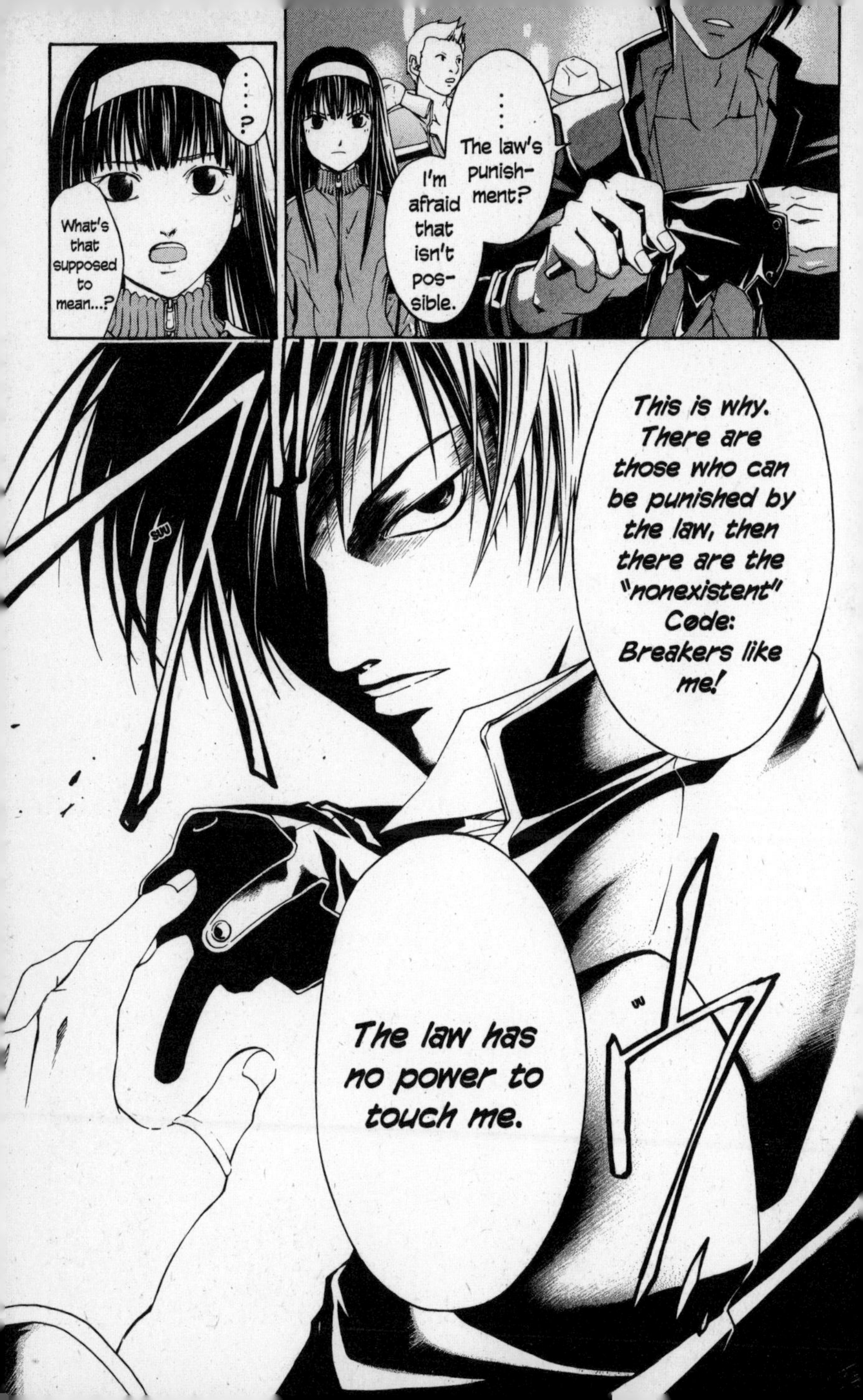
...
The law's punishment?
I'm afraid that isn't possible.
....?
What's that supposed to mean...?
This is why. There are those who can be punished by the law, then there are the "nonexistent" Code: Breakers like me!
The law has no power to touch me.

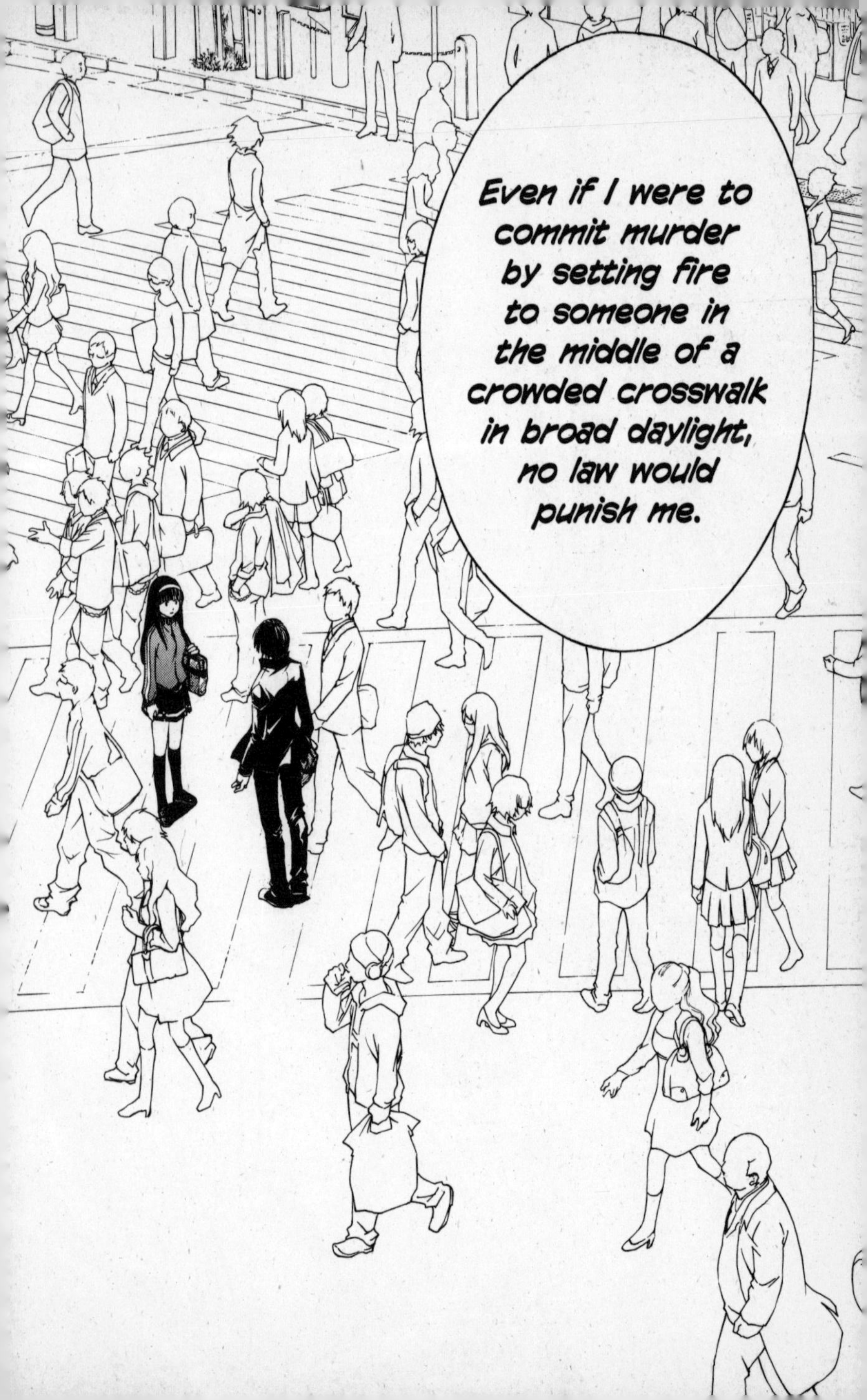
Even if I were to commit murder by setting fire to someone in the middle of a crowded crosswalk in broad daylight, no law would punish me.

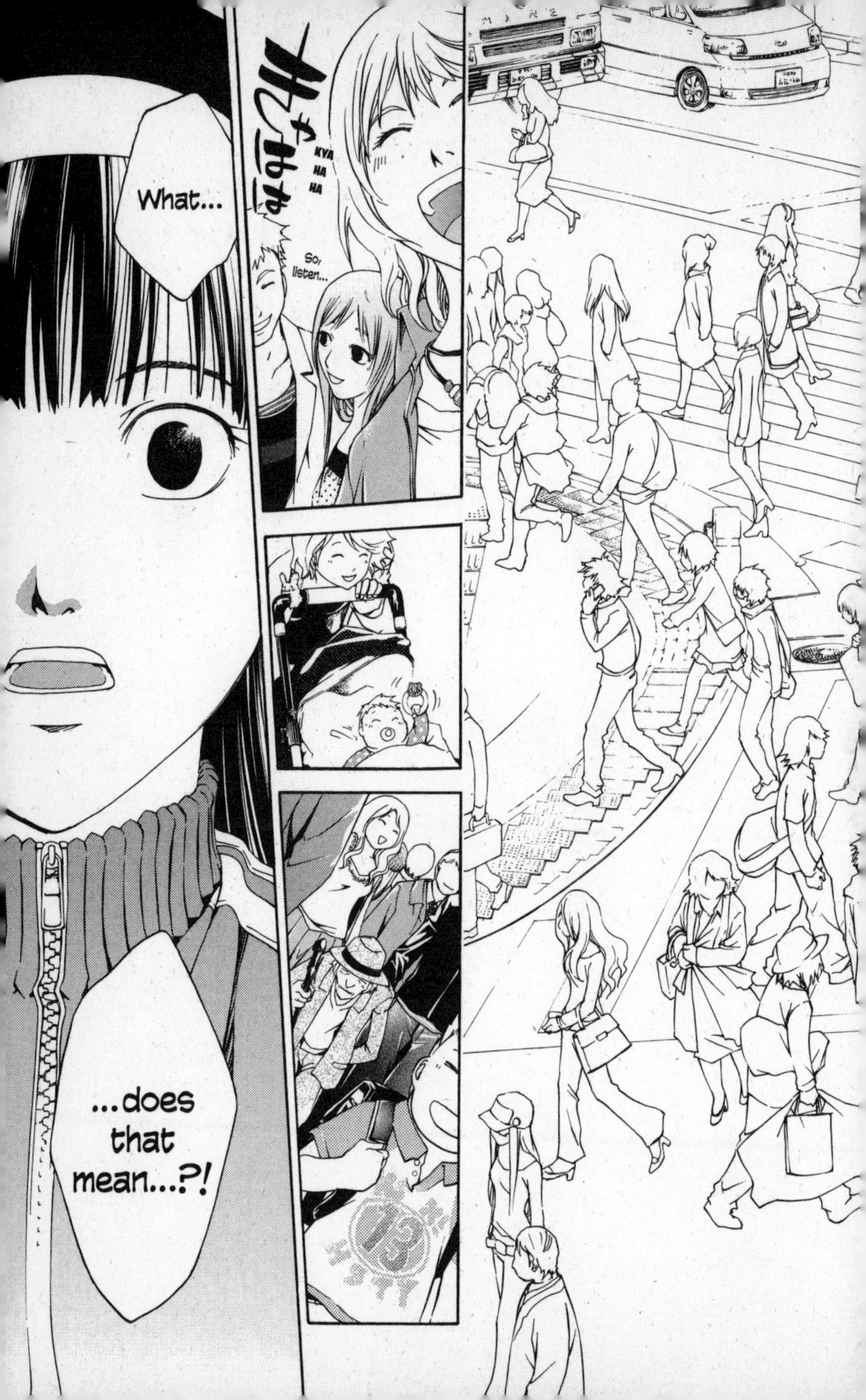
KYA HA HA
So, listen...
What...
...does that mean...?!

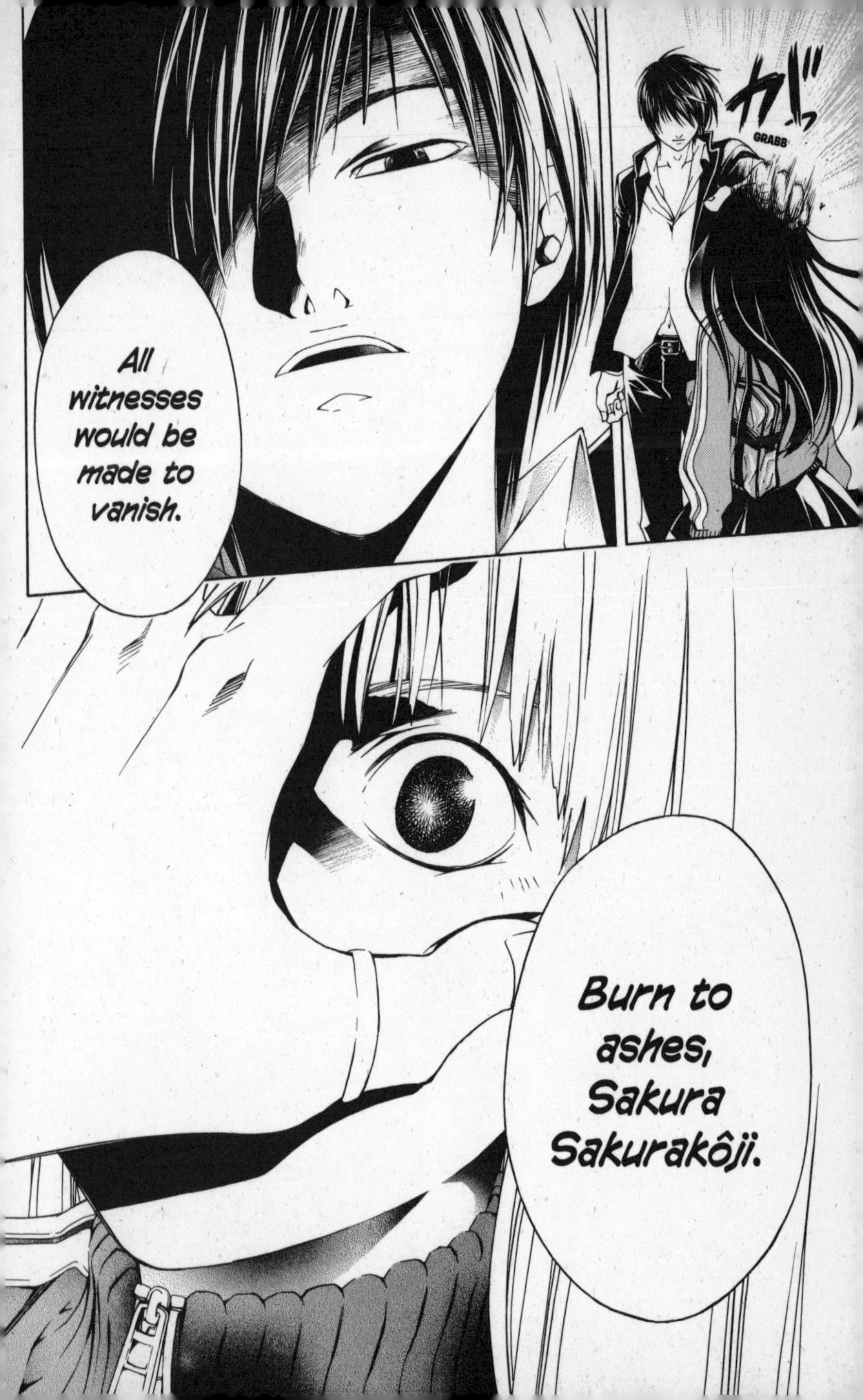
GRABB
All witnesses would be made to vanish.
Burn to ashes, Sakura Sakurakôji.

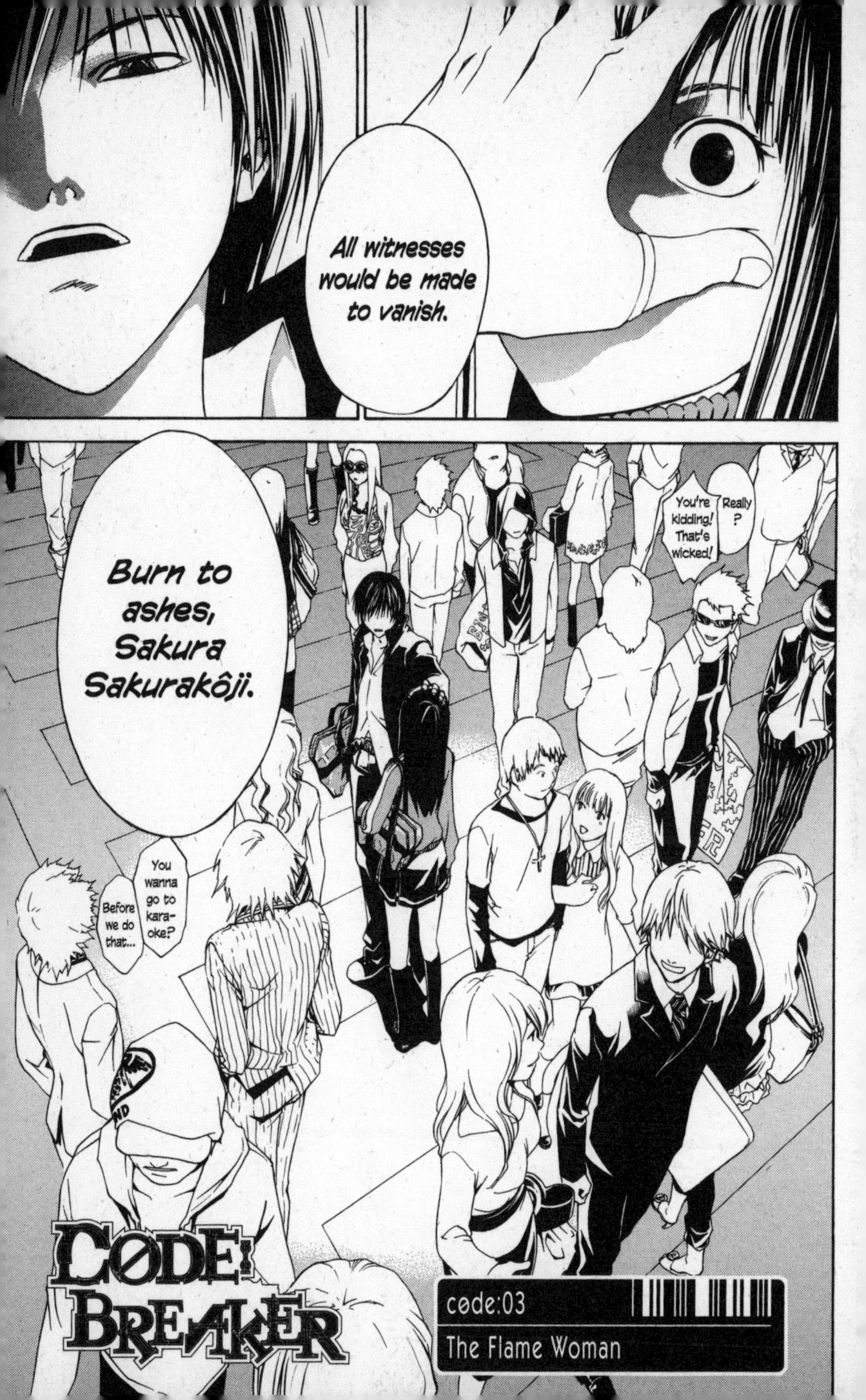
All witnesses would be made to vanish.
Really?
You're kidding! That's wicked!
Burn to ashes, Sakura Sakurakôji.
You wanna go to karaoke?
Before we do that...
CODE:BREAKER
code:03
The Flame Woman

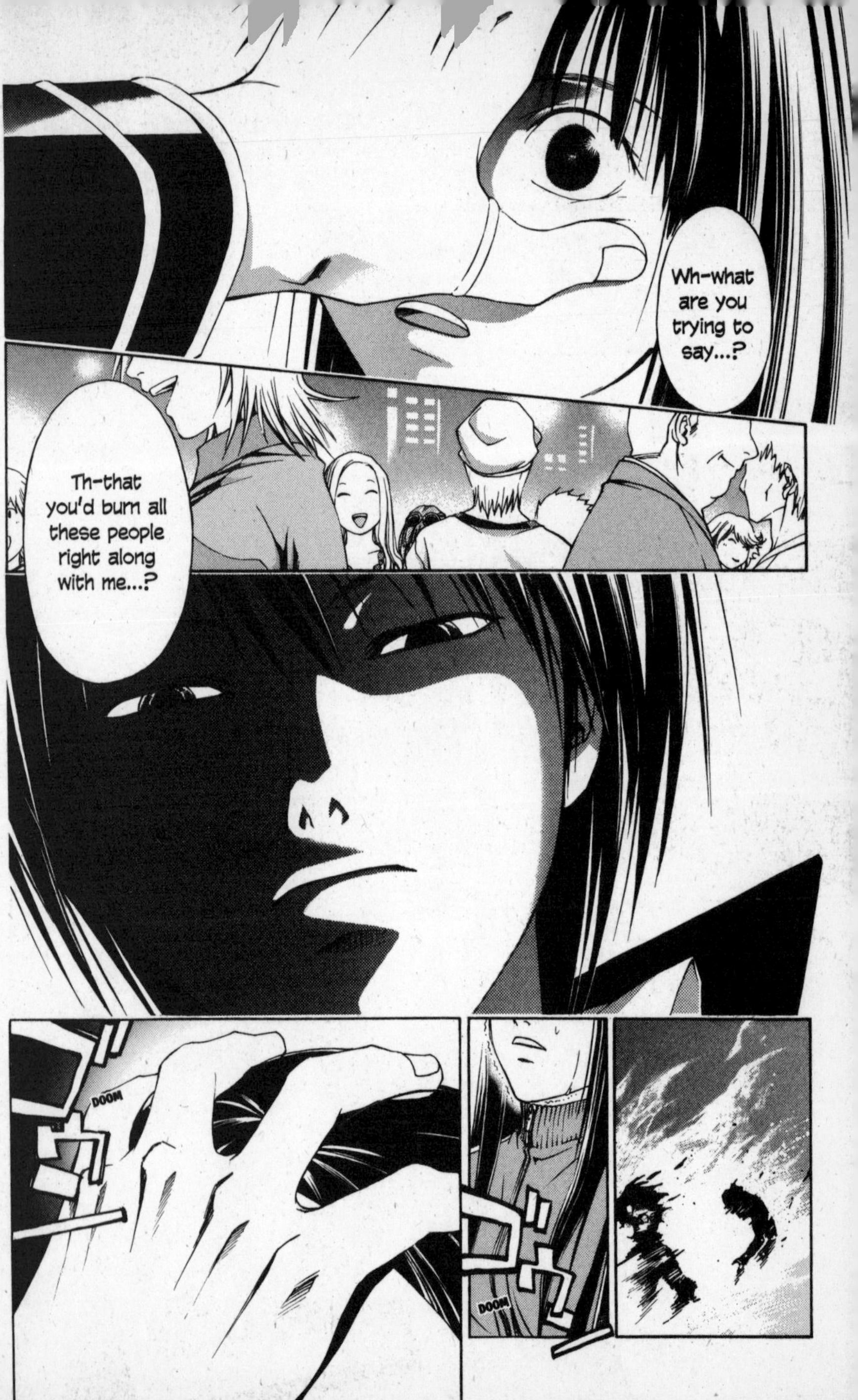
Wh-what are you trying to say...?
Th-that you'd burn all these people right along with me...?
DOOM
DOOM

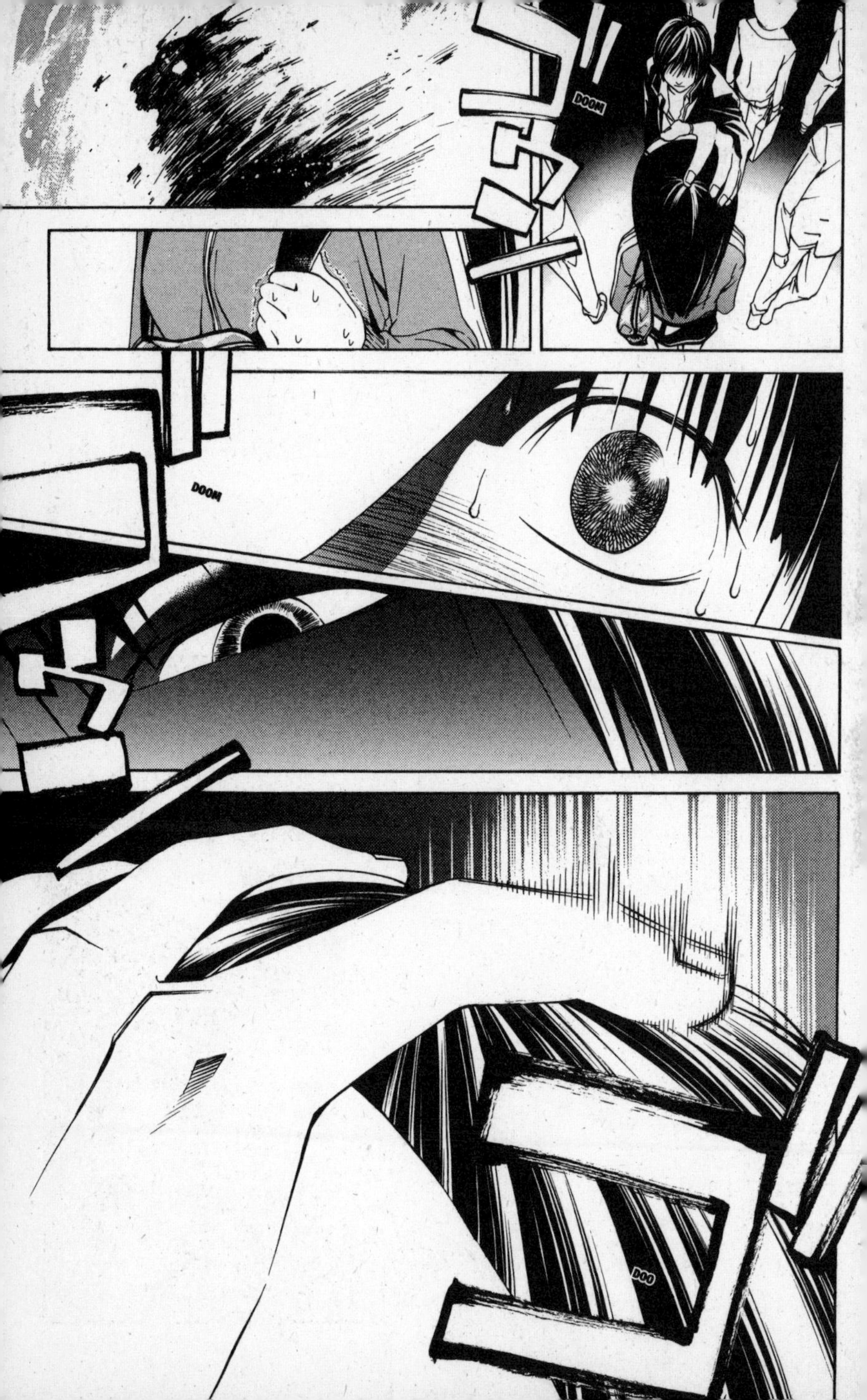
DOOM
DOOM
DOO

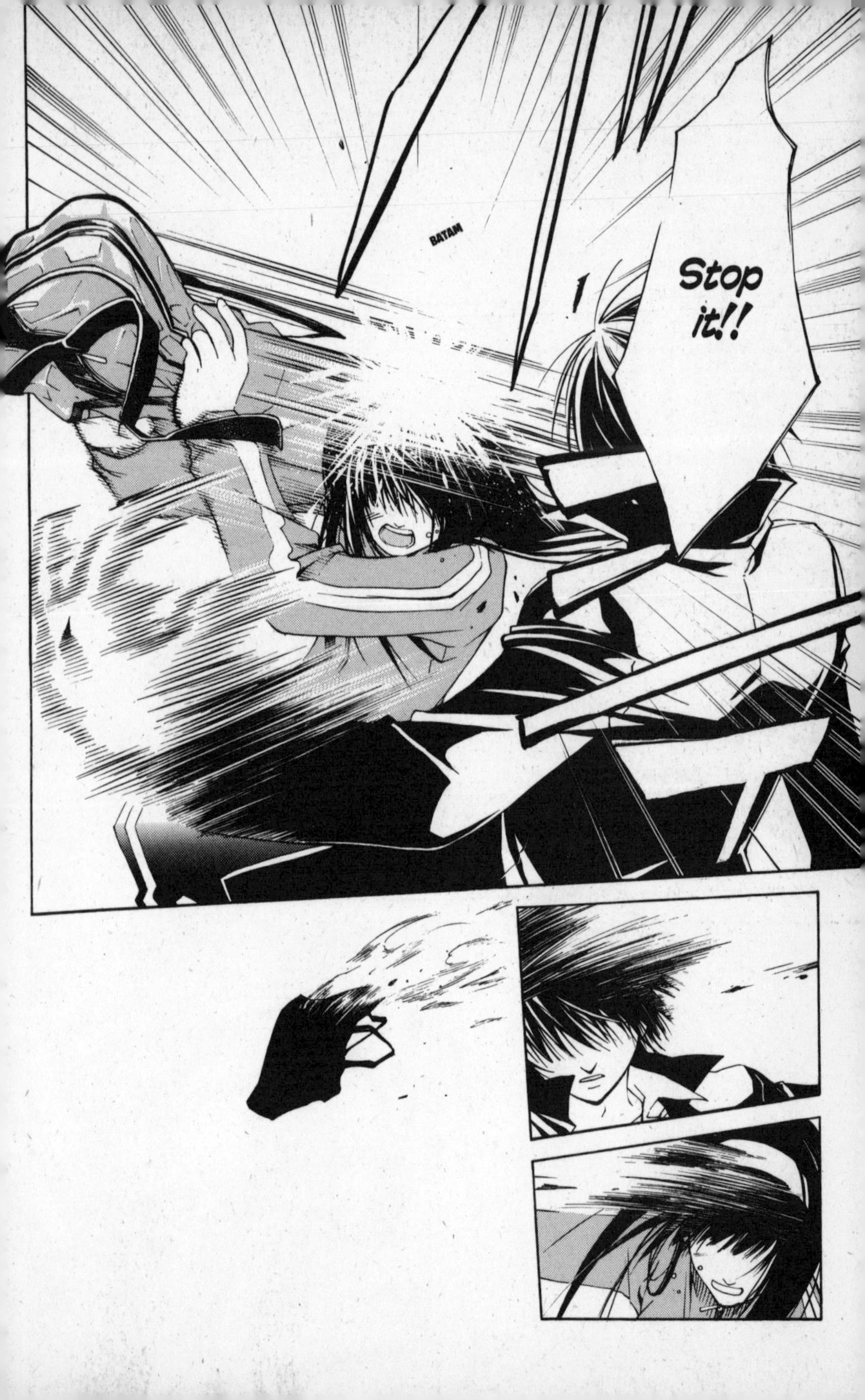
Stop it!!
BATAM

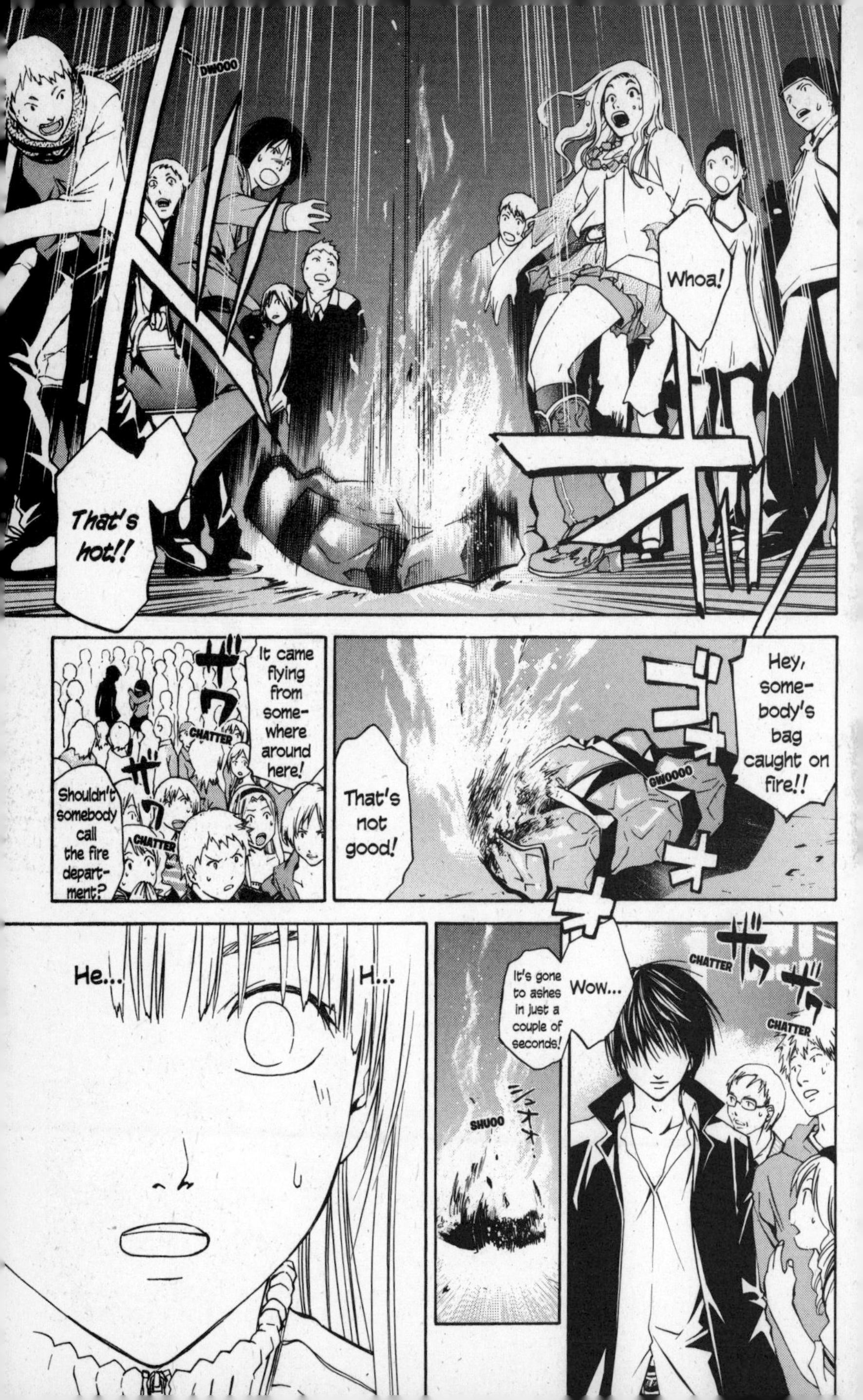
DWOOO
Whoa!
That's hot!!
Hey, somebody's bag caught on fire!!
GWOOOO
That's not good!
It came flying from somewhere around here!
CHATTER
Shouldn't somebody call the fire department?
CHATTER
CHATTER
CHATTER
Wow...
It's gone to ashes in just a couple of seconds!
SHUOO
H...
He...

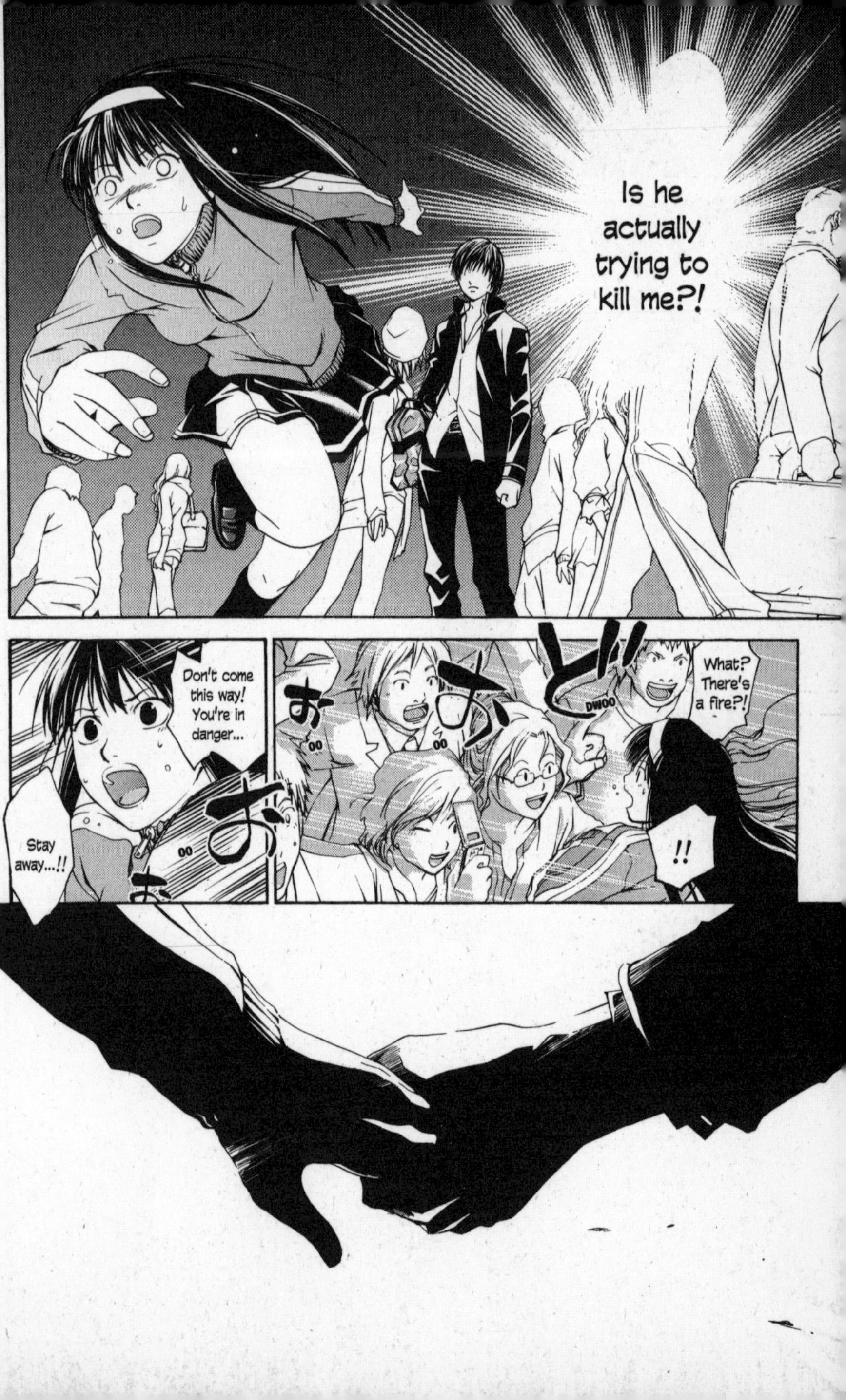
Is he actually trying to kill me?!
What? There's a fire?!
DWOO
OO
OO
!!
Don't come this way! You're in danger...
OO
Stay away...!!

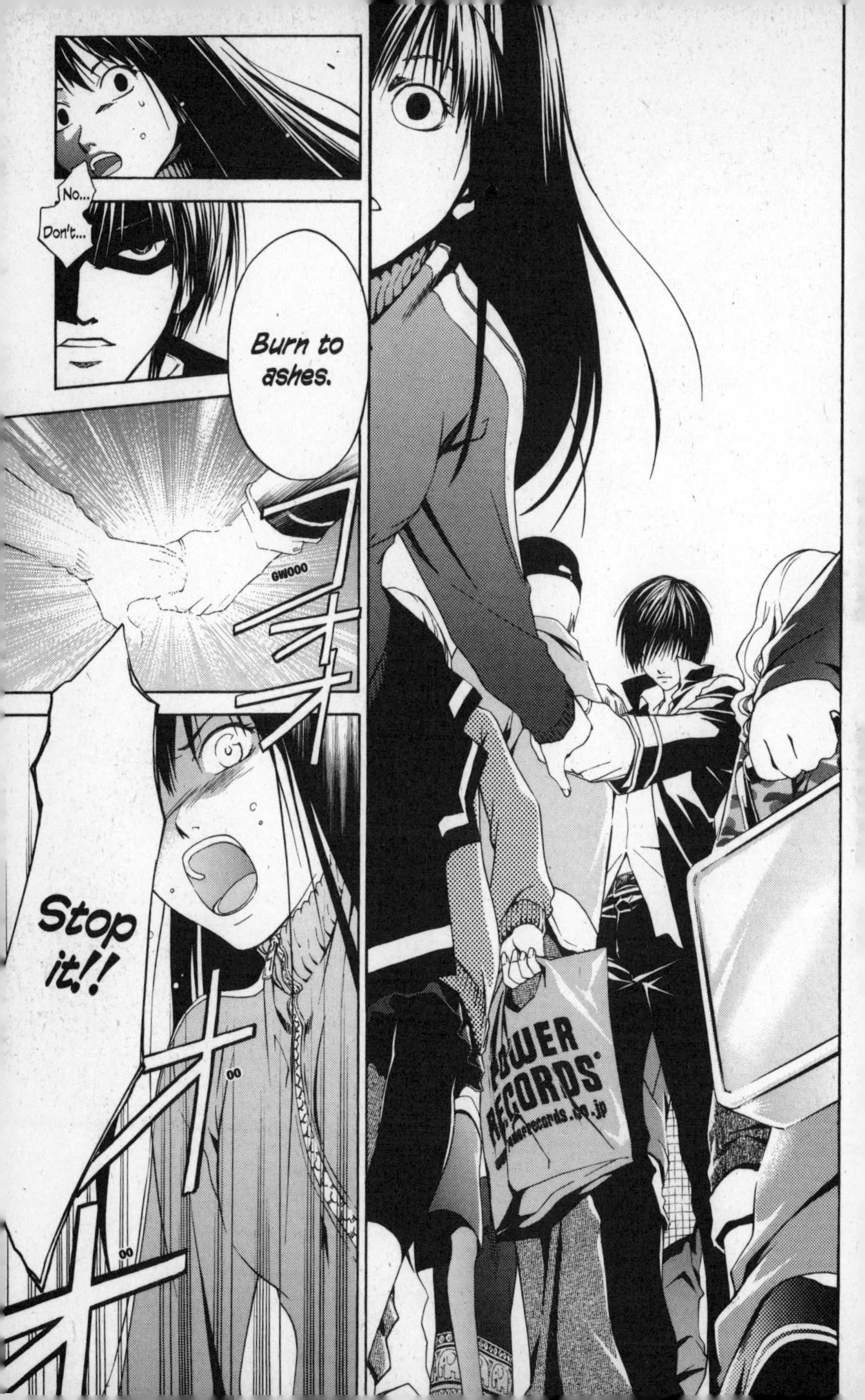
POWER RECORDS
No...
Don't...
Burn to ashes.
GWOOO
Stop it!!

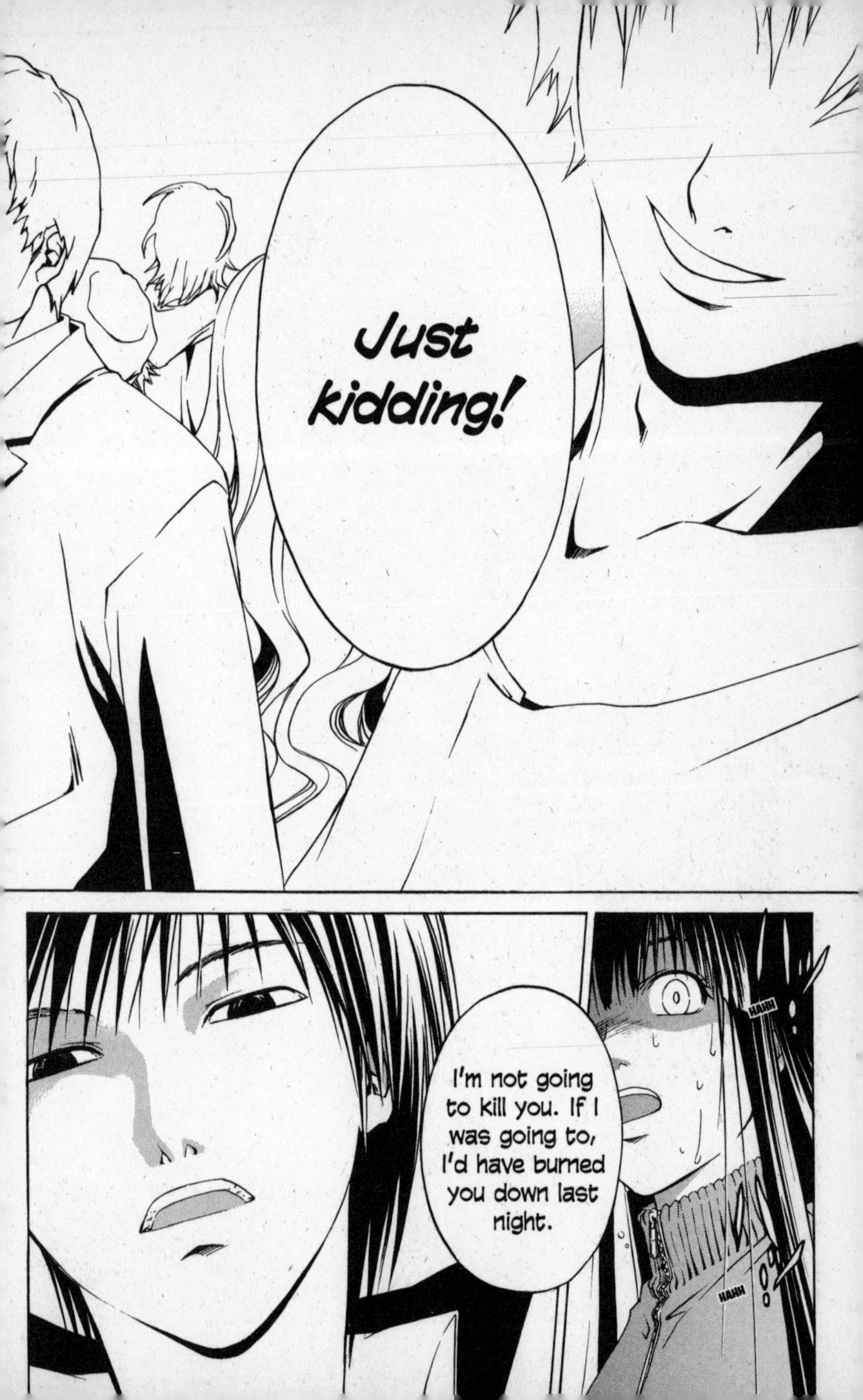
Just kidding!
HAHH
HAHH
I'm not going to kill you. If I was going to, I'd have burned you down last night.

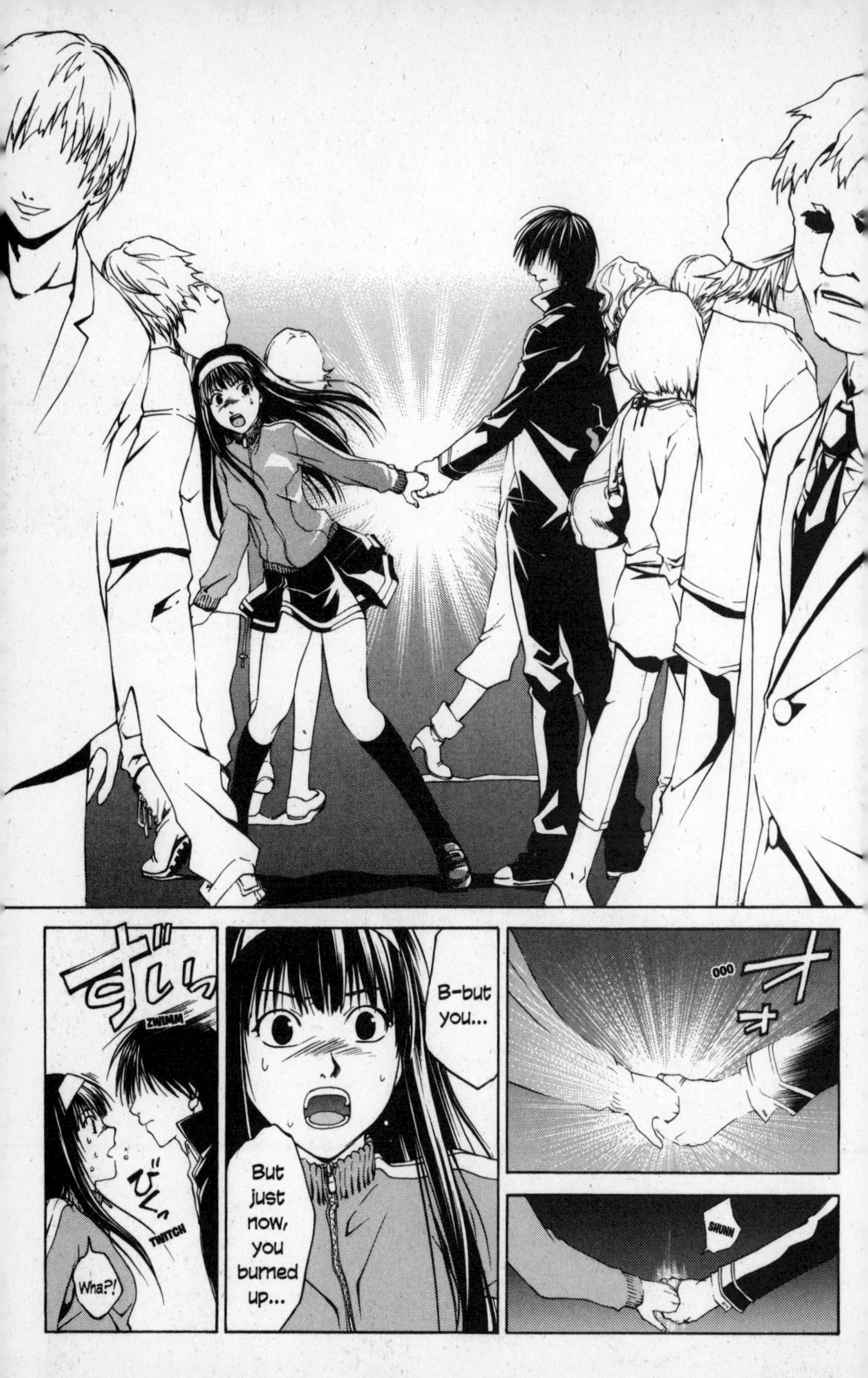
ooo
SHUNN
B-but you...
But just now, you burned up...
ZWIMM
TWITCH
Wha?!

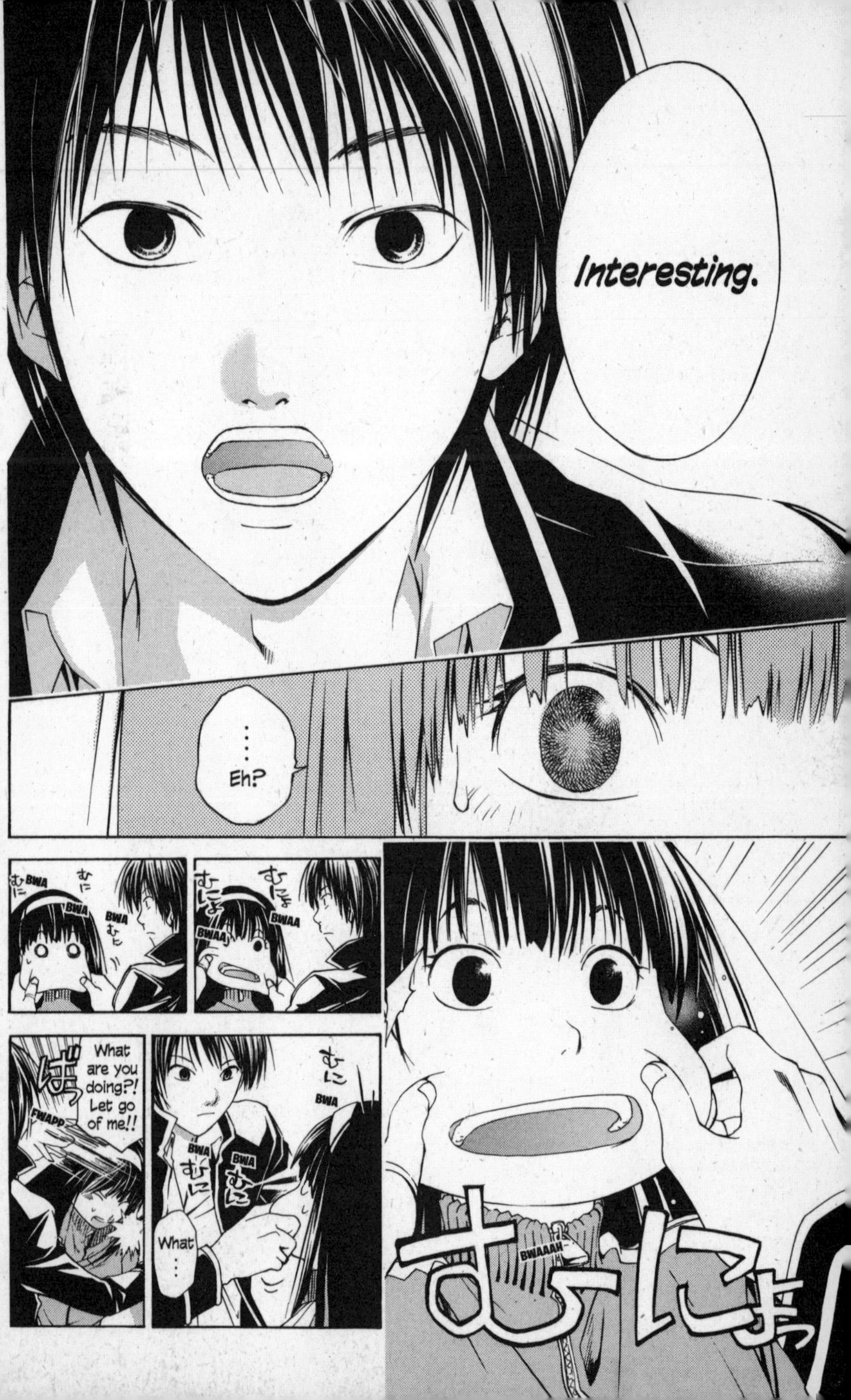
Interesting.
...... Eh?
BWAAAH-
むにょっ
BWAA
BWAA
BWA
BWA
BWA
BWA
BWA
BWA
What ...
What are you doing?! Let go of me!!
FWAPP

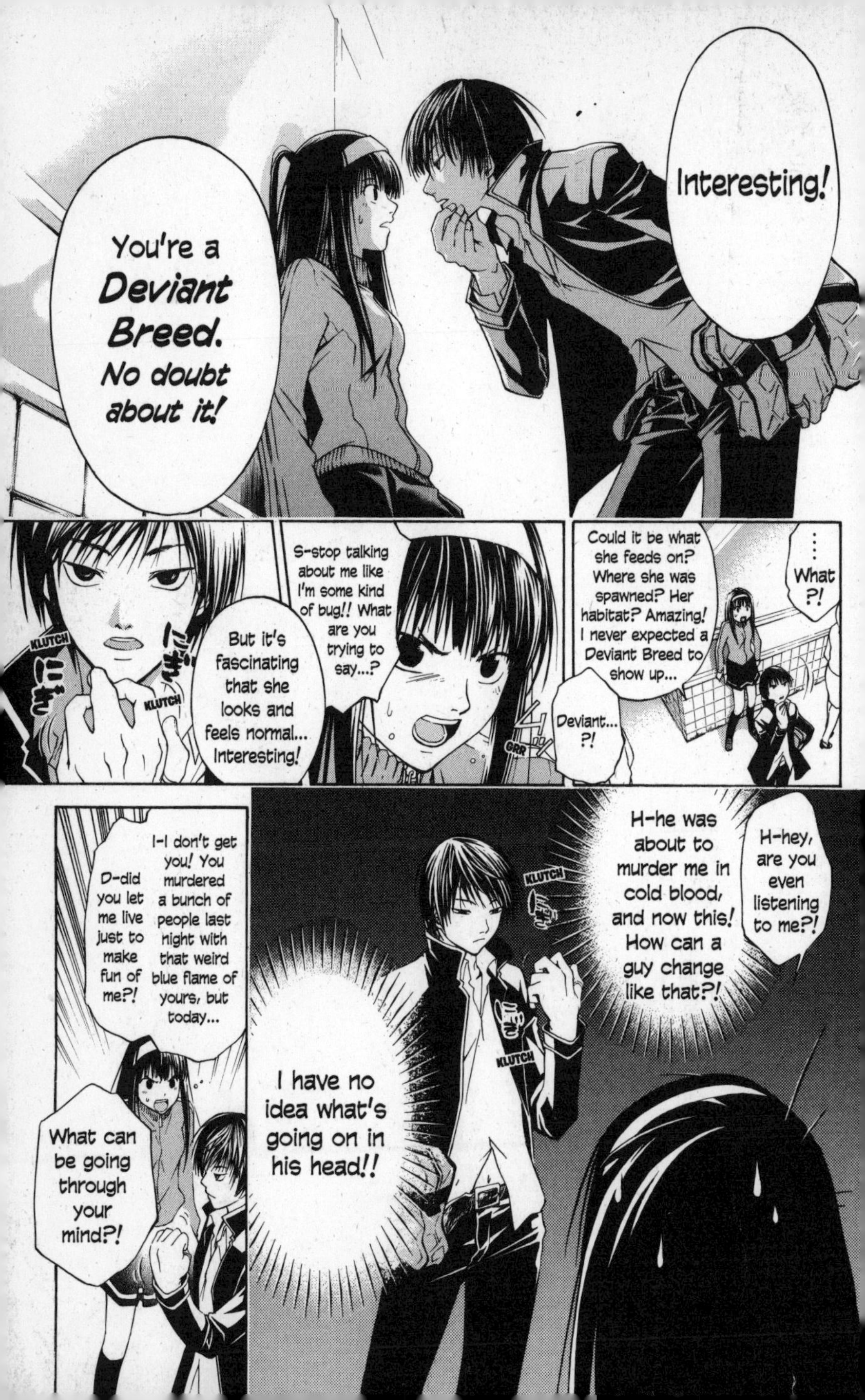
Interesting!
You're a Deviant Breed. No doubt about it!
... What ?!
Could it be what she feeds on? Where she was spawned? Her habitat? Amazing! I never expected a Deviant Breed to show up...
Deviant... ?!
S-stop talking about me like I'm some kind of bug!! What are you trying to say...?
GRR
But it's fascinating that she looks and feels normal... Interesting!
KLUTCH
KLUTCH
H-hey, are you even listening to me?!
H-he was about to murder me in cold blood, and now this! How can a guy change like that?!
KLUTCH
KLUTCH
I have no idea what's going on in his head!!
I-I don't get you! You murdered a bunch of people last night with that weird blue flame of yours, but today...
D-did you let me live just to make fun of me?!
What can be going through your mind?!

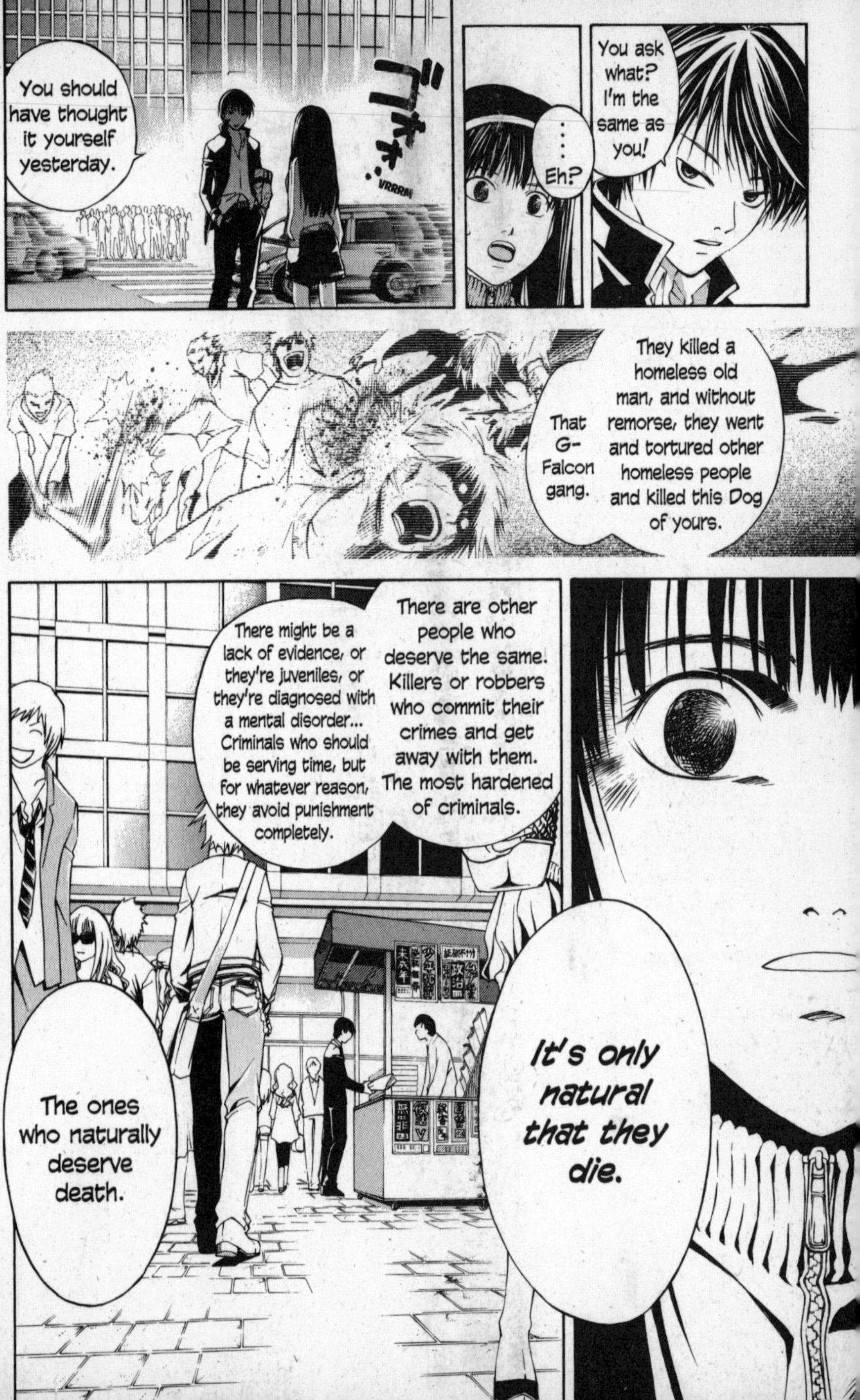
You ask what? I'm the same as you!
......Eh?
You should have thought it yourself yesterday.
ゴォォ
VRRRM
That G-Falcon gang.
They killed a homeless old man, and without remorse, they went and tortured other homeless people and killed this Dog of yours.
There are other people who deserve the same. Killers or robbers who commit their crimes and get away with them. The most hardened of criminals.
There might be a lack of evidence, or they're juveniles, or they're diagnosed with a mental disorder... Criminals who should be serving time, but for whatever reason, they avoid punishment completely.
The ones who naturally deserve death.
It's only natural that they die.

It's my job to clean out those pests.
I'm here to maintain this false peace that you people so happily live under.
FLASH
We are the evil that punishes the evil the law fails to punish. That's us, the Code: Breakers.

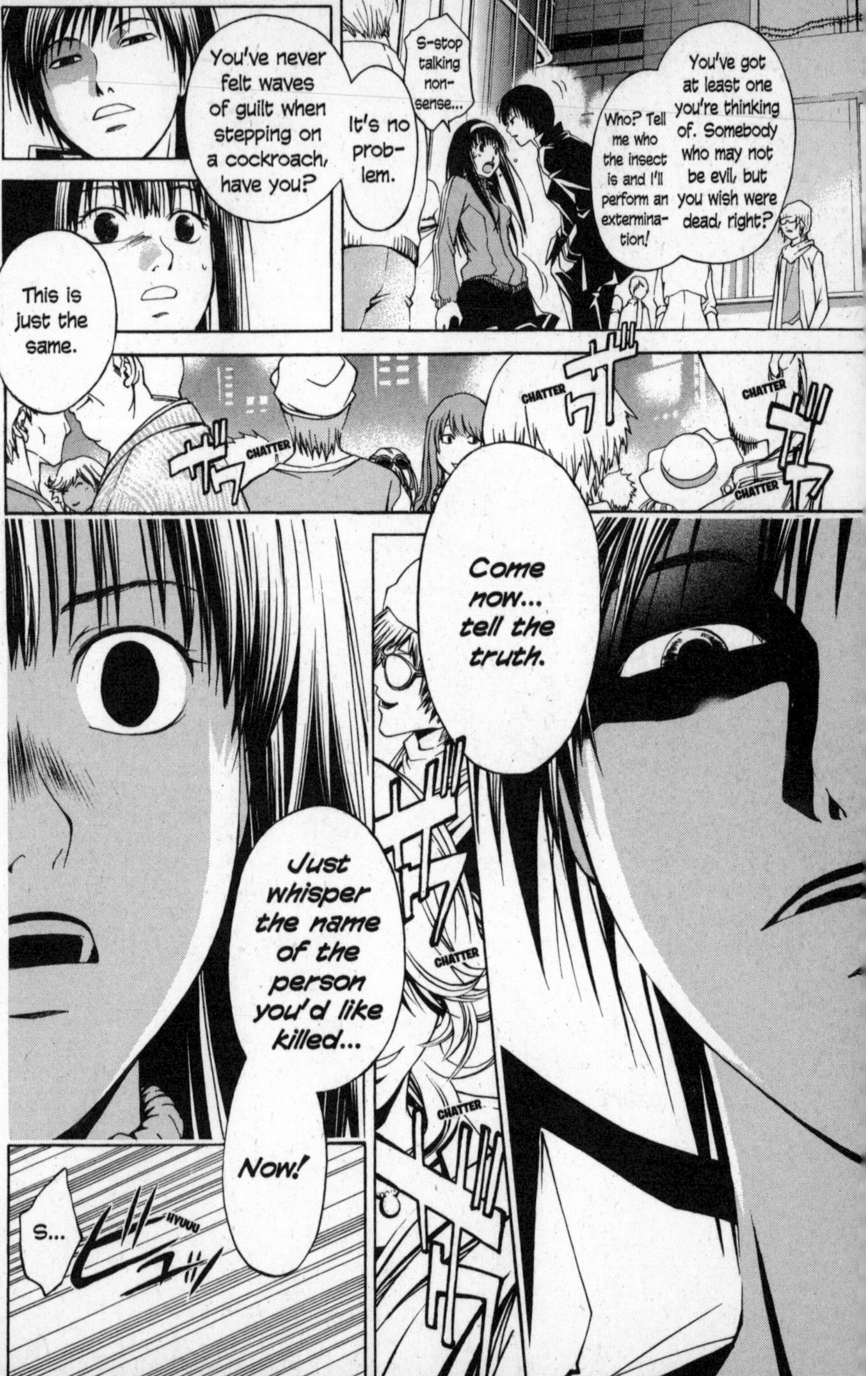

You've got at least one you're thinking of. Somebody who may not be evil, but you wish were dead, right?
Who? Tell me who the insect is and I'll perform an extermination!
S-stop talking non-sense...
It's no prob-lem.
You've never felt waves of guilt when stepping on a cockroach, have you?
This is just the same.
CHATTER
CHATTER
CHATTER
CHATTER
Come now... tell the truth.
Just whisper the name of the person you'd like killed...
CHATTER
CHATTER
Now!
S...
HYUUU

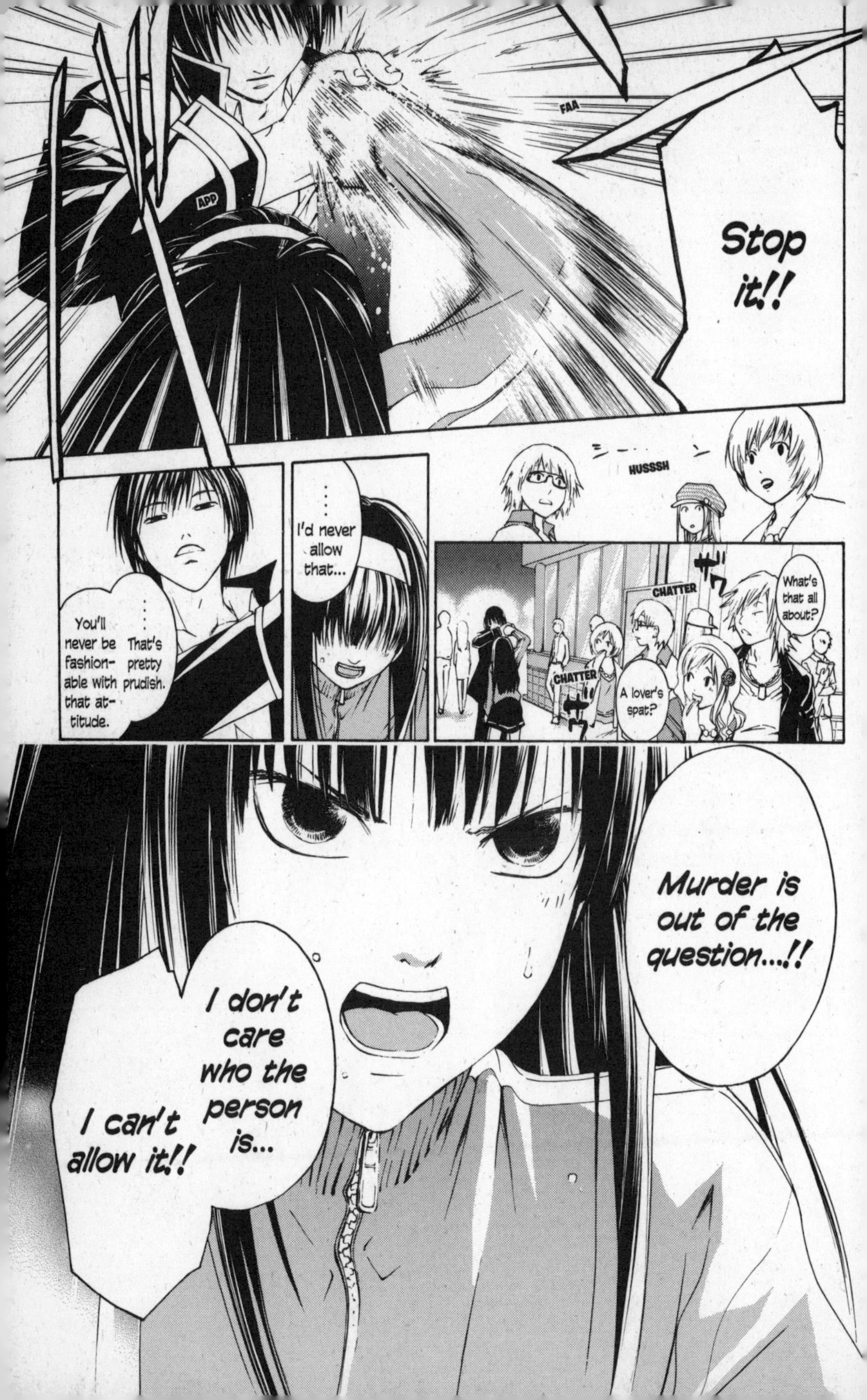
Stop it!!
FAA
APP
HUSSSH
What's that all about?
CHATTER
CHATTER
A lover's spat?
... I'd never allow that...
... That's pretty prudish.
You'll never be fashion-able with that at-titude.
Murder is out of the question...!!
I don't care who the person is...
I can't allow it!!

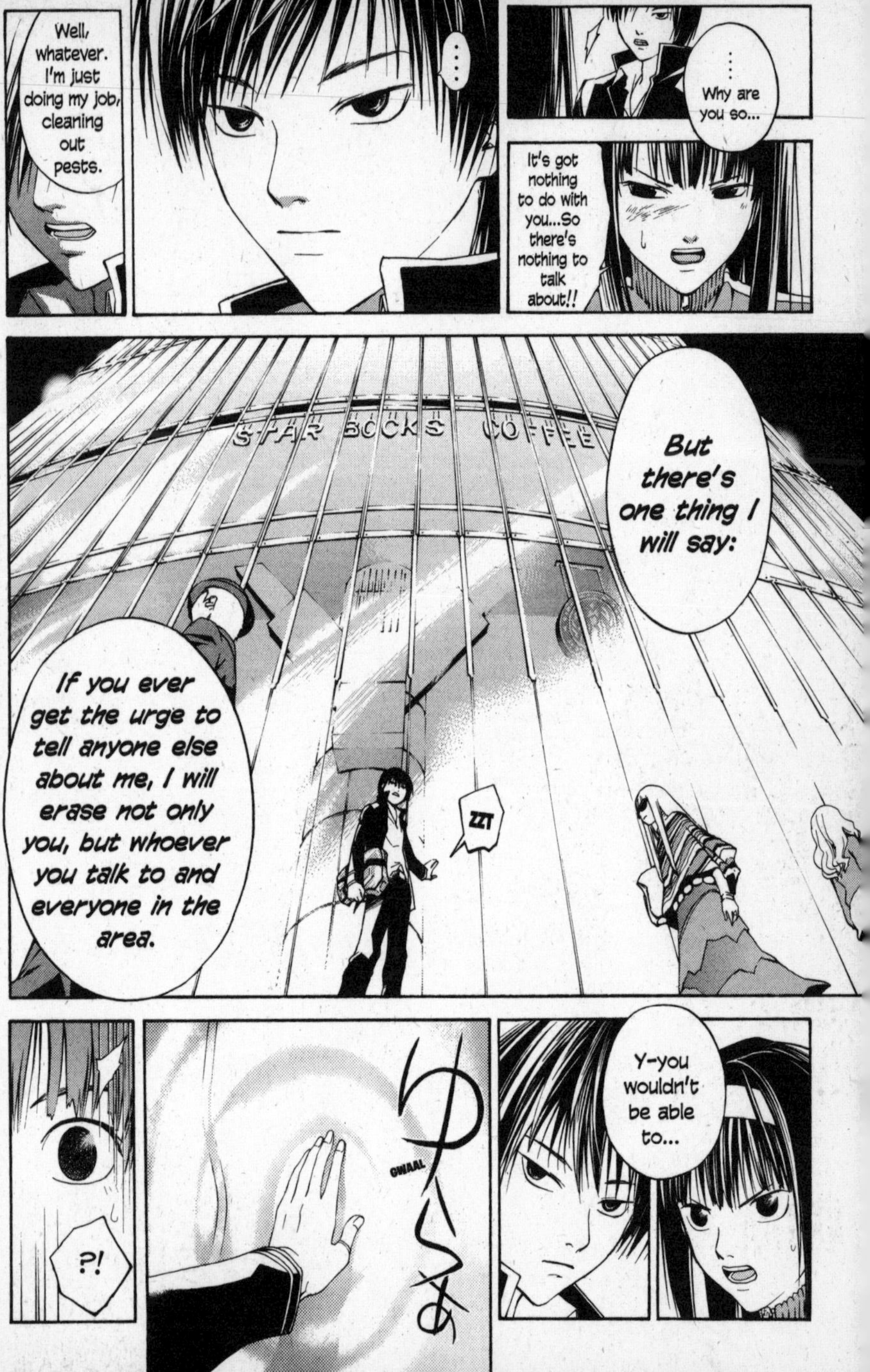
…
Why are you so...
It's got nothing to do with you...So there's nothing to talk about!!
…
Well, whatever. I'm just doing my job, cleaning out pests.
STAR BOCKS COFFEE
But there's one thing I will say:
If you ever get the urge to tell anyone else about me, I will erase not only you, but whoever you talk to and everyone in the area.
ZZT
Y-you wouldn't be able to...
GWAAL
?!

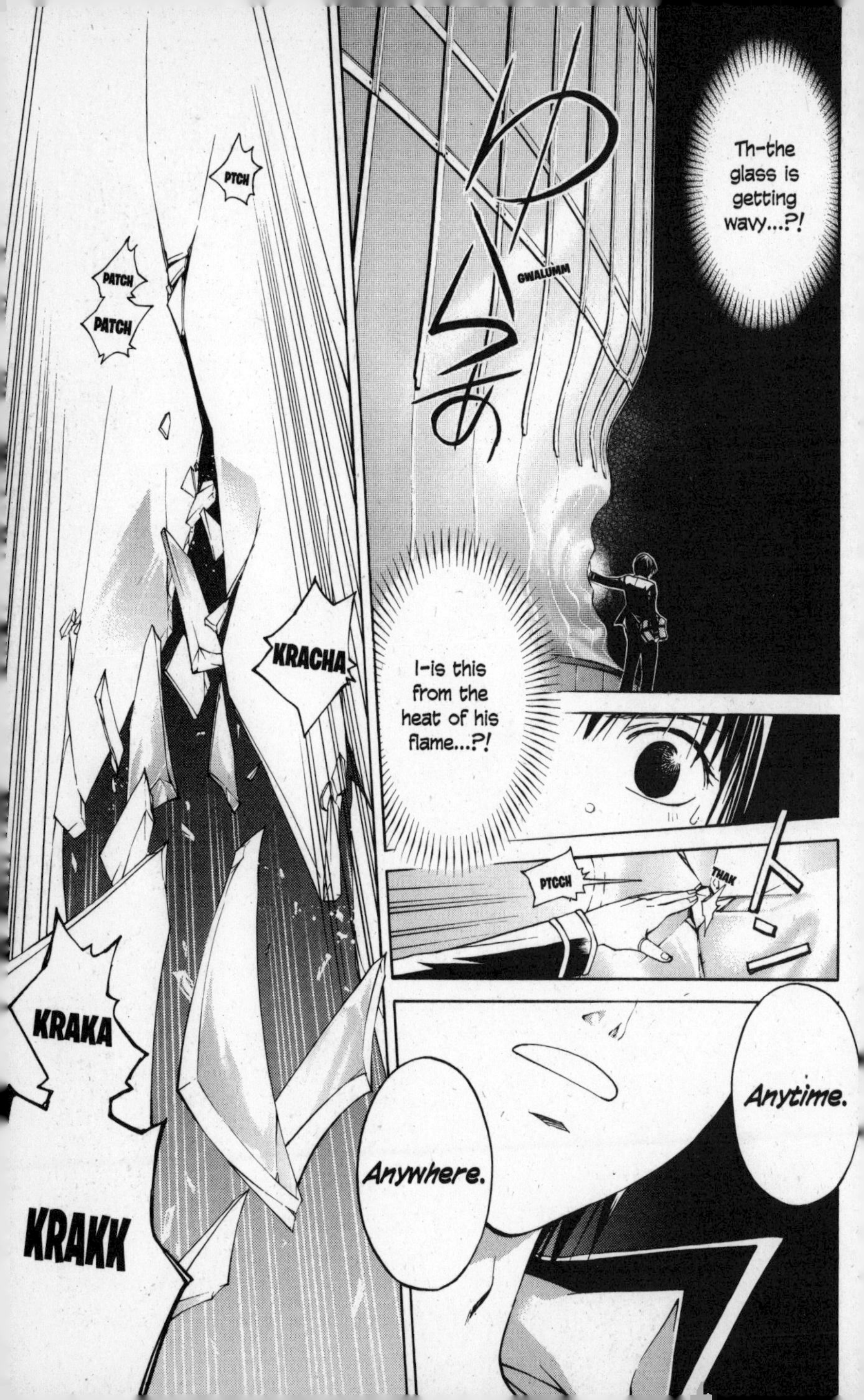
Th-the glass is getting wavy...?!
ゆらあ
GWALUMM
I-is this from the heat of his flame...?!
PTCCH
THAK
Anytime.
Anywhere.
PTCH
PATCH
PATCH
KRACHA
KRAKA
KRAKK

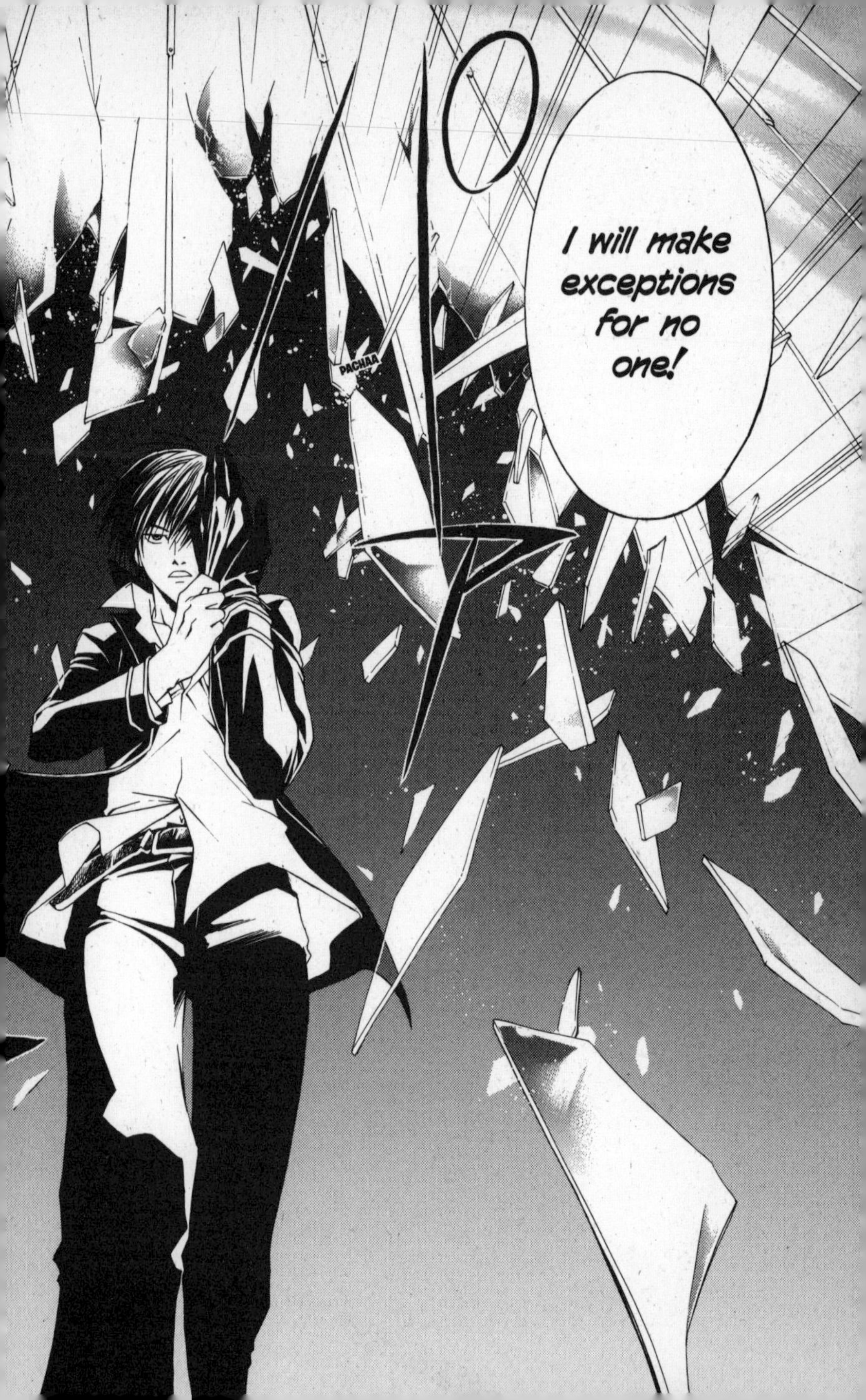
I will make exceptions for no one!
PACHAA

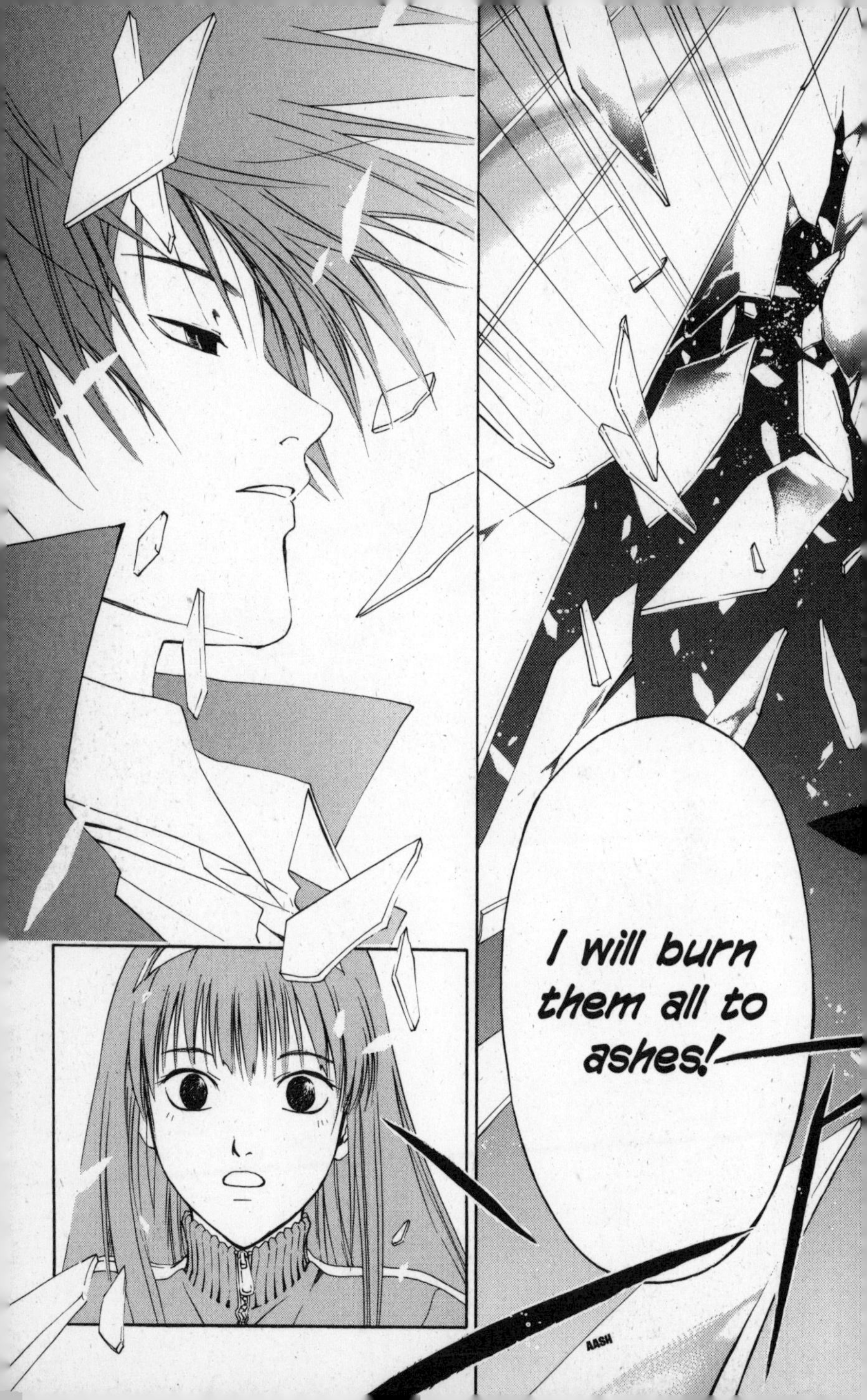
I will burn them all to ashes!
AASH

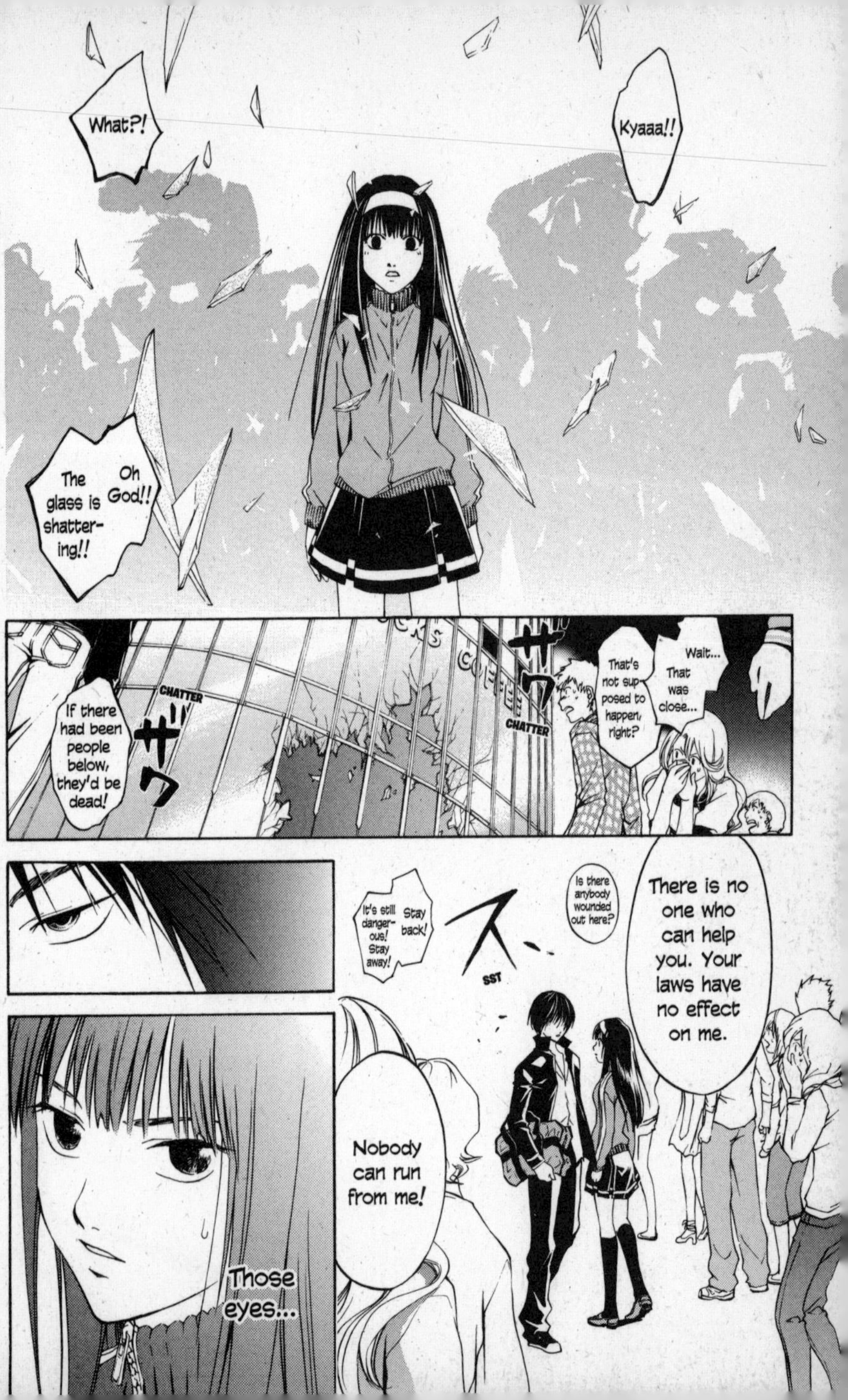
Kyaaa!!
What?!
Oh God!! The glass is shattering!!
Wait... That was close...
That's not supposed to happen, right?
CHATTER
CHATTER
If there had been people below, they'd be dead!
There is no one who can help you. Your laws have no effect on me.
Is there anybody wounded out here?
Stay back! It's still dangerous! Stay away!
SST
Nobody can run from me!
Those eyes...

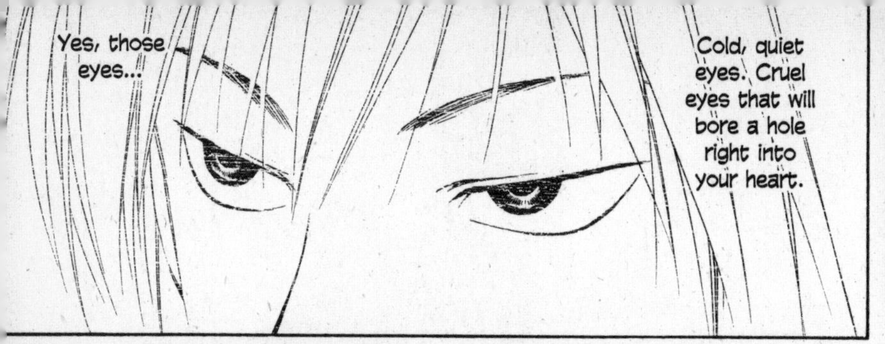
Cold, quiet eyes. Cruel eyes that will bore a hole right into your heart.
Yes, those eyes...
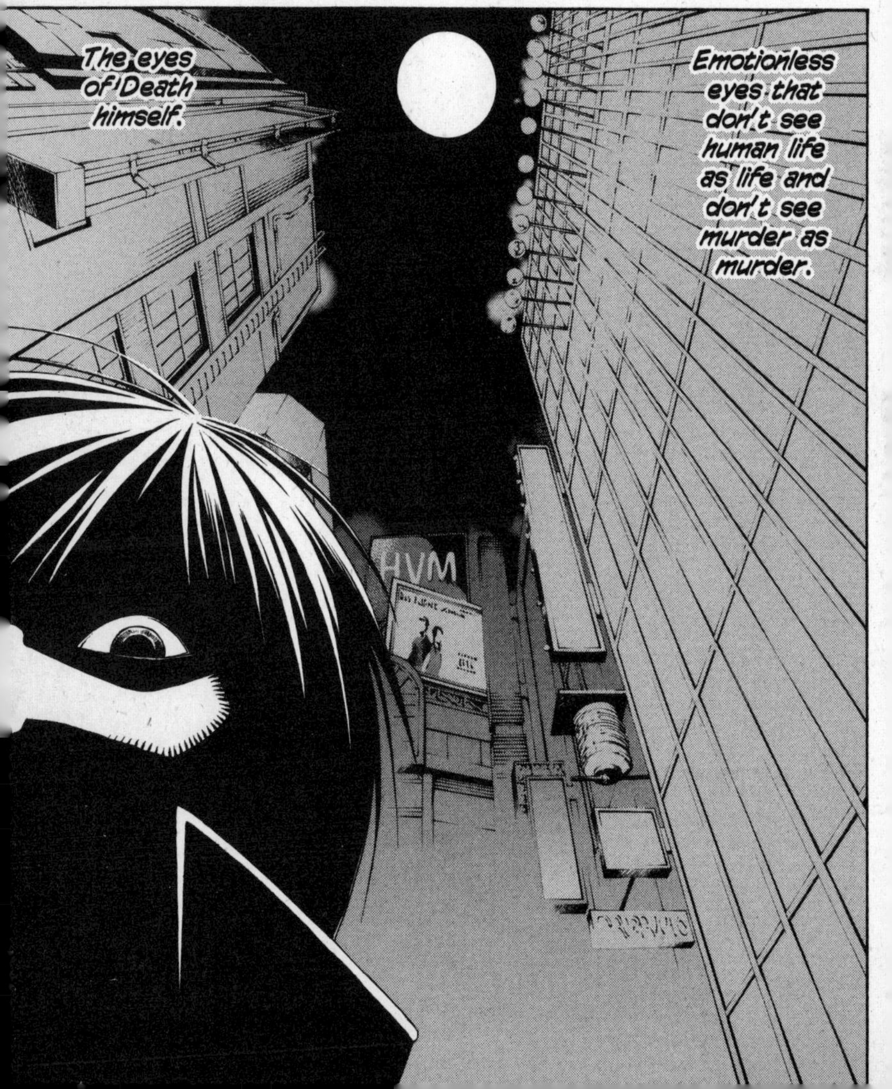
Emotionless eyes that don't see human life as life and don't see murder as murder.
The eyes of Death himself.
HVM

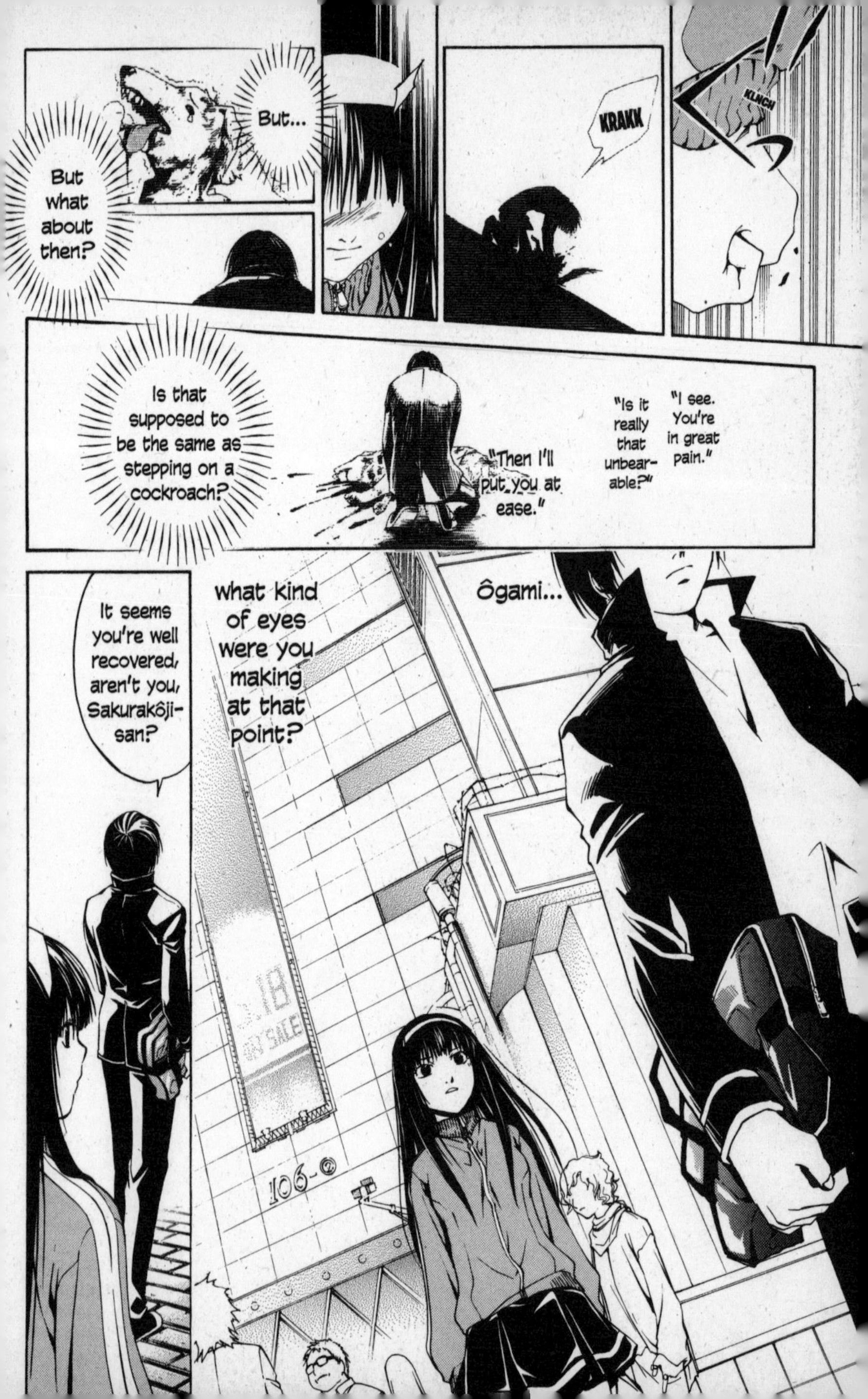
KLNCH
KRAKK
But...
But what about then?
"I see. You're in great pain."
"Is it really that unbearable?"
"Then I'll put you at ease."
Is that supposed to be the same as stepping on a cockroach?
Ôgami...
what kind of eyes were you making at that point?
It seems you're well recovered, aren't you, Sakurakôji-san?

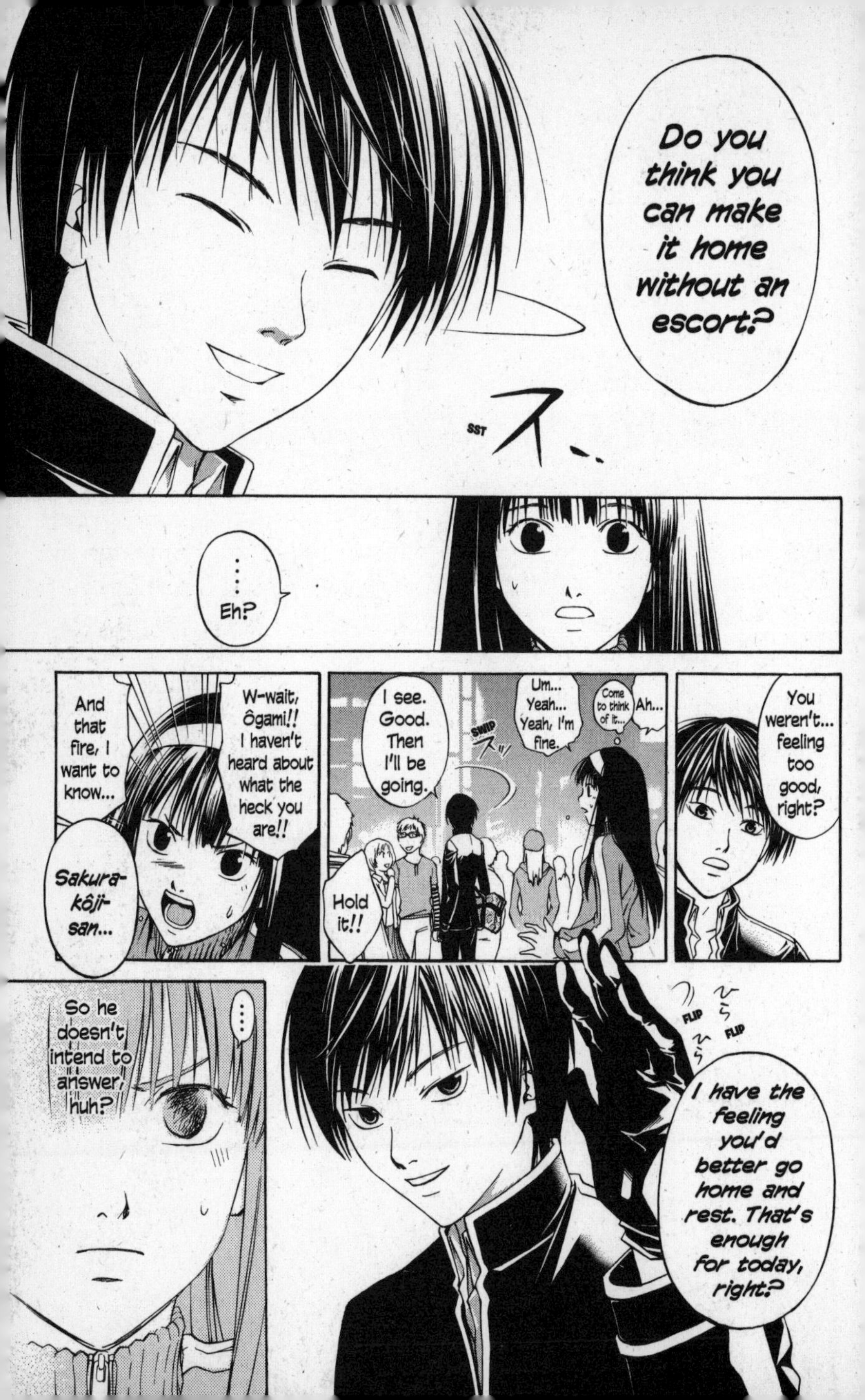
Do you think you can make it home without an escort?
SST
......
Eh?
You weren't... feeling too good, right?
Ah...
Come to think of it...
Um... Yeah... Yeah, I'm fine.
SWIP
I see. Good. Then I'll be going.
Hold it!!
W-wait, Ôgami!! I haven't heard about what the heck you are!!
And that fire, I want to know...
Sakura-kôji-san...
FLIP
FLIP
I have the feeling you'd better go home and rest. That's enough for today, right?
....
So he doesn't intend to answer, huh?

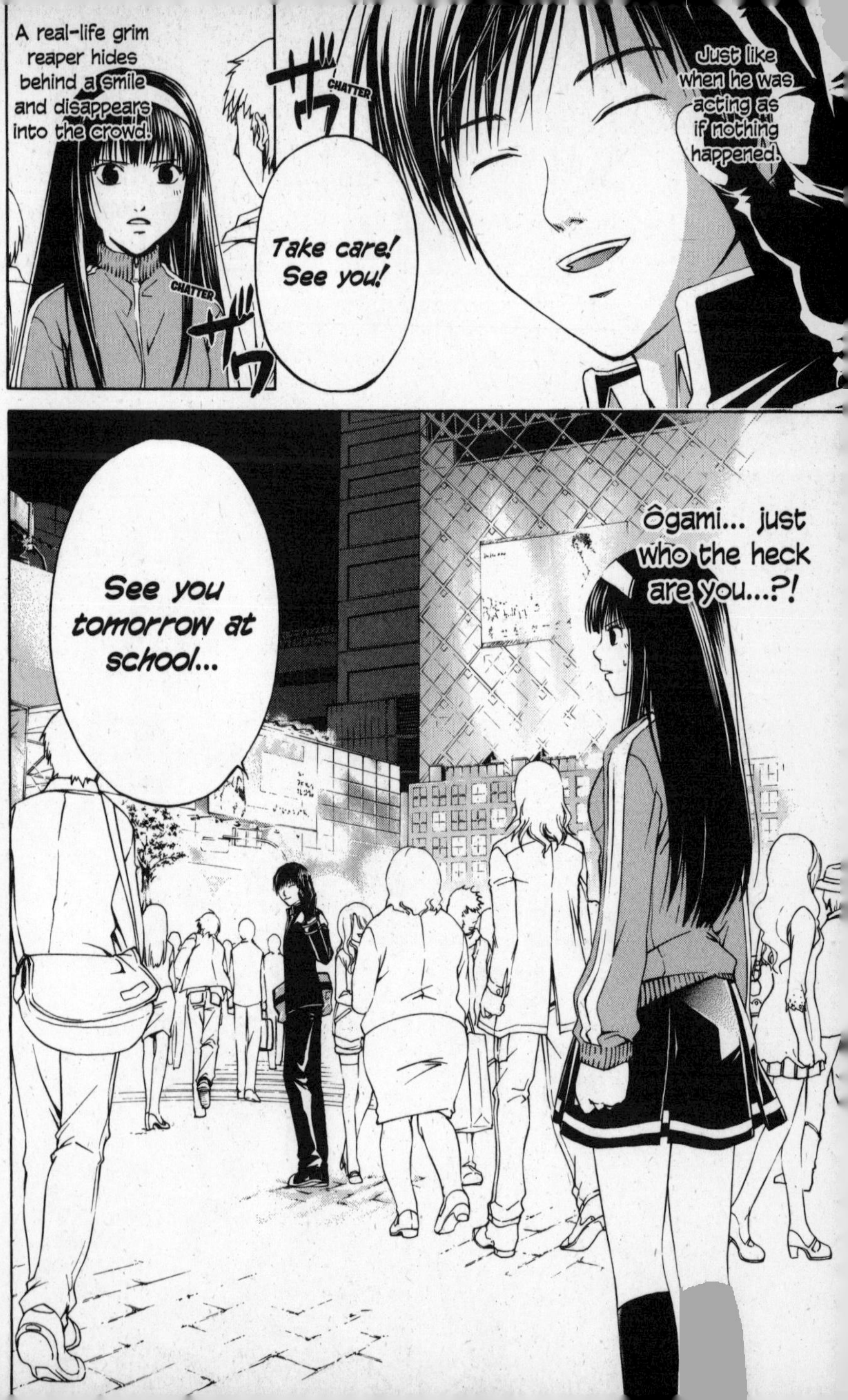
Just like when he was acting as if nothing happened.
Take care! See you!
CHATTER
A real-life grim reaper hides behind a smile and disappears into the crowd.
CHATTER
Ôgami... just who the heck are you...?!
See you tomorrow at school...

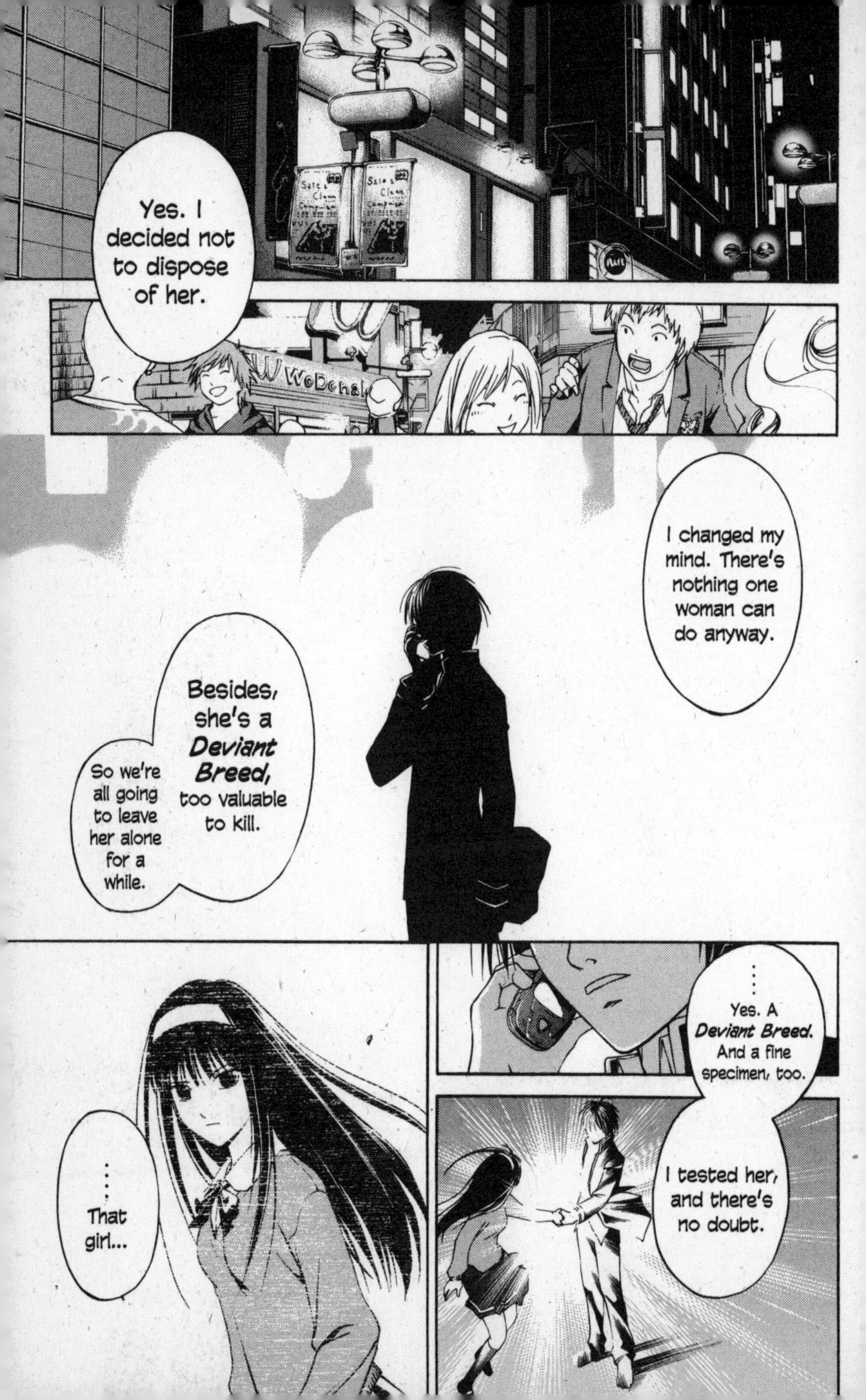
Yes. I decided not to dispose of her.
I changed my mind. There's nothing one woman can do anyway.
Besides, she's a *Deviant Breed,* too valuable to kill.
So we're all going to leave her alone for a while.
... Yes. A *Deviant Breed.* And a fine specimen, too.
I tested her, and there's no doubt.
... That girl...

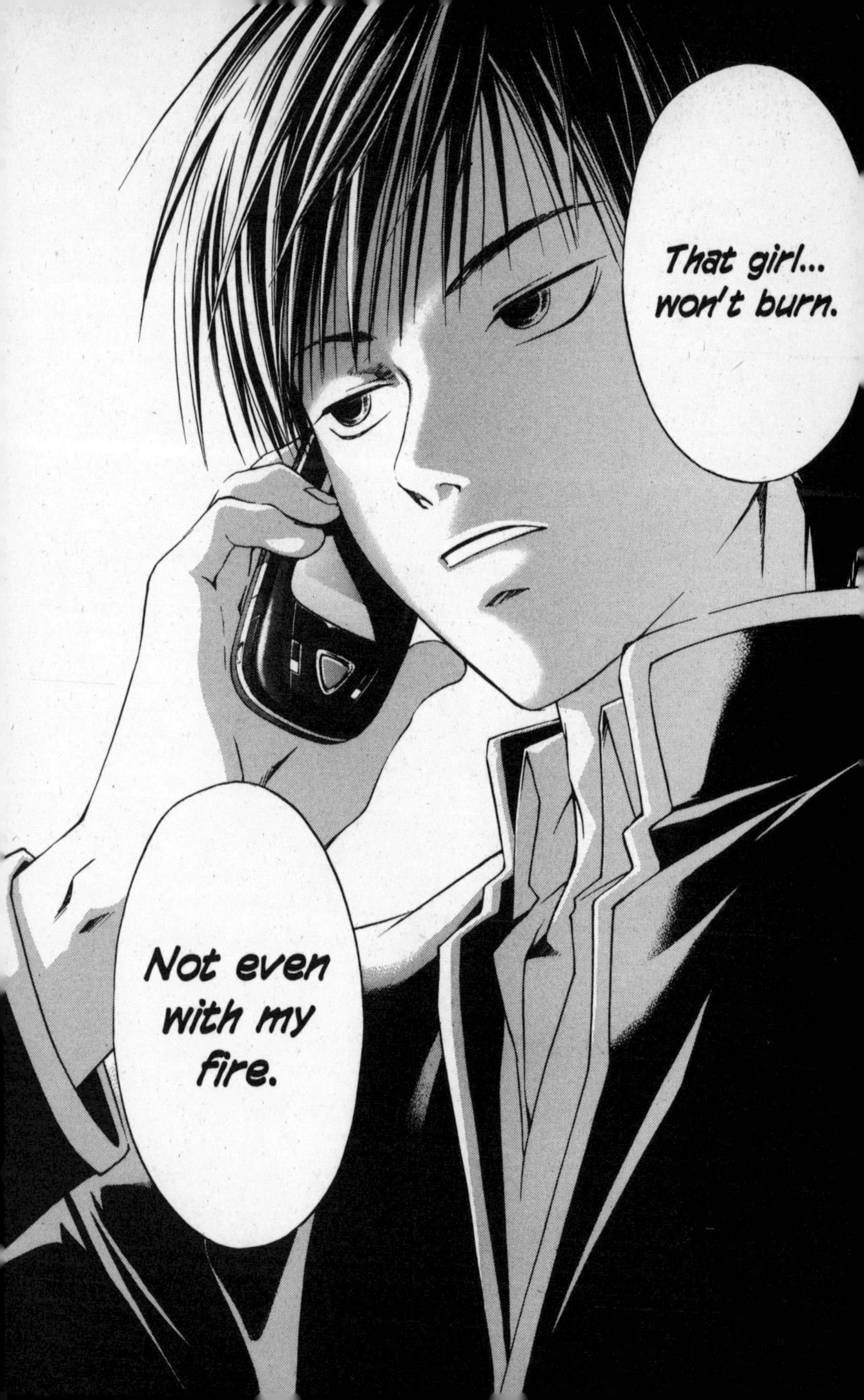
That girl... won't burn.
Not even with my fire.

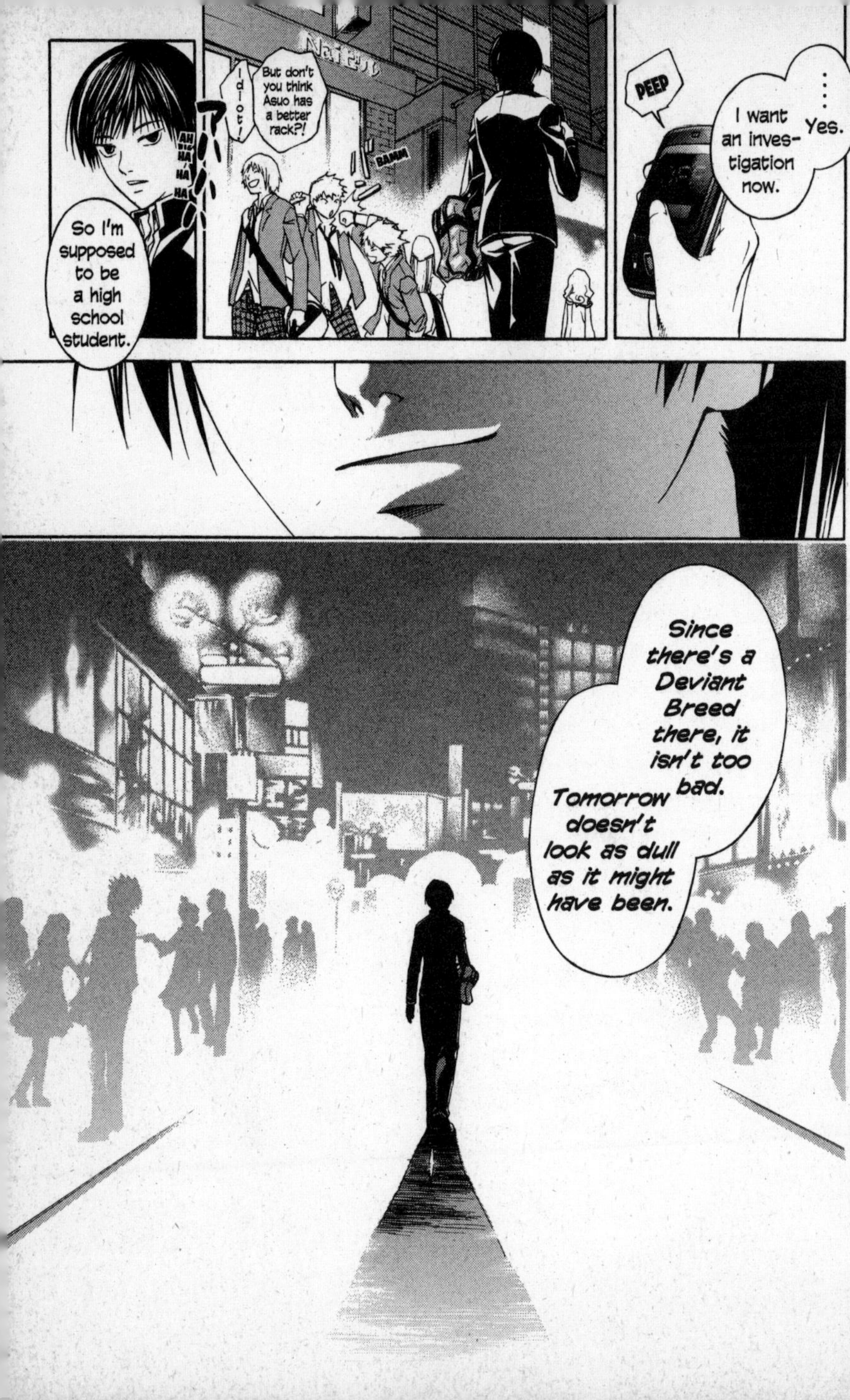

.... Yes.
I want an investigation now.
PEEP
But don't you think Asuo has a better rack?!
Idiot!
BAMM
AH HA HA HA
So I'm supposed to be a high school student.
Since there's a Deviant Breed there, it isn't too bad.
Tomorrow doesn't look as dull as it might have been.

Kamijyo Info

Yo! It's Akimine Kamijyo! Nice to meet you! I want to take this opportunity to thank you for picking up *Code:Breaker*, volume 1! And if you have fun reading it, that would make me very happy!

This manga falls right into the genre of the Dark Hero. But these days, the term "Dark Hero" is rather vague and undefined, or at least that's how Kamijyo thinks of it.

Whether you agree or disagree with the opinions of Ôgami or Sakura or any of the other characters is strictly up to you! My intention is to draw my stories without succumbing to one particular position.

There are three themes to this Code: Breaker manga. But they'll remain a secret for now!! I have the feeling that the readers will have no problem picking up on them from the manga.

Ôgami Mystery

The transfer student, Rei Ôgami is a little mysterious.
Maeshun (Maeda), a classmate from 1-B.
WHOOSH
Heh! I can do the glove thing, too!
Just wait for the introduction of Maeshun and other 1-B classmates in Volume 2!
That's what happens when you wear a glove for a year without a rest!
AAAN
MWAA
Whoa, Maeshun! That stinks of old sweat!
And the Ôgami mystery deepens even further.
How does he keep his gloves from stinking?
MWAAN

← Continued on P.197

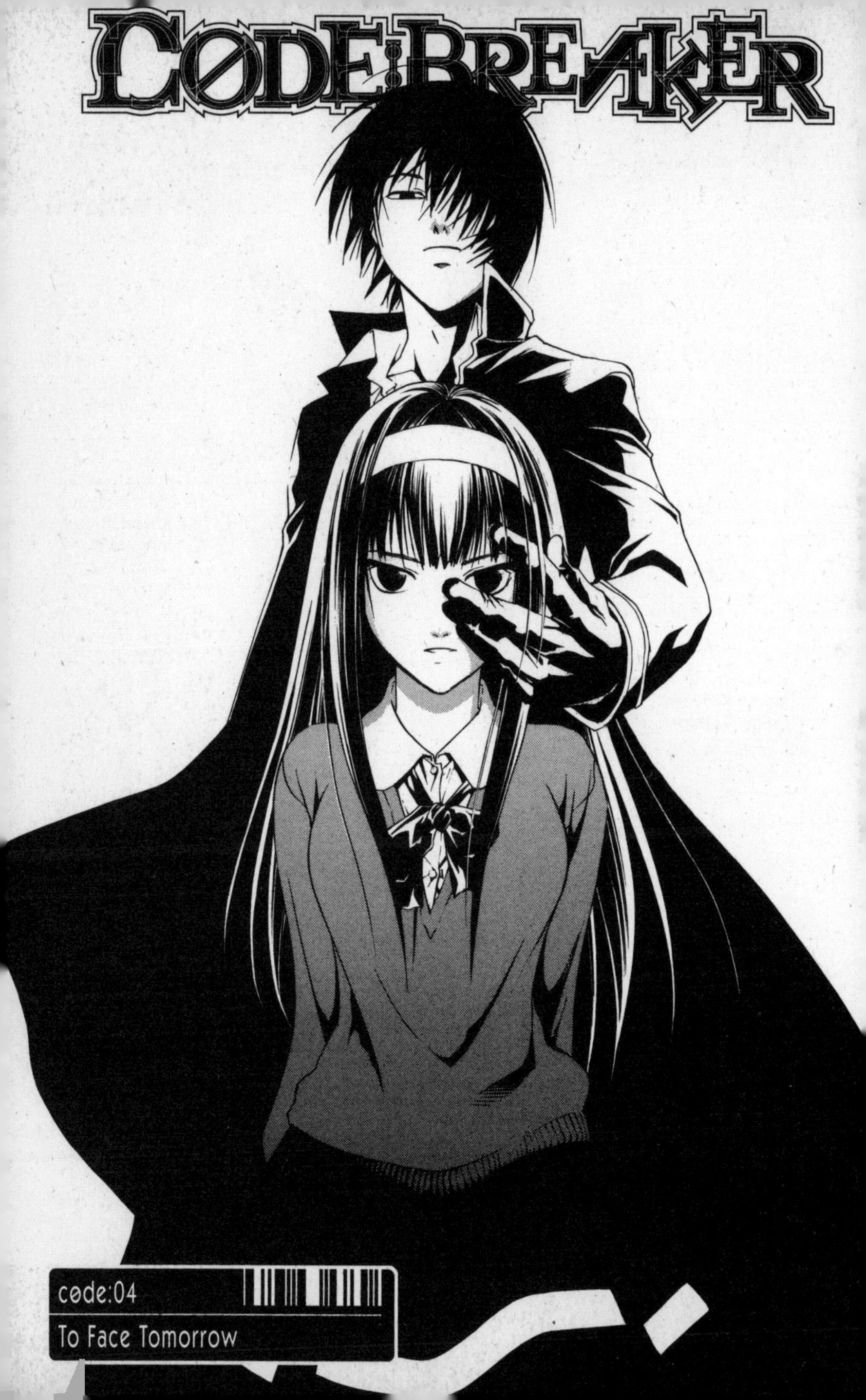
CODE:BREAKER
code:04
To Face Tomorrow

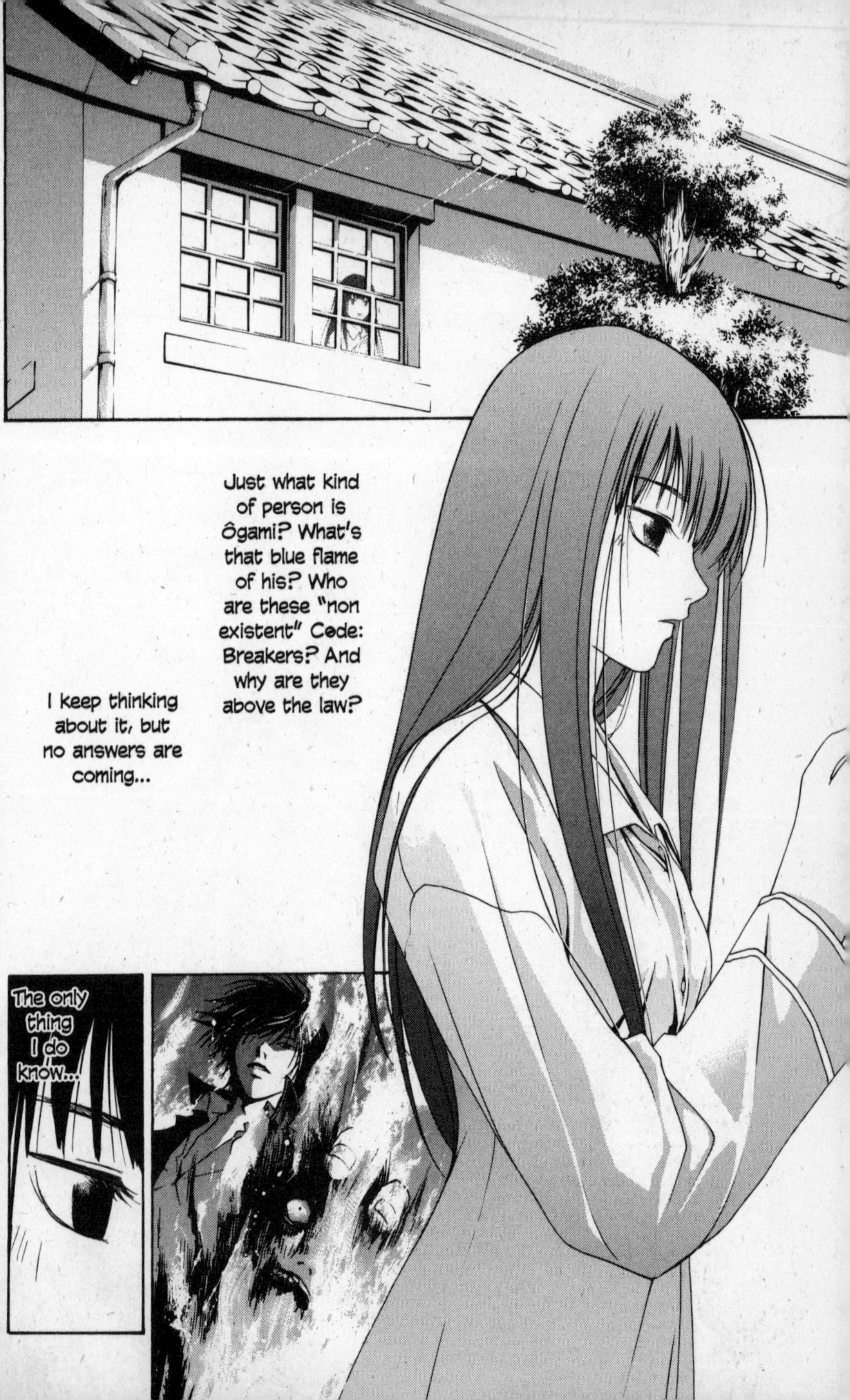
Just what kind of person is Ôgami? What's that blue flame of his? Who are these "non existent" Code: Breakers? And why are they above the law?
I keep thinking about it, but no answers are coming...
The only thing I do know...

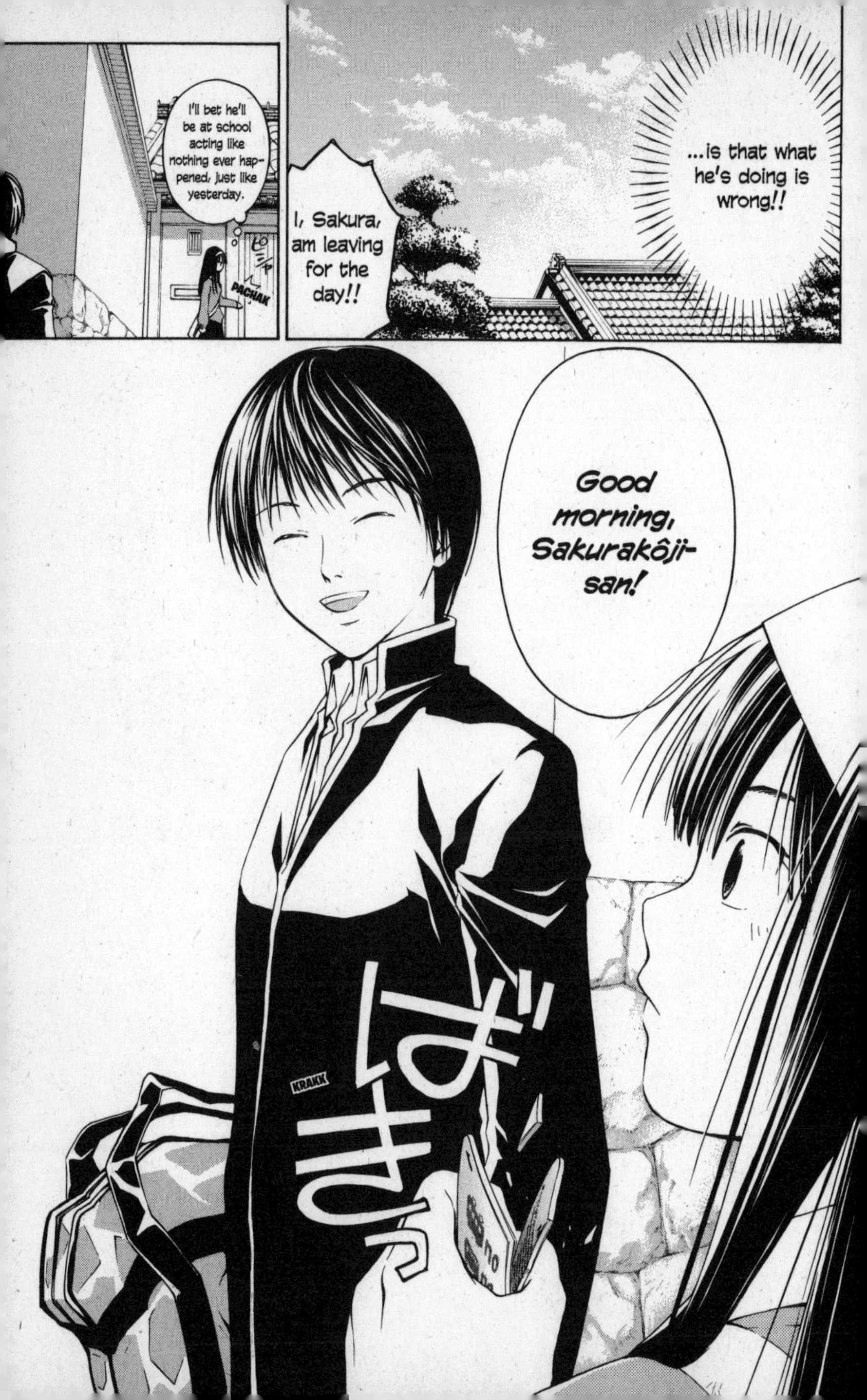
...is that what he's doing is wrong!!
I, Sakura, am leaving for the day!!
I'll bet he'll be at school acting like nothing ever hap-pened, just like yesterday.
PACHAK
Good morning, Sakurakôji-san!
KRAKK
ぼきっ

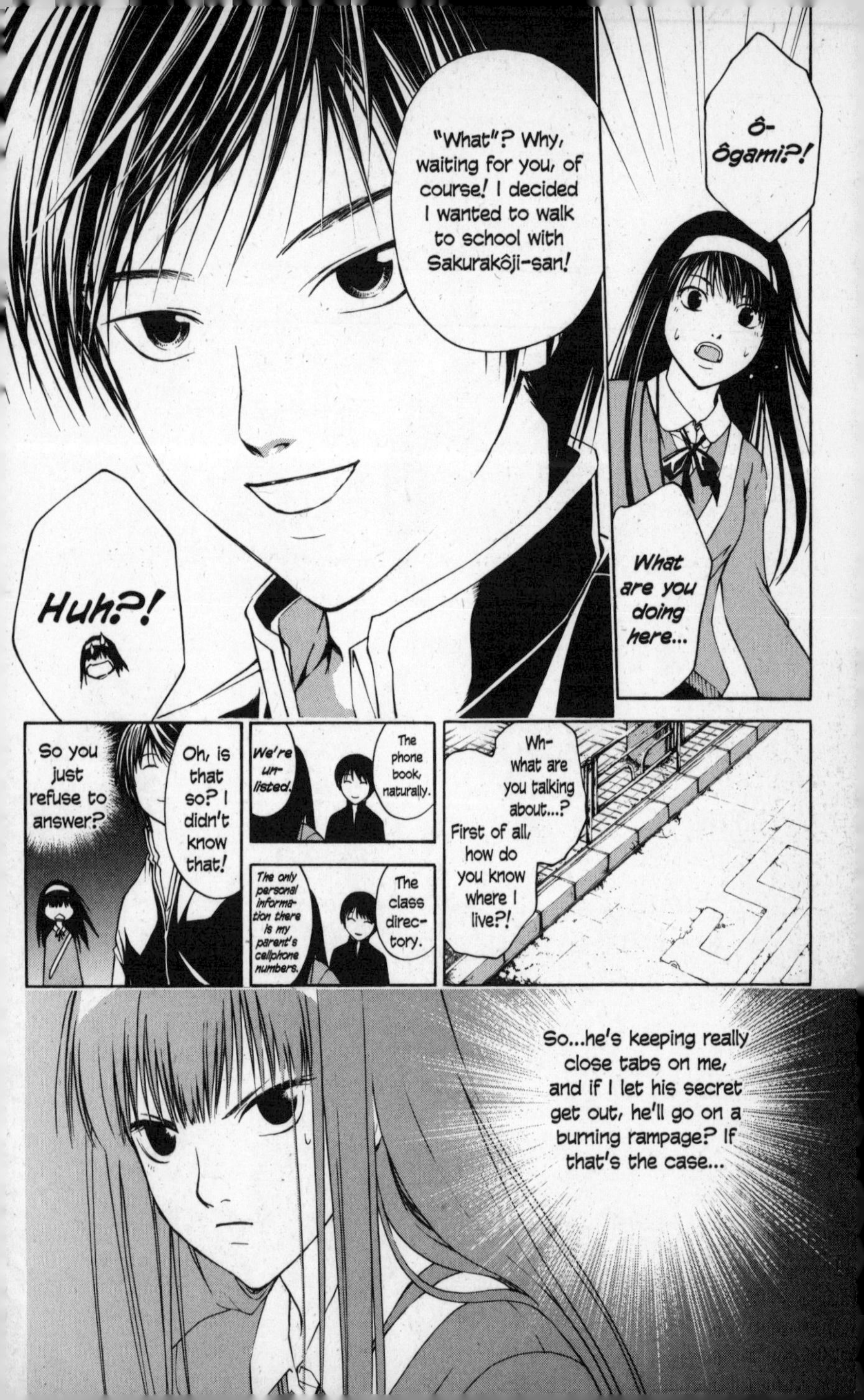
Ô-ôgami?!
What are you doing here...
"What"? Why, waiting for you, of course! I decided I wanted to walk to school with Sakurakôji-san!
Huh?!
Wh- what are you talking about...? First of all, how do you know where I live?!
The phone book, naturally.
We're un-listed.
The class directory.
The only personal information there is my parent's cellphone numbers.
Oh, is that so? I didn't know that!
So you just refuse to answer?
So...he's keeping really close tabs on me, and if I let his secret get out, he'll go on a burning rampage? If that's the case...

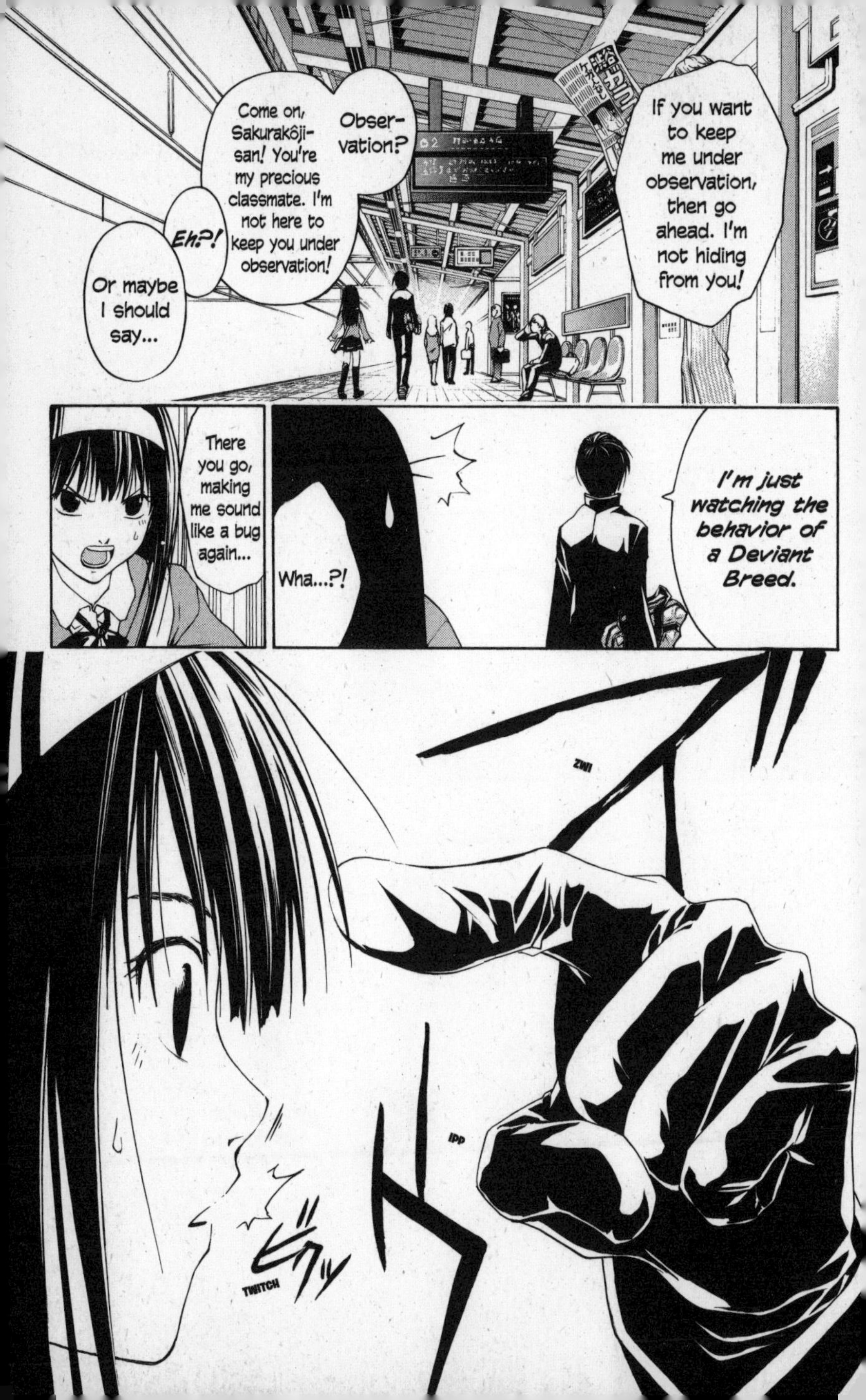
If you want to keep me under observation, then go ahead. I'm not hiding from you!
Observation?
Come on, Sakurakôji-san! You're my precious classmate. I'm not here to keep you under observation!
Eh?!
Or maybe I should say...
I'm just watching the behavior of a Deviant Breed.
Wha...?!
There you go, making me sound like a bug again...
ZWI
IPP
TWITCH

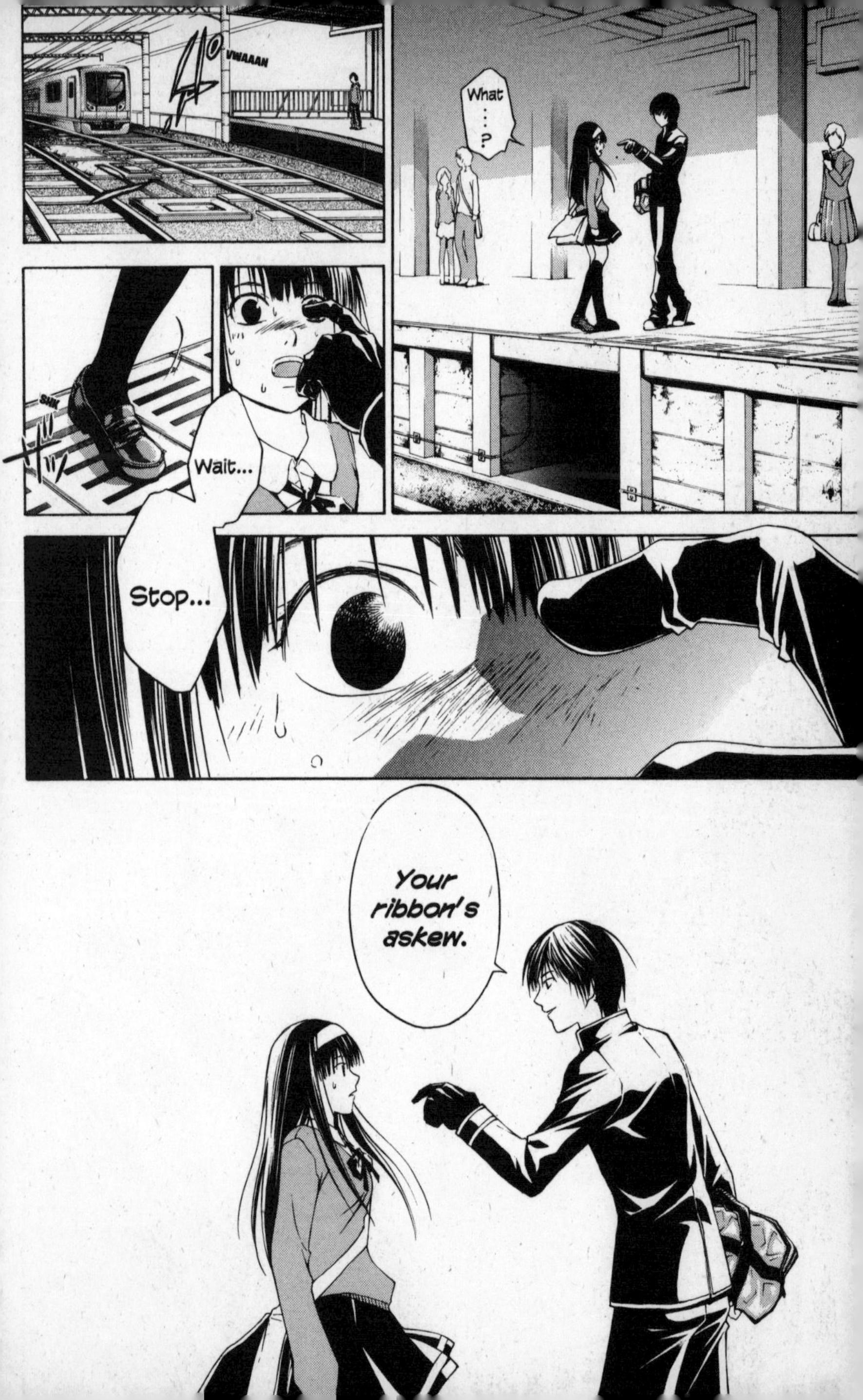
What...?
VWAAAN
Wait...
SHK
Stop...
Your ribbon's askew.

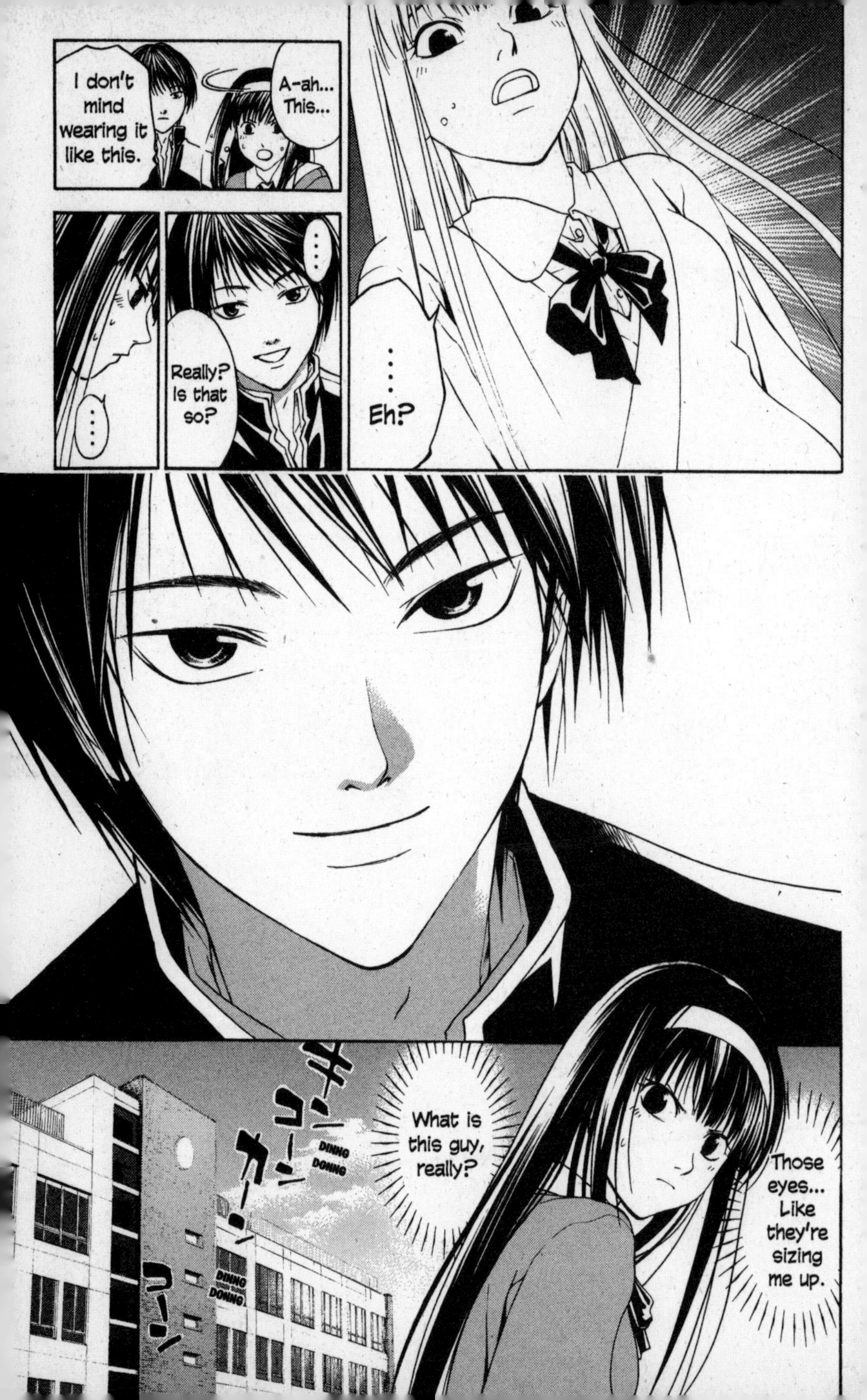
....
Eh?
A-ah... This...
I don't mind wearing it like this.
....
Really? Is that so?
....
Those eyes... Like they're sizing me up.
What is this guy, really?
DINNG DONNG
DINNG DONNG

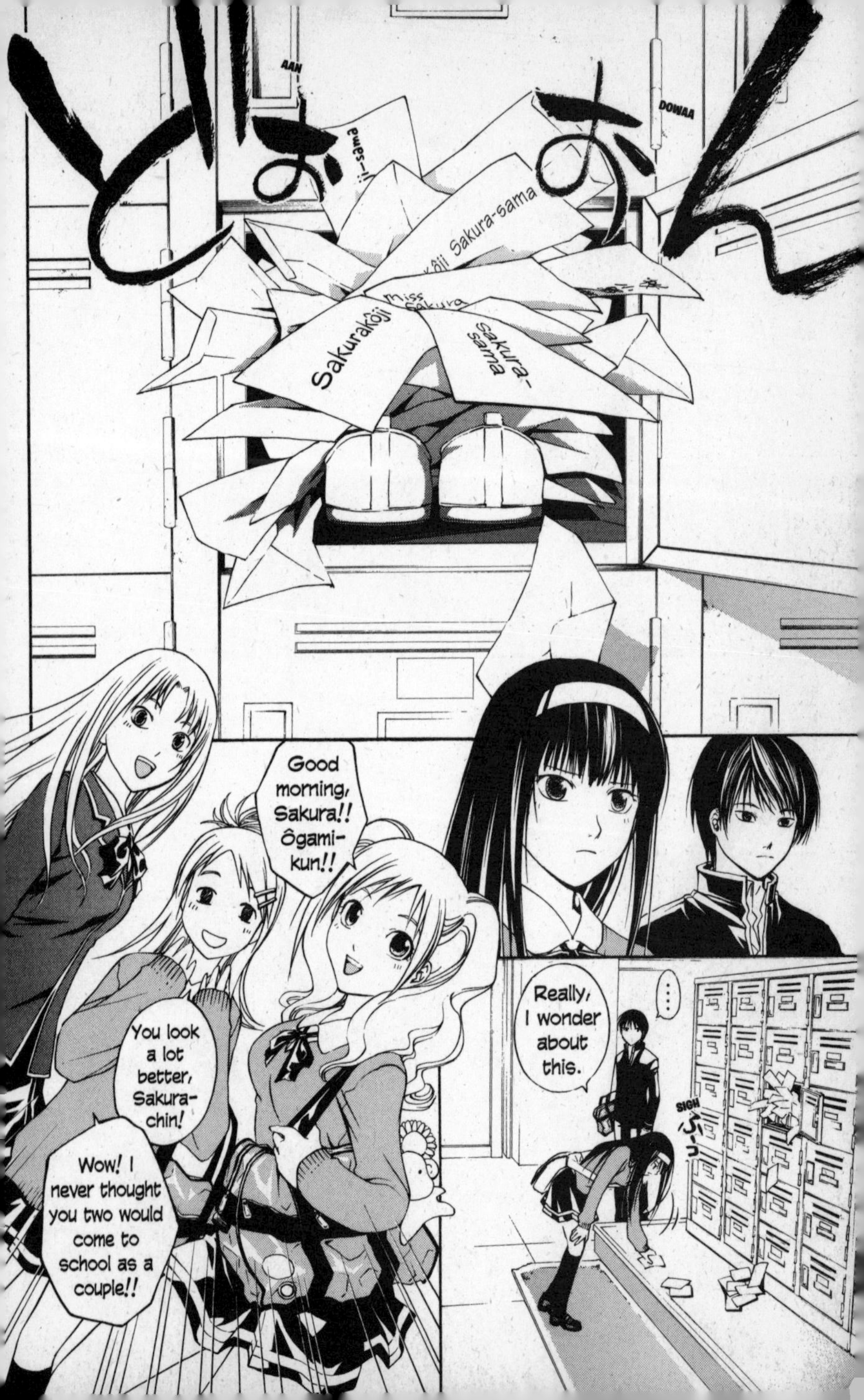

DOWAA
AAN
ji-sama
Sakura-sama
kōji Sakura-sama
Miss Sakura
Sakurakōji
Sakura-sama
. . .
Really, I wonder about this.
SIGH
Good morning, Sakura!! Ôgami-kun!!
You look a lot better, Sakura-chin!
Wow! I never thought you two would come to school as a couple!!

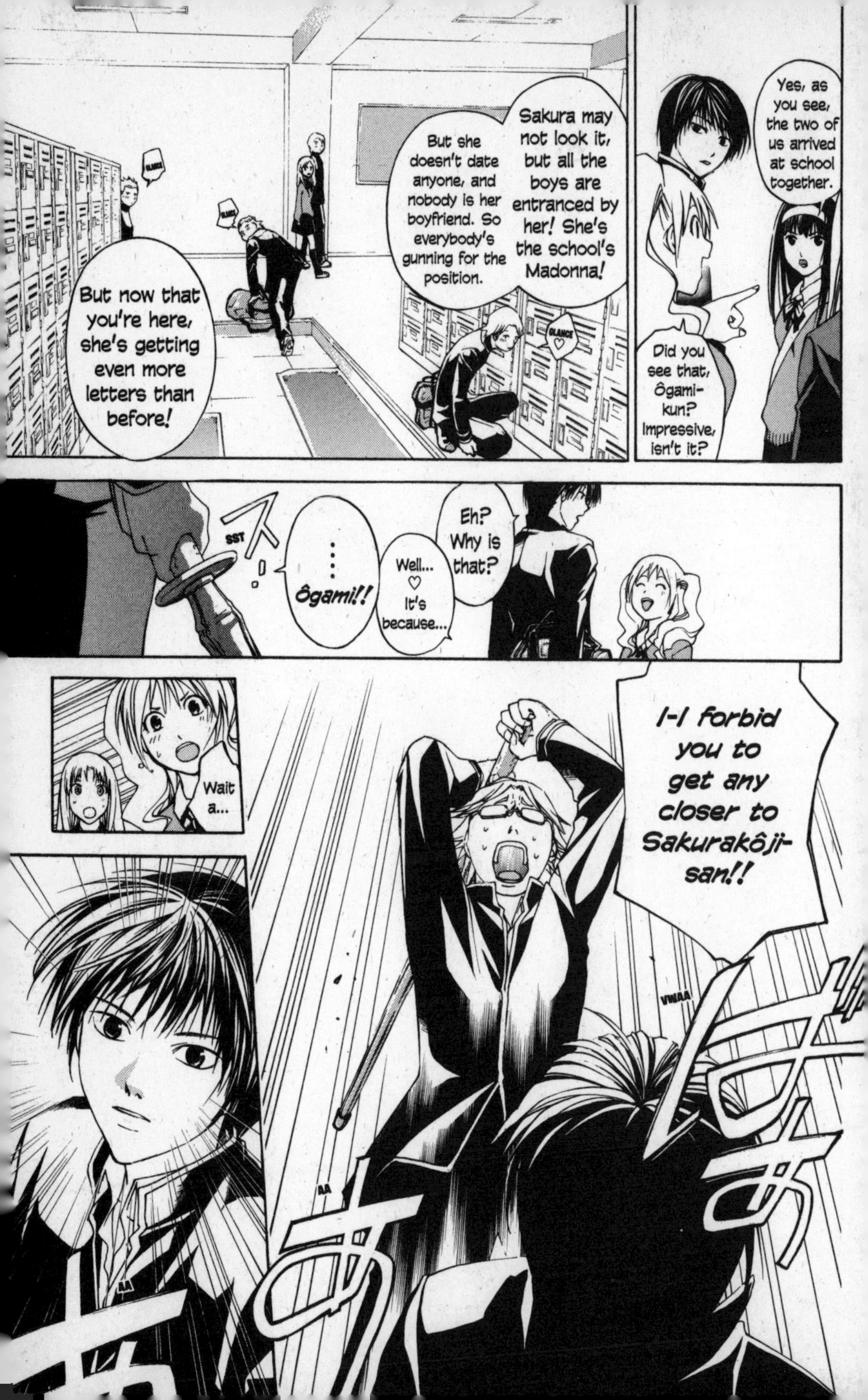
Yes, as you see, the two of us arrived at school together.
Did you see that, Ôgami-kun? Impressive, isn't it?
Sakura may not look it, but all the boys are entranced by her! She's the school's Madonna!
But she doesn't date anyone, and nobody is her boyfriend. So everybody's gunning for the position.
GLANCE
GLANCE
GLANCE
GLANCE
But now that you're here, she's getting even more letters than before!
Eh? Why is that?
Well... ♡ It's because...
...Ôgami!!
SST
I-I forbid you to get any closer to Sakurakôji-san!!
Wait a...
VWAA
AA
AA

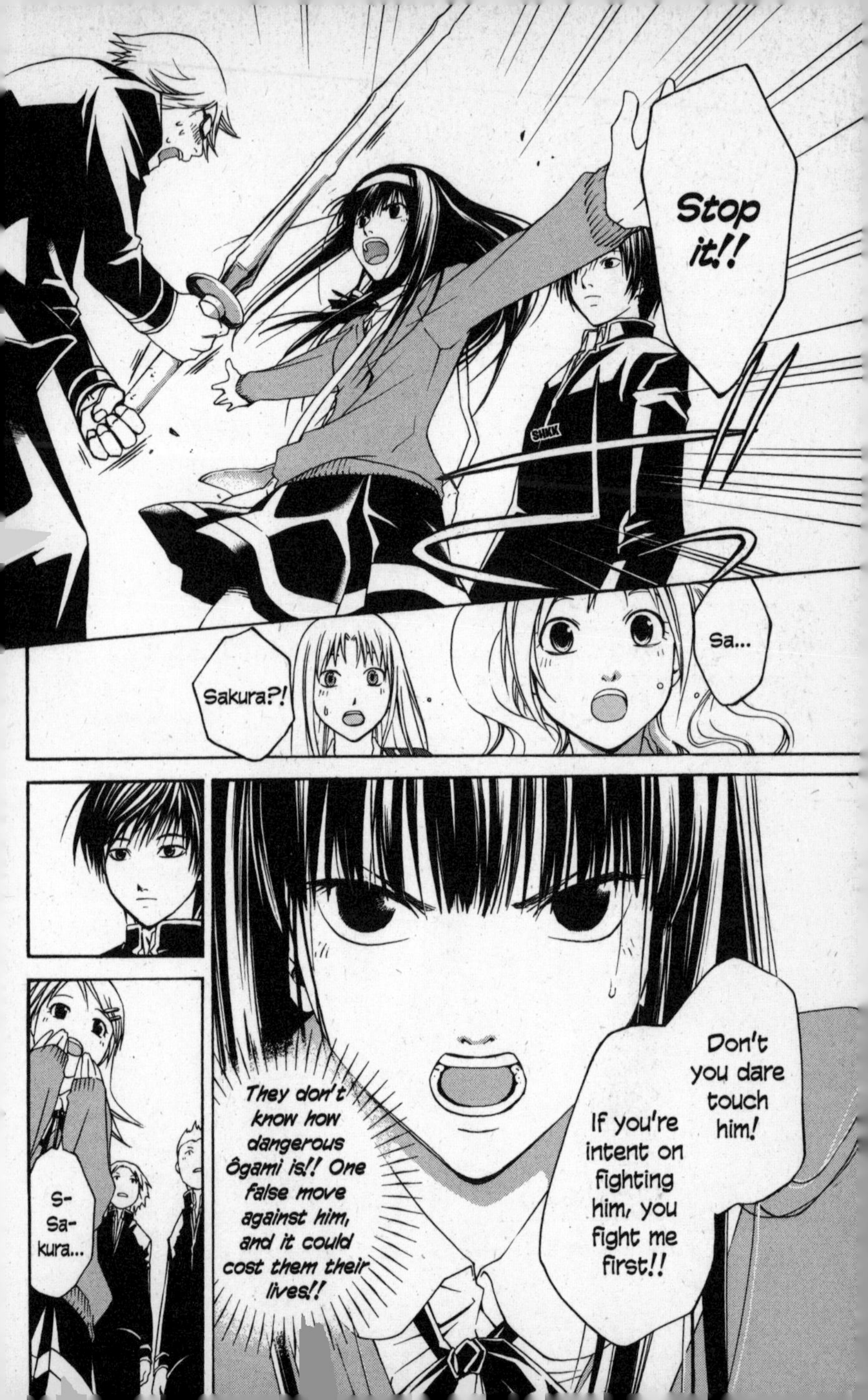
Stop it!!
SHKK
Sa...
Sakura?!
Don't you dare touch him!
If you're intent on fighting him, you fight me first!!
They don't know how dangerous Ôgami is!! One false move against him, and it could cost them their lives!!
S-Sa-kura...

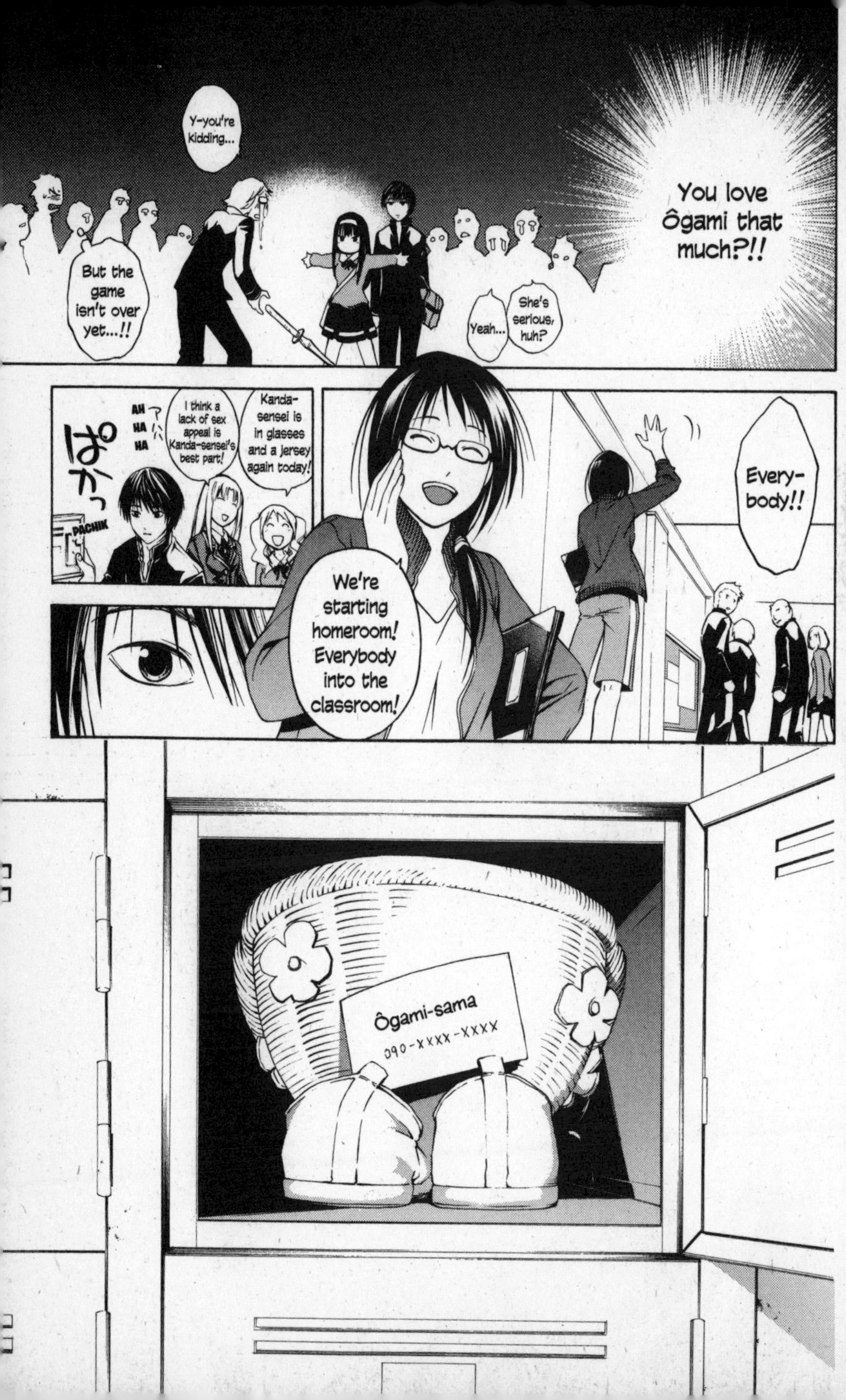
You love Ôgami that much?!!
She's serious, huh?
Yeah...
Y-you're kidding...
But the game isn't over yet...!!
Every-body!!
We're starting homeroom! Everybody into the classroom!
Kanda-sensei is in glasses and a jersey again today!
I think a lack of sex appeal is Kanda-sensei's best part!
アハハ
AH HA HA
ぱかっ
PACHIK
Ôgami-sama
090-XXXX-XXXX

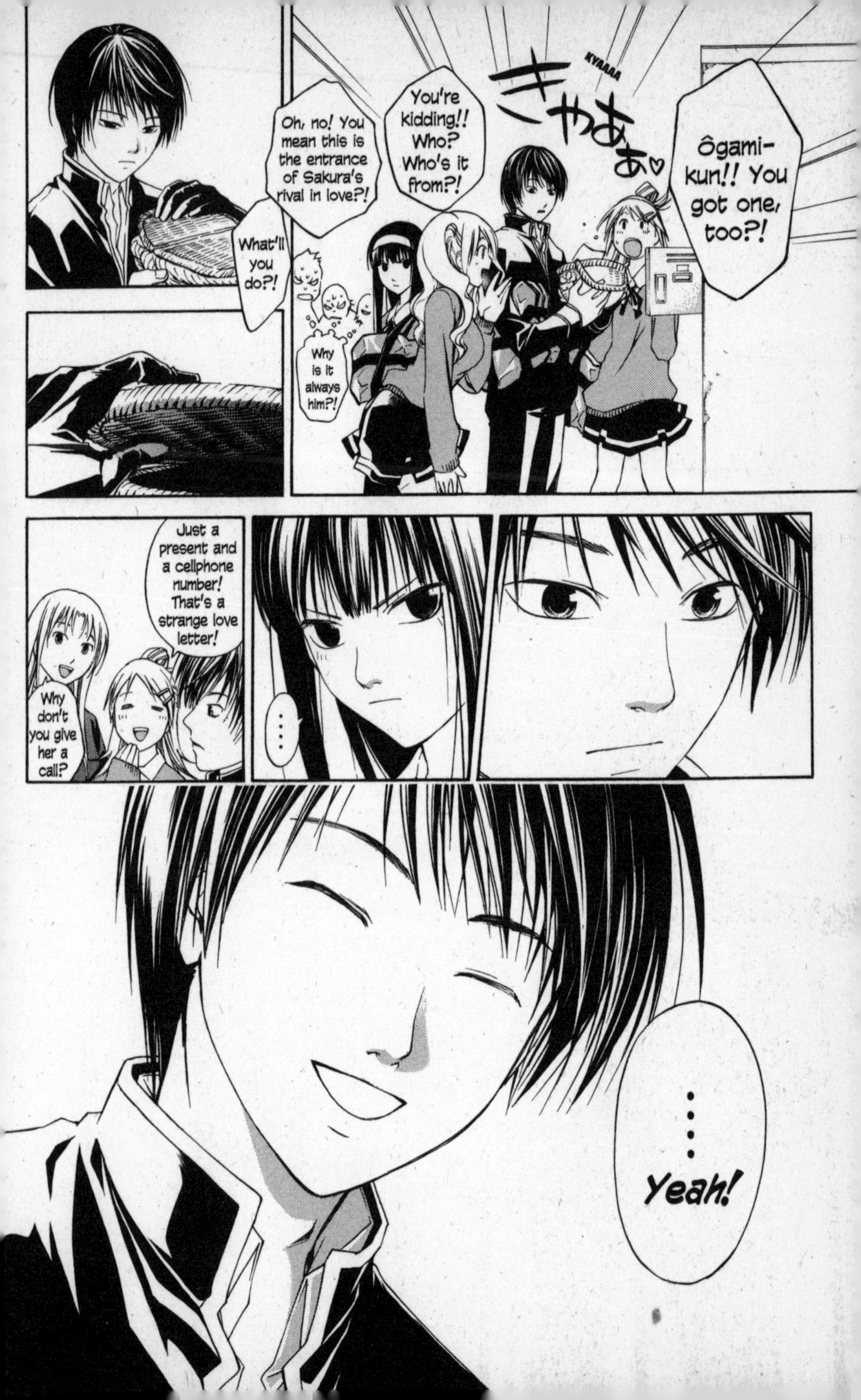
Ôgami-kun!! You got one, too?!
きゃああ♡
KYAAAA
You're kidding!! Who? Who's it from?!
Oh, no! You mean this is the entrance of Sakura's rival in love?!
What'll you do?!
Why is it always him?!
....
Just a present and a cellphone number! That's a strange love letter!
Why don't you give her a call?
....
Yeah!

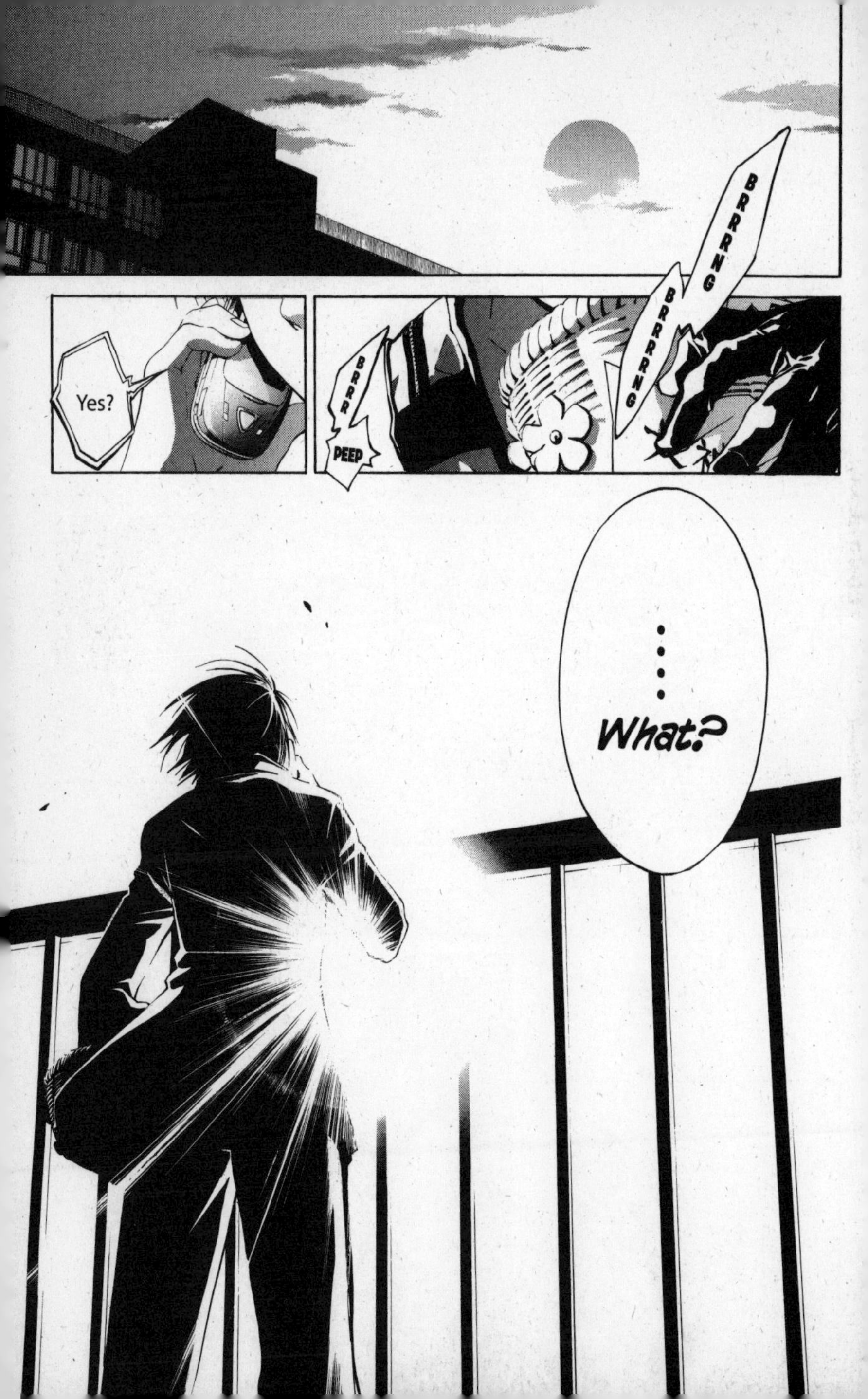
BRRRRNG
BRRRRRNG
BRRR
PEEP
Yes?
....
What?

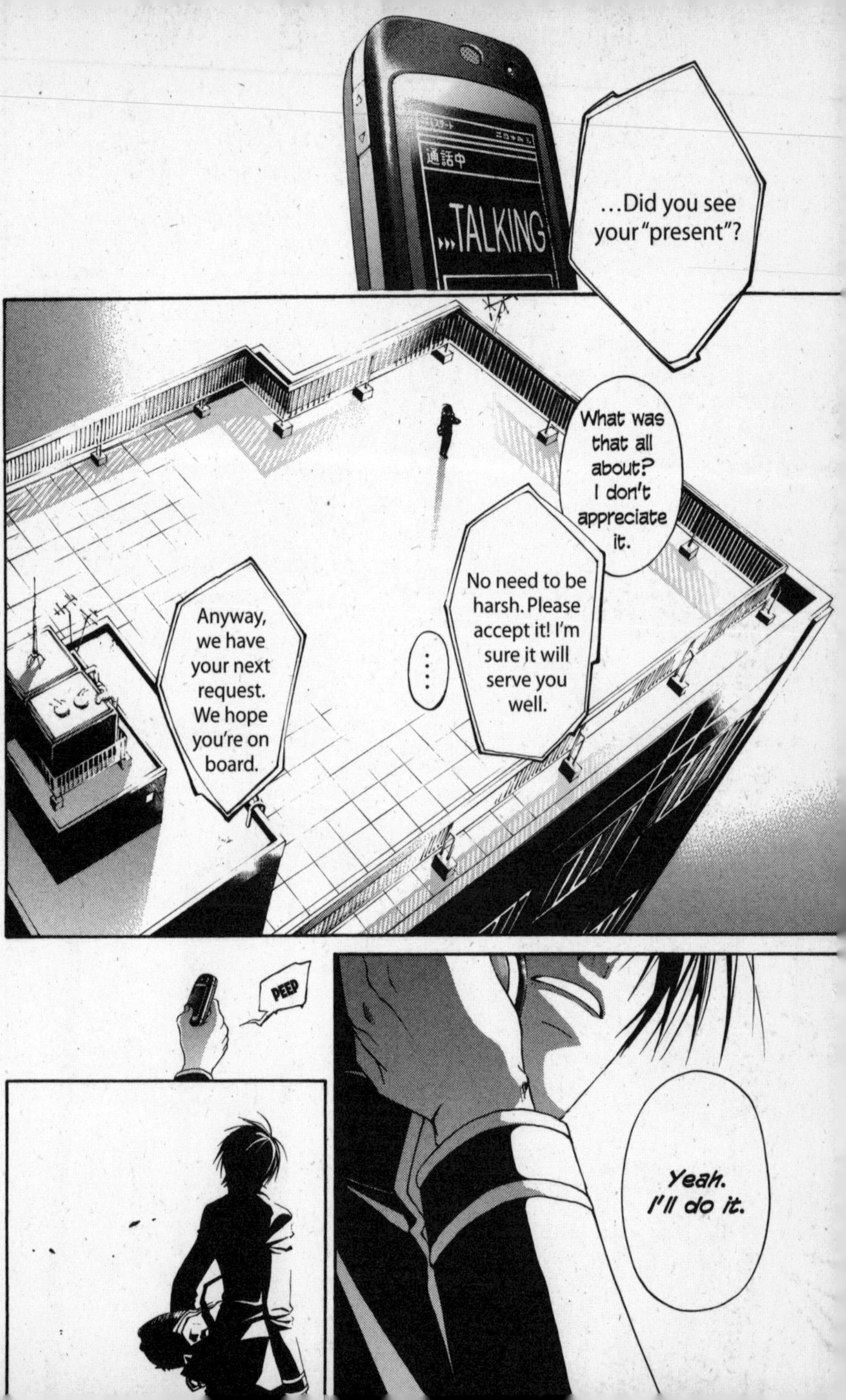
通話中
...TALKING
...Did you see your "present"?
What was that all about? I don't appreciate it.
No need to be harsh. Please accept it! I'm sure it will serve you well.
....
Anyway, we have your next request. We hope you're on board.
Yeah. I'll do it.
PEEP

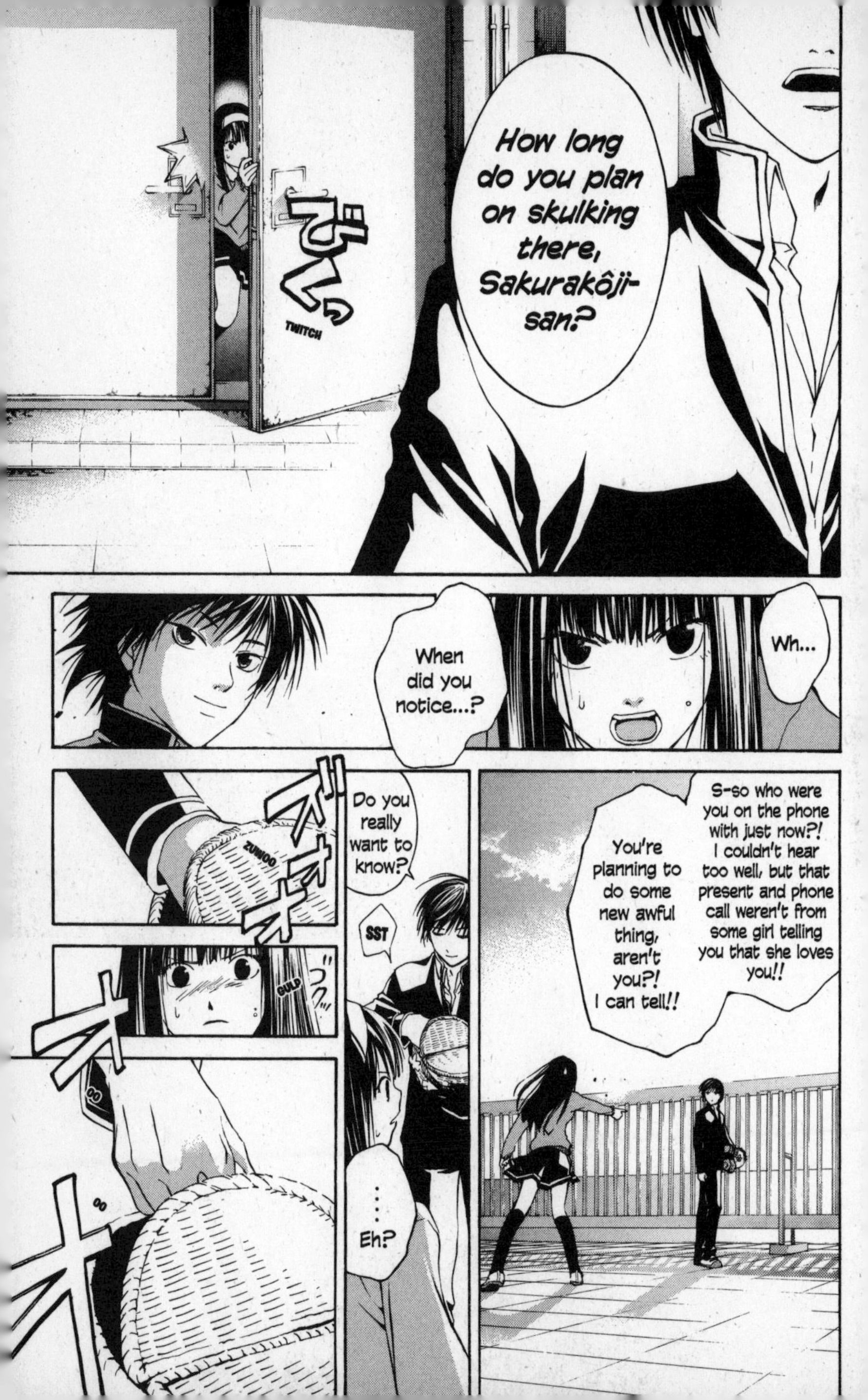
How long do you plan on skulking there, Sakurakôji-san?
TWITCH
Wh...
When did you notice...?
S-so who were you on the phone with just now?! I couldn't hear too well, but that present and phone call weren't from some girl telling you that she loves you!!
You're planning to do some new awful thing, aren't you?! I can tell!!
Do you really want to know?
ZUMOO
SST
GULP
...Eh?

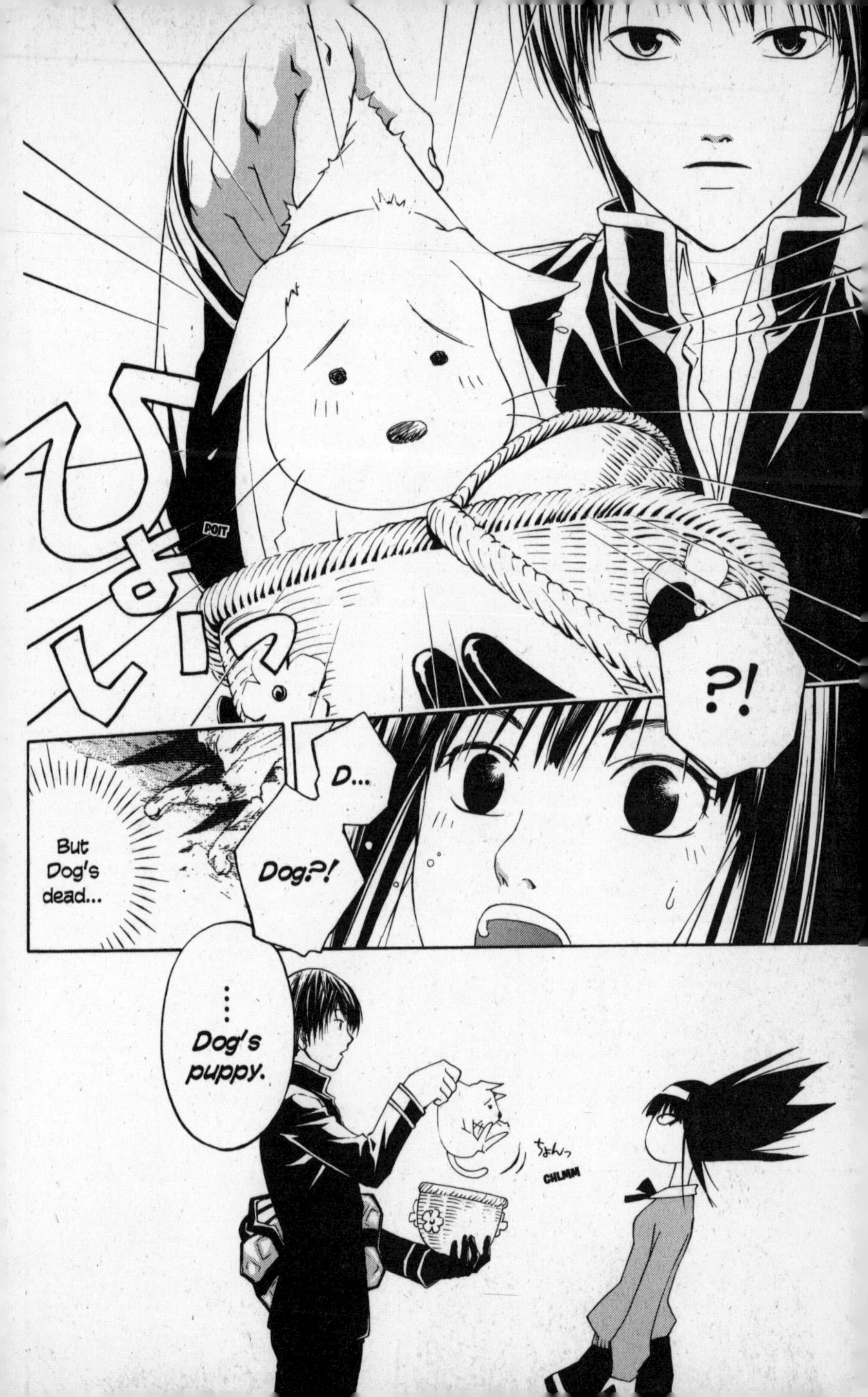
?!
ひょいっ
POIT
D...
Dog?!
But Dog's dead...
... Dog's puppy.
ちょんっ
CHLMM

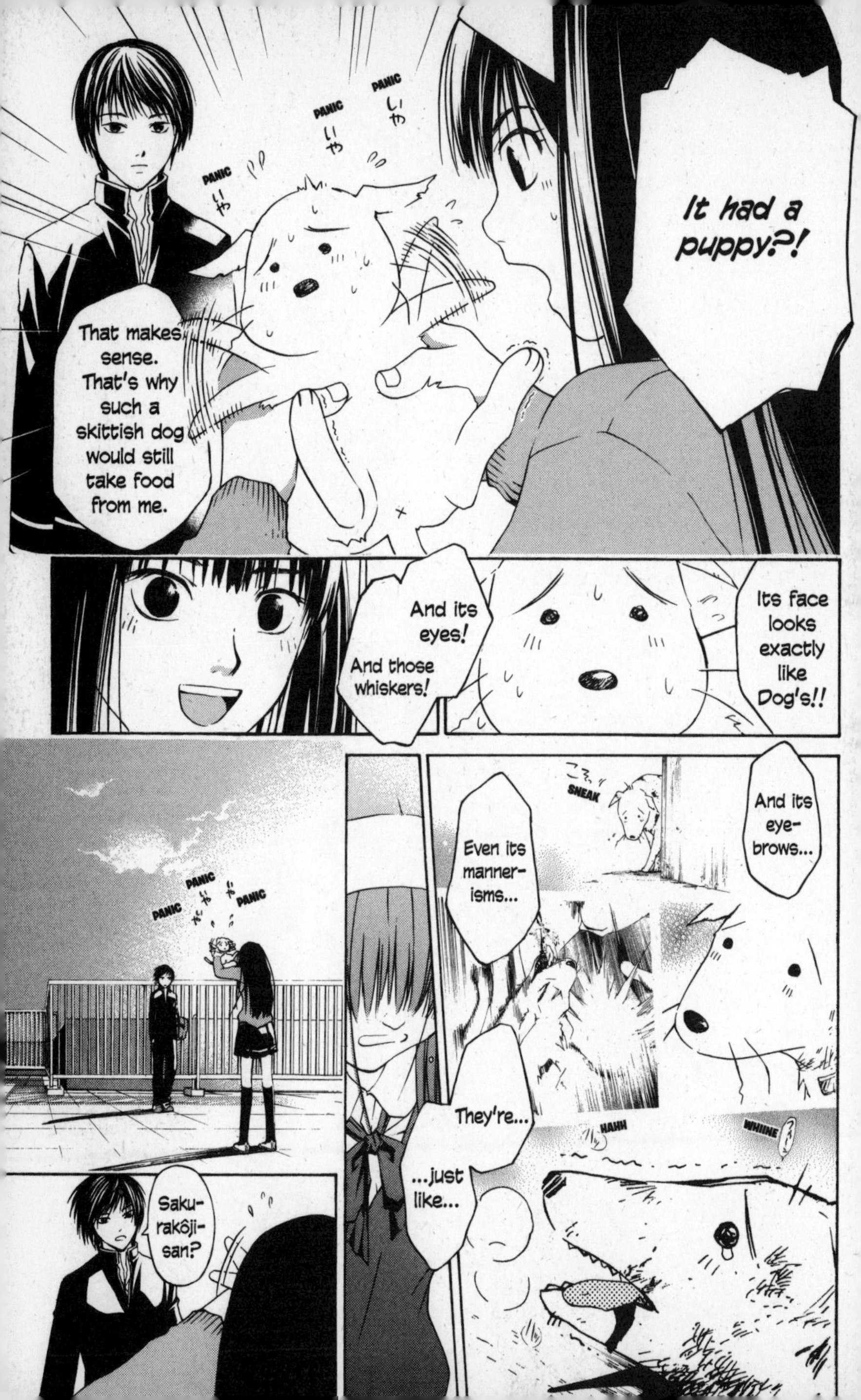
It had a puppy?!
PANIC
いや
PANIC
いや
PANIC
いや
That makes sense. That's why such a skittish dog would still take food from me.
Its face looks exactly like Dog's!!
And its eyes!
And those whiskers!
And its eye-brows...
SNEAK
Even its manner-isms...
WHIINE
HAHH
They're...
...just like...
PANIC
PANIC
PANIC
Saku-rakôji-san?

Forgive me...
I always thought your mother...
...was a coward, but...
Sh-she tried to save my life...
GRAA
and then...
LIKK
I'm so sorry!!
If I had been even a little better...
...you'd still have...

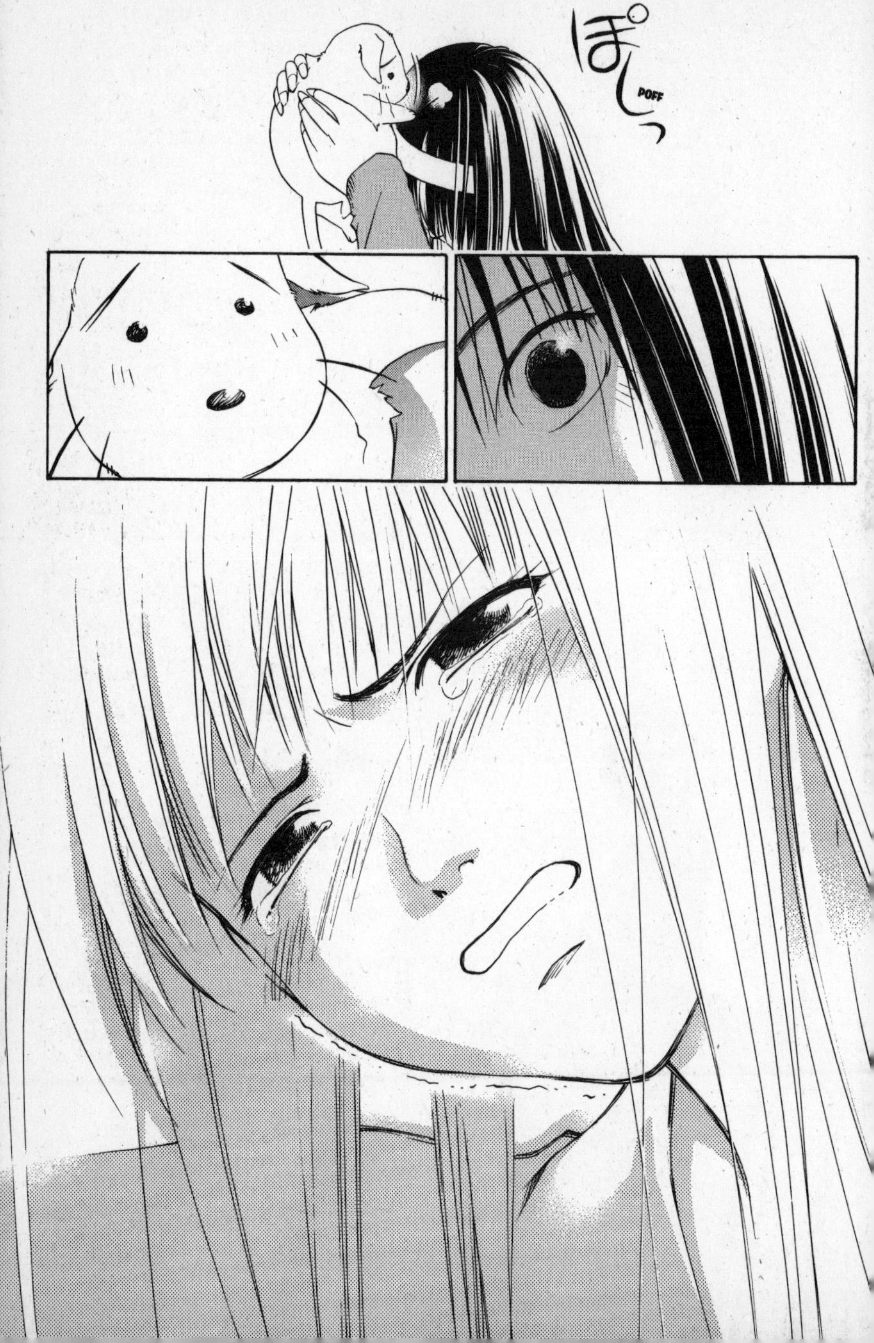
ぽしっ
POFF

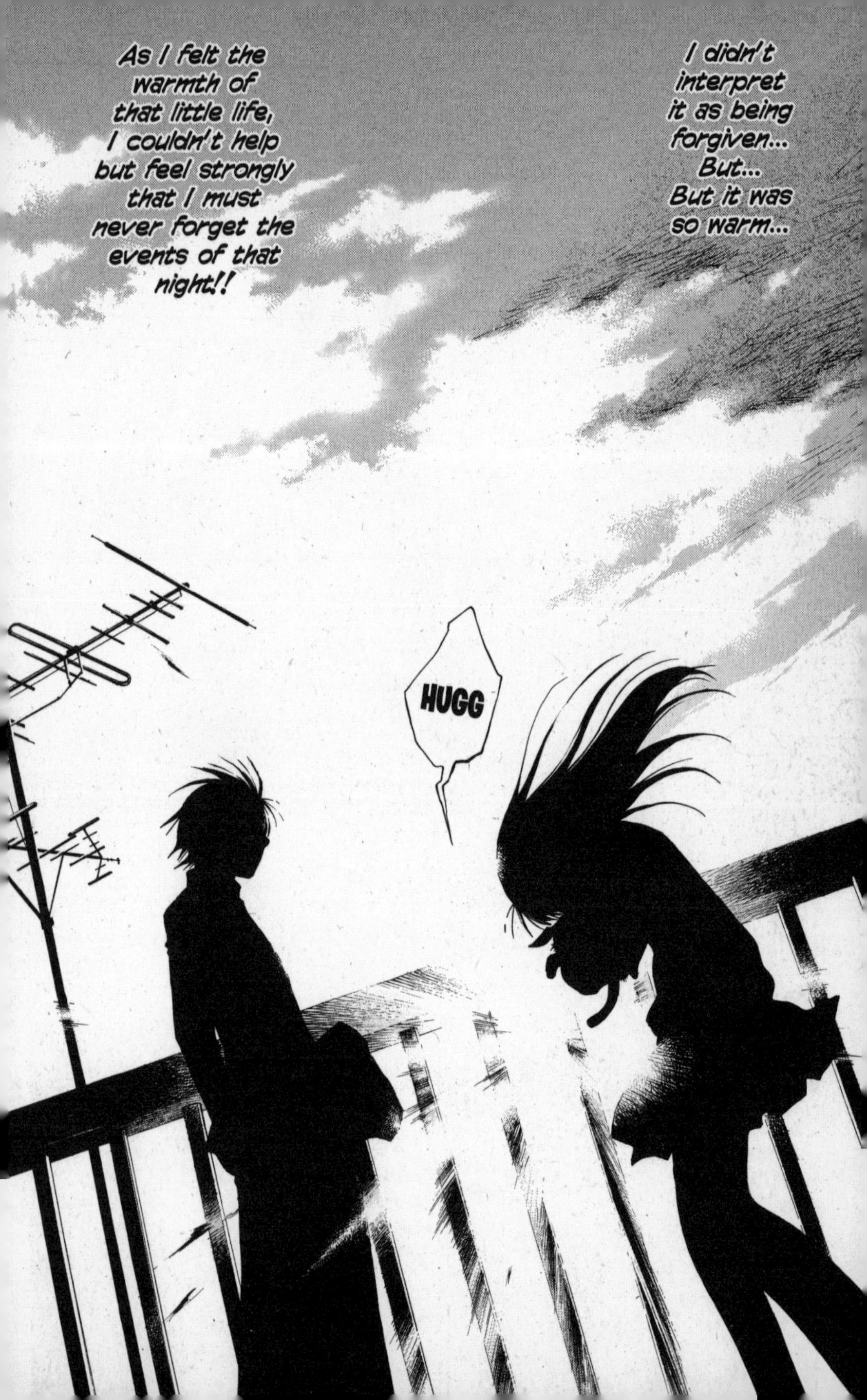
I didn't interpret it as being forgiven... But... But it was so warm...
As I felt the warmth of that little life, I couldn't help but feel strongly that I must never forget the events of that night!!
HUGG

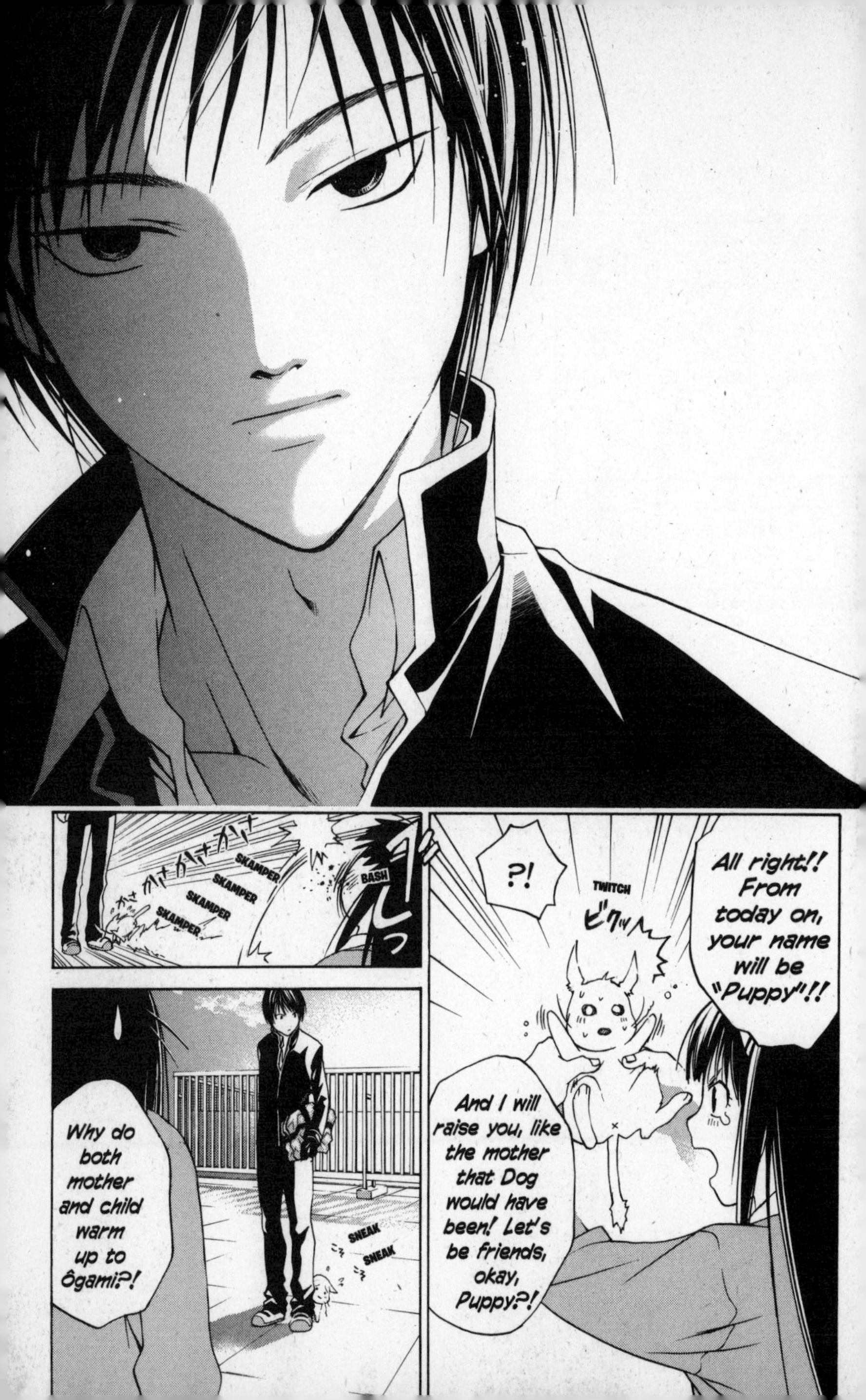
?!
TWITCH
ビクッ
All right!! From today on, your name will be "Puppy"!!
And I will raise you, like the mother that Dog would have been! Let's be friends, okay, Puppy?!
SKAMPER
SKAMPER
SKAMPER
SKAMPER
BASH
Why do both mother and child warm up to Ôgami?!
SNEAK
SNEAK

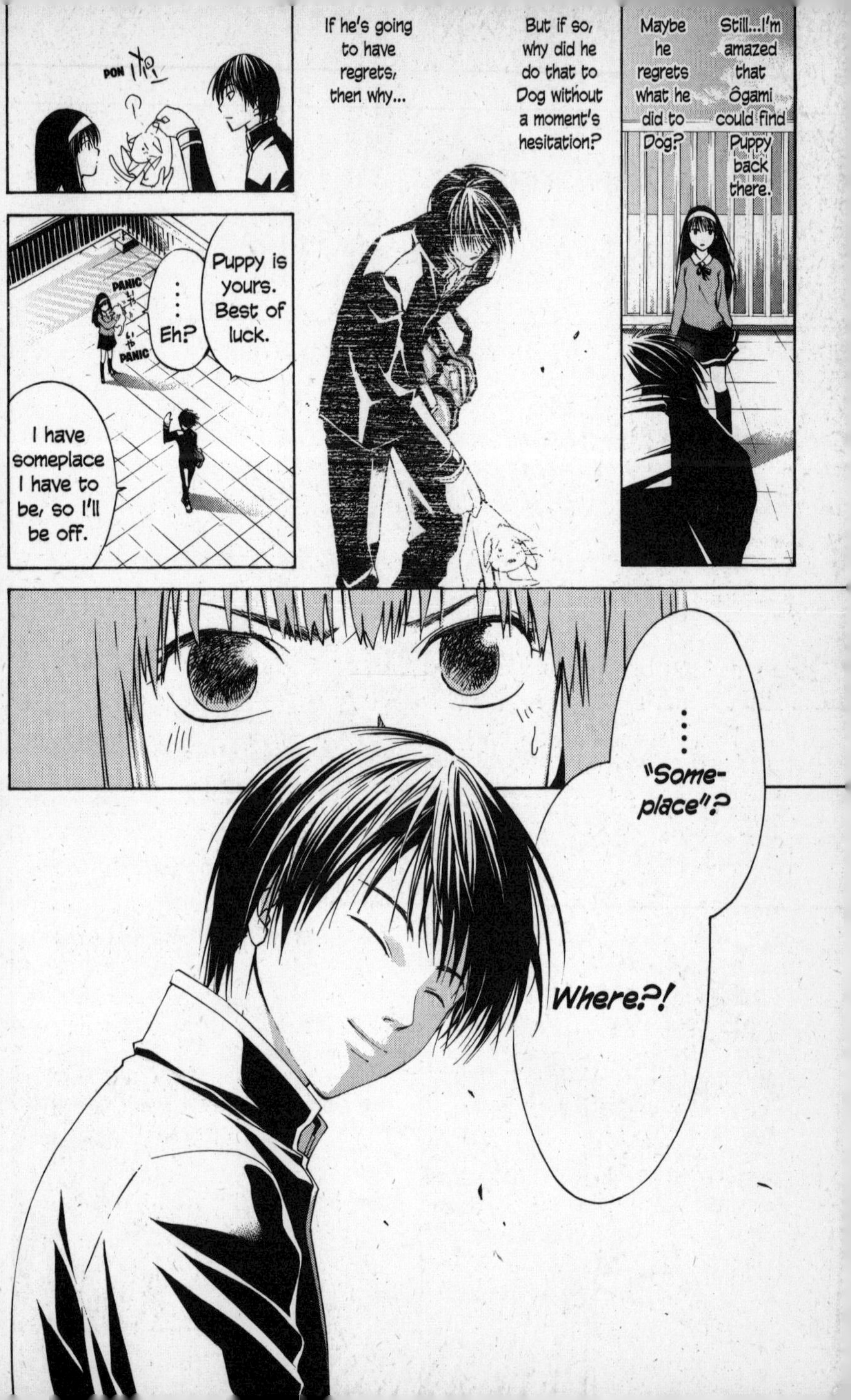
Still...I'm amazed that Ôgami could find Puppy back there.
Maybe he regrets what he did to Dog?
But if so, why did he do that to Dog without a moment's hesitation?
If he's going to have regrets, then why...
PON
Puppy is yours. Best of luck.
... Eh?
PANIC
PANIC
I have someplace I have to be, so I'll be off.
... "Some-place"?
Where?!

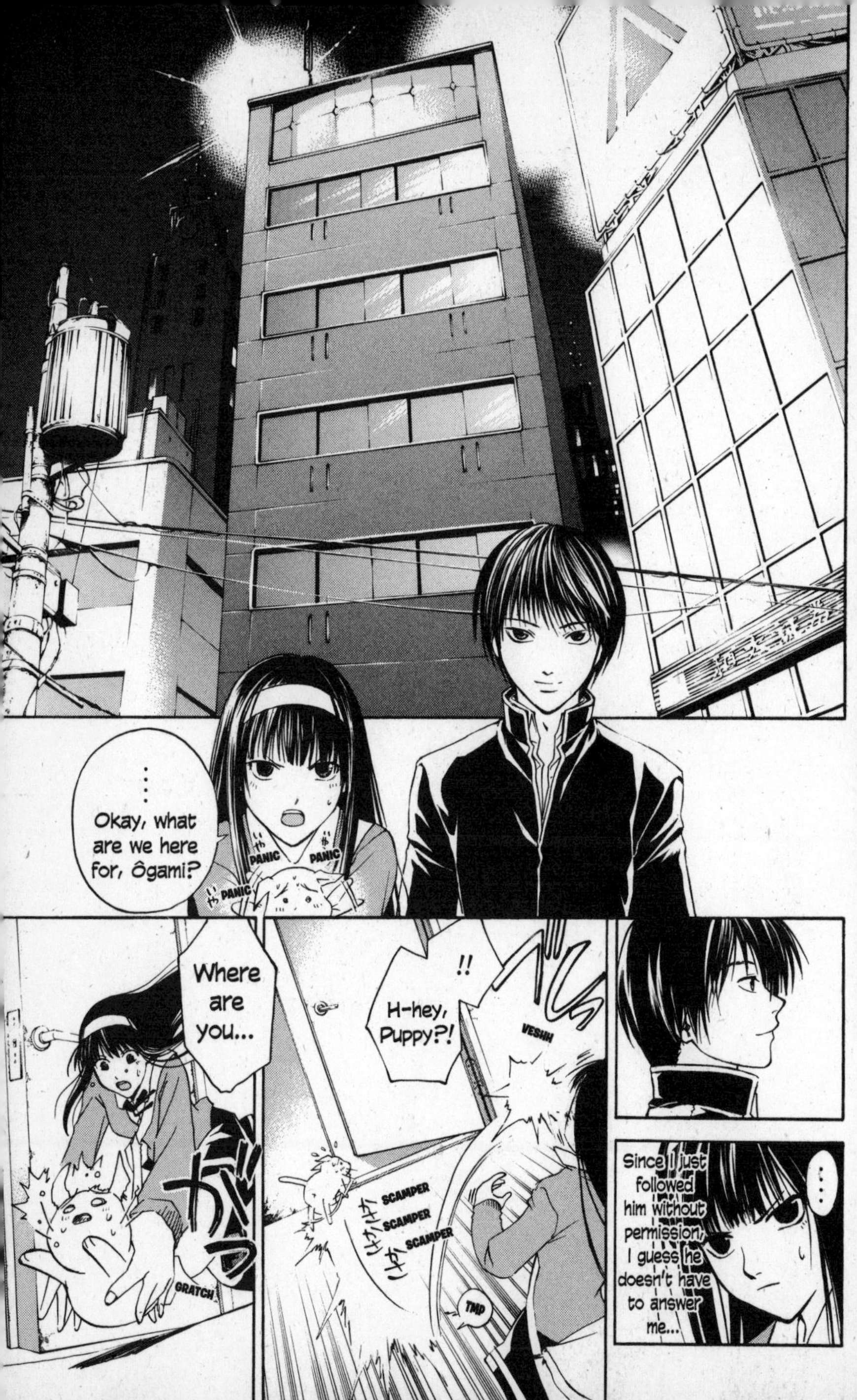
. . . .
Okay, what are we here for, Ôgami?
PANIC
PANIC
PANIC
. . .
Since I just followed him without permission, I guess he doesn't have to answer me...
!!
H-hey, Puppy?!
VESHH
SCAMPER
SCAMPER
SCAMPER
TMP
Where are you...
GRATCH

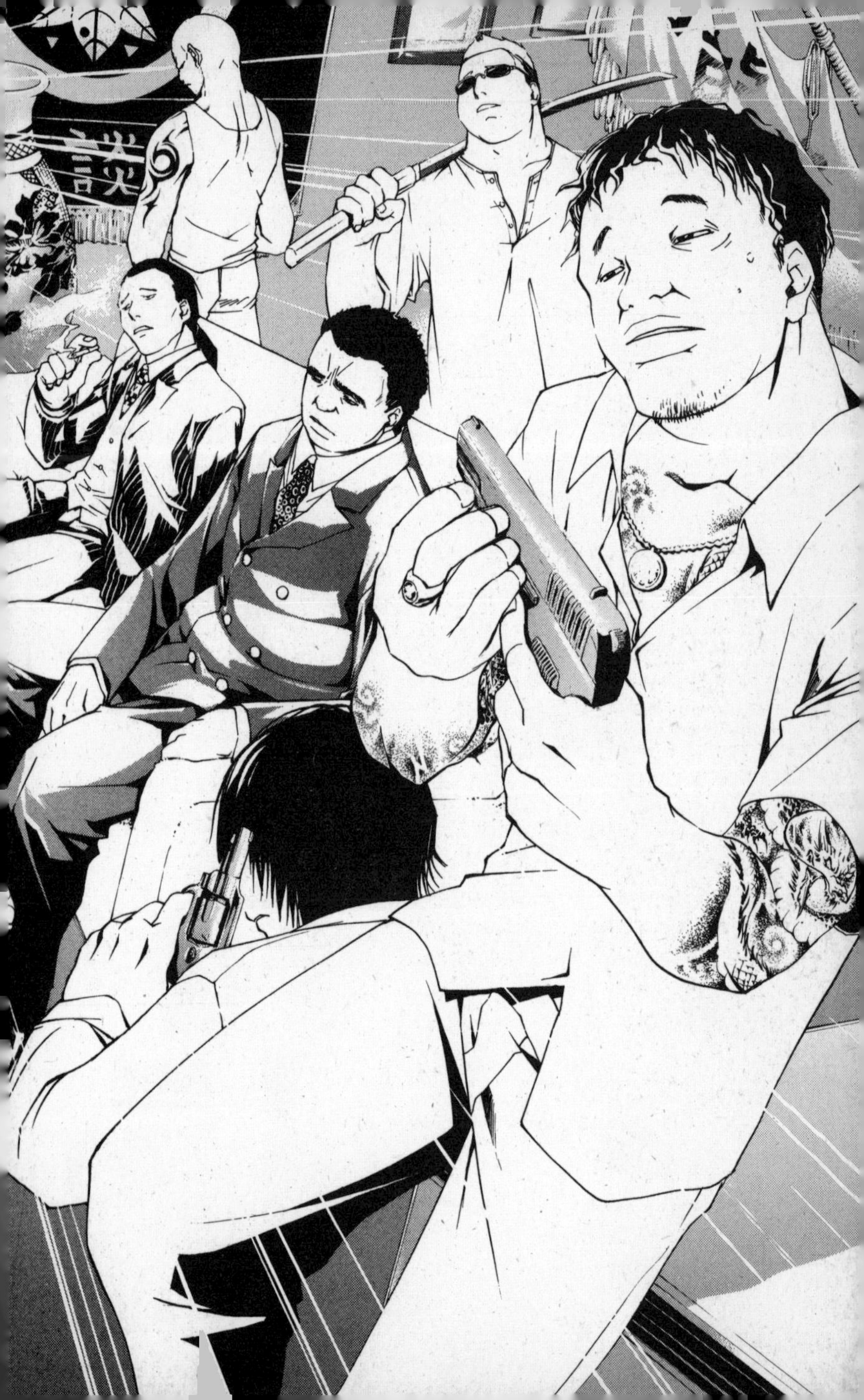

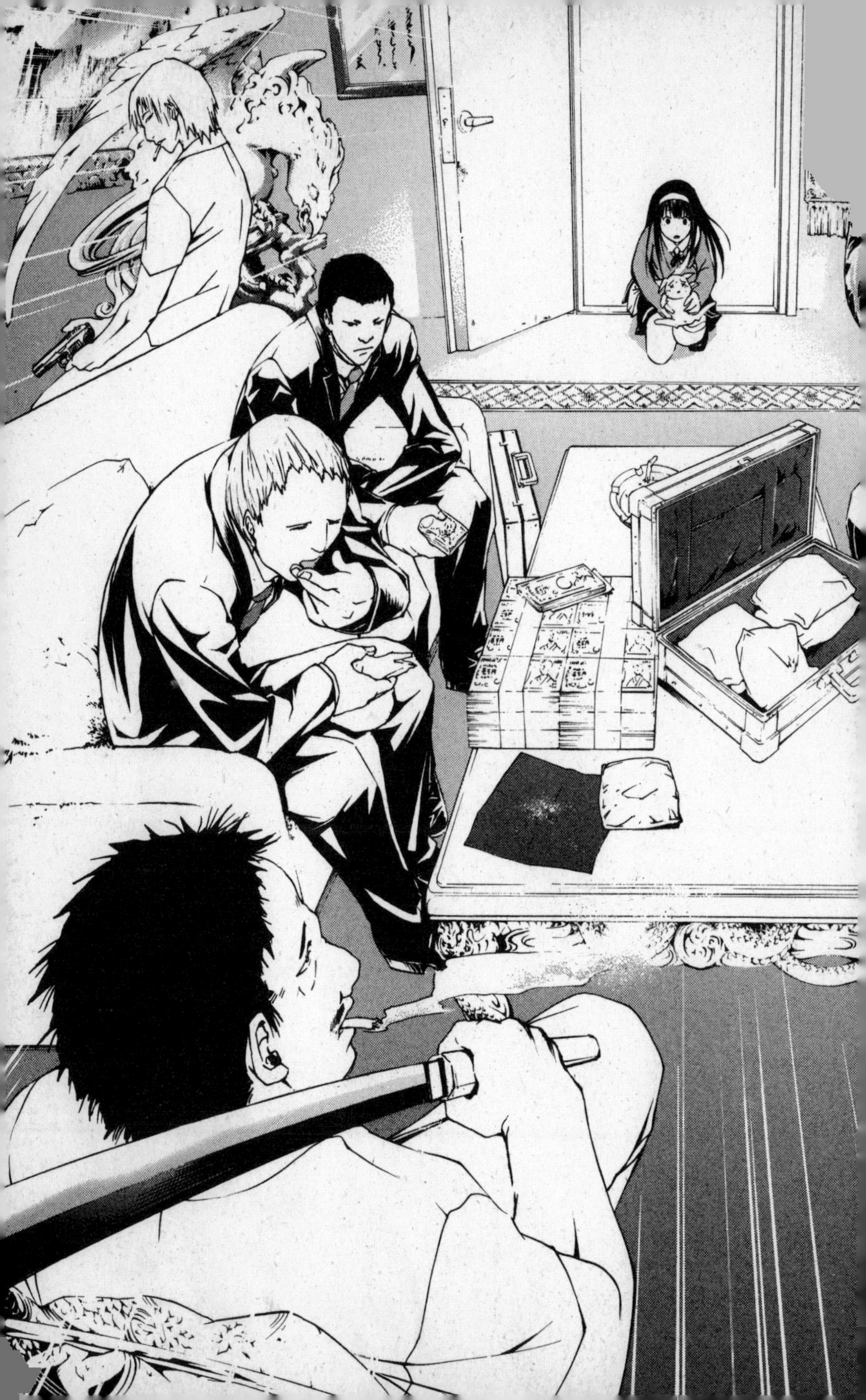

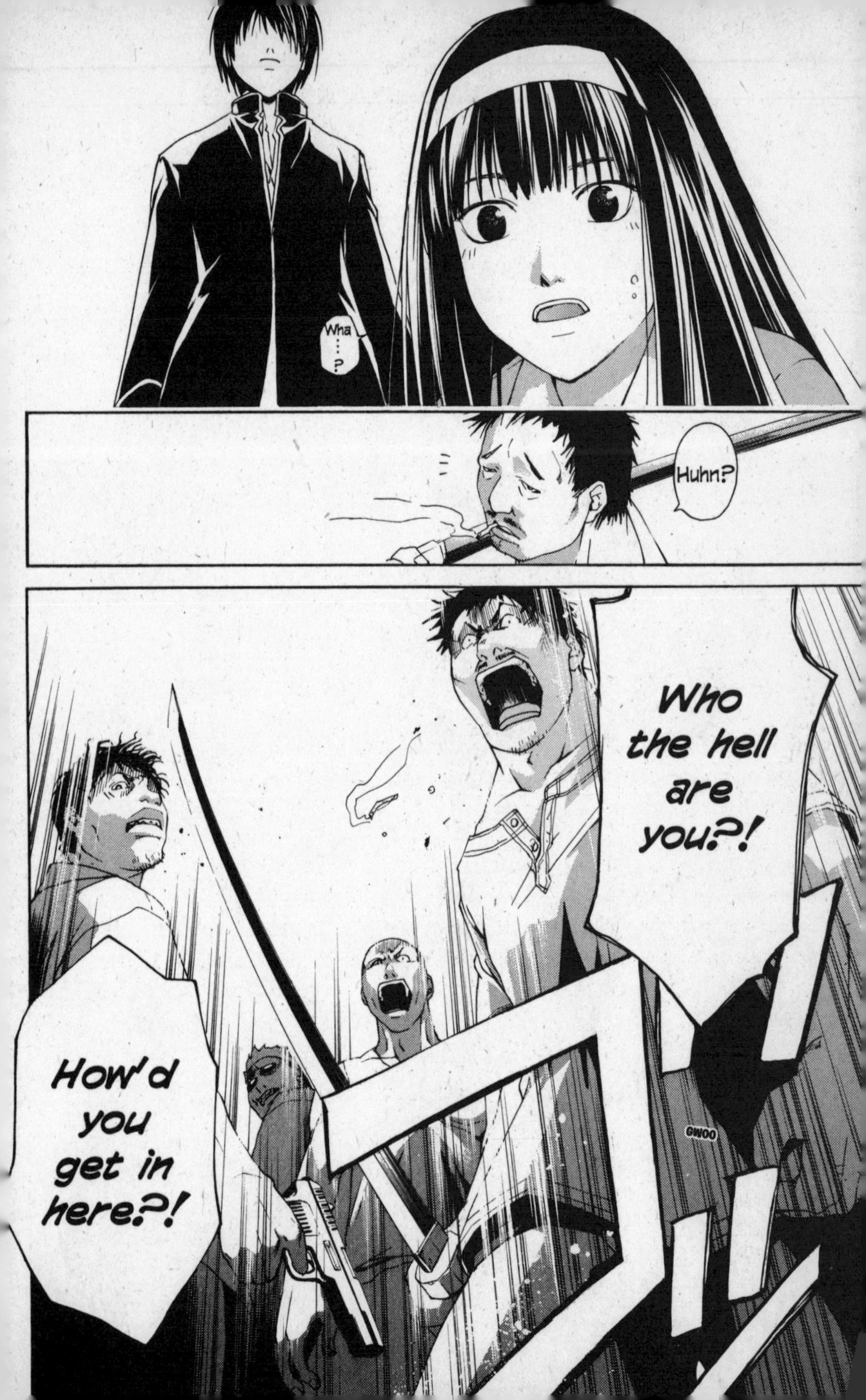
Wha...?
Huhn?
Who the hell are you?!
How'd you get in here?!
GWOO

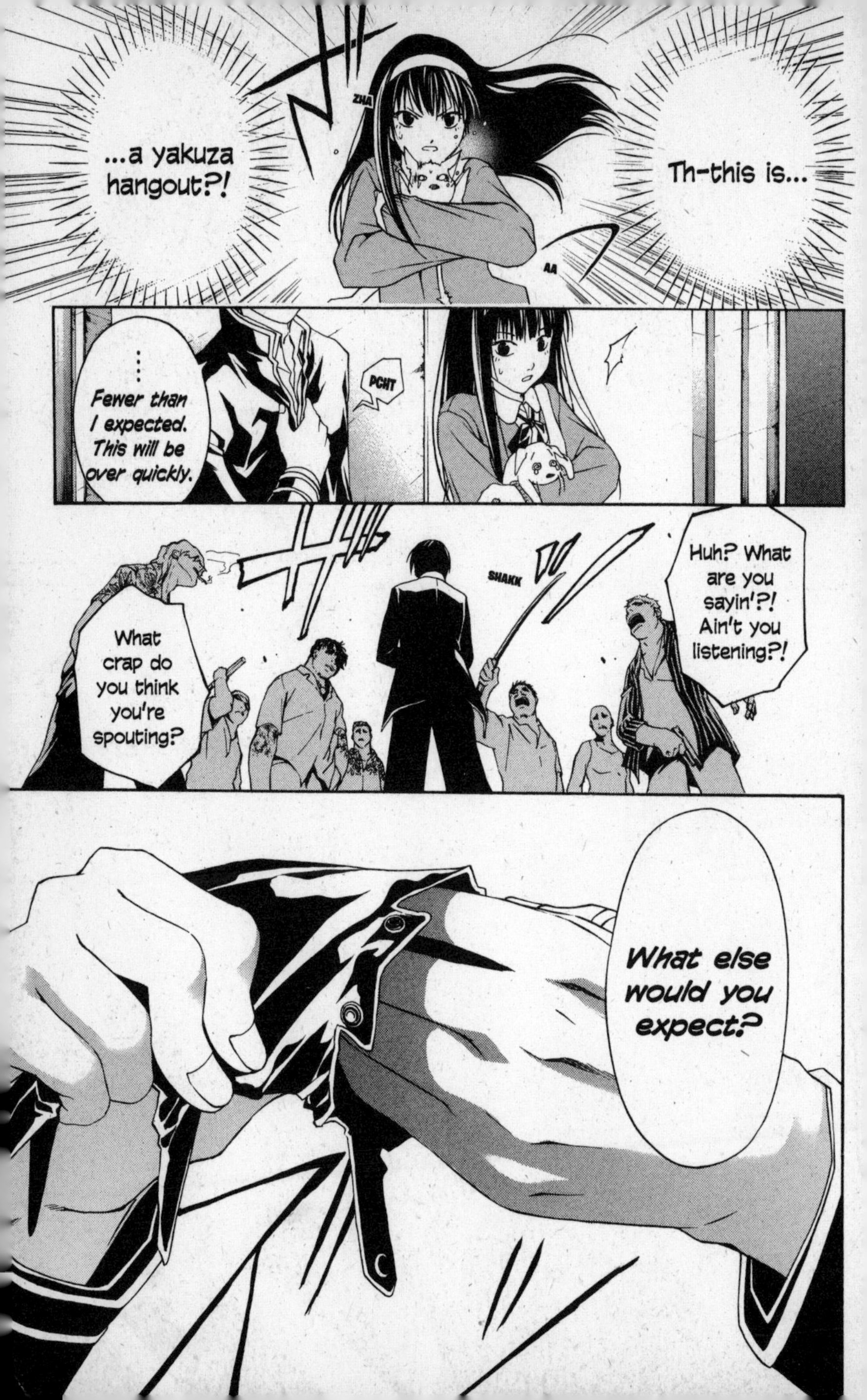
Th-this is...
ZHA
...a yakuza hangout?!
AA
PCHT
... Fewer than I expected. This will be over quickly.
Huh? What are you sayin'?! Ain't you listening?!
SHAKK
What crap do you think you're spouting?
What else would you expect?

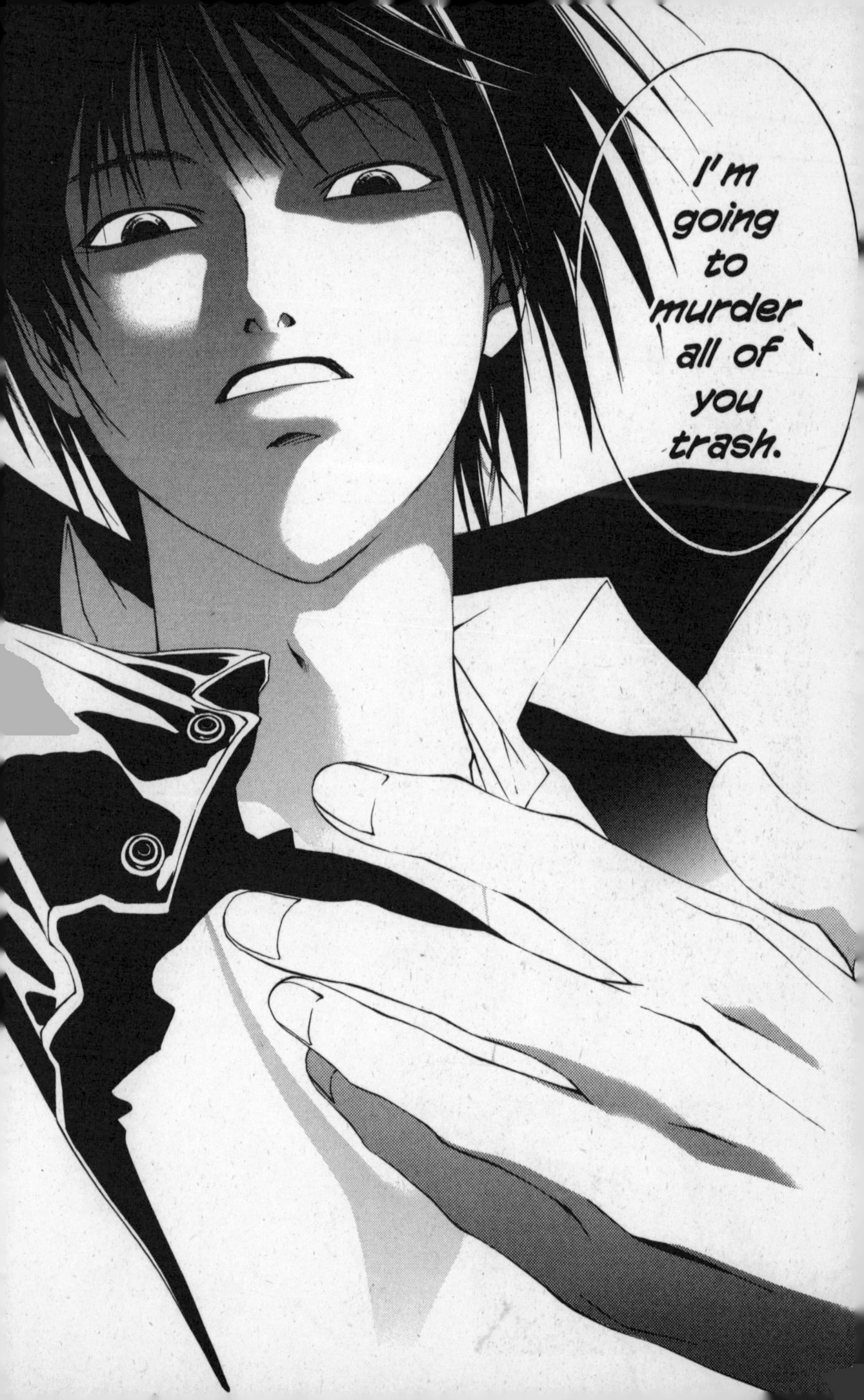
I'm going to murder all of you trash.

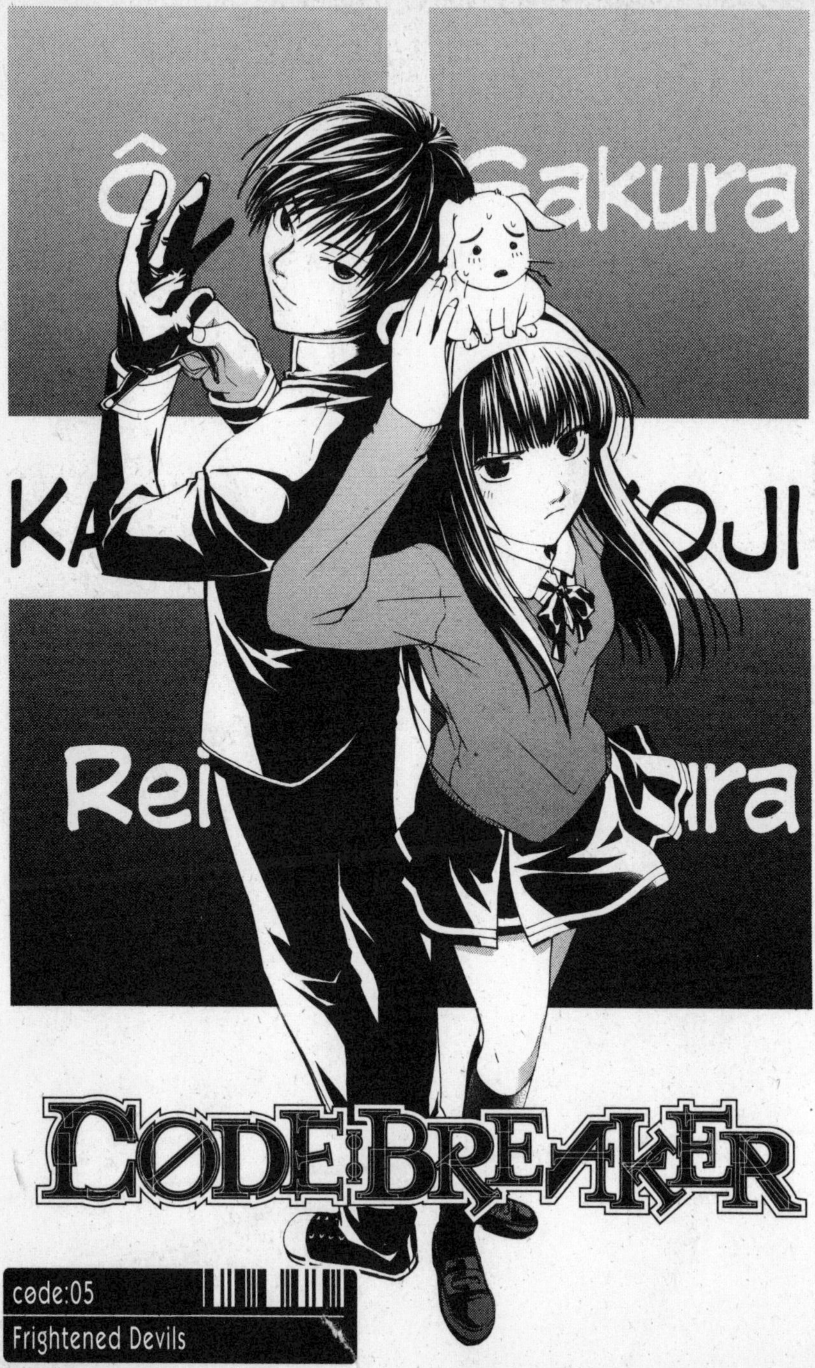

ô
Sakura
KA
OJI
Rei
ra
CODE:BREAKER
code:05
Frightened Devils

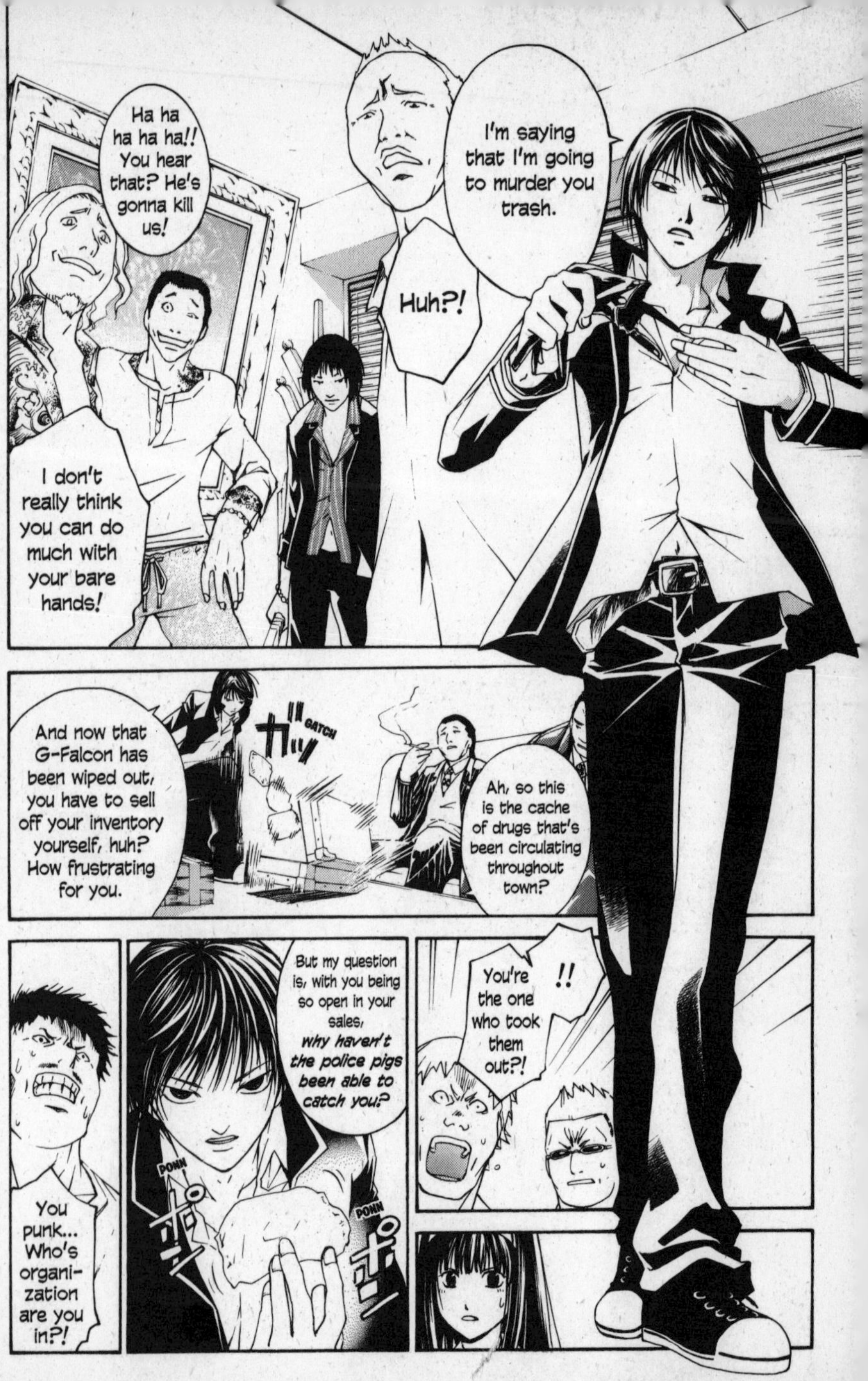

I'm saying that I'm going to murder you trash.
Huh?!
Ha ha ha ha ha!! You hear that? He's gonna kill us!
I don't really think you can do much with your bare hands!
Ah, so this is the cache of drugs that's been circulating throughout town?
ガッ CATCH
And now that G-Falcon has been wiped out, you have to sell off your inventory yourself, huh? How frustrating for you.
You're the one who took them out?!
!!
But my question is, with you being so open in your sales, *why haven't the police pigs been able to catch you?*
PONN ポン
PONN ポン
You punk... Who's organi-zation are you in?!

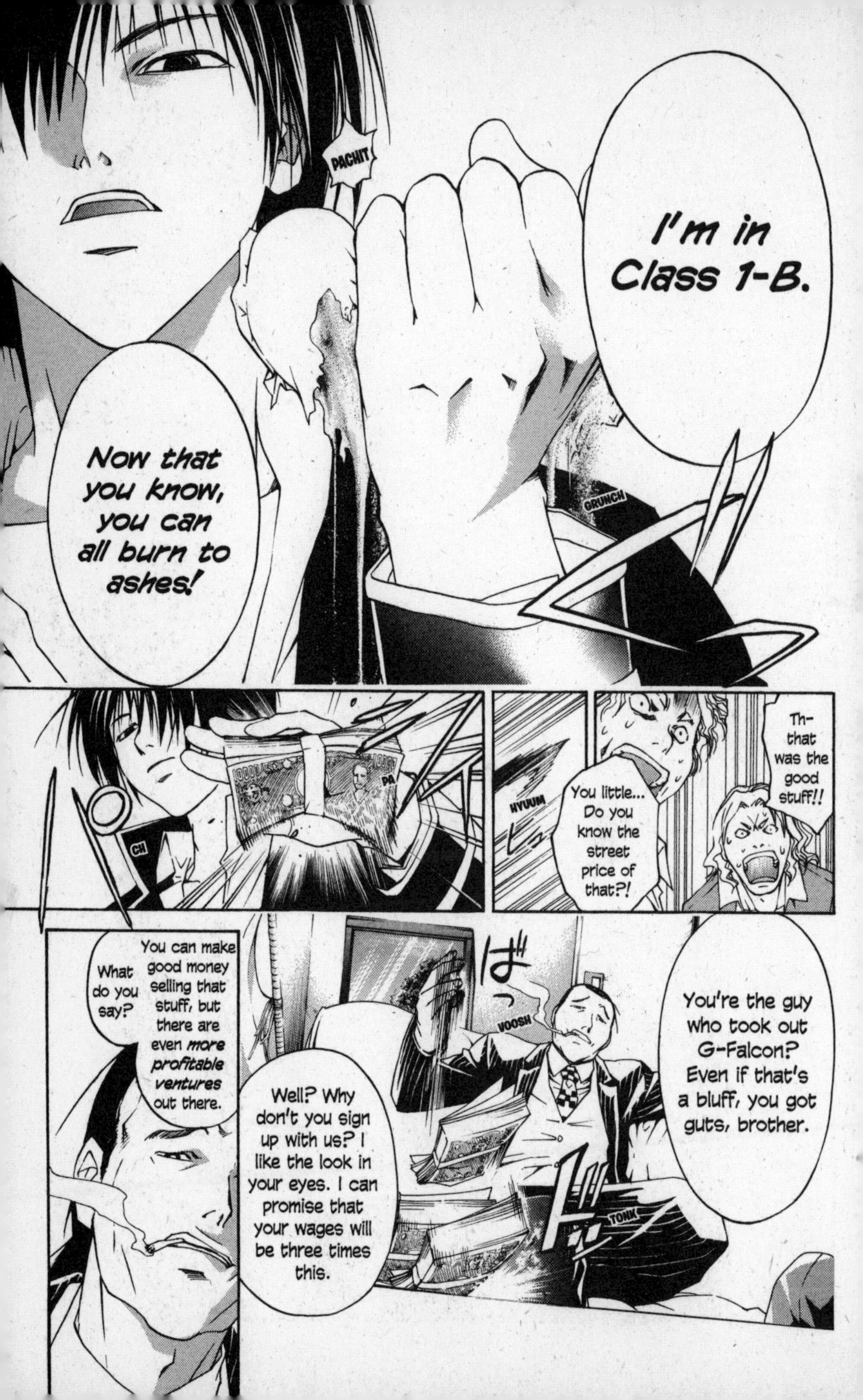
I'm in Class 1-B.
PACHIT
GRUNCH
Now that you know, you can all burn to ashes!
Th- that was the good stuff!!
You little... Do you know the street price of that?!
HYUUM
PA
CH
You're the guy who took out G-Falcon? Even if that's a bluff, you got guts, brother.
ばっ
VOOSH
TONK
Well? Why don't you sign up with us? I like the look in your eyes. I can promise that your wages will be three times this.
You can make good money selling that stuff, but there are even *more profitable ventures* out there.
What do you say?

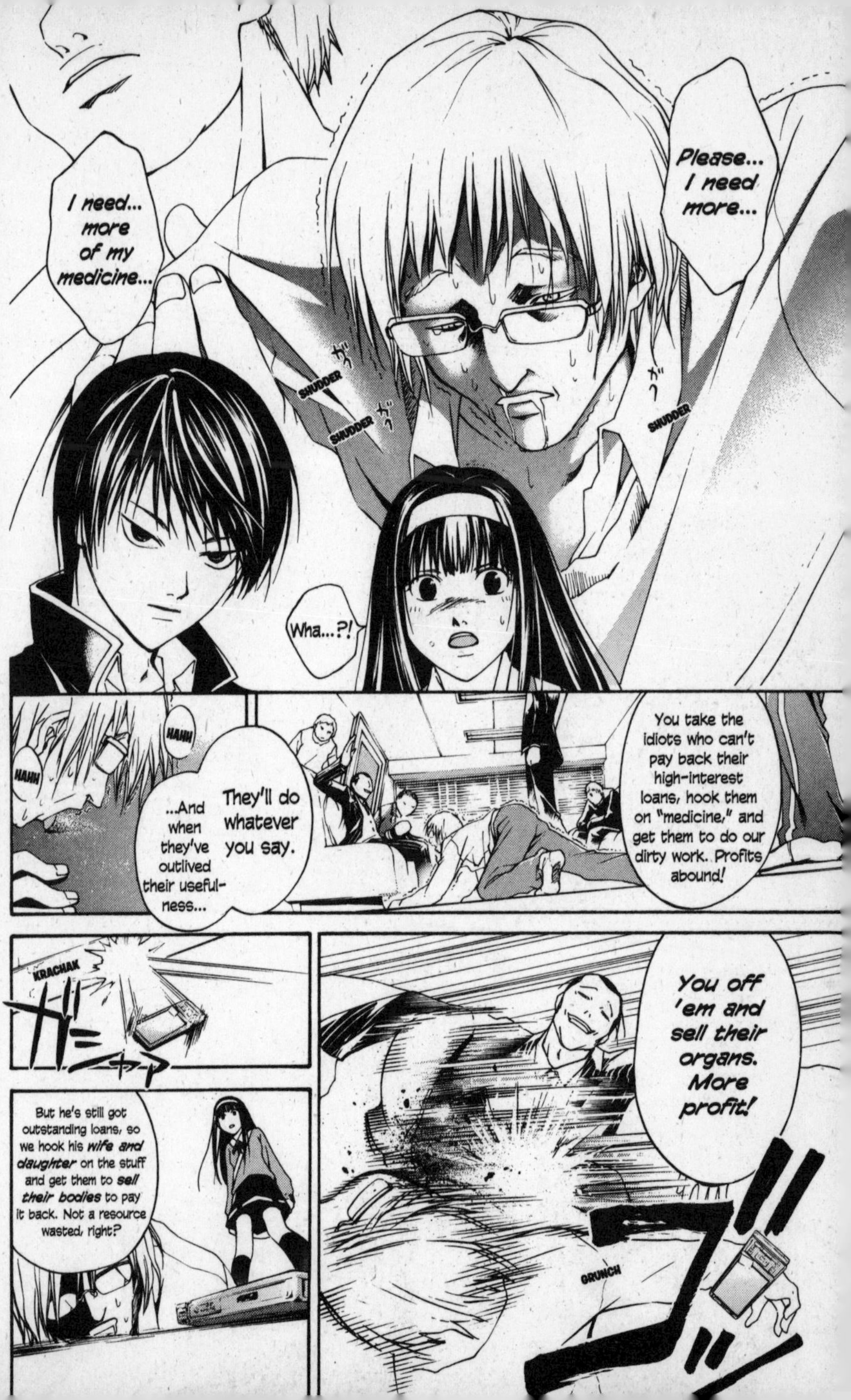
Please... I need more...
I need... more of my medicine...
SHUDDER
SHUDDER
SHUDDER
Wha...?!
You take the idiots who can't pay back their high-interest loans, hook them on "medicine," and get them to do our dirty work. Profits abound!
They'll do whatever you say.
...And when they've outlived their usefulness...
HANH
HANH
You off 'em and sell their organs. More profit!
GRUNCH
KRACHAK
But he's still got outstanding loans, so we hook his *wife and daughter* on the stuff and get them to *sell their bodies* to pay it back. Not a resource wasted, right?

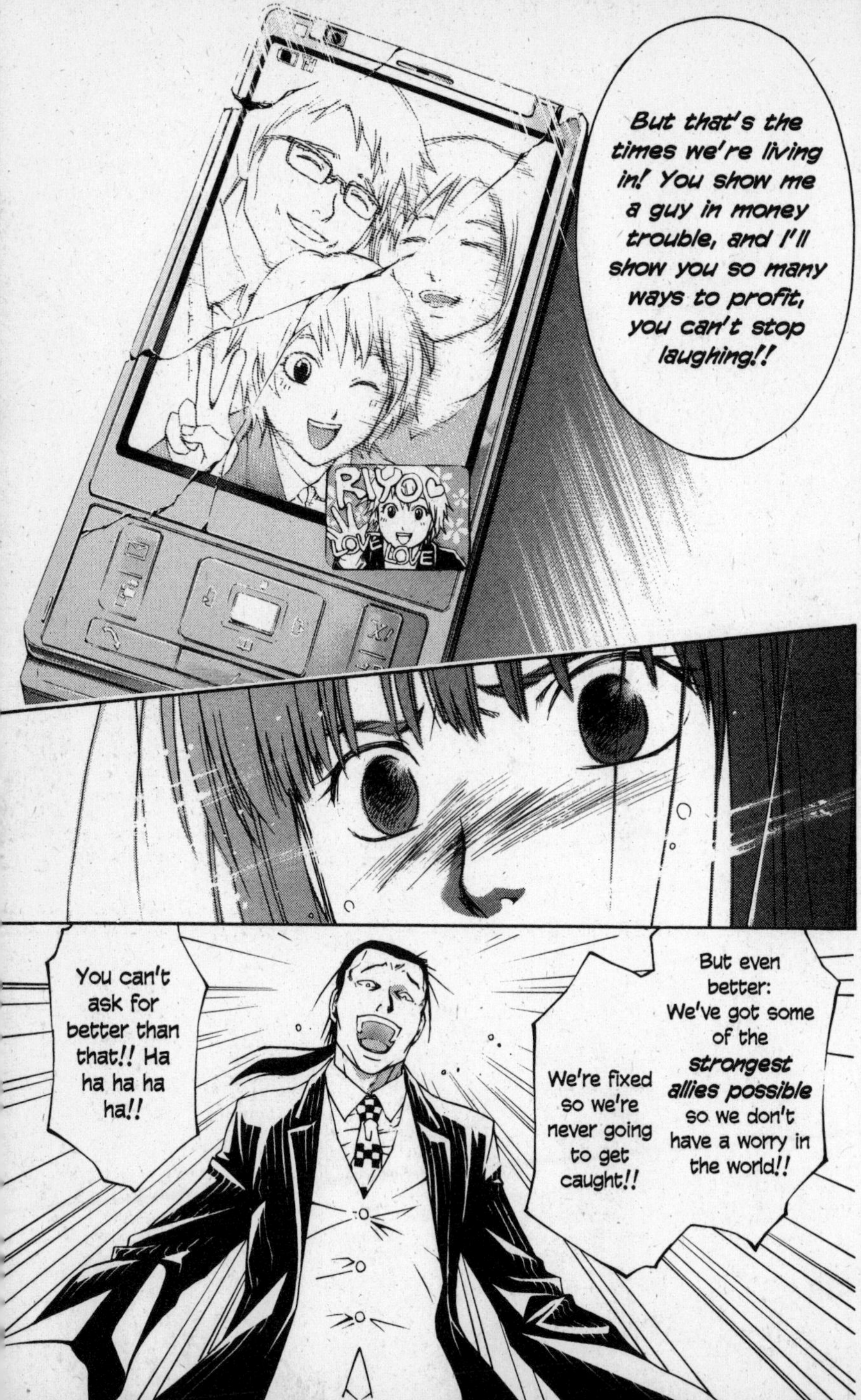
But that's the times we're living in! You show me a guy in money trouble, and I'll show you so many ways to profit, you can't stop laughing!!
RIYO
LOVE LOVE
But even better: We've got some of the **strongest allies possible** so we don't have a worry in the world!!
We're fixed so we're never going to get caught!!
You can't ask for better than that!! Ha ha ha ha ha!!

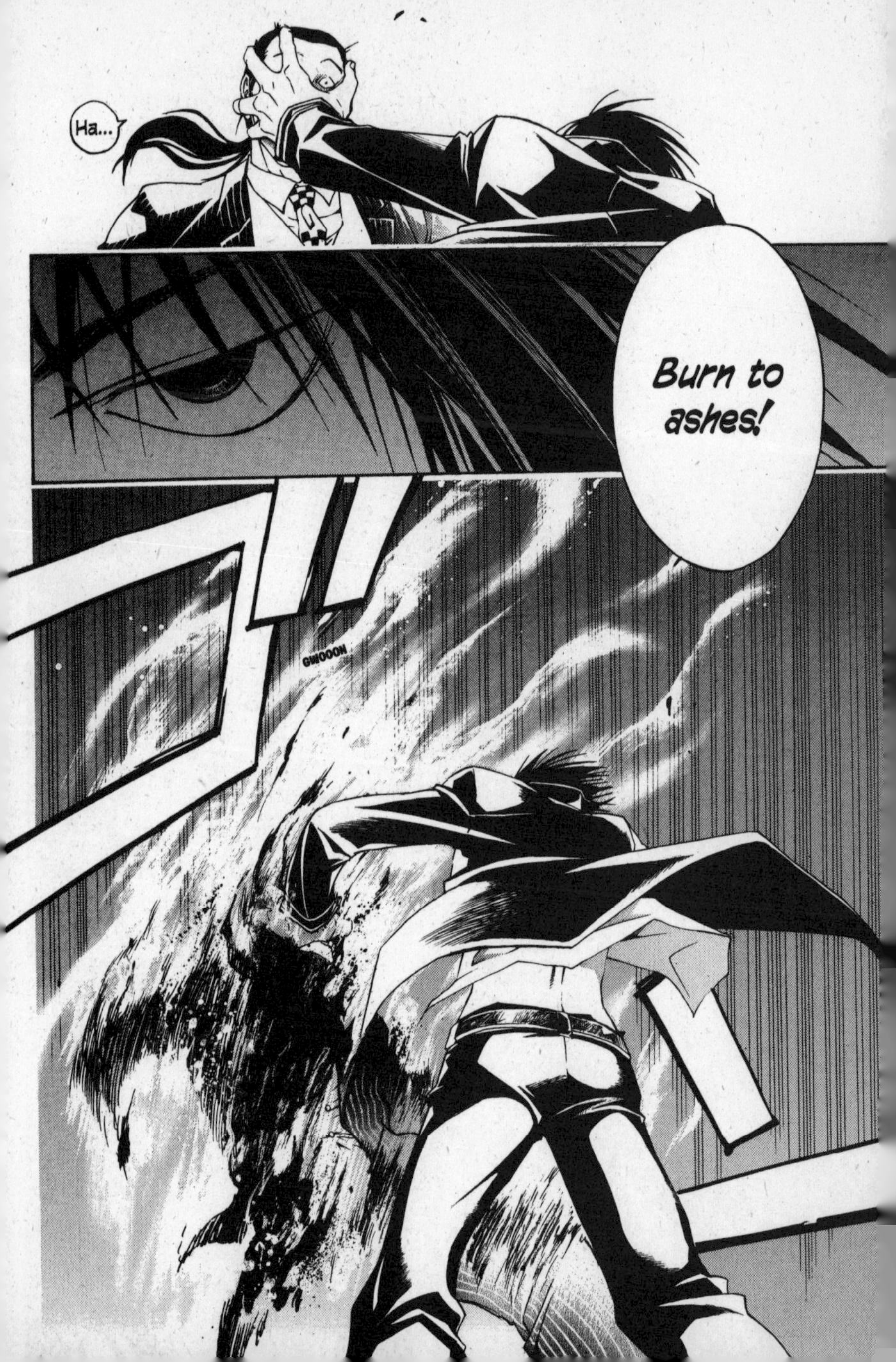
Ha...
Burn to ashes!
GWOOON

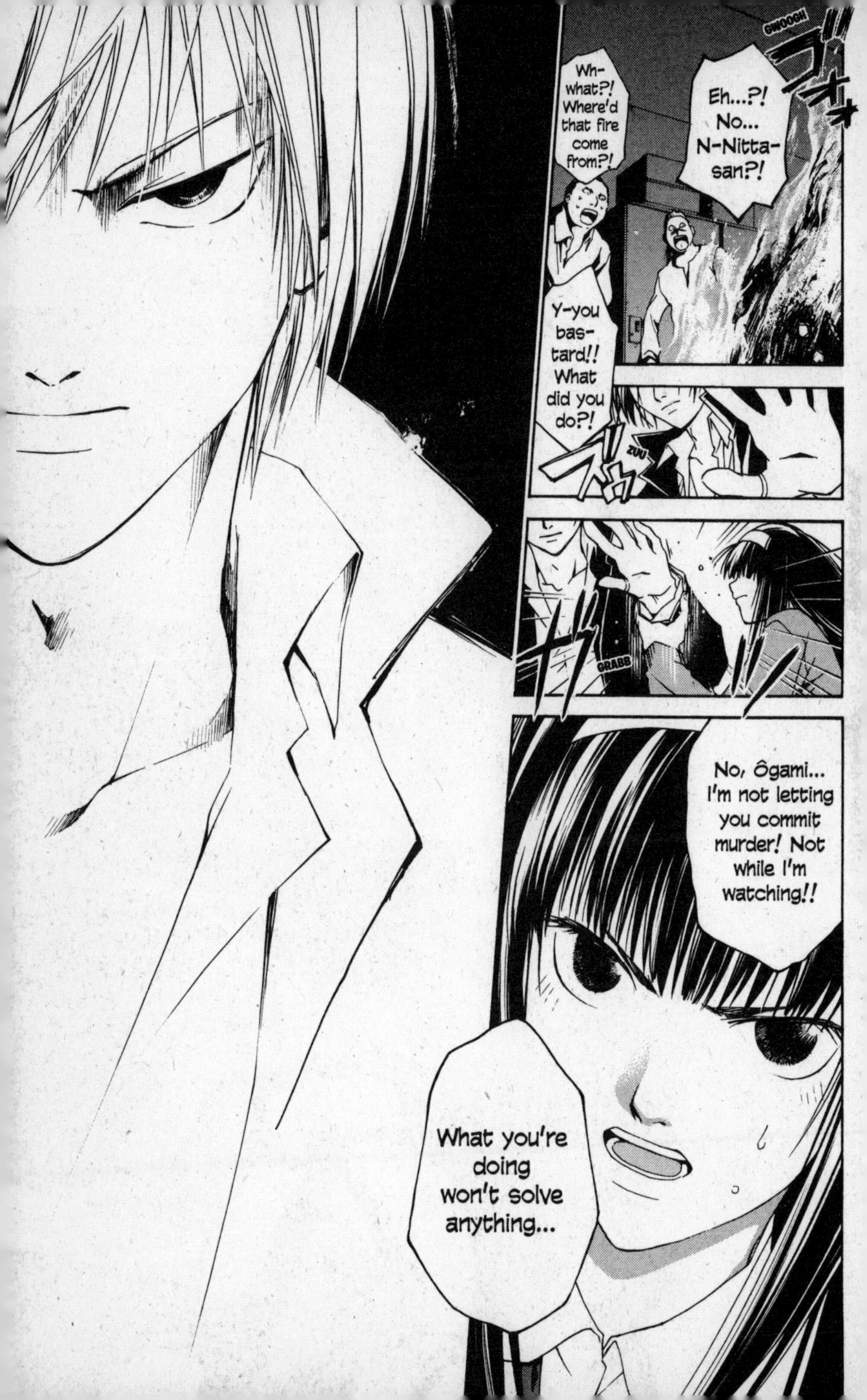
GWOOGH
Eh...?! No... N-Nitta-san?!
Wh-what?! Where'd that fire come from?!
Y-you bastard!! What did you do?!
ZUU
GRABB
No, Ôgami... I'm not letting you commit murder! Not while I'm watching!!
What you're doing won't solve anything...

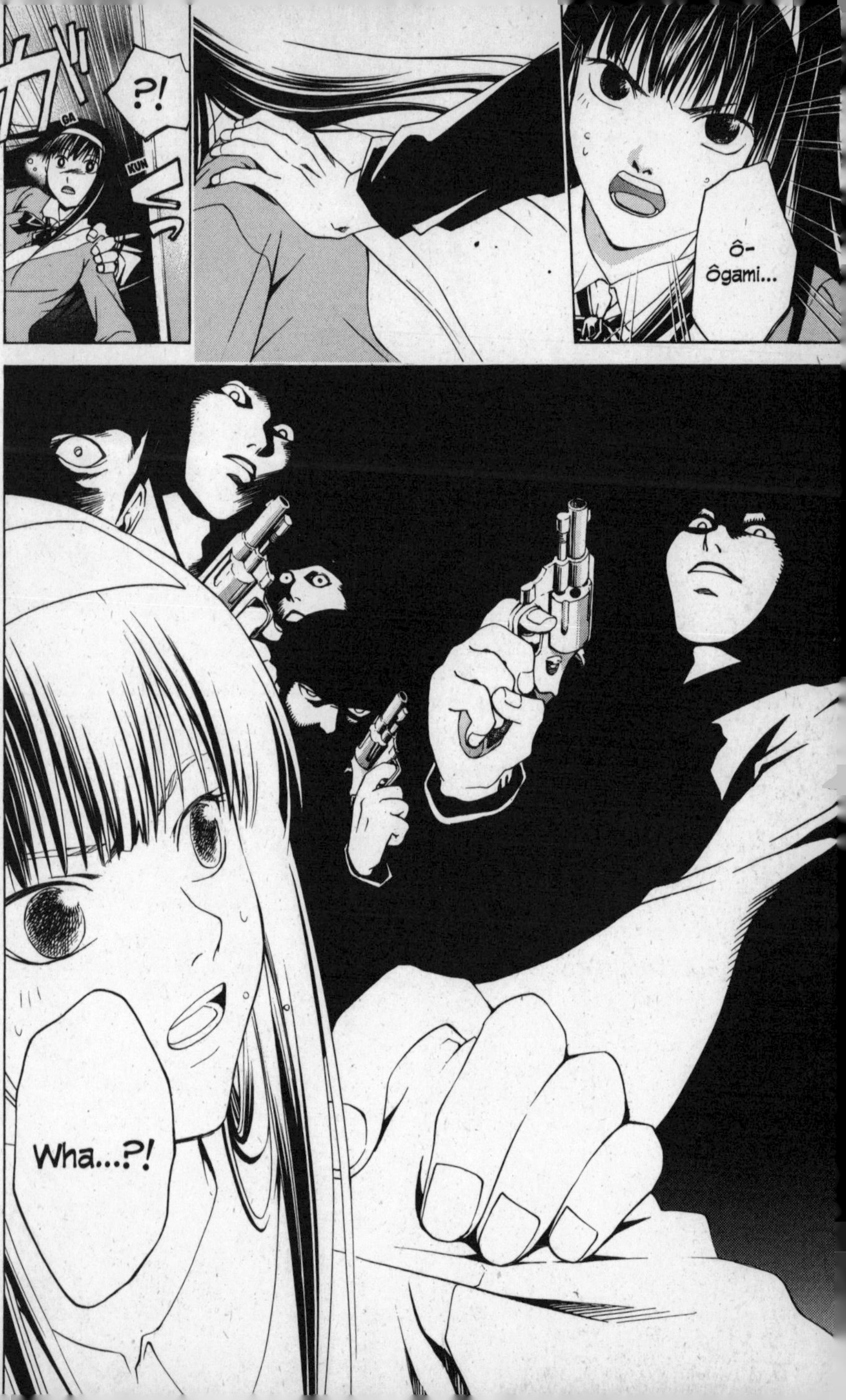
Ô-
Ôgami...
ガッ
GA
?!
KUN
Wha...?!

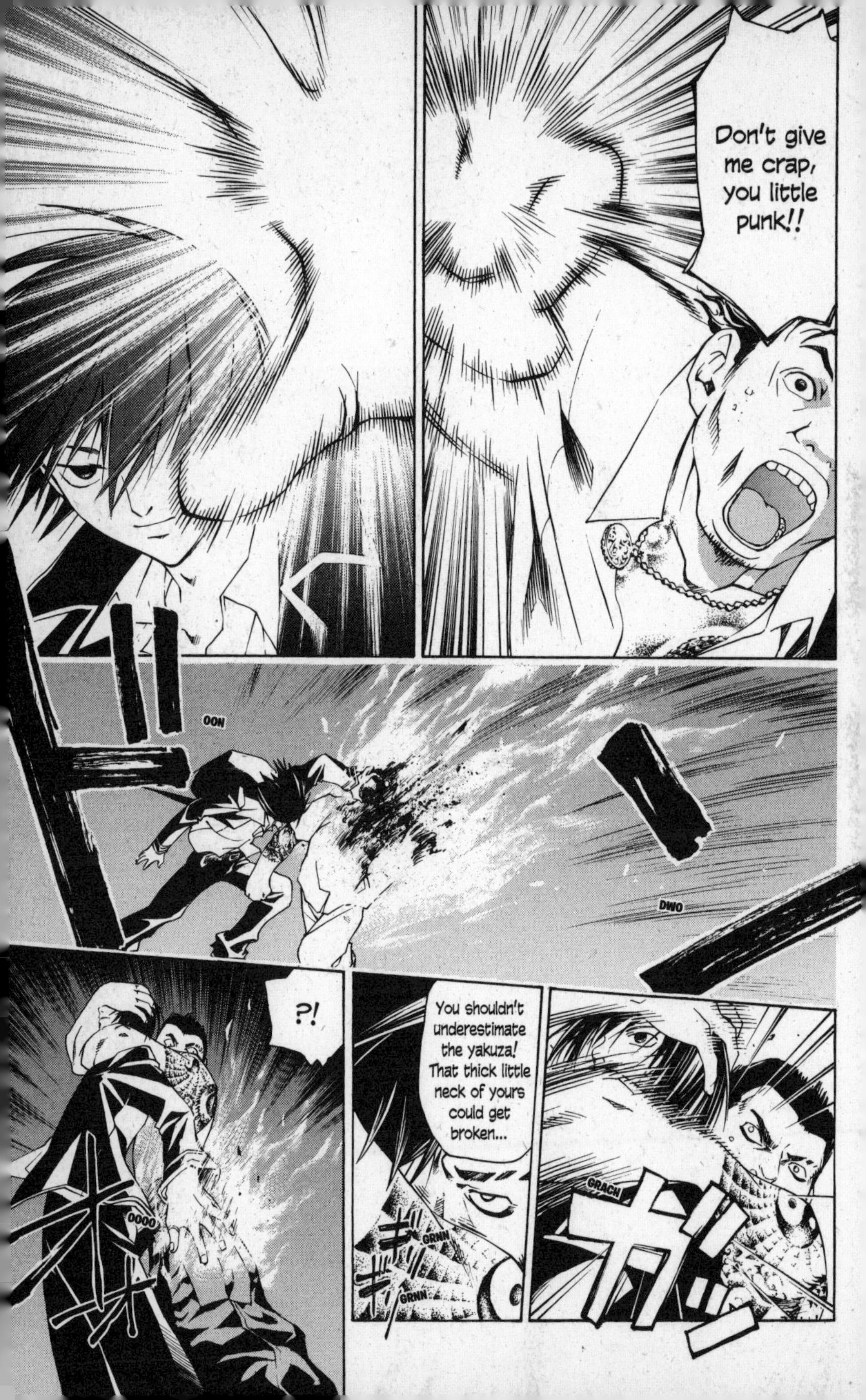
Don't give me crap, you little punk!!
DWO
OON
GRACH
You shouldn't underestimate the yakuza! That thick little neck of yours could get broken...
GRNN
GRNN
?!
OOOO

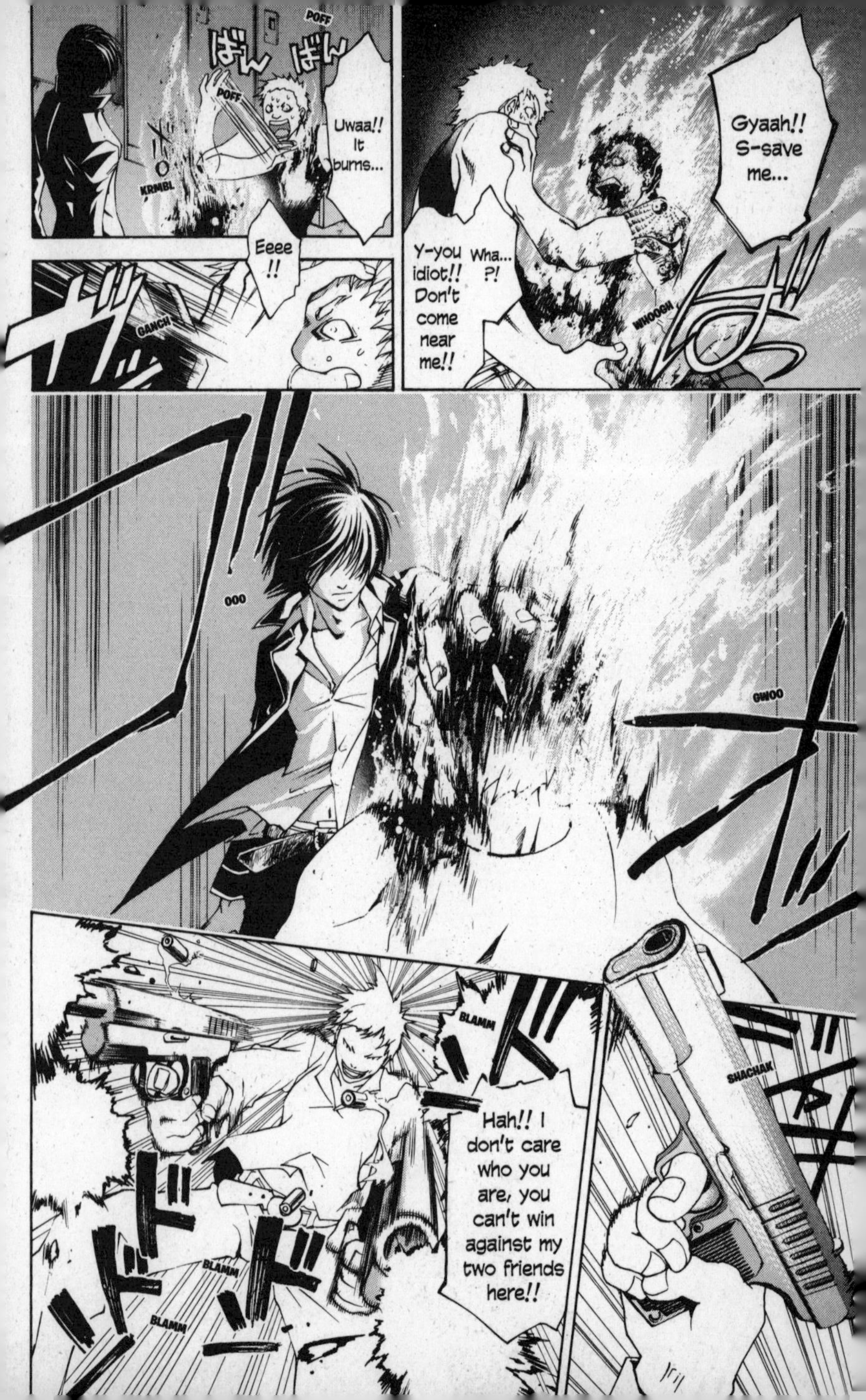

Gyaah!! S-save me...
WHOOGH
Wha...?!
Y-you idiot!! Don't come near me!!
POFF
ばん ばん
Uwaa!! It burns...
POFF
KRMBL
Eeee!!
GANCH
GWOO
OOO
SHACHAK
BLAMM
Hah!! I don't care who you are, you can't win against my two friends here!!
BLAMM
BLAMM

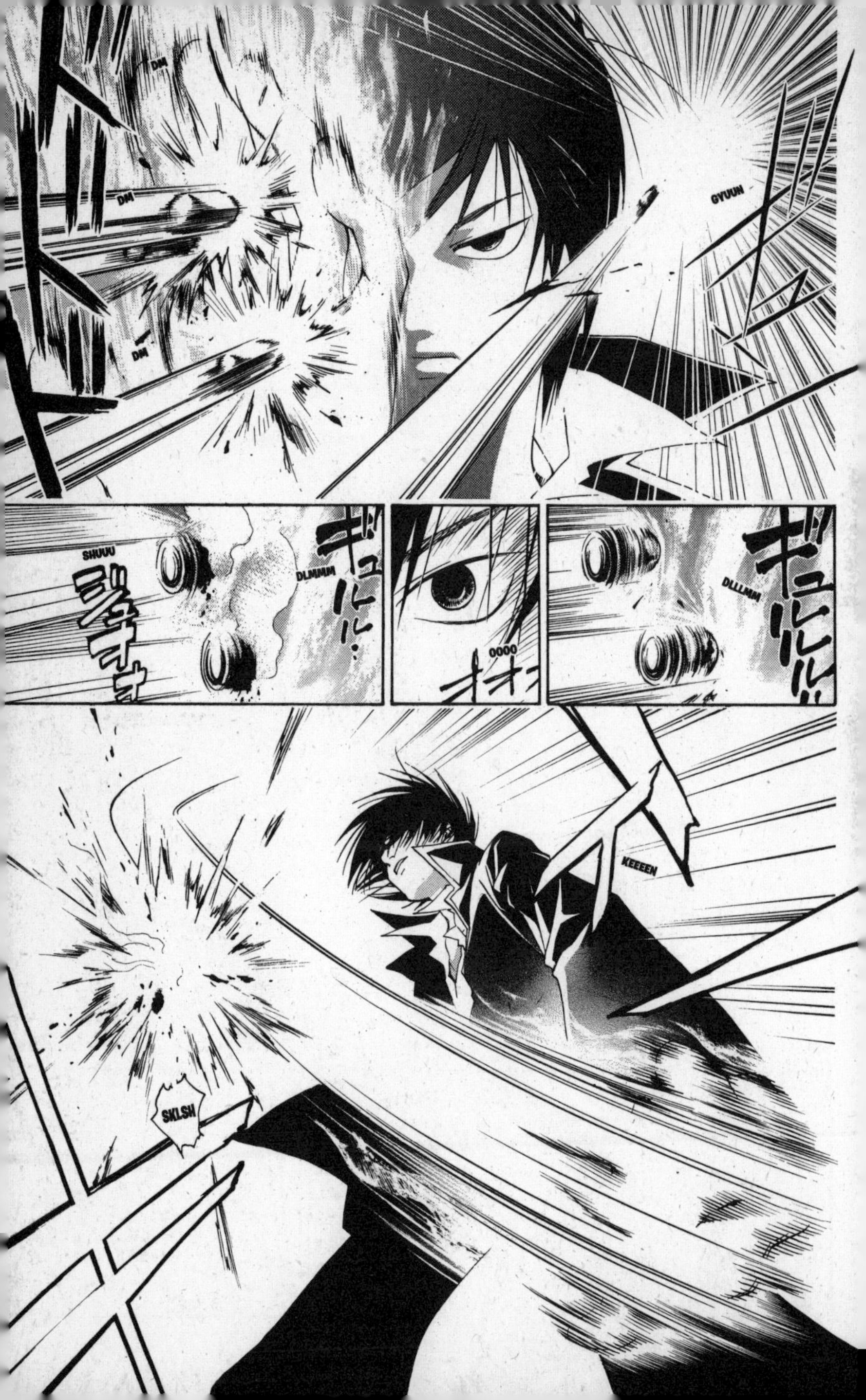
GYUUN
DM
DM
DM
ギュルルル
DLLLMM
OOOO
オオオ
ギュルル・
DLMMM
SHUUU
ジュオオ
KEEEEN
SKLSH

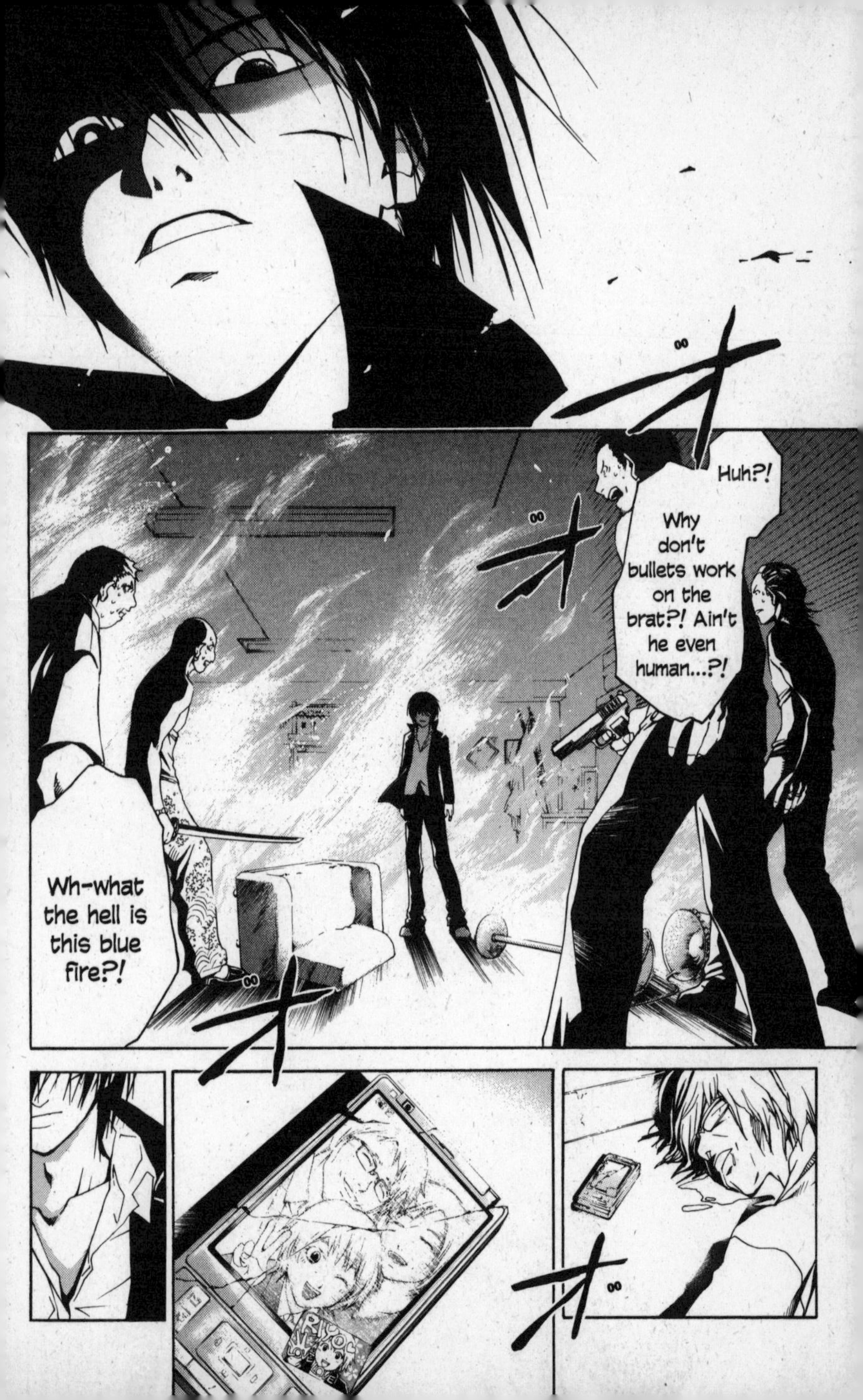
Huh?!
Why don't bullets work on the brat?! Ain't he even human...?!
Wh-what the hell is this blue fire?!

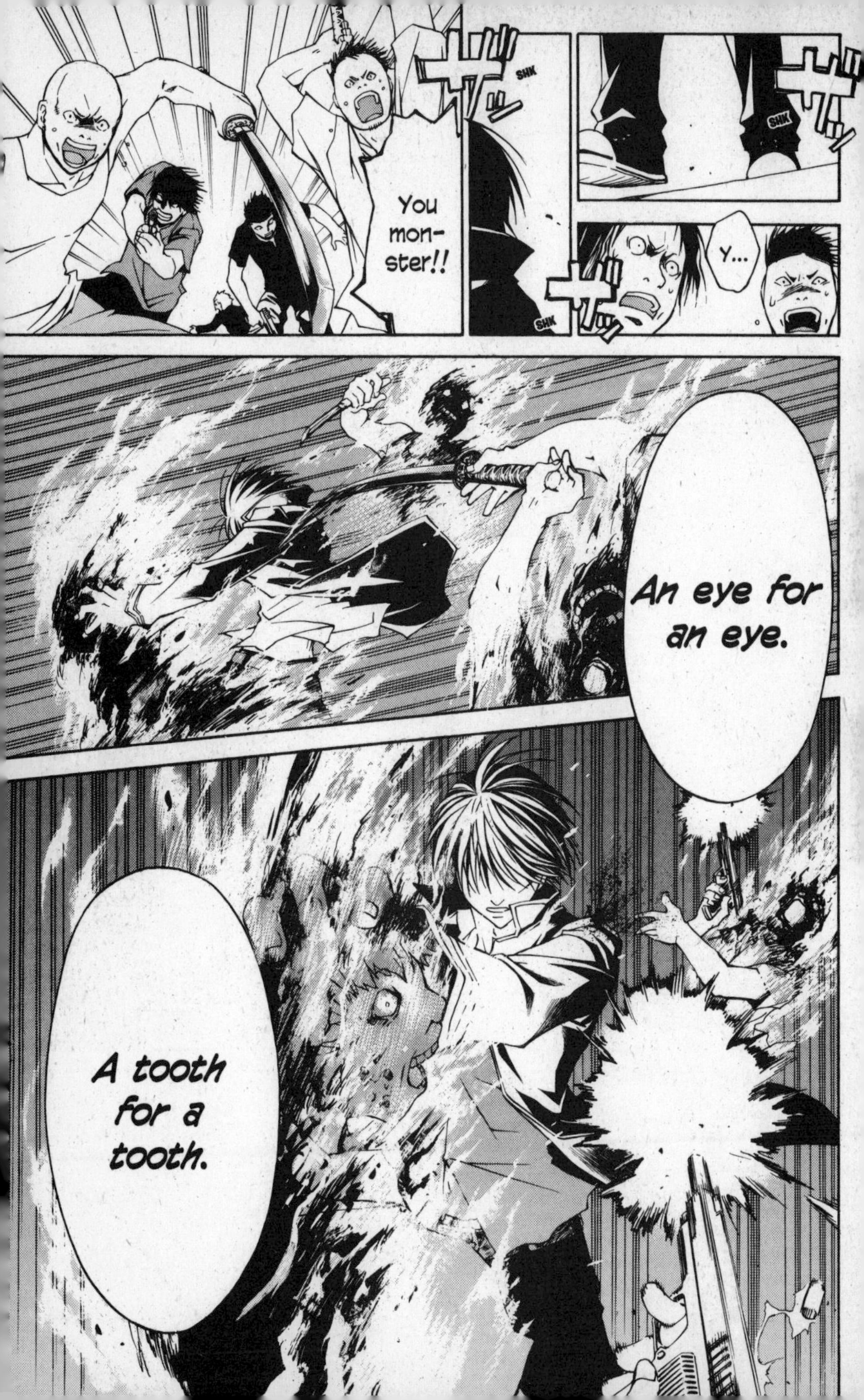
SHK
Y...
SHK
SHK
You monster!!
An eye for an eye.
A tooth for a tooth.

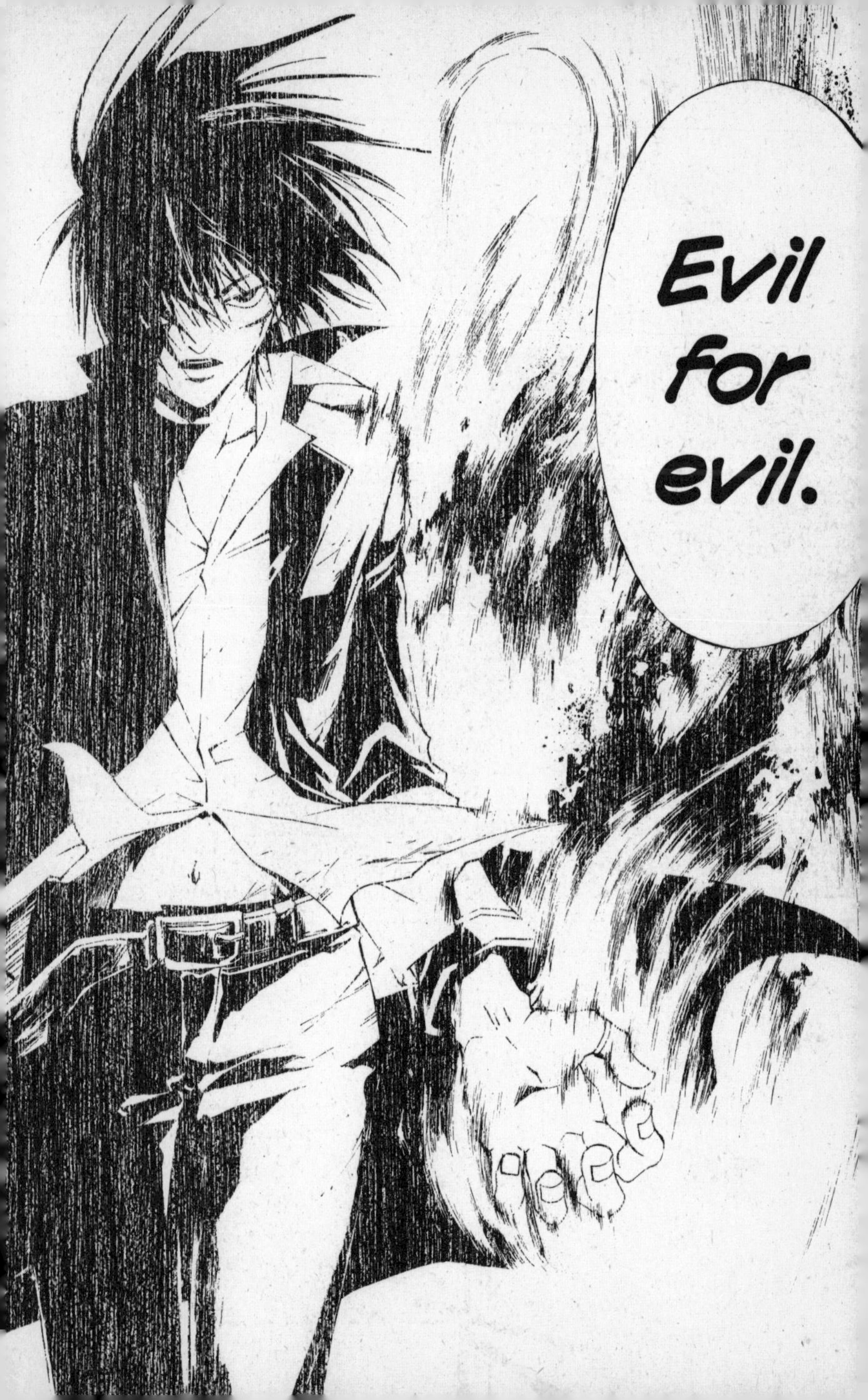
Evil for evil.

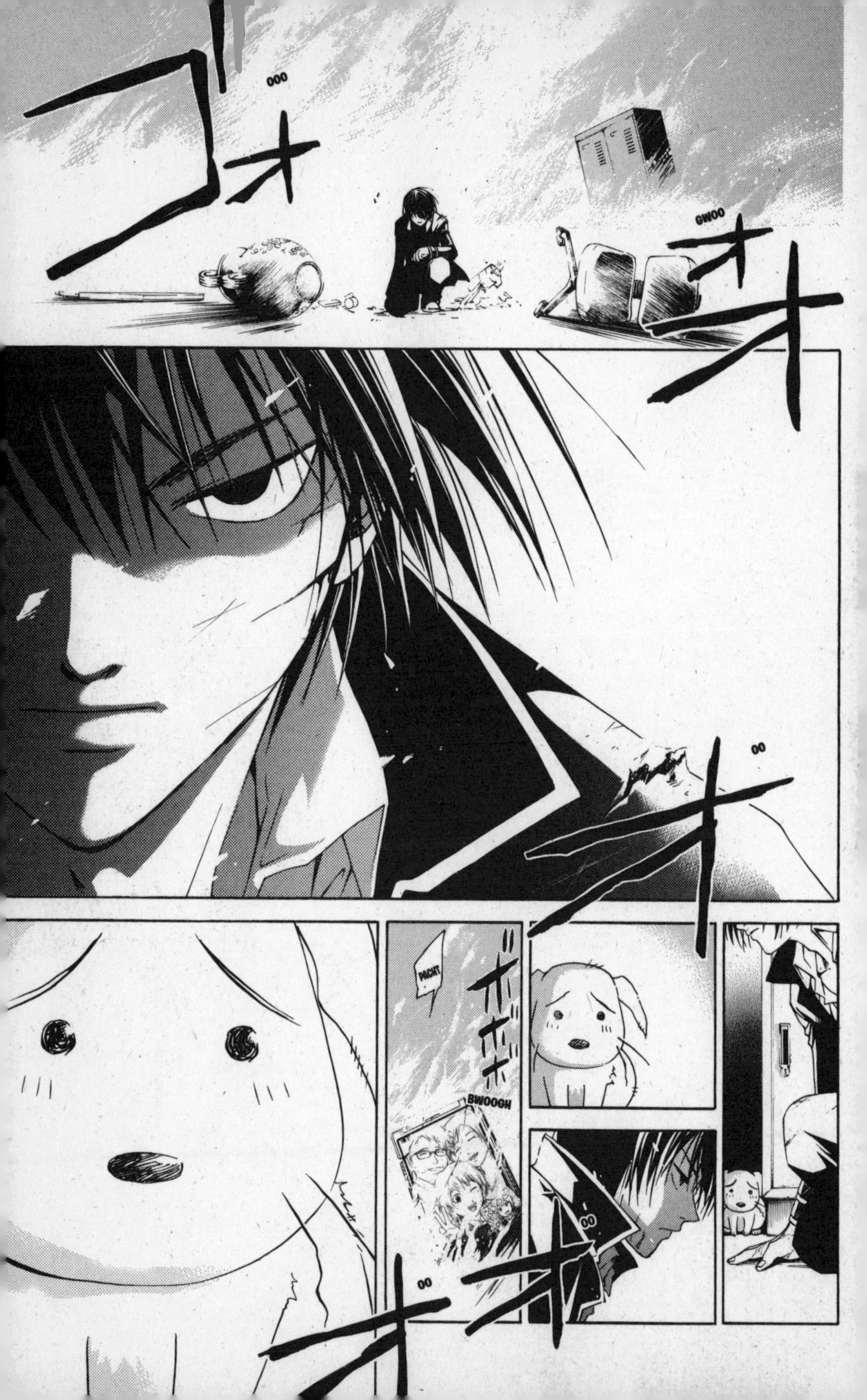
GWOO
OOO
OO
OO
PACHT
BWOOGH
OO

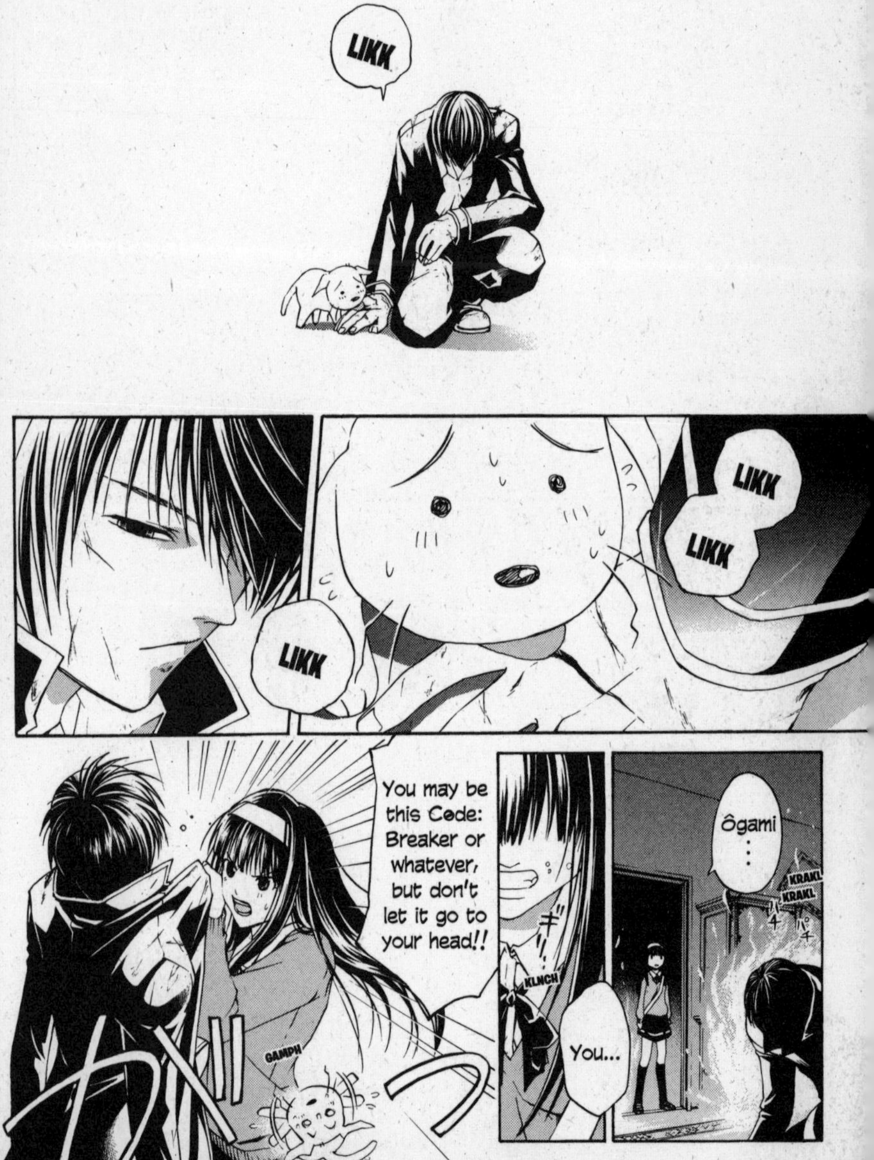
LIKK
LIKK
LIKK
LIKK
Ôgami...
KRAKL
KRAKL
KLNCH
You...
You may be this Code: Breaker or whatever, but don't let it go to your head!!
GAMPH

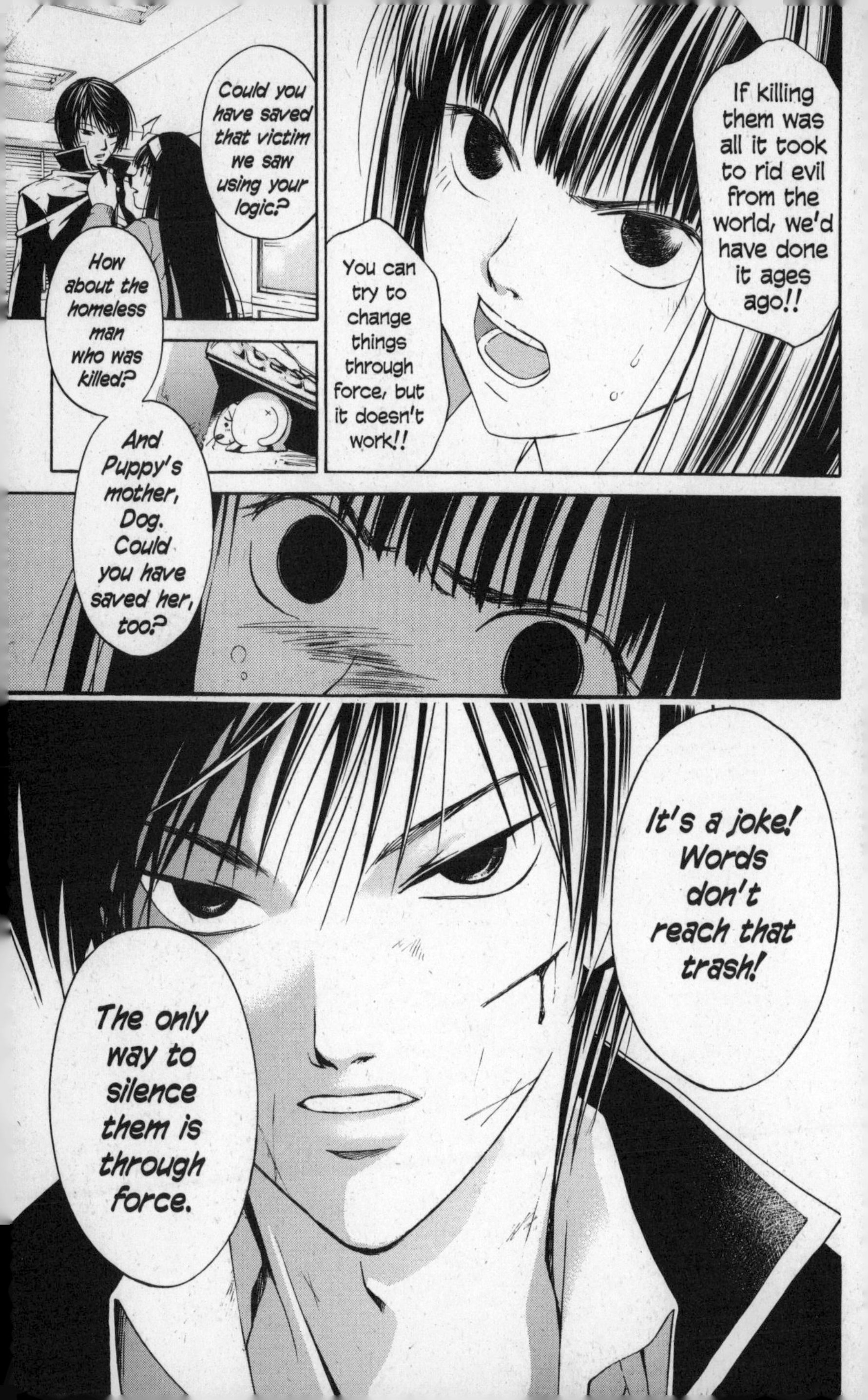
If killing them was all it took to rid evil from the world, we'd have done it ages ago!!
You can try to change things through force, but it doesn't work!!
Could you have saved that victim we saw using your logic?
How about the homeless man who was killed?
And Puppy's mother, Dog. Could you have saved her, too?
It's a joke! Words don't reach that trash!
The only way to silence them is through force.

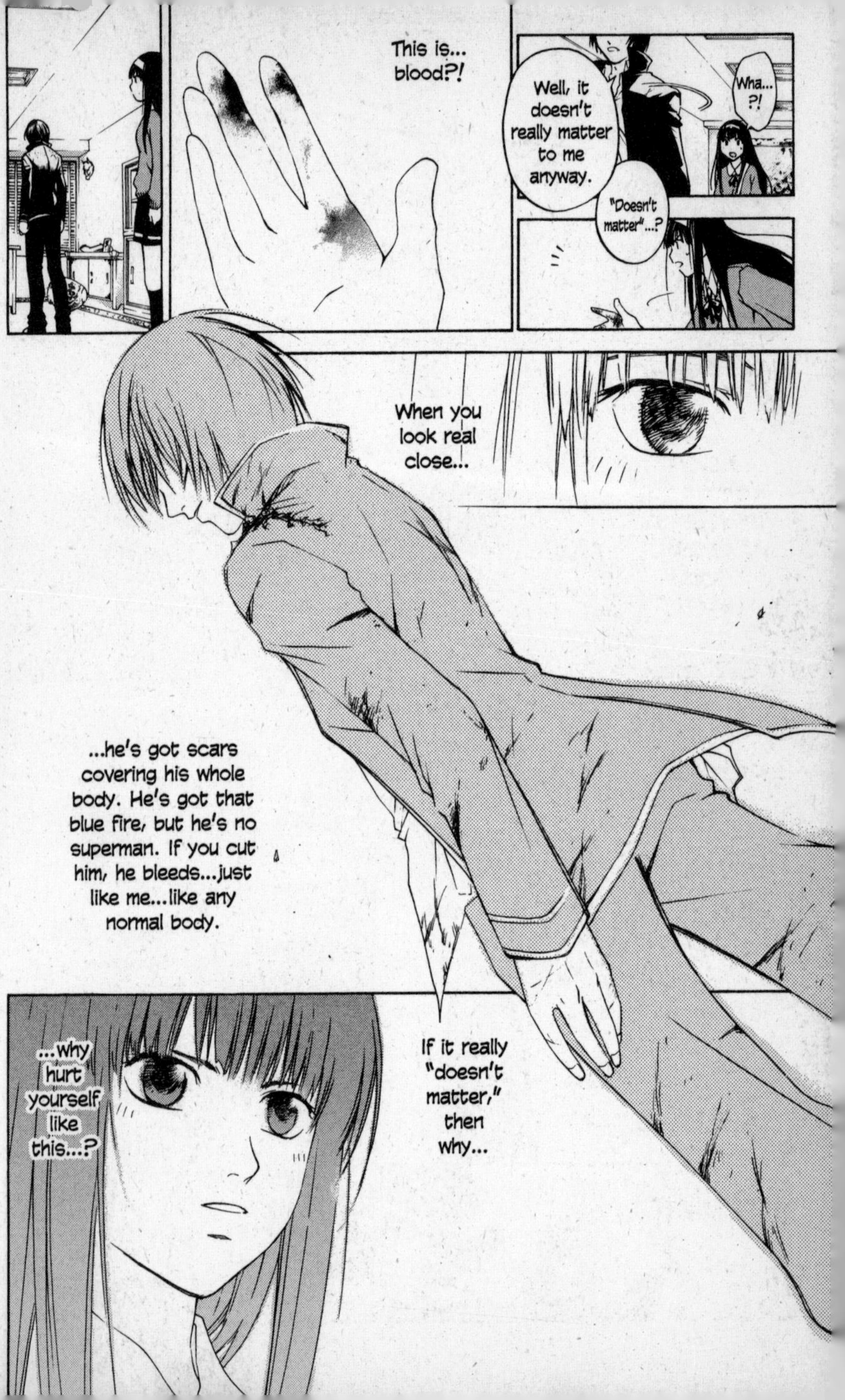
Well, it doesn't really matter to me anyway.
Wha...?!
"Doesn't matter"...?
This is... blood?!
When you look real close...
...he's got scars covering his whole body. He's got that blue fire, but he's no superman. If you cut him, he bleeds...just like me...like any normal body.
If it really "doesn't matter," then why...
...why hurt yourself like this...?

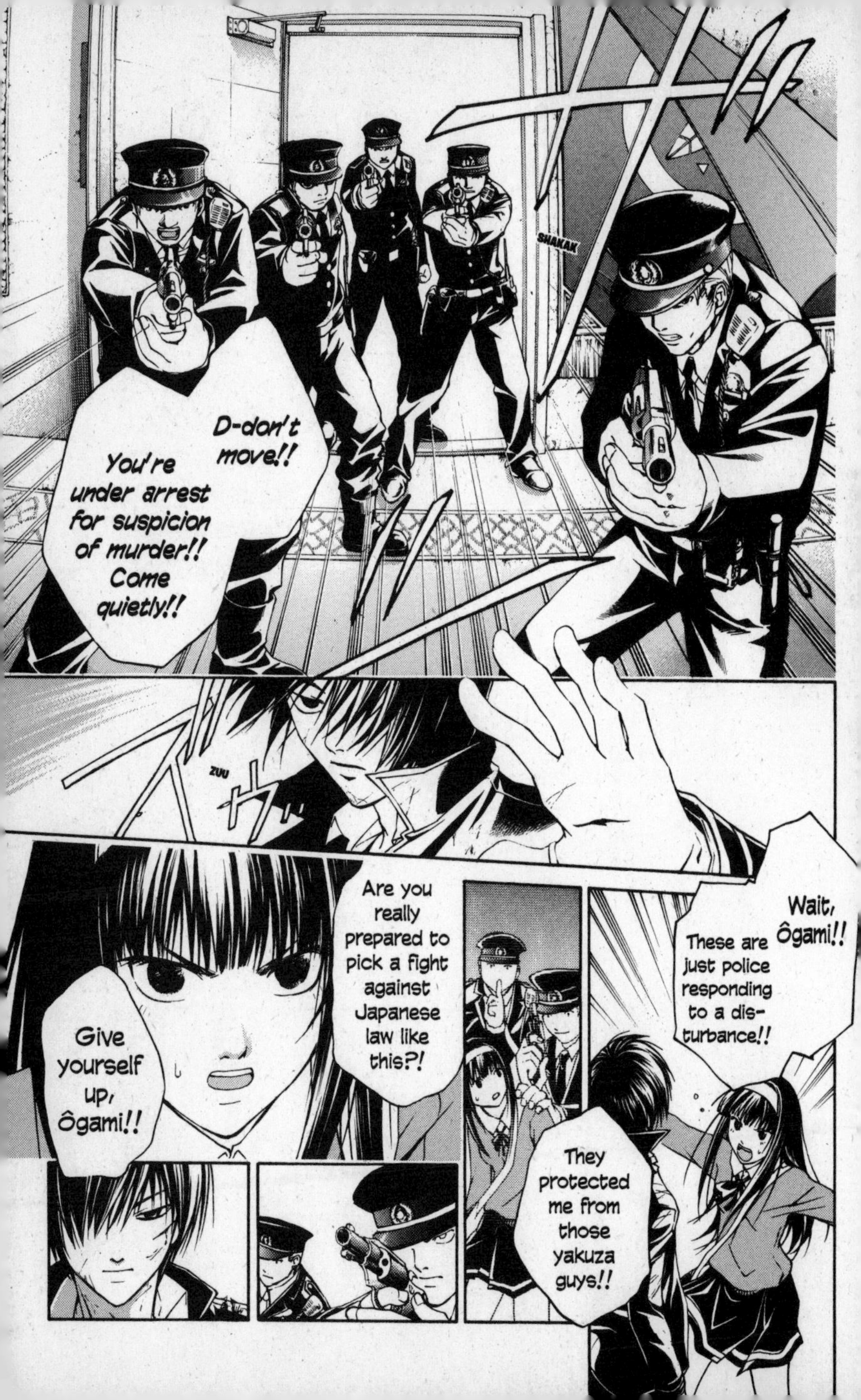
SHAKAK
D-don't move!!
You're under arrest for suspicion of murder!! Come quietly!!
ZUU
Wait, Ôgami!!
These are just police responding to a disturbance!!
They protected me from those yakuza guys!!
Are you really prepared to pick a fight against Japanese law like this?!
Give yourself up, Ôgami!!

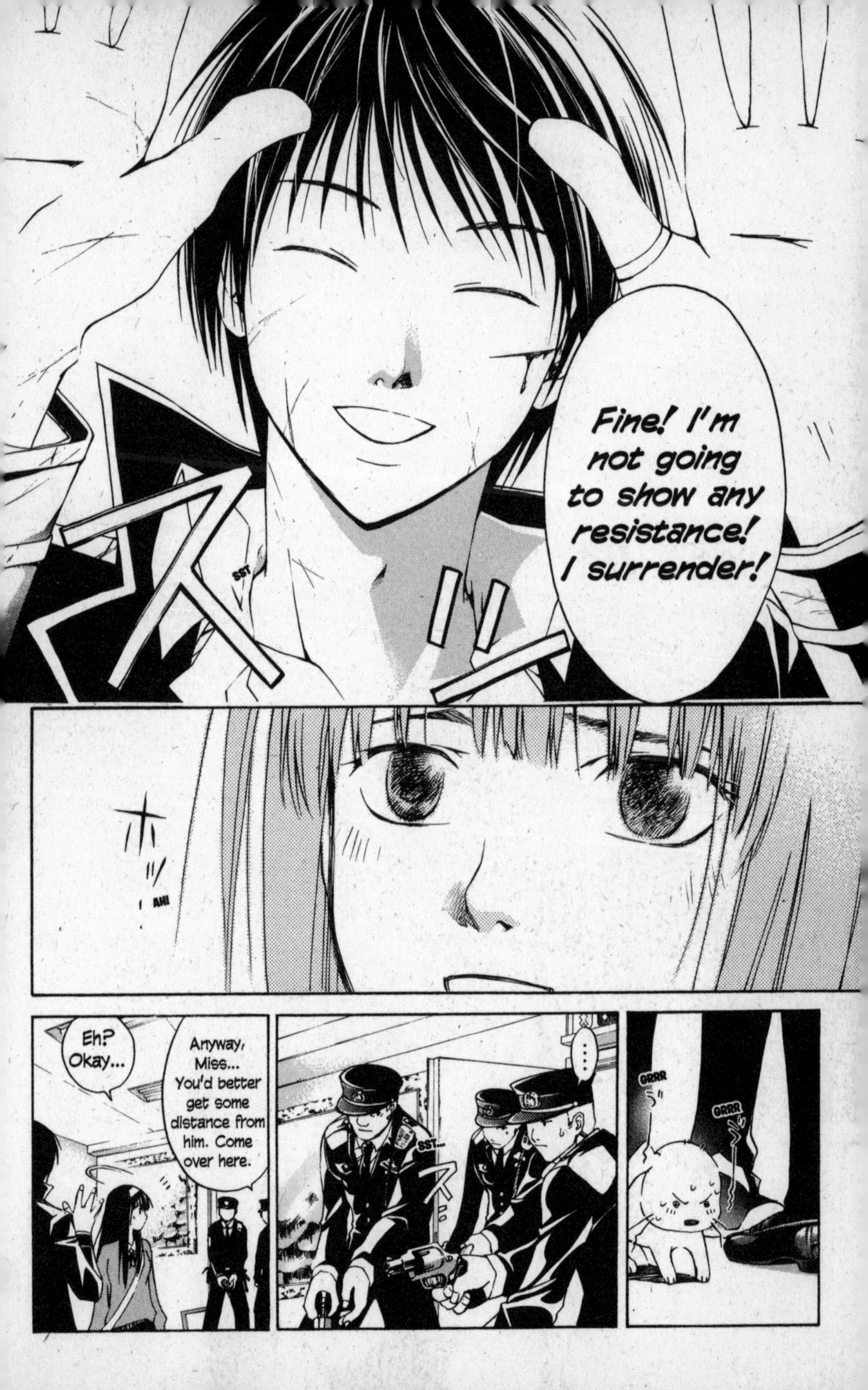
Fine! I'm not going to show any resistance! I surrender!
SST
AH!
GRRR
GRRR
...
SST...
Anyway, Miss... You'd better get some distance from him. Come over here.
Eh? Okay...

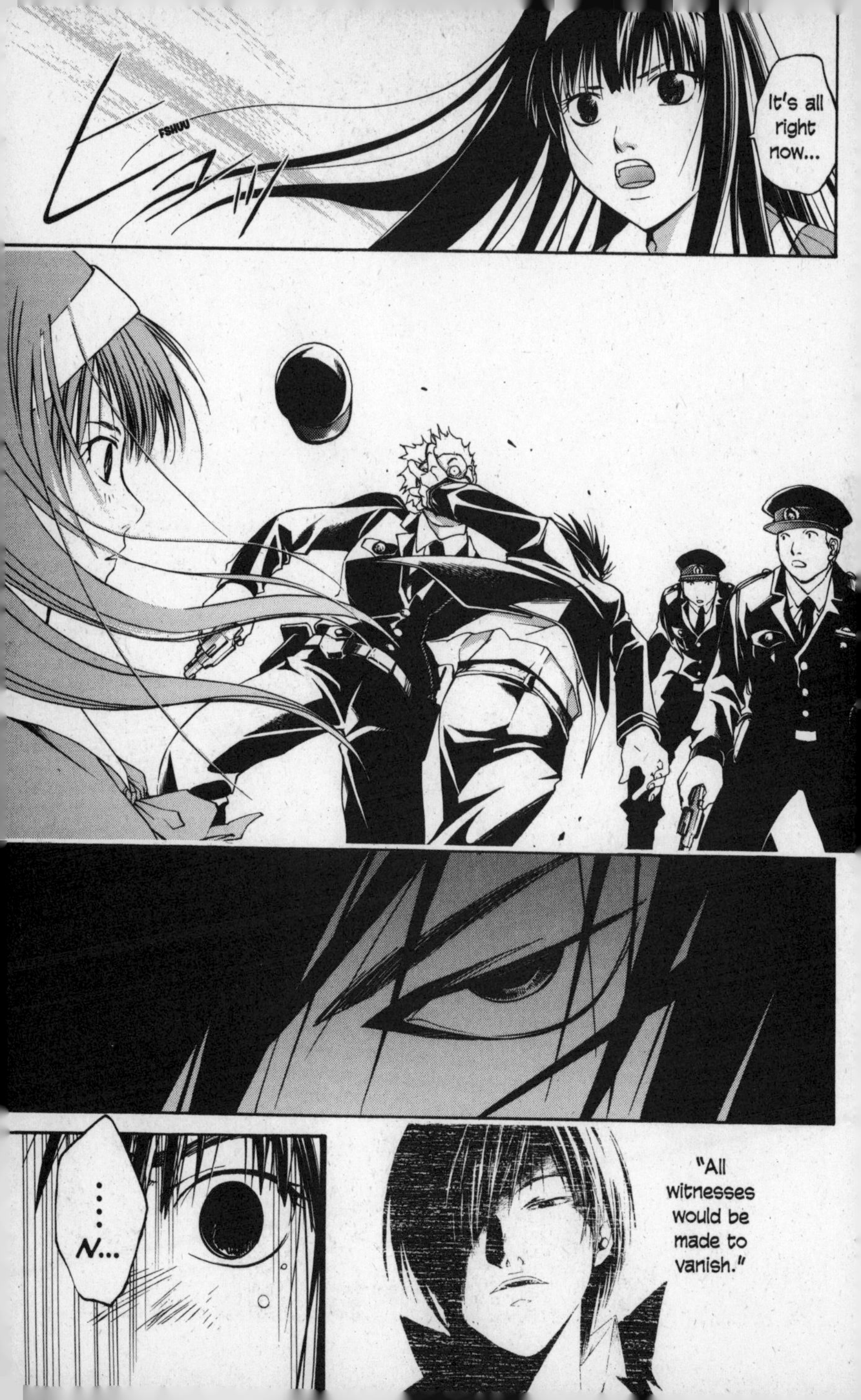
It's all right now...
FSHUU
"All witnesses would be made to vanish."
.... N...

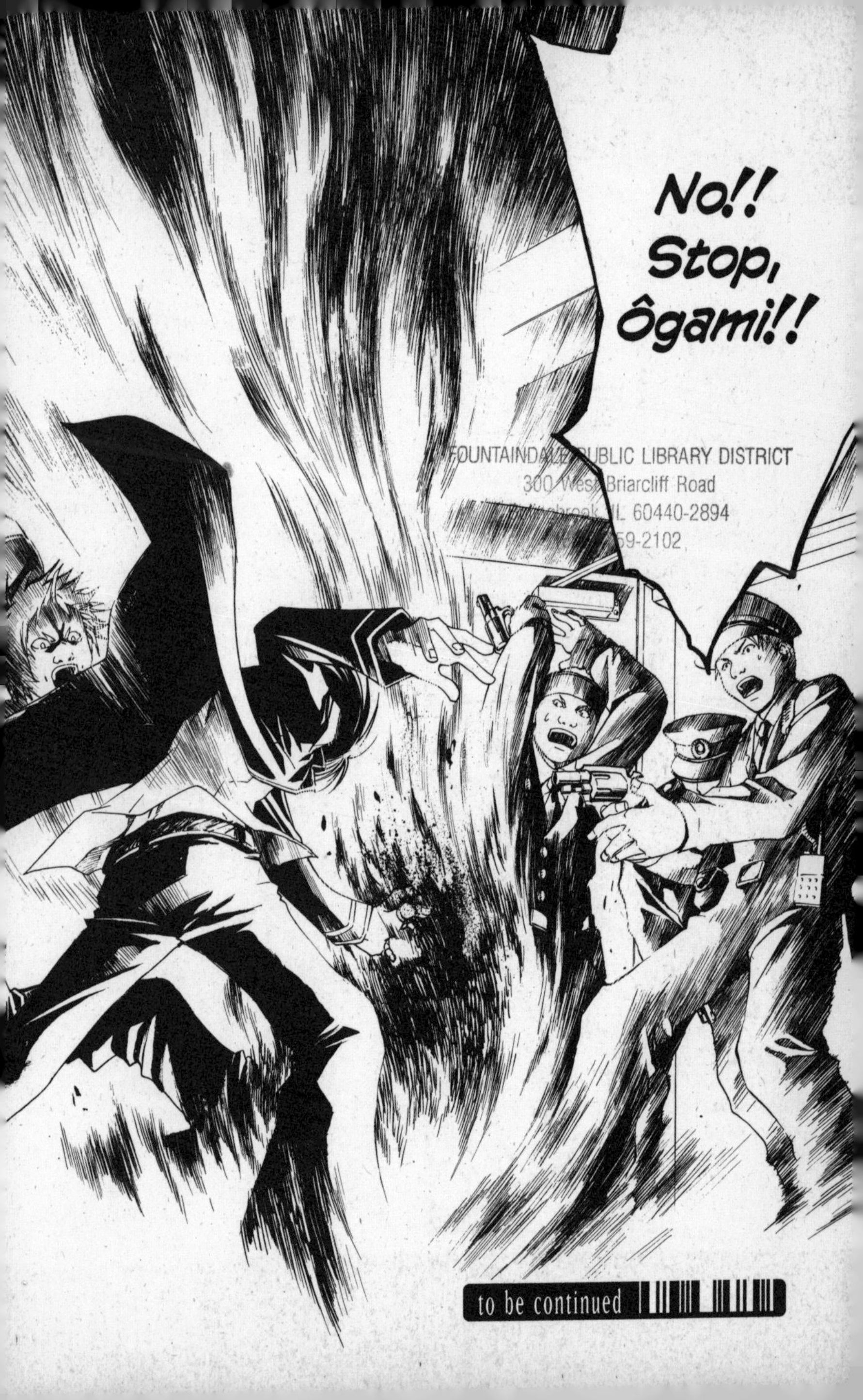
No!! Stop, ôgami!!
to be continued

Kamijyo Info

The Fate of a School Idol

After being attacked by G-Falcon, Sakura heads directly to school, so...
...she goes in a jersey that she had in her bag.
I know that nobody attends school wearing a jersey, and I'll attract everyone's attention, but I have bigger worries than that.
GLANCE
GLANCE
GLANCE
The next day...
Finally, I'm back in a regular school uniform!
Hm?
I just had to dress the way Sakurakōji-san did yesterday!
KYAAA
KYAA
Here I am in my jersey!
...
The look was just too cute!
The "look" had caught on.

Now, in volume 2, the story moves in big new directions. What kind of person is Ôgami?! And how will Sakura react to him...?! How about new characters? What about Puppy?! (ha ha) There will be a lot of high school life and Rei's job in volume 2!! Let's meet again there!

Thanks to everyone who sent me letters or presents! The very core of my energy comes from your support and words of encouragement! And just like you wanted, we're going to revive the Postcard Corner!! Please take up Kamijyo's challenge!!

Continued on the back cover!

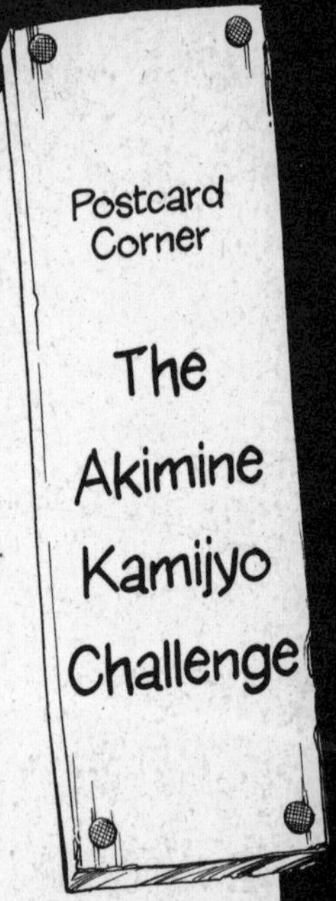
Postcard Corner
The Akimine Kamijyo Challenge

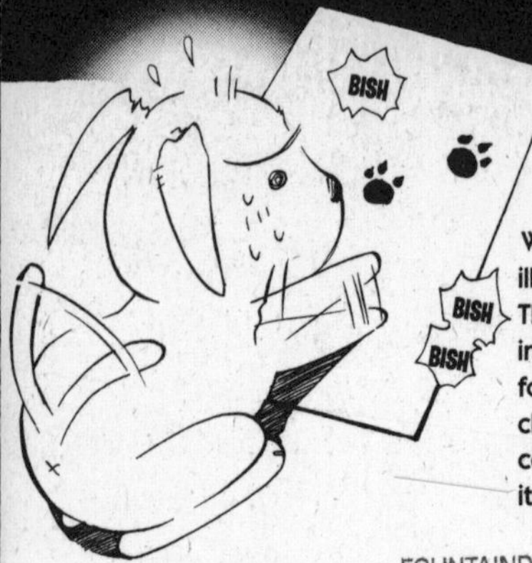
BISH
BISH
BISH

A Call Requesting Your Work!

We're looking for your illustrations of *Code:Breaker*! The best ones we receive will be included in the graphic novels for *Code:Breaker*! And the ones chosen will also receive a special commemorative *Code:Breaker* item!

Send it to:
Del Rey Manga
1745 Broadway, 24-2
New York, NY 10019

* All illustrations should be in pen and sent on postcard stock!
* Send along your questions and letters of support to Kamijyo, too!!

No matter what, I'm always grateful to my respected and beloved father and late mother!

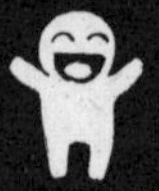

■ STAFF

Shiba Tateoka, Shô Yashioka, Kazuki Hirako, Joriimanma, Takehiko Yamashita, A. Taniguchi

■ COMICS DESIGN

Masashi Hisamochi

■ Thanks to my cousin Y., H.-senpai, Big Sis, M-chan x 2, my older cousin, all the part-time workers at the photo-typesetting place, everybody at DaiNippon Printing, all the self-effacing people in the editorial department who insisted that I don't have to mention their names (ha ha), and to all of the countless other people, thank you so much!!

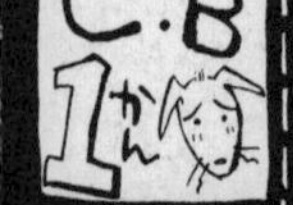
C:B
1かん

And a new "non existent" Code: Breaker makes his entrance!!

Just as Ôgami reveals his true intentions, an "Evil" that had remained hidden reveals itself!!

Plunge deeper into the story!

CODE: BREAKER

The "deeper" volume 2 goes on sale in the fall!!

Translation Notes

Japanese is a tricky language for most Westerners, and translation is often more art than science. For your edification and reading pleasure, here are notes on some of the places where we could have gone in a different direction with our translation of the work, or where a Japanese cultural reference is used.

The Transfer Student in the Dramas, page 24

One of the most-used clichés in Japanese high school drama is the "transfer student" who suddenly arrives to shake up the established order of love relationships or high school politics.

Confession of Love, page 25

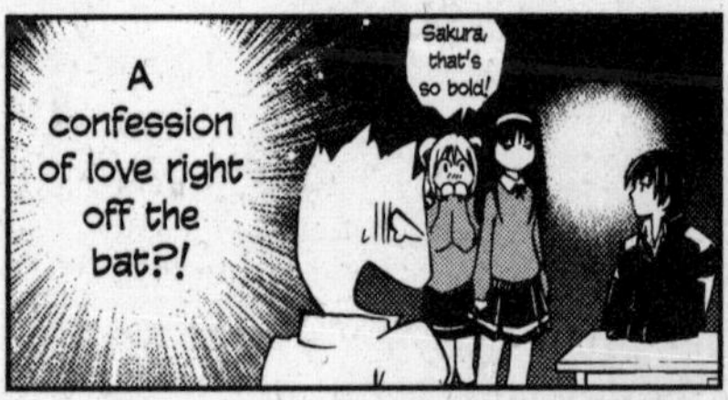
Sakura, that's so bold!
A confession of love right off the bat?!

A rite of passage for anyone who has a crush in Japan seems to be the confession of love. It usually involves asking the person to go someplace private where one admits, in one form or another, that one likes the person.

Tacks in His Slippers, page 30

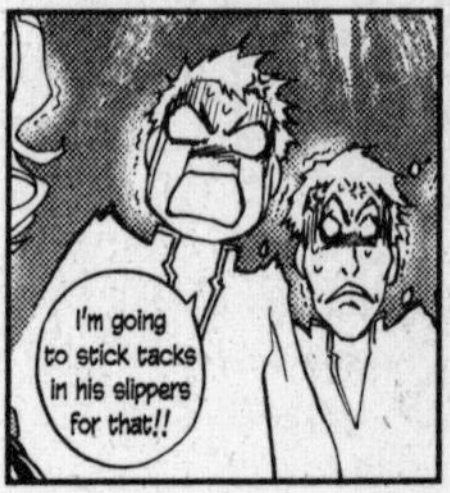
I'm going to stick tacks in his slippers for that!!

Just like love letters can be left in one's shoe locker (see note on page 201), other not-so-welcome things can be left there as well. One of the nastier tricks has been to leave tacks, pointy end facing up, taped to the inside sole section of a rival's slipper, so the rival will impale him- or herself when putting on the slipper.

WC, page 30

For those who have never encountered this term, WC stands for "water closet" and is a somewhat outdated term for bathroom that is still used in Japan.

Walking Three Steps Behind, page 106

In Japan's medieval times (until the mid-1800s), it was the Japanese custom for women to walk three steps behind their husbands. After the Meiji Restoration and Japan's rush to catch up to the modern world, this custom began to fade, and now it is almost nonexistent (but still romantically idealized).

Shibuya, page 107
One of the "city centers" of Tokyo (others include the Ginza, Shinjuku, Ueno, Ikebukuro, etc.), and best known for its fashionable shops, theaters, restaurants, clubs, and other outlets mainly oriented toward young people. It is considered one of the great date spots of Tokyo.

Sakurakôji
Miss Sakura
Sakura-sama

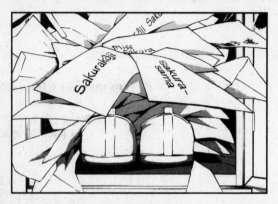

Love Letters in the Shoe Locker, page 154
One of the traditional ways to leave a love letter in a Japanese school is to leave it in the recipient's shoe locker. (We refer to it as a locker, but it is hardly ever locked.) All students use their shoe locker each time they enter or leave the building, so it is a place one can be sure one's notes will be found. Other, not-so-welcome messages may be left there as well (see Tacks in His Slippers, page 200).

Sakura-chin, page 154
There are many cute honorifics that are similar to "-chan," which is listed in the honorifics section at the front of this book. Some, such as "-chin" and "-tan," are very widespread and one comes upon them often.

Ôgami-sama
090-XXXX-XXXX

090-xxxx-xxxx, page 157
If you substitute the Xs for numbers, the format is what cellphone numbers look like in Japan. Cellphones bought in the Tokyo area start with the 090 prefix.

TOMARE!

[STOP!]

You're going the wrong way!

Manga is a completely different type of reading experience.

To start at the *beginning*, go to the *end*!

That's right! Authentic manga is read the traditional Japanese way— from right to left. Exactly the *opposite* of how American books are read. It's easy to follow: Just go to the other end of the book, and read each page—and each panel—from the right side to the left side, starting at the top right. Now you're experiencing manga as it was meant to be!